THE GOOD GERMANS

THE GOOD GERMANS

Catrine Clay

WEIDENFELD & NICOLSON

First published in Great Britain in 2020 by Weidenfeld & Nicolson
an imprint of The Orion Publishing Group Ltd
Carmelite House, 50 Victoria Embankment
London EC4Y 0DZ

An Hachette UK Company

3 5 7 9 10 8 6 4

A CIP catalogue record for this book is
available from the British Library.

ISBN (Hardback) 978 1 4746 0787 2
ISBN (Export Trade Paperback) 978 1 47460 788 9
ISBN (eBook) 978 1 4746 0790 2

Typeset by Input Data Services Ltd, Somerset
Printed in Great Britain by Clays Ltd, Elcograf S.p.A.

www.weidenfeldandnicolson.co.uk
www.orionbooks.co.uk

Anthony Sheil
(1933–2017)
Agent, and friend

CONTENTS

AUTHOR'S NOTE

Translations from the German are the author's own. The dialogue is invented, but never the content.

Introduction

THE GOOD GERMANS

My father always said there were no Good Germans. I suppose you can understand it: he fought them for five years during the Second World War. In fact, that view was widespread among his generation: there was something wrong with the German psyche, a sort of Teutonic fatal flaw. At first, I didn't take much notice – too busy with my own life. Later I got to thinking: but surely there were Germans and there were Nazis and they were not the same thing. Later still, I learned that two-thirds of Germans – some twenty million people – had never voted for the Nazi Party, as the National Socialist German Workers' Party was known. The near hysterical crowds featured in the newsreels of the time, screaming *Sieg Heil!* and throwing bouquets of flowers as Hitler drove past in his black Mercedes, never amounted to more than a few hundred thousand. The membership of the Nazi Party when they came to power through a fateful coalition of right-wing parties in 1933, was some two million. For them Hitler was their Führer, the man who would lead them out of their desperate lives following Germany's humiliating defeat in the First World War and the chaos of the Weimar years which followed. But what of those two-thirds of Germans who did not vote for the Nazis and had to live through the Nazi terror regime, then the Second World War, and then, once it was all over, suffer the opprobrium of the whole world as more and more of the atrocities perpetrated by the Nazis became public knowledge, extermination camps and all? Not to mention their own feelings of guilt, because many of those Good Germans ended up believing it had all been their fault. What of them?

I've been working on the Nazi period off and on for many years, first at the BBC making history documentaries, then in writing books. Now I've come to the subject which has been hovering all these years: what of those two thirds? How would I have managed if I'd had to live through that terror regime – any terror regime for that matter – knowing that even the slightest indication that I wasn't a committed

Nazi could have lost me my job or got me sent me to a concentration camp. Or shot. Or hanged. Or guillotined. What would any of us do?

Within just six months of the *Machtergreifung*, the 'seizure of power', on 30 January 1933, Germany's democracy had been replaced by the Nazi regime: no more political parties, trade unions, independent judiciary, civil service, free press or independent churches. The policy of *Gleichschaltung*, brought in by March 1933, meant those who were not politically aligned – teachers, doctors, civil servants – were removed from their jobs and, if they persisted in opposing the regime, arrested, sent to a concentration camp, 'shot while trying to escape' or simply shot on the spot. Many Jews had already lost their jobs. The *Volksgericht*, the People's Court, was set up early in 1934 as an alternative legal system to bypass the traditional judicial system, specifically for acts of treason. Treason could be anything from not giving the Heil Hitler salute with sufficient zeal, to taking part in a full-scale plot to assassinate Hitler.

War was always part of the grand plan for the Nazis, as Hitler wrote in *Mein Kampf* as early as 1925, in order to gain *Lebensraum*, the space for living necessary to bring about the triumph of the Master Race and what Hitler referred to as the Thousand Year German Reich, or Third Reich, the natural successor to the Holy Roman Empire (First Reich) and the German Empire (Second Reich).

As the terror regime took hold, most of those Germans who weren't Nazis just tried to keep their heads down and protect their families – they moved to the country or pretended to support the regime to avoid being denounced by neighbours, and they tried to work out what was really happening in the Reich, surrounded as they were by Nazi propaganda and fake news. But hundreds of thousands of Germans, mostly unknown, decided to resist the regime in large ways and small: Communists, Social Democrats, Catholics, Protestants, Quakers and Jehovah's Witnesses, teachers, shopkeepers, Prussian aristocrats, priests, army officers, factory workers, mothers, grandfathers – each risking their lives every day during that time, a period which lasted no more than twelve years, but which cost millions of lives.

Once power gets into the wrong hands there is little the individual can do.

So I decided to write a book about those Good Germans who tried to resist the Nazis in small ways and large. But how? I didn't want to write the big history again – the one about Hitler and Himmler and

Goebbels. I wanted to write about people like you and me. Reverse things: write the small history big and the big history small. But where to find such small, personal stories of quiet courage – the unknown stories, based on memoirs, many unpublished? Luckily my years of interest stood me in good stead: I knew where to look. And I speak German.

This is not to ignore the famous stories of resistance to Nazi rule, like the White Rose Group in Munich, but more to show that there were hundreds of thousands of other, unknown people acting at the same time. So the book starts in 1932, in the lead-up to the January 1933 *Machtergreifung*, and ends in 1946 when everything – the terror regime, the war, all the destruction and downfall and the millions of dead – was over, though far from done.

I decided on six characters, making them as wide a selection as possible: workers and aristocrats, Communists and conservatives, women and men, young and old. Because their actions inevitably affected the people around them, they are not seen in isolation but as part of their families: a brother and sister; a wife; a father with three children; an only son; the parents of a Communist pioneer daughter. Their stories are interwoven throughout the book, each experiencing the big events of Nazi history as they unfold in their own small lives. Good Germans, all.

THE GOOD GERMANS

BERNT ENGELMANN is a schoolboy living in Düsseldorf in 1932 at the start of this story. His father is a businessman, his mother a housewife. He is an only child. The family is an ordinary German family, generally Social Democrat but not especially political or religious. They join a local clandestine resistance group made up of people like themselves – a teacher, a tailor, a lawyer, a pastor, and led by Tante Ney, Aunt Ney, who runs the bakery and café on the corner of their street, welcoming everyone, including local Nazis who never suspect this old woman who used to treat them well in their poor days, before they rose and rose to unheard-of positions of power and influence. The Engelmanns' reason: they simply cannot countenance what they see happening all around them under the new terror regime. And for that they risk their lives.

FABIAN VON SCHLABRENDORFF is a law student in Berlin, serious-minded and quietly determined. His father died when Fabian was 16 and his mother was left to bring up her five children on her own. The family are anti-Nazi from the very beginning. When we first meet Fabian, in 1933, after the Nazi *Machtergreifung*, he is walking across Berlin in search of a man he doesn't know and has never met – a man from a very different background to his own privileged one: Ernst Niekisch, the editor of a magazine called *Widerstand*, Resistance. Fabian is looking for like-minded people to start fighting the Nazis, whoever they are. Among the secret resisters the traditional class divisions are breaking down, factory worker and Prussian aristocrat working hand in hand, finding they have much more in common than they ever realised.

RUDOLF DITZEN is a middle-aged man, already famous as the author Hans Fallada, best known for his novel *Alone in Berlin*. But he is also a morphine addict, drinker, liar and womaniser who killed a friend in a duel when he was young and has done time in prison for embezzlement. He has been in several clinics and lunatic asylums, trying to cure him of his addictions. Rudolf is married to the strong and long-suffering Suse and they have three young children. They live in Carwitz, a rural hamlet in Mecklenburg in northern Germany, where Rudolf writes furiously day and night, chain-smoking all the way. His subject, time and again, is the decent little people of Germany who have somehow to manage their difficult lives. This is his act of resistance – reaching out to his readers. Not for him acts of great courage. '*I am a weak man, but not a bad man,*' he wrote to his mother. The problem for Rudolf is how to keep going under this Nazi terror regime – without making too many compromises and still remaining true to his liberal convictions.

IRMA THÄLMANN is thirteen in 1932, the daughter of Ernst Thälmann, the charismatic leader of the KPD German Communist Party. In 1933, Thälmann is immediately arrested with some 10,000 other Communists. He will spend eleven and a half years in solitary confinement before being vengefully executed just before the Russians arrive, in March 1945. Irma is an only child living with her mother, Rosa, in Hamburg, with both grandfathers – old Communist comrades – living not far away. Irma is a fighter, the very image of her father. She'd rather get beaten every day at school than give the Heil Hitler salute. Mother and daughter are active resisters throughout, till the Gestapo finally catch up with them. Meanwhile, there are rare visits to her father, and occasional letters, and his speeches which they read again and again. '*We know a land where there is no Fascism,*' Ernst Thälmann declaimed, '*a land where it would be unthinkable for the Fascist hounds to practise murder on the streets, carrying out their bloody actions in the working-class districts. It is called the Soviet Union!*'

FRITZ-DIETLOF VON DER SCHULENBURG (FRITZI) is getting married to Charlotte when we first meet him in March 1933. He is 31, a Prussian aristocrat – energetic, clever, popular, idealistic – and a convinced Nazi. Like so many Germans from any background, he is still smarting from the brutal and humiliating terms of the Treaty of Versailles following defeat in the First World War. And from the wholesale collapse of the German economy after the Wall Street Crash of 1929. He hopes the National Socialists will make Germany great again. He believes in their stated Socialist aims. The day before Fritzi's wedding Hermann Göring summons him to a meeting. The Nazis need top men on side. So pleased is Göring with the young, clever Count, he takes him into the next room to meet the Führer. But by 1934, Fritzi is already having doubts, strongly encouraged by his sister, Tisa – the passionate Socialist in their family of Nazis. By 1938, Fritzi has joined General Beck's secret group of resisters and is ready to lose his life for the cause.

JULIUS LEBER was a leading Social Democrat in the Reichstag before the Nazis came to power, when they immediately banned all political parties other than their own. *'Two hours after our victory Dr Leber will be hanging from a lamp post in the market square!'* jeered the Nazis in Lübeck, Leber's home town. But Leber, a large, ebullient, tough man isn't easily frightened. When the result of the right-wing coalition is broadcast, handing Hitler and the Nazis their *Machtergreifung*, he goes out on the town and gets drunk. In the early hours he gets into a street brawl with some local Nazis, after which he is arrested and incarcerated indefinitely. His devoted wife, Annedore, when refused a visiting permit, finds a spot on a nearby rooftop, to watch him during his daily hour of exercise in the prison yard. When he's finally let out in 1937 – after being repeatedly beaten and tortured – the Nazis think they'll have no more trouble from Dr Leber. But he goes straight back to the fight, knowing full well what it will likely cost him in the end.

CHAPTER ONE

THE SWASTIKA

Bernt Engelmann was greeted by a surprising sight when he arrived at his *Gymnasium*, grammar school, one Monday morning in May 1932. A swastika flag was flying high up on a turret of the school building for all to see. The playground was full of students and teachers gazing upwards, astonished. A senior master said: 'Get that thing down at once! It's a disgrace!' The janitor just grinned. He couldn't find the key to the turret, he said. Then they saw a shaming sight: their French teacher Dr Levy, who only had one arm, was clambering out of a dormer window and groping his way across the roof. He climbed the fire ladder and somehow hauled himself over the iron railing surrounding the turret, and tore the flag down. They knew it was Dr Levy because they could see the empty sleeve of his jacket flapping. The playground burst into applause, all but a few who booed and hissed. Bernt's class had French for the second period that day, but Dr Levy never said a word, just carried on with his irregular verbs as though nothing had happened. Except that, when he slid the front blackboard across to write on the one behind, he found the words '*Salope Juif!*' scrawled there in bold white chalk. He turned to face the class. 'Did one of you write that? No? – I believe you.' He went on to explain that '*salope*' meant 'sow', so, being feminine, '*Juif*' should have been '*Juive*'. Then he took the sponge and wiped it off, replacing it with '*Manchot Juif*'. *Manchot* was the French term, he explained, for a veteran of the war who had lost an arm. As he had, in 1917, at the Battle of Arras.

Bernt was twelve at the time, and when he got home for the midday meal he told his parents what had happened. His father was a businessman in imports and exports, his mother a busy housewife. They were average middle-class Social Democrats and Bernt, their only child, had grown up during the virtual civil war of the Weimar Republic when the paramilitary Fascist Freikorps, essentially private armies formed of war veterans, routinely fought pitched street battles with the Communists and Socialists, the pavements covered in blood.

The Engelmann parents were shocked by what Bernt told them, even more so that evening when it transpired that the school principal, a suspected Nazi sympathiser, instead of punishing the perpetrators, had suspended Dr Levy 'until further notice'. Bernt's father nodded, 'That's the sort of thing that happens these days.'

Still, in the Reichstag elections that November 1932, the Nazis' National Socialist Party lost 34 seats, failing to get the majority it needed, in spite of a massive propaganda campaign orchestrated by Dr Joseph Goebbels, with all the usual staged events: blaring loud-speakers, declamatory speeches, military bands, marching Freikorps, hearty singing and night-time torchlight processions. And the usual street violence.

Bernt's father, listening to the election results on the wireless in the front room of their house in the suburbs of Düsseldorf, thought the outcome showed that Germans had some sense after all. But he spoke too soon. Through a series of dubious right-wing coalitions, Hitler was appointed Chancellor of Germany in President Hindenburg's government on 30 January 1933. The Engelmanns had a friend who was a doctor working in the emergency department of their local hospital. He told them they'd been completely overwhelmed that evening with the injured, many of them seriously wounded. The triumphant Nazis had gone on a rampage of violence, attacking Communists,

Socialists and Jews with anything they could lay their hands on – steel balls covered in leather, knuckle-dusters, horse-whips – and this in Düsseldorf where the Social Democrats traditionally had the upper hand. Apparently Felix Fechenbach, editor of the *Volksblatt*, the Social Democrat paper, was badly beaten, then arrested and taken into 'protective police custody'. Later, they heard he'd been shot 'while trying to escape'.

On 30 January 1933, the Engelmann family stayed safe at home, like two-thirds of the population and quite unlike that remaining third, filmed for the newsreels by Dr Goebbels' propaganda machine, cheering hysterically as their Führer drove through the streets of Berlin in his open-topped car, hand raised in the Hitler salute. Bernt's father shook his head and went into the other room to listen to the wireless broadcast: '*Like a blazing fire the news spreads across Germany! Adolf Hitler is Chancellor of the Reich! A million hearts are aflame. Rejoicing and gratitude pour forth . . . . A procession of thousands is streaming up Wilhelm Strasse, a hundred thousand voices shouting joyously "Sieg Heil! Sieg Heil!" into the night.*' Herr Engelmann sunk his head in his hands. It was unbelievable – even the voice of the commentator was different: louder, more strident. 'They will destroy everything, law, order, civilisation, everything we value,' he said.

The Reichstag was in uproar after the election, called in desperation by the Weimar government, still beset with the economic and social problems following Germany's defeat in the Great War of 1914–18 and the punishing terms of the 1919 Treaty of Versailles which followed, and made even worse by yet another disastrous economic crisis caused by the 1929 Wall Street Crash. The worst year had been 1923 when hyper-inflation was so high people were paying a million marks for a sack of potatoes. Following the Dawes Plan of 1924 – which fixed German war reparations at 50 billion gold marks, agreed a loan from America and negotiated the withdrawal of French and Belgian troops from the Ruhr so the German coal and steel industry could recover – the economy had gradually steadied. Until the reverberations of the Wall Street Crash, at which point everything was up in the air again. The result: constant disruption by violent extremists, both left and right, the Left blaming the Capitalists, the Right blaming the Communists and the Jews. By 1930 there was another plan, the Young Plan, reducing repayments by 20 per cent, but the Volk, the ordinary people, were close to starvation by then, with everyone looking for a saviour.

In the previous July 1932 election the NSDAP, Nazi Party, had won a huge 37.27 per cent of the vote and 230 of 584 seats, and there was every expectation that they might reach the 293 seats needed for a majority at the next election, especially if Dr Goebbels continued his good work. To everyone's amazement the turnout for the November election was over 80 per cent of the population, which said something important about the feelings of the German people at the time, though no one knew quite what.

But it was the Communist KPD, led by the charismatic Ernst Thälmann, pointing constantly to the dangers and volatility of the Capitalist system, which quite unexpectedly gained 11 seats, while the Nazis and Social Democrats lost theirs. Deputies in the Reichstag were stunned, Thälmann and his comrades triumphant: at last the working man had woken to the fact that only the uncompromising Communists had the answer, and that the Social Democrats' endless political compromises had let them down. By 1932 there were six million unemployed in the Reich and 27,000 farmers had gone to the wall. In Berlin, three-quarters of the population lived in a single room, children and all. The democracy of the Weimar years had manifestly failed to solve the desperate poverty, political chaos and deep post-war disillusionment. So, apart from those traditional patriots who voted for the conservative DNVP, the German National People's Party, Germans turned to more extreme political parties to solve their problems, polarising the nation even more. The workers tended to vote Left, either SPD, Social Democratic Party, or the Communist KPD, but now they shifted decisively to the Communists, with the Social Democrats losing 12 seats. The workers constituted 45.9 per cent of the population, but only 28 per cent of them voted for the Nazi Party. It was the lower middle class, shopkeepers and white collar workers who voted for the Nazis, making up a quarter of the Party's membership even though they were only 12 per cent of the population.

Hitler decided it was time to employ other means as soon as possible: ban Democracy, ban the Reichstag, ban the Communists and the Socialists, blame and kill the Jews. Anyone who had ears to listen or eyes to read Hitler's political manifesto *Mein Kampf*, 'My Struggle', published in two volumes in 1925 and 1927, could have foreseen it. There was a whole chapter on Eastern Policy. The racially pure German Volk would need *Lebensraum*, Hitler wrote, land to live in, and that would come from expansion to the East, into Poland and

Russia, and this, of necessity, meant war. Not just against the non-Aryan, subhuman Slav, but also against Communism.

As to the Jews in Germany: 'As soon as I have the power, I shall have gallows after gallows erected, for example in Munich on the Marienplatz,' Hitler told his cronies in one of his private table talks in the early 1920s. 'Then the Jews will be hanged, one after another, and they will stay hanging until they stink. They will stay hanging as long as hygienically possible. As soon as they are untied, then the next group will follow and that will continue until the last Jew in Munich is exterminated. Exactly the same procedure will be followed in other cities until Germany is cleansed of the last Jew!'

In Hamburg Ernst Thälmann meanwhile addressed his own comrades, at a Communist mass gathering on 10 July 1932. 'There is no greater or more shameful lie to the masses than when they are told: the Fascists will soon enough run out of steam, just let them carry on. Any such comment must be noted and rejected in the strongest terms. It is a slap in the face to all anti-Fascists and social democratic workers ... We are witnessing a growing Fascist movement in Germany, an increase in Fascism in the workplace and within our military, and an increase in their votes. They not only employ the most brutal methods to suppress the worker, but also prepare for a war against the Soviet Union.'

In Berlin, a *referendar* law student, Fabian von Schlabrendorff, was trying to make sense of what was happening to the Germany he knew and loved. Fabian was 25, dark-haired, serious-minded, clever, bespectacled, with the quiet confidence bestowed by a happy childhood. His family was Prussian nobility, though not one of the foremost like the Bismarcks or the Moltkes, nor were they even especially well-off. But everyone knew everyone else in those circles, many loosely related too. The families owned large country estates, sometimes entire villages, their titles of *Graf* or *Freiherr* or *Baron* passing seamlessly from father to eldest son. Apart from running their estates, the fathers might also hold positions high up in the Prussian Civil Service or hold rank in the Prussian army. Politically, they tended to be conservative, voting for the DNVP, German National People's Party, or the Centre Party, and as a class they believed in the traditional values of honour and patriotism, family, duty, social responsibility, decency and the natural order of things, whereby the Prussian nobility stood above, and the rest of the Volk somewhere below.

Theirs was a paternalistic society, and all the better for it, they agreed. On Sundays the whole family attended church, mostly Protestant but some Catholic, taking up the front pews, with their villagers and estate workers standing respectfully in the rows behind. The turbulent years of the Weimar Republic had left them with extremely mixed feelings about democracy. They were used to Kaisers and their hero was Bismarck, iron fist and all. The Republic was too weak they felt, leaving the Reich and the Volk in confusion and conflict. So they held firmly to their Prussian heritage, their kith and kin. If their sons didn't enter one of the regiments in the Prussian army they would likely begin their studies in Law, after attending a *Gymnasium* and getting a good grounding in the Classics – the Law being the gateway to everything else.

This was Fabian's story. By 1932 he was living in the family's apartment in Berlin and continuing his law studies. The Schlabrendorffs were Prussian soldiers on both sides, but Fabian was minded to make his future elsewhere, perhaps in a legal department of the Prussian Civil Service. He entertained rather left-wing views for someone of his background and he was determined to make his own way. In fact, he had little choice in this – his father, twenty years older than his mother, had died when Fabian was sixteen. He was the only boy, with four sisters, and their mother had to struggle to make ends meet. Fabian's father had been traditional in his views, holding little sympathy for the Weimar Republic. As a soldier, he knew Germany needed a strong leader and a strong army. Few of his fellow army officers would have disagreed, but not many shared his reasons: that the army's first and last task was to avoid war – not to make it.

Fabian was just a boy in 1914 when the Great War broke out, but he remembered the heady jubilation. Not his father: 'The German Reich will lose this war,' he'd warned, 'and the monarchy with it.' Everyone thought von Schlabrendorff was giving vent to his well-known pessimism, but as times got harder, food scarcer and victories fewer, people saw that he was right. When he died, he left Fabian a copy of Oswald Spengler's *Der Untergang des Abendlandes*, The Decline of the West, the book everyone was reading at the time, written in the shadow of war. Fabian kept it with him always. It gave him spiritual guidance for the rest of his life.

If Fabian's father was a silent man, his mother was the polar opposite: a born talker, and not very circumspect about it either. When her husband warned that Germany would lose the war, she told anyone who cared to listen, causing quite a stir. She was energetic, vivacious, warm, rebellious by temperament, and adored by all five children. And by her quiet husband, who, called in to account for his wife's unpatriotic talk, refused to apologise for her, saying she was entitled to her opinions like anyone else. Frau von Schlabrendorff became a fervent Nazi-hater early on. Some years later the Nazis tried to award her the Cross of Honour of the German Mother. To gain such a medal you had to prove your racial purity back to the grandparents and have at least four children. It was known derisively by the man in the street as the Order of the Rabbit. Frau von Schlabrendorff had five children and was living in straitened circumstances since her husband died. As such, she might have been awarded something more than just a medal – a larger apartment perhaps, recently 'vacated' by a Jewish family. But when the local Nazi officials came to congratulate her, Frau von Schlabrendorff greeted them with: 'I suppose you've come to take me away to a concentration camp!' And that was that.

So, on that day in 1932, Fabian was walking across Berlin in search of a man he didn't know and was unlikely to meet in the normal course of events, their social backgrounds being entirely different. He'd come across a journal titled *Widerstand*, Resistance, edited by Ernst Niekisch, a leading light of a movement called National Bolshevism.

This was loosely linked to the KPD Communist Party, and brought together disparate forces in Germany which all, for their varied reasons, rejected the terms of the Treaty of Versailles, preferred Soviet to American power, yet also supported German nationalism. Fabian knew that Niekisch had helped to set up the short-lived Bavarian Soviet Republic in 1919 during the virtual civil war which engulfed Germany following the war, and that he'd served a term in prison for his support of the revolution in Bavaria, and he knew that Niekisch was nominally a member of the SPD, but that he rejected their stated pacifism and was therefore expelled from the party in 1926. Which was when he started *Widerstand*. In 1932 he published a pamphlet, *Hitler, ein deutsches Verhängnis*, Hitler, Germany's Fateful Downfall, an outspoken attack on Nazism. And this is why Fabian was now seeking him out.

Fabian had read *Mein Kampf* in Halle, the university where he'd started his law studies. Halle was an odd choice for a young man with left-wing leanings because, even then, it was a hotbed of right-wing extremism, with a flourishing local Nazi Party. But Onkel Alfred, his mother's only brother, lived there. Onkel Alfred was a steadying influence, always the same, one of those people liked and respected by everyone whatever their background or political leanings. He was a senior civil servant, a liberal, and a confirmed bachelor. In 1933, when the Nazis were still keen to appear on the right side of the law, they offered him the job of President of Police in Halle, but he refused. That showed Fabian you could be an official in the Third Reich but not give way to the Nazis. And Onkel Alfred never did give way, even as late as 1944, when he publicly supported friends involved in the 20 July Plot to assassinate Hitler. Likewise, when Fabian was finally arrested and incarcerated in the Gestapo headquarters in Prince Albrecht Strasse, Onkel Alfred travelled from Halle to Berlin to visit him.

Fabian had started his law studies at Halle at his uncle's instigation because it was an excellent university with a renowned library – where he found *Mein Kampf*. Any doubts he may have had were instantly banished: from now on he would fight the Nazis however he could. But where to start? His relations and friends all came from similar Prussian backgrounds and, in 1932, most were still in search of a strong leader to release them from the chaos of Weimar democracy. Doggedly, Fabian searched around for people with other views and other aims. By the time he transferred to Berlin to pursue the next stage of his law studies, he'd discovered *Widerstand*.

Ernst Niekisch wasn't expecting anyone when he heard a knock at his door in the Hallesches Ufer district of Berlin, an ordinary sort of place a long way from the elegant district where the Schlabrendorffs had their apartment. When Niekisch opened the door he saw a young man standing there – obviously Prussian nobility because these things can't easily be disguised and quickly confirmed once Fabian began speaking. In his educated, cultured way, he apologised with a quick bow for his unannounced arrival, introduced himself and explained his reasons for coming. For his part, Fabian saw before him a short, stocky, middle-aged, middle-class man with a tough, determined face. 'He was probably the most important man ever to step into my life. *Les extremes se touchent*,' as he put it later, referring to the powerful attraction of opposites. The two got on immediately and it stayed like that until the day Niekisch died.

Once inside the house, Fabian quickly saw he'd done the right thing and found the right man. Niekisch had a fine way with words and he spoke them openly and directly, only concerned to put across his views with force and clarity. He never spoke down to Fabian even though he was just a young student, but quickly set out to convince him there was another way of looking at things. For Fabian it was his first proper encounter with a heart and soul republican. Up till now he'd only read about the kind of views held by Niekisch, which he recognised as loosely Marxist, but nationalist rather than internationalist. Now the man was there, in the flesh, and Fabian knew for certain a new world stood before him. Years later he still vividly remembered that first encounter.

'How did you find me?' asked Niekisch.

'In *Widerstand*.'

That told Niekisch he didn't have to start with the basics – this young man already knew them. Unlikely as it seemed, Fabian von Schlabrendorff had come to the same conclusion as himself: that Hitler and the Nazis were a force of chaos and destruction for Germany and that they had to be resisted at all costs. Niekisch thought a new era had to emerge out of the Weimar chaos, an era of the proletariat, of the working man, to counteract Hitler's populism with all its talk of Volk and race and war. And its hatred of the Jews. Fabian wondered briefly if Niekisch had some Jewish blood. Possibly. As to the proletariat, as far as Fabian could see, many of them were putting their hopes in the Nazis.

'Do you think Hitler's a kind of Napoleon III?' he asked.

'No, no,' said Niekisch. 'More Napoleon I. He'll draw the whole world into war. He'll start with great victories, waving that swastika flag, before the final inevitable downfall and destruction.' He said that in 1932, Fabian later reminded himself, long before all the downfall and destruction.

Fabian realised he had a lot to learn. To his surprise Niekisch was no admirer of Gustav Stresemann, the Weimar politician who served as both chancellor and foreign minister in the 1920s, guiding Germany through the crisis of hyperinflation caused by the harsh terms of the Treaty of Versailles. Like most Democrats, Schlabrendorff had admired how Stresemann, working with the Western Allies, was able to reduce the sum of war reparations, converting some into payment of raw materials such as coal and pig iron, and for his part in the negotiations between Germany and France over France's retreat from their occupation of Germany's industrial area of the Ruhr. But National Bolshevist Niekisch didn't agree. He was not impressed by this flirtation with the Western Allies, the very people who'd imposed such crippling terms on Germany. He preferred the terms of the 1922 Treaty of Rapallo between Germany and the new Soviet Socialist Republic whereby the two governments agreed to cooperate to meet the economic needs of both, each renouncing territorial and financial claims. Publicly, the two sides had agreed to re-establish diplomatic relations. In secret, by 1926, they had also agreed some military cooperation.

As secrets go, this was a big one. Niekisch was never for pacifism, and he deeply resented the fact that Germany was forbidden to rearm by the Treaty of Versailles, save for a basic army of no more than 100,000 men. By the time Fabian met him, Niekisch was acting as a secret liaison between Germany and Soviet Russia, working with Karl Radek, a Communist who'd returned to Germany from Moscow in 1923 and started putting out feelers towards the remaining stump of the *Reichswehr*, German army. The plan was to secretly build up a panzer regiment and a fledgling Luftwaffe in Russia, blatantly breaking the terms of the Treaty of Versailles. How far the plans succeeded remains unclear, but one thing is certain: Niekisch enjoyed the protection of the German military well into the Nazi era. Of course, Fabian only discovered this later. For the time being, he was simply looking for others who felt as he did about the dangers of Nazism. The Volk was well and good, as Niekisch was wont to say, but it was only the State which had the right to rule. Fabian, with his Prussian background, could only agree.

If all this was clear to Fabian, it was extremely unclear to a man called Rudolf Ditzen. Variously described as a thief, a liar, an alcoholic, a drug addict and a womaniser, Rudolf lived on his nerves and was in a constant state of depression. Some said it dated back to a serious accident when he was a boy which left him with headaches, dizzy spells and trouble sleeping. Others said he was just born like that, causing trouble for his parents from the start. When he was eighteen he underwent the first of many stays in a lunatic asylum after accidentally killing a friend in a duel – the result of a suicide pact which went wrong. In the 1920s, he did two short stints in prison for embezzlement.

The Ditzens were a typical middle-class family – the father a local magistrate in Greifswald, a town on the Baltic coast, the mother a housewife presiding over a household of four children with the help of a nursemaid and two servants. Rudolf was their third child, the one they never understood. Year after year, they tried to influence him, guide him, support him, often financially in later years, all to no avail. Rudolf careered from one crisis to another, often suicidal, always trouble. His teachers described him as 'a decadent person, who seemed almost weary of life, who felt himself above the law'. Arrogant too, noted the school principal. It was especially puzzling because the parents were good, decent people. They liked books and music. They played the piano. They took their children to museums and the zoo. They had no idea what to do with their wayward son. By the time Rudolf finished studying at the *Gymnasium* and the university, they just hoped and prayed he'd get a decent job, find a good wife, settle down. Instead, things only got worse. Rudolf drank more and more, became addicted to morphine and cocaine, smoked like a chimney, stayed out all hours, sometimes all night. He was plagued by a chronic restlessness. He couldn't sleep. He seemed to hate his parents.

By now the family was living in Leipzig following the father's promotion to the Supreme Court. Rudolf cast around for something to do. If nothing else, he had to earn some money. His father gave him a small allowance, but it was nothing like enough to cover his expensive tastes. Finally he found a job as a steward on a local country estate. Then came the 1914–18 war where he was not deemed fit enough to serve, and another job on another estate in Pomerania. The work suited him. He liked the farm workers, the ordinary people, and he liked the countryside, the woods, the fields, the solitude. It didn't change him, nothing could do that, but it suited him. Above all, it gave him time to do what he'd always wanted to do and knew he could do – write.

'All this time – and I only discovered this decades later – I was learning, learning to become what I was going to be one day: a writer ... endless rows of chattering women weeding beet or lifting potatoes and I heard these women and young girls chatting away all day.' The same went for the boss and the dairymen and the labourers. 'I learned how they talked and what they talked about, and because I was just a lowly employee myself, they weren't shy with me.'

Rudolf started to write, without a publisher and without any clear plan. But gradually he found his subject: the ordinary Volk, the '*Anständigen*', decent people, the ones who were struggling to survive in the economic and political chaos of post-war Germany. He chose Hans Fallada as his *nom de plume*, the name of a horse in one of the Grimms' fairy tales, a horse who always told the truth – a nice touch given his own slippery nature. 'Everything in my life ends up in my books,' he told a radio interview in 1946. And this, in fact, is how Rudolf told the world the truth about what was going on in Germany: through his writing, if not always through his actions.

The 1920s were as dramatic and chaotic for Rudolf as they were for Germany itself. One of Rudolf's brothers had been killed in the war, a devastating blow to all of them. In addition, Herr Ditzen's war bond investments were badly affected by Germany's defeat, resulting in a reduction of Rudolf's allowance. Where once the family enjoyed long summer holidays and winter skiing in the Alps, by the summer of 1923, with raging hyperinflation adding to their financial problems, they could only afford a short holiday, not least because of the expense of travel. 'The fourth-class railway tickets cost 58,000 marks on the way there and 580,000 marks on the way back. The next day the price would have been 2,320,000 marks,' as Herr Ditzen wrote to his son.

Bad news awaited them when they got home. In July Rudolf, perhaps making up for the shortfall in his allowance, was sentenced to six months in prison for embezzlement. His addictions to morphine and alcohol and tobacco all had to be paid for, after all. In August 1923 there was a general strike and the government fell. In Hamburg there was a short-lived Communist uprising, and in Munich the fledgling Nazi Party instigated the 'Beer-hall' putsch. Gustav Stresemann was soon replaced as chancellor, though not as foreign minister, and the next government was forced to bring in emergency legislation to try and quell the violent civil unrest.

Rudolf was sunken-faced and sallow-skinned due to his addictions and his chronic chain smoking. But he was like a cork on the high seas, tossed this way and that but somehow always bouncing back to the surface. By 1924, he'd found a publisher, Ernst Rowohlt. Large in build and temperament, humorous, generous, Rowohlt was a man who could walk into any room and be immediately surrounded by friends. A publisher to his fingertips, he supported his writers through thick and thin. From jail, Rudolf airily asked Rowohlt to send him six volumes of Balzac. Rowohlt sent the books, adding a jovial note: the postage alone had cost him 116,760,000,000 marks. Rowohlt knew Rudolf was trouble, but he could also see that he was an exceptional writer. In December, he paid Rudolf 100 gold marks, the first of many advances and loans he would give him over the years.

In prison, Rudolf was busy learning Oscar Wilde's 'Ballad of Reading Jail' by heart. Because of the emergency, the cell meant for one was full to bursting. By day he worked at chopping wood, by night he read and wrote till the light faded and the cockroaches emerged. Unfortunately, to gain favour with the prison guards, he grassed on his fellow jail-birds. 'But that's life,' he wrote to a friend, careless. 'I have to survive. Let stronger men be heroes and martyrs. I only have enough talent to be a small-scale coward.' If the stint in prison was meant to teach him a lesson, it didn't. He was hardly out and hardly into his new job on yet another country estate when he disappeared, along with 14,000 marks out of the till. Later he forged a cheque for 10,000 marks, and stole a further 5,000 marks. Then he gave himself up. He pleaded guilty to all charges and was sentenced to two and a half years in prison. 'A thoroughly degenerate psychopath,' noted the magistrate.

As far as Rudolf was concerned prison was good news. The one thing he didn't want was to end up in another lunatic asylum. In prison he could read and write. And perhaps even kick his addictions. He was already working on another novel, and now, guided by Rowohlt, he was writing essays and articles as well. He was increasingly concerned with the subject of the decent little man, struggling, poor, unfairly blamed and put upon, flung this way and that by fate and by political circumstances over which he had no control.

Based on his own experience, he took up the cause of prison reform. 'Prisoners who have served long sentences should not be released without adequate provision,' he wrote in one of his articles. In his own case the system worked well: when he was released in February 1928 the prisoners' welfare found him a job and accommodation in Hamburg. There he joined the SPD and started attending the Order of the Good Templar, an abstinence society, which helped him to give up his drugs. And there he met Suse Issel, aged twenty-seven, doing voluntary work – fair-haired, sweet-natured, strong. Who changed his life.

The Issels were part of the 'Anständigen' decent people Rudolf was minded to defend. Suse worked as a milliner and belonged to a trade union. Politically the family were Social Democrats, still hoping for a better world and a fairer society. The SPD did well in the 1928 elections, just before the Wall Street Crash, becoming the largest party in the Reichstag, reflecting the fact that the government was finally managing to bring some stability to the economy. The Nazis' NSDAP only got 2.6 per cent of the vote.

Herr Ditzen's finances began to recover along with everyone else's.

Rudolf wrote asking for more money to support his new life as a writer. Against his better judgement but keen to give his son a chance especially now that he had a publisher, Herr Ditzen agreed on a sum of 150 marks a month – on condition he wrote to his mother regularly, enclosing a detailed budget. Rudolf bought a second-hand typewriter and set to work in his new lodgings in Hasselbrook Strasse. He did some typing work for extra money, and wrote to Rowohlt enquiring after some work in his publishing office. Later he moved back to Neumünster in Schleswig Holstein, where he'd been living before prison, but he wrote to Suse every day and visited Hamburg regularly. By December, they were engaged, the wedding set for April. 'I have never been so happy in my whole life,' Rudolf wrote to a friend.

In Neumünster, he got some work on a local newspaper, writing up local events in the town and the surrounding countryside, and reviewing films. It earned him some money, but more than that, it gave him the material for his next book, which first alerted the general reading public to Hans Fallada. Titled *Bauern, Bonzen und Bomben* (Farmers, Functionaries and Fireworks), and published in 1931, it was the story of a small provincial town, its people and its newspaper, and by Rudolf's own account it was completely different to any of his previous novels: much more political, committed to the 'little man' buffeted by fate. It was Rudolf's way of making his views felt. If he wasn't strong or courageous enough to act, he could still write, and reach millions of people in doing so. The book was really about 'poor Germany' not just 'poor farmers', as he wrote to his sister Elizabeth.

So here comes Tredup, on the first page of the book, in threadbare black coat and black felt hat, striding furiously along the street to his meagre job, selling advertising space on the local *Chronicle* newspaper, outraged at the unfairness and ignominies of his life. When he comes into the office the secretary looks up briefly, sees who it is, and goes back to reading her romance. 'Don't be like that Clara, Clarabella, Clarissiama,' he protests, reminding her that he saw her coming out of the Grotto past midnight. 'Well, if I'm to live off what he pays me!' is her shameless reply. His readers knew what that meant: so many women had been reduced to prostitution to make ends meet after the latest economic crisis. Tredup asks after the boss's wife. 'Sozzled?' Yes. Out cold drunk in the courtyard, skirts up to her knickers, for all to see. To amuse themselves Tredup and his two colleagues Wenk and Stuff come up with alternative titles for the newspaper: the *Daily Smear, Swastika Sell-out, Shit-house Square, Fart-in-a-phone-box, Read-it-and-Sleep, Scandal Sheet*. Apparently the police superintendent who used to vote SPD, now a Nazi, was caught red-handed having it off with one of the cleaners that night in the *Rathaus*, the Town Hall. 'They were doing it on the Mayor's desk.' Naturally that wouldn't make the pages of the *Chronicle*, he being the police superintendent and a Nazi to boot. Let's face it: there was corruption everywhere.

No wonder the reading public was thrilled by Hans Fallada. They recognised their own lives, described with sharp humour and humanity. They could see it and, thanks to the writer's brilliant way with dialogue and voices, they could hear it too. The next scene hit home. Two bailiffs are on their way to Farmer P. They're off to auction two oxen because Farmer P can't pay his taxes. Another bankrupt. 'I make them homeless after 1,000 years,' the senior tells his junior. The book had turned its attention to the Land Volk movement – an association of small farmers who'd banded together to protest about the effects of the economic crisis on their lives, driving 27,000 of them into bankruptcy. Schleswig Holstein, where the imaginary *Chronicle* existed and the real Ditzens lived, was especially affected. The farmers couldn't get a proper price for their milk, meat, butter or vegetables. They were falling into debt and unable to pay their taxes. Bankruptcy swiftly followed, with families who'd tilled the same land for generations becoming 'homeless after 1,000 years' as Rudolf's bailiff said. The same applied to local small businesses. By 1930, following the shock waves of the Wall Street Crash, the NSDAP vote had increased from 4 per cent to 27 per cent in Schleswig Holstein, the highest political shift in the land.

Meanwhile Rudolf Ditzen, now thirty-five, was happy for the first time in his life. Suse was the perfect wife for him, strong, calm and a good housewife. With her help, he cut out drinking and continued to resist the temptations of morphine and cocaine, limiting himself to chain-smoking. During the day he wrote, in the evenings he read aloud to Suse while she did the darning. His book was well reviewed and was actually making money. They were able to move to the Moabit district of Berlin, renting two furnished rooms with their own kitchen – which was just as well since they had their first child now, a boy called Uli, named after Rudolf's brother killed in the war. Rudolf's parents, daring to hope their son's life was finally steadying, upped his allowance. Better still, Rowohlt was able to offer Rudolf a part-time job in the Reviews Department at the office, earning 250 marks a month. Every morning he took the train from Bellevue station then walked the last stretch to Passauer Strasse, starting work at 9am, ending at 2pm. When he got home he played with Uli. Then he wrote till late into the night, chain-smoking. Life really couldn't have been much better. At least for the time being.

In Hamburg, on 10 July 1932, Irma Thälmann, aged thirteen, was having her hair done by her mother in preparation for their big outing. Her father, Ernst Thälmann, the charismatic leader of the KPD, the German Communist Party, had already left the house, accompanied by his comrades and bodyguard, for the Platz in the centre of the city, where he was going to address the crowds of workers gathered there. It was the first time Irma was allowed to attend such a mass meeting, dangerous as they usually were. She had already proved her dedication to the cause, her fervour fuelled by her devotion and profound admiration of her father. She'd insisted on joining the Red Young Pioneers when she was six, though the normal age was nine. By the time she was eleven she was one of the leaders. When Thälmann looked at his daughter, his and Rosa's only child, he felt he looked at himself.

'My parents often told me what terrible poverty there was in 1919 when I was born, in Hamburg-Eppendorf, Siemssenstrasse 4. Deep snow on the ground, and no coal or wood to be had, our rooms ice cold,' Irma would write in her memoir years later.

Apparently her father always promised her mother that things would change. 'A million children freezing like ours here now. And myself unemployed like nearly all other dockworkers and millions of other German workers.' The only way the Thälmanns survived was with the help of friends and comrades and a small stipend from his trade union where he was treasurer.

The flat was always a hive of activity, Irma recalled, nearly all of it political – discussions, planning, conspiracies, plenty of secrets. Irma was told never to talk to anyone in the street about what went on in their home. It was too dangerous. How could a child tell between friend and foe? They didn't want her to know there were spies every-where watching every movement *Vater* made.

She remembered being at home alone one evening when her parents were out at a meeting. Their flat was on the ground floor and she was in bed, fast asleep, when some men broke in, turned the cupboards and desk upside-down, looking for incriminating political material. She slept through it all. When her parents came home they asked her, what happened? She had no idea. She never forgot their dis-tressed expressions. Rosa should never have left her alone, she knew, but this was a most important meeting at a time of virtual civil war between Left and Right, and to Irma's parents' politics, the Fight and the Party had to come first. Later that same year, Irma and *Mutti* were already in bed, *Vater* out at yet another meeting, when the Freikorps 'Consul' unit threw a hand grenade through the window of their front room. It's just the way things were in those days.

'My father was a fighter,' Irma wrote. One evening, coming home at 2am from a meeting in a Hamburg suburb, he saw a suspicious guy lurking, and beat him up. It was no contest. Ernst Thälmann was built like a tank and honed by years of street battle. Then another guy ran up to stop him. Apparently the one lying on the ground was a com-rade, one of many placed at intervals on Thälmann's route between the station and home, to give him protection from the Freikorps. No one had thought to tell him. They often laughed about it later, during rare evenings when Thälmann was home and not working on a speech or lecture, when they'd sit round the table, mother, father and daughter, and Irma learned the lessons she'd hold to for the rest of her life. They were magical evenings full of passionate talk and plenty of laughter. Sometimes her father would suddenly pull Irma up from the table and dance round the kitchen with her.

Summer Sundays were the best. *Vater* would say they were going to the Blankenese, which was a beach on the Elbe where many Hamburg workers met to recover after a hard week, swimming, playing ball games, talking, discussing. Everyone knew everyone. *Vater* would be sitting there on the bank, happy among his friends and talking to the dock workers, hearing their worries, getting information, offering practical advice. And playing with the children. 'Sport makes happiness,' he'd say, 'but it's also necessary to strengthen us for our daily battles.' There were members of the SPD there too, and non-politicals, all Hamburg workers. They formed discussion groups, and there were often great disagreements when *Vater* intervened. 'Think about it!' he'd tell them. 'The five fingers of your hand couldn't achieve much on their own. Only when they're made into a fist do they have power!'

Ernst Thälmann was full of energy and exuberance, always ready to fight. But it was clear the family had to move to a safer flat, not on a ground floor. So Irma's mother Rosa went searching everywhere on foot – there wasn't enough money for trams. Her father's modest expenses were funded by the Party, but not Rosa's. Not many landlords wanted Ernst Thälmann in their buildings, but she never gave up. That was Rosa. As determined and committed in her way as her husband. Finally, she found rooms on a first floor in Tarpenbeck Strasse, near the centre of the city.

Their new home quickly became another meeting place for the fighters, filled with constant activity and noisy discussion. In October 1923, Thälmann had led the great Hamburg Uprising, the workers from the docks and the factories protesting against the lack of bread and employment and the hard repression by the authorities. It lasted three days and three nights and Irma, aged four at the time, never forgot it. Women and children helped build the barricades using whatever they could find: stones, garden gates, trees, even furniture. There were hardly any weapons. Only a few of the 'partisans', as Irma's father called them, had rifles, firing on the police from the rooftops. The police had tanks as well as guns and many fighters were killed. 'They attacked, were felled, and they attacked again, they never gave up,' Irma recalled, nostalgic for those heady days. But there was no support for the KPD workers from the SPD, so the chance for change was lost. Hundreds of workers, men and women, were arrested, and many died at the hands of the right-wing Freikorps.

On 9 November there was a mass demonstration at the Ohlsdorf cemetery to honour the dead. In spite of the danger a stream of workers arrived. Irma's father was warned he'd be arrested if he appeared, but of course he went and addressed the workers. Irma went too. 'I went with mother. Great crowds were making their way to the cemetery. They were threatened by the commandos and the lorries of heavily armed police at the gates and more police and criminal investigators in the cemetery. But the workers were well organised. Each comrade on protection duty knew exactly where to stand and what his job was. My father was nowhere to be seen. Suddenly cheering rose from somewhere in middle of the crowd. He appeared from nowhere and spoke in their midst, dispelling all sadness and praising the workers of Hamburg for their courage to great cheers, and then, just as suddenly, he disappeared into the masses, protected by an unbreakable chain of comrades.'

From 1924 onwards, Thälmann spent a lot of time in Berlin, taking up his position as KPD member in the Reichstag. Irma asked if she and her mother could move to Berlin too, but her father said no: his heart and home were in Hamburg, with the dock workers.

'*Vater* often travelled to the Soviet Union. When I was nine he came came back from Leningrad one day, and *Mutti* and I went to pick him up. Lots of comrades were there to meet him too and once he'd finished talking to them, he whispered in my ear: "I've brought you something fine." He gave us his suitcase to take home and came along later. We didn't open the case but were excited. He waited till we'd eaten, then unpacked. I got a Pioneer outfit with red neckerchief and white blouse and a skirt. *Mutti* helped me put it on and showed *Vater*. "In the Soviet Union the young Pioneers have rules, and once you wear the uniform, you have to obey the rules," he told Irma. 'All my friends were envious. I explained that the red neckerchief's three corners were a symbol of the three parts of the Communist Party, and the knot bound them fast. He also brought me some picture books. And some beautiful wooden jigsaws of the Kremlin and the red flag.'

Irma's favourite evenings were when *Vater* had the time and inclination to sit at the kitchen table telling stories about his childhood. 'Remember, Hamburg was a great city, a Hansa Stadt, free state, within the monarchy when I was growing up,' he'd tell Irma and Rosa who'd heard it all before but still liked to hear it all again. 'Blohm and Voss Shipbuilders alone employed 10,000 dock workers building those great ocean liners for the Hamburg-America Line. There were powerful trade unions and worker organisations, social as well as political. Hamburg had a million inhabitants and we were trading across the world: rubber, wool, jute, copper, zinc, oil, and products from our factories like margarine, chocolate and cigarettes. We had cotton mills and breweries. The greatest industrial output in the Reich.

But of course they were all Capitalist enterprises with no interest or care for their workers who came in from the country, from Schleswig, Mecklenburg, Friesland, farmers and sailors and builders – strong, intelligent types, who were soon demanding their rights, striking and demonstrating. The Capitalists and authorities came down hard on them, imprisoning them, and putting them on their Black List. That's what happened to *Grossvater*, Grandpapa, you know. And when he got out of prison the only way he could provide for us was to go round the streets with a cart selling potatoes and coal. Then a horse and cart. Then the cellar shop. It didn't stop him being politically active. Nothing could do that.' You could hear the deep admiration in *Vater*'s voice.

Talking in that spellbinding way of his, Irma listening wide-eyed, he said he had to help his own *Vater* from the age of seven, getting up at 4am on market days, looking after the horse, delivering door to door, in deepest snow of winter or the boiling heat of summer. He was good at school but had to leave at 14. There just wasn't the money. As soon as he could he was off, as a stoker on one of the big ships to America. There he worked on a farm near New York. America taught him a thing or two about the workings of the Capitalist system, he said, laughing. Such riches. Such poverty. The farm employed negroes and their children weren't allowed to play with the white farmer's children. Even the negro children had to work hard.

When he came back to Hamburg he joined the Transport Workers Trade Union, threw himself into it, organising strikes and demonstrations. Soon he was the treasurer, then the branch leader, finally the leader. Sometimes strikes lasted for weeks, 18,000 workers all out, all holding together. Every spare minute he studied books on political theory. And went to meetings. He loved the company and good company in general. He was twenty-eight when the Great War broke out. He described it as a victory for the Imperialists over the working man. The Left, including the Social Democrats, were against the war. But the Thyssens and the bankers and the Imperialists and Junkers won, he told Irma, and they got their war. That's what the youth of Europe, on all sides, was sacrificed for! The Munition Kings and Finance Princes. It was a terrible thing for the workers, a painful disillusionment, he said. He himself spent two-and-a-half years at the Front, first at the Somme, then the Aisne. He was forbidden home leave. That's how the Imperialists solved their problem with the politically active worker

– kept them at the Front, getting killed. He was wounded twice. But still no home leave. He quoted Karl Liebknecht: 'The main enemy of every people lies in their own country. The main enemy of the German Volk is in Germany itself: German Imperialism, the party of war.'

Finally, in summer 1917, he got home leave. He used the short time to read up about the Russian Revolution and revolution in Germany. He joined the Independent Social Democrats and voted against the war. Later he left, taking 42,000 members into the Communist Party with him. In 1917 the sailors mutinied at Wilhelmshaven. Then came the October Revolution. He was back at the Front by then, having to be careful with his anti-war activities, as he knew he was under surveillance. Another year with no home leave followed. When he finally returned to Hamburg, in autumn 1918, he found starvation everywhere and strikes in the docks. Karl Liebknecht and Rosa Luxemburg were in prison, later murdered. 'Europe had become a hell,' he said. 'Millions of dead, millions of wounded, nameless suffering, hunger . . . while the winners of the war – the Captains of Industry and the armaments factories made more and more profits.'

On 5 November 1918 the Hamburg dock workers laid down their tools and marched on the city centre. In Hamburg alone there were eight different Freikorps units, fighting the Communists in the streets. They had names like 'Werewolf', 'Fredericus Rex' and 'Black Hunter', filled with demoralised soldiers – politically right-wing, certainly, but above all demoralised, with no jobs and nowhere else to go. They decided the left-voting working class was the reason Germany lost the war. And the Jews. They called it the stab in the back. They hated democracy. They wanted a military dictatorship. It was they who formed the foundations and structure of the Nazi party. Then came the right-wing Kapp Putsch. To their shame, the government briefly fled to Stuttgart, but the German Volk stood up to them, answering the call for a general strike, downing all tools – no trains or trams, no factories, no lorries, no businesses, no ships setting sail, no dock workers. It was over in days. The failure of that revolution was due to the fact that the leaders of the German proletariat were divided, Vater explained to Irma.

By the time she was thirteen Irma was a hardened revolutionary. She'd been in the Young Pioneers for seven years and witnessed for herself the poverty of families whose fathers were unemployed or who'd been killed in the uprisings or street battles. Every Christmas she'd brought toys and food to those starving families, donated by the Party. Now, on 10 July 1932, wearing her Young Pioneers' uniform, she was part of the throng of workers making their way to the Platz for the anti-Fascist rally, holding tight to her mother's hand so as not to get lost in the crowd. Her father had gone ahead as usual, protected by the comrades. The mood was electric with anticipation. The workers didn't care about the Freikorps or the police who were standing by with guns and fists at the ready. They just wanted to hear the voice of their great leader.

Suddenly a great cheer went up. Thälmann appeared in their midst, out of nowhere, as usual. And then he began to speak, using a megaphone: Don't believe the Social Democrats when they tell you that even if the Fascists get into power, they won't last. No! This was a shameless lie! The Fascists will never give up power once they have it, and they will prepare for another war. 'Everywhere we see not only the hard repression of the working man, but also preparation for war against the Soviet Union,' he warned. What Germany needed was national, social and political freedom, not war. 'We know a land where there is no Fascism, a land where it would be unthinkable for the Fascists to practise murder on the streets, carrying out their bloody actions in the working-class districts. It is called the Soviet Union!' Irma cheered and cheered along with all the rest. 'So we continue our fight against Fascism, closely bound together with the international proletariat!'

CHAPTER TWO

THE NAZIS TAKE POWER

Fritz-Dietlof Count von der Schulenburg got married on 11 March 1933. He was thirty-one. His bride was Charlotte Kotelmann – a perfect match in every way. The day before the wedding he was called in for a meeting with Hermann Göring, now busily employed creating the *Geheime Staatspolizei* – the Gestapo, the secret police designed to eradicate all opponents of the Nazis. Having joined the NSDAP as member 291342 a year before, the Count was seen as one of the up-and-coming, well-connected young men the Nazis were keen to attract – a proper Prussian aristocrat no less, clever, and with plenty of old-world charm. The meeting got off to a bad start, however, when Göring, lavishly attired in one of his smart uniforms, berated the young Count for his sloppy dress. Von der Schulenburg, with aristocratic disdain and in fact not much money, brushed the rebuke off easily, and after some further discussion Göring invited him to meet the Führer and some of his cronies. This was an unexpected honour and meant that everyone waiting back at the Count's family apartment in Berlin – his parents, four brothers and sister, Tisa – were getting worried that Fritz-Dietlof would be late for his *Polterabend*, stag night. Göring presented Schulenburg to the Führer as 'the wild Count', indicating the casual dress, but Hitler didn't pay much attention, having more important matters on his mind.

Fritzi, as he was known to his family and friends, managed to get back to the apartment just in time for the celebration. The next day the happy couple were married at the *Dreifaltigkeitskirche*, Holy Trinity Church, the bride in white with a bouquet of lilies, the groom in his morning suit and silk top hat. His three older brothers, Johann Albrecht, Wolf Werner, known as Wolfi, and Adolf Heinrich, known as Heini, were all enthusiastic members of the Nazi Party, as were the parents. Only Wilhelm, Fritzi's younger brother, held back. And Tisa, his sister. Tisa was anti-Nazi from the first.

Charlotte was of a mind to support her new husband, whatever he did. She was seven years younger than him and had given up her Philology studies to marry. His parents couldn't have been happier. Charlotte was everything they could have wished of a daughter-in-law: loving, attractive, intelligent without being too clever, happy-natured, wanting nothing more than to be a good wife and mother. Shortly before their marriage, Charlotte had visited Fritzi in Königsberg where he'd been posted straight after the *Machtergreifung*, the Nazi power grab. He'd found himself a nice apartment there, he wrote to Charlotte, half an hour by train from Königsberg, in a beautiful and quiet country setting, just how he liked it, away from all the hustle and bustle and political infighting. He wrote to her almost every day, long letters and short, the long ones often about his political and social hopes and aspirations. She was his soulmate to the last. He reminded her that she'd married a dedicated worker who would never have a lot of time for her. 'But when I'm with you, you have my entire joy and love.' As though to prove the point, he called off the long honeymoon they'd planned, replacing it with a few days at Schloss Tressow, the family estate in Mecklenburg in northern Germany. She didn't mind. Snapshots taken of them at that time show a couple seated on the grass in a park, arms wrapped around one another, crazily in love.

The odd one out in the Schulenburg family was Tisa. She and Fritzi had grown up doing everything together, there being only eighteen months between them – but more than that because they were kindred spirits. Fritzi was different from their three elder brothers, more sensitive, more clever and altogether more to Tisa's liking. When she was born, on 7 December 1903 at Tressow, their father called his four small sons into his study to ask them what name they might give her. The four boys didn't know any girls' names. '*Rosenkranz*', rose-wreath, suggested one of them, trying his best. In the event she was named Elizabeth Karoline Mary Margarete Veronika. Tisa for short. From the start Tisa went her own way. No one in the family understood her. Except Fritzi.

Fritzi wasn't born at Tressow but in London where his father, Count Friedrich Bernhard von der Schulenburg, was military attaché at the Court of St James. His parents, who were close friends of the Kaiser, loved London: the place, the people, the banquets and balls, the country house weekends – in fact all of Court life in a vibrant international city. Potsdam, Schulenburg's regimental home, was a small garrison town by comparison. But the family wasn't often in Potsdam, moving from one provincial town to another following the father's postings. Home was Tressow. Tressow they loved. Fritzi and Tisa shared a room there till Fritzi was sent off to school, and they shared the nursery with Heini, where only English was spoken with Vicky the English nurse-maid. Later they shared a governess, Miss Bull, a vicar's daughter from the north of England who took a dislike to Fritzi for no discernible reason other than perhaps his precociousness: from early on Fritzi was a touch arrogant.

'Fritz-Dietlof von der Schulenburg, I'll box your ears!' she'd say. And did. Or she locked him in the dark cupboard under the stairs. 'Tell Mama!' said Tisa, but proud Fritzi never would. Afterwards they'd escape into the parkland surrounding the Schloss, climbing trees, running races with their brothers, playing in the stables, sledging in the winter, bathing in the lake in the summer, and going on their daily walk with Miss Bull through the fields and the woods, Tisa in her English smocks, the boys in their sailor suits. Tisa did everything the boys did, refusing to be left out. 'You're like a boy!' they accused her. But only Tisa was allowed to sit on the silk chair in her mother's bedroom in the mornings watching Maria brush *Mutti*'s hair.

In 1911 their father was transferred from one of his provincial postings back to Army High Command in Berlin. Now his trousers bore the wide red stripe down the side and his boots were high and black and shiny. He had very blue eyes, their *Vater*, with bushy eyebrows and a handlebar moustache. He could laugh heartily but he was strict too. They only saw him at the evening meal when they had to sit up straight and stay silent. Once Fritzi, the rebel, broke the silence and spoke. *Vater* frowned. To everyone's amazement, Fritzi said: 'I can look like that too!' knitting his brows. That got him punished. Perhaps he wasn't allowed to go to Circus Busch with its Chinese acrobats and fire-eaters, or perhaps he couldn't go roller-skating, Tisa couldn't remember. But it was soon forgotten and they were off with their brothers, jumping on the back of trams or riding the electric U-Bahn, exploring Berlin, newly vibrant following the unification of Germany and the rapid growth of the economy in the early years of the twentieth century. Sometimes they were lucky and persuaded their grandfather, the Bismarck one on their mother's side, to take them for a drive in his automobile which could go at 20 kilometres an hour. But holidays were always spent at Tressow where they quickly reverted to the ways of country life. The estate had several villages attached and one of Tisa and Fritzi's favourite activities was to accompany their mother when she paid a villager a visit, perhaps one of the old people living in the almshouses built for them by their father at the turn of the century. But whatever they did, be it Berlin, Potsdam or Tressow, Fritzi and Tisa did it together.

The day came when Fritzi had to join his brothers at the *Gymnasium*. Tisa, the girl, had to stay home. She begged and begged to be allowed to go to school too, and later she was allowed to attend the local art school, because Tisa loved to draw and paint. But by then Germany was embroiled in the Great War, with their father and two of her brothers already at the Front and Heini soon to join them, all three brothers volunteering at the first opportunity. Their mother cried and their father warned of the senselessness of war, but nothing could stop them. By the end of the war the father, who'd advised making peace as early as 1916, came home exhausted and bitter, and retreated to his room. Johann Albrecht and Wolfi were wounded. Heini returned hardened and disillusioned.

Fritzi was too young to fight. But he did *Grenzenschutz* border patrol on the new Eastern frontier with Poland and experienced first-hand the poverty and despair of the ordinary people, the ones who suffered most from the Reich's defeat. He was billeted with a farming family so poor they ate their potatoes straight from one big dish in the middle of the kitchen table – no plates, and often no food either. Later, in Berlin, he fought the Communist Spartacus League on the barricades. When he came home Tisa found him changed – sharper, less talkative, more determined. And so thin his mother at first didn't recognise her own son walking along the country road back to Tressow.

After recuperating, Fritzi went to the University of Göttingen. He took Law and *Staatswissenschaft*, Political Science, preparing himself for a life in the Prussian Civil Service, very much in the Schulenburg tradition on both sides of the family. He read everything he could lay his hands on, including Marx and Lenin. Engulfed by political and economic crises, he and his student comrades drank and discussed late into the night, always battling with the same question: what to do to save the German Reich?

He was the natural leader of the group, humorous, well-read and sceptical of quick solutions. He decided to go into training, for the self-discipline and to toughen himself up: body-building, fencing, swimming. To Tisa's surprise, he joined the student fraternity. It shocked her because it seemed to go against everything they'd talked about before: the urgent need for political change and reform of the old traditional ways in order to create a fairer society. But Fritzi being Fritzi didn't just join the fraternity, he got himself into a duel, resulting in a deep scar on his left cheek, which he had for the rest of his life. Tisa meanwhile drew and painted and flirted with the new ideas of Socialism during those early Weimar years. Her parents worried. Why was she so different to the rest of the family? So argumentative? So rebellious? So unfeminine? How would she ever find a husband with views like that?

By the time Fritzi and Charlotte got engaged in June 1932, he'd taken the usual steps along the Prussian Civil Service path. He showed early signs of promise and was quickly promoted. Off his own bat, he decided to get a transfer to Recklinghausen in the industrial and largely Catholic west Germany to see for himself how bad things were there. And things were very bad indeed, with every kind of social problem and unemployment even higher than in Prussia. The administrative paperwork piled up on his desk, but Fritzi was never one to get bogged down by that. He did the minimum, quickly and effectively, preferring to be out and about checking matters for himself. He made a point of meeting the workers and the unemployed, Socialists and Communists, and personally helped out some families financially. Everyone, including Fritzi himself, blamed the situation on the punishing terms of the Treaty of Versailles – and many of those he talked to preferred the Russians to the Western Allies.

By autumn 1932, Fritzi had been transferred to Heiligenbeil in East Prussia. The fishermen there were suffering from the Haff sickness, caused by eating contaminated fish. They couldn't work to earn a living and feed their starving families. No one in the administration was doing anything about it. Fritzi easily discovered the cause: polluted water from the local factories. He arranged a meeting with the factory bosses who refused to comply. When he warned them of disciplinary action, they still refused, knowing that this was just a junior official and the senior ones would surely turn a blind eye, as they always had. Fritzi demanded a meeting with the big boss, Landrat Gramsch, who referred the matter upwards.

It was Fritzi's deep conviction that the Civil Service was there to serve not just the state, but the Volk, whether at local, regional or national level. 'I want to feel Germany's need as my own, carry the longings of millions of unhappy Germans in my own heart, and work for them, as though it were my own fate,' he wrote to a friend. 'I feel that I'm bound tightly to Germany with a deep love. I feel her pain and her need as though it were my own. And I see it as the highest duty, worth giving up a person's life, to fight for it, and to sacrifice oneself for it.'

What the country needed, Fritzi was convinced, was strong, good leadership. A Führer. He joined discussion groups, went to meetings, gave lectures, did everything he could to help the Volk. And if his convictions meant taking on the big landowners or the factory bosses or the local administrators, so be it.

The Nazi propaganda machine, orchestrated by Joseph Goebbels, was making a strong impression, and nowhere more so than in East Prussia where the farmers' Land Volk movement, which Rudolf Ditzen had written about so vividly, was on the march.

'I've become a National Socialist as a result of experiencing circumstances in Northern Germany, where the Party has become a Volk movement,' Fritzi wrote to Charlotte. 'There are good leaders there too. Because I've realised there's no other flag under which this can be achieved. I know the shadow side of the Party. I know many of the local leaders aren't great. But everything is on the move. It looks as though the Prussian and North German way will be able to win through.'

Fritzi was deeply impressed by Gregor Strasser who was on the Left of the Party – a man of intellect who was nevertheless of and for the

Volk. The economy would be reorganised by the Nazis, said Strasser, reining in the big banks who'd got them into so much trouble. They would have German Socialism – not the Capitalism of the Western Allies nor the Communism of the Russians.

When Hitler came to Königsberg to give one of his *Führer-Rede* talks, Fritzi was there, all ears. 'Hitler spoke mesmerisingly,' he wrote to Charlotte, 'deeply serious, everything he says is alive and lived. Here is a man who believes in something, and believes every word he says, and has stayed unpretentious about everything. This is a man who has become a real Führer but has nevertheless not cut himself off from us, the Volk. He may have made mistakes and have weaknesses. But he is the prophet, the educator, the man to believe in, for the millions.'

Goebbels came too, in April 1932, and again Fritzi was impressed. To his delight Goebbels stated categorically that National Socialism was based on Old Prussian values. 'The ideas we hold are Prussian. The aims, which we mean to achieve in a more modern fashion, are those of Friedrich Wilhelm I, Friedrich the Great, and Bismarck. The Volk wants us to bring back these Prussian values of State government.' How could idealistic Fritzi have known that Goebbels, the day before, had written in his diary: 'The fight for Prussia (in the forthcoming elections) is almost over. It's proceeding apace. We have fourteen more days to achieve our aim. It's a master-stroke of propaganda.'

And so, in January 1933, Hitler became Chancellor of Germany. And everything changed overnight. It only took five days from the *Machtergreifung* for the Nazis to pass the Law for the Protection of State and People, which restricted press freedom and freedom of assembly. On 22 February, 50,000 auxiliary 'policemen' were created, mostly attached to the *Sturmabteilung*, SA, the Nazis' paramilitary force since the early days, unleashing a wave of violence across the country against Communists and Socialists. The KPD Communist headquarters in Berlin was raided and ransacked. On 27 February came the Reichstag fire, which the Nazis claimed was the work of Communists. In reprisal, 10,000 Communists were arrested. Hitler passed another Law for the Protection of People and State the following day, giving him emergency powers to 'restore order'.

All freedom of speech and assembly and the press were now suspended. The police were given powers to arrest and detain suspects indefinitely. By March, Oranienburg and Dachau concentration camps had been set up as prison/work camps for political opponents of the regime taken into 'protective custody'. Germany had become a Police State.

On 23 March, following the elections held on 5 March, came the Enabling Act. From now on laws could be passed without the

consent of the Reichstag, effectively making Germany a dictatorship. *Gleichschaltung* was immediately put into action, requiring total political and cultural alignment with Nazi ideology. Anyone who resisted – teachers, lawyers, businessmen, doctors, factory foremen – were now in danger of losing their jobs. *Gleichschaltung* was the key to everything, allowing the Nazis to hound any opponent of the regime, however small. The first of April marked the first boycott of Jewish shops and businesses, their doctors' surgeries and legal practices. Six days later, the Law for the Restoration of the Professional Civil Service was passed, purging it of all 'unreliable' political elements, including in the universities. On 2 May, the Trade Unions were dissolved. 10 May saw the burning of 'degenerate' books. On 22 June, the SPD, the Social Democrats, were officially banned, their assets seized. Three thousand prominent Socialists were arrested. The Party fled abroad, first to Prague, then Paris, and finally, in 1941, after the Nazis subjugated France, to London. By July 1933, all political parties except the Nazi Party had been disbanded in Germany. And the Protestant churches were amalgamated to form a single 'Reich Church'. Six months is all it took.

Back in Hamburg, Irma Thälmann, now fourteen, was distraught. Her father, Ernst Thälmann, leader of the German Communists, had been arrested in Berlin on 3 March at the KPD Party headquarters. Many wondered why it hadn't happened sooner, but the Nazis held back from arresting someone so powerful in their first month for fear of civil unrest. They knew they needed time to win the people over. Hardly a third of the population had voted for them in the November election.

The newsreels of hysterical crowds cheering Hitler as his car made its triumphal way through the streets of Berlin after 30 January 1933 were as much thanks to Goebbels' dark arts as a reflection of the feelings of the majority of the German people, most of whom stayed quietly at home, keeping their heads down, hoping for the best. Arresting Ernst Thälmann, the most charismatic and popular of leaders, would have been a dangerous mistake. Even after Thälmann addressed a secret meeting of the Central Committee at an undisclosed location near Berlin on 3 February, he wasn't arrested. The comrades had warned him not to address the meeting but to disappear underground or into exile as others had done. Instead he made a four-hour speech, only occasionally consulting his notes, urging the parties of the Left to unite in order to fight the new regime. He regretted not having called for unity earlier, but no one foresaw the Nazi seizure of power, achieved by a fateful collusion of right-wing parties.

Thälmann warned that the Nazis would stop at nothing to defeat their political opponents. He reminded them of the Armament Kings, men like German industrialists Krupp and Thyssen who bank-rolled the Nazi Party, the SA and the SS, and who were supporting war, intending to reap the profits. He talked about the meetings his own Party were organising on local and district levels to plan their counter-attack. He was confident they were gaining ground. He praised the *Bauernhilfe* programme, when the comrades and the Young Pioneers went into the countryside to help out the farmers who were starving and in debt, working side by side with them in the fields. In the villages, the children didn't have enough milk to drink and no warm clothes or even shoes in winter, he accused, with the result they often didn't go to school. There were many stillbirths and many cases of tuberculosis. The great landowners were using the farm workers as cheap labour. And what did the reactionary parties in the Reichstag vote for? *Osthilfe!* Giving the wealthy *Junker* landowners millions in subsidies! The Capitalist land agents might speak of democratic elections and freedom of choice, he continued, but the young Communist workers lost their jobs if they were found canvassing for Thälmann; farm boys and apprentices were beaten up and arrested if they were found distributing leaflets or magazines. Still they got six million votes in the November election! The only solution was a revolutionary overthrow – a bitter fight to the end.

When he came home to Hamburg to join his dock worker comrades he told Irma and Rosa all about the meeting. And about the workers' response when the Party called on them to come out into the streets and demonstrate against the Fascists. That was on 25 January, a bitterly cold day, he said. But they came, in their thousands, marching past Karl-Liebknecht Haus, the Communist Party Headquarters, eight abreast, singing, for hour upon hour, while he and the delegates of the Central Committee stood to salute them, fists clenched. The Berlin police patrolled the march and with each new song they jumped from their lorries and beat the demonstrators up. But the columns always reformed – if the front was beaten up the middle sang, and if the middle, then the back sang. Finally they were surrounded and cornered by the police and made to stand, captured in a square, for hours, in the freezing cold. But they never lost courage and never stopped singing. It was the most powerful and profound thing he'd ever experienced, he told Irma and Rosa. 'It's a terrible disaster for our *Vaterland*, that the working class is split,' he admitted. He knew, too late, what part he'd played in that.

The Nazis didn't arrest Thälmann till after the Reichstag fire, a staged event, as witnessed by Herbert von Bismarck, the former Prussian Interior Minister – the only Secretary of State taken on by Hitler from the previous administration. Bismarck didn't last long in his post, but long enough to confirm the actual facts of the fire rather than the lies. In his ministerial role, he'd immediately gone to the Reichstag and inspected everything, including the underground tunnel which led directly from the Reichstag to Reich President Göring's home. He talked to all the fire officers and came to the certain con-clusion that the fire was the work of the Nazis themselves, not the Communists, as they claimed. That evening, he joined Hitler, Göring and Goebbels at a meeting and found an atmosphere of jubilation and self-congratulation, Goebbels, in high good humour, constantly rub-bing his hands in glee, Göring grinning. Bismarck knew he couldn't remain in his post now, but he also knew he had to be careful. He told them that he had to tend to the family estates in Pomerania. In the coded wording of the times, this was understood to mean he'd retire to the country and make no trouble. But it didn't stop him talking to trusted friends in secret.

The public had no idea what was happening. In every town and city, the loudspeakers, newspaper headlines and radio broadcasts blared out the propaganda, just as Goebbels planned, whipping the people up into a hysteria of anti-Communism. It was a plot against the state, they said, requiring immediate emergency legislation. Of the 10,000 Communists arrested across the Reich 1,500 lived in Berlin. All were rounded up, dragged from their homes or their places of work, many shot on the spot. Leaders of local Party districts and regions or factory and dockyard cells were arrested first, to destroy the Party structure. Then it was every man or woman who showed signs of resistance.

Whole working-class areas were cordoned off, with control posts set up at the boundaries. The SA and SS, helped by the local police, went from house to house, searching everywhere – attics, cellars, garden sheds – turning everything upside down. The raids went on through-out the summer and into the autumn. Once in Gestapo custody, tor-ture was routine. 'What type of mistreatment had taken place cannot be said with certainty on the basis of the autopsy. But the positioning of the bleeding which is formed like riding britches lets us suppose that probably the dead man had been bent over,' read one courageous Nuremberg coroner's report on 18 August 1933. 'The collection of blood on the soles of the feet leads us to assume a mistreatment similar to Oriental "Bastonade".'

The prisons were overflowing. And now, finally, the Nazis felt con-fident to arrest Ernst Thälmann, which they did, locking him up in solitary confinement indefinitely.

At first Irma and Rosa knew nothing. Berlin was far away and there was so much confusion. In the past, whenever *Vater* was on the run from the police, he'd stay with comrade families, never more than a night or two at a time. So perhaps he was hiding out with them again, Irma and Rosa hoped and prayed when they heard of the sweeping arrest of Communists after the Reichstag fire. Perhaps he would re-appear in a few days, unannounced, as he had so often before.

On 5 March, Rosa went to the polling station to vote in the snap election called by the Nazis to demonstrate they now had the people behind them. It turned out to be the last so-called democratic election before Hitler's dictatorship. At the polling station she met a com-rade who walked part of the way home with her. When no one was around he told her the rumour: Thälmann had been arrested two days earlier and was now in solitary confinement at Gestapo Headquarters in Berlin.

'What's up, Rosa?' asked *Grossvater* Thälmann as soon as she walked through the door.

She told them what the comrade had said. 'I don't know what's going to happen now.' She was close to tears.

Grossvater Thälmann lived with them. Rosa's father lived not far away. They were both good old fighters for the cause.

'Don't be sad. How can you believe such a thing?' said Irma. 'We'd know if it was true. We'd get news from one of the comrades if father can't write to us!'

But the next day it was in the newspapers: *Thälmann arrested!* The reports made less of the fact that, in spite of all the violence and intim-idation, the Communist Party still polled 4,850,000 votes and won 85 seats in the election. The Nazis took immediate action: on 6 March all KPD activities were banned, and three days later there were no more KPD delegates left in the Reichstag.

The Thälmann family heard nothing until the end of March when a comrade who'd escaped capture told them everything. He suggested *Mutti* go with him to Berlin, so the next day they took the train together, leaving Irma and *Grossvater* alone at home in Hamburg. Rosa was away for five weeks. They were the hardest weeks of Irma's childhood, she wrote later – not knowing anything, just scraps of news here and there. The only thing that saved her was her grandfather's steadfast attitude and the fact that so many other Hamburg families were in the same position, many of them literally starving now that the breadwinner was in prison. Some of Irma's friends had come home from school to find both parents arrested.

On 24 March 1933 the *Frankfurter Zeitung*, one of the last newspapers with some semblance of press freedom, reported on the speech in the Reichstag by Otto Wels, the leader of the Social Democrats, about the Nazis' *Enabling Act*. Wels was the only member of the Reichstag with the courage to speak out against it, in a long speech defending the principles of Social Democracy.

'In this historic hour, we German Social Democrats solemnly pledge ourselves to the principles of humanity and justice, of freedom and socialism. No Enabling Act gives you the power to destroy ideas that are eternal and indestructible. After all, you yourselves have professed your adherence to Socialism,' he challenged. 'You can take our lives and our freedom, but you cannot take our honour,' he ended, turning to face Hitler directly.

'The veiled voice sounded very serious,' reported the *Frankfurter Zeitung*, 'the speech given in the most difficult situation imaginable – decent, brave, at times even slightly aggressive. One felt the whole misfortune which has today come over this well-meaning but luckless party . . . During the last words of Wels's speech, the Chancellor jumped up and hurried to the rostrum. A thunderstorm burst over the Social Democratic Party, the like of which we have never witnessed in all the years in the Reichstag. How Hitler can debate! Without trouble he found the arguments to talk down the opposition amidst stormy applause from the Brownshirts . . .'

Nevertheless, all the Social Democrats present voted against the law though some were absent, mostly in prison. By 22 June, the Social

Democratic Party had been banned; by July, after thousands more arrests, the Party fled abroad.

Rudolf Ditzen was briefly arrested along with many of his Social Democrat friends during that spring of 1933. It wasn't for long – but long enough to put the fear of God in him. As he said himself, he was a coward, not made of the stuff of heroes. He'd just published his first best-seller and the Nazis, who had liked his book about a provincial newspaper and the farmers in the Land Volk movement, seeing it as an attack on the economic chaos of Weimar, wanted him on side. Goebbels' attitude was, why waste such a talent? 'Masterly,' he'd called the Land Volk book. Rudolf was appalled: 'I reject the notion that I have written a novel about farmers and I certainly don't want to be identified with the extreme right,' he wrote to his mother in one of his dutiful letters home.

The next book, the best-seller, came just in time. Money had been tight for the Ditzens again, Rudolf spending too much as usual, and they'd been forced to move out of central Berlin to the suburb of Neuenhagen, into a small house with two bedrooms. But it had a cellar and a garden, giving Uli, now two, somewhere to play. And there was a bit of land next to the garden where Suse, who was pregnant again, could plant her vegetables and fruit bushes. Her friend Lore gave them two beds. Privately Suse was pleased Rudolf no longer had easy access to the wild life led in Berlin by many of his friends, including Rowohlt, drinking and carousing late into the night in the bars and cabarets for which Berlin was famous.

For Rudolf, still working in Rowohlt's office, the move to Neuenhagen meant getting up at five in the morning and not returning till six in the evening. Except on those occasions when he couldn't resist the delights of Berlin's sleazy night life when he might arrive home at any hour, or not at all. But usually he came home on time, played with Uli, had something to eat, then worked like a maniac, chain-smoking and drinking endless cups of coffee, banging out the chapters of his next book on his typewriter or, more often, by hand, till past midnight. Somehow he fitted in writing short stories for the magazines as well, to keep them afloat financially, but also because it came so easily to him, thinking up these tales about the decent, struggling people who had become his constant subject now. It was his way of making a stand, fighting for the little man, who was his reader as well as his subject.

Rudolf wasn't the only one. In the early months of 1932, before the Nazi *Machtergreifung* when the press still had freedom, the magazine *Berliner Illustrierte Zeitung* produced two powerful pieces of photo reportage, the first about soaring unemployment, the second about the crisis in homelessness. 'Bank clerk, wife and child' was the caption to one of Ernst Thormann's accompanying photographs. It showed the family living in their one room, like thousands of others. The bank clerk sits on a chair in the foreground reading his newspaper in his neat jacket and tie, hair carefully combed, shoes highly polished. His back is squeezed up against the wardrobe on the left wall, his knees touch the baby's iron cot in front and his elbow touches the parental bedstead behind, beside which, on the only other chair in the room, sits his wife, with the child on her knee, looking out of the window. There is just room for a dresser between the child's cot and the wife's chair, for the few necessities of life. The only way for the wife or child to leave the room would be for the husband to get up and let them by. The kitchen was shared by everyone in the building. And this was a clerk, a man with a white-collar job, not one of the unemployed. By 1932, following the Wall Street Crash, there were six million unemployed, two out of every three workers in Germany.

'It all looks so dismal and everyone I know, office workers like myself, trembles at the thought of the day each month when we can be issued with notice of dismissal,' Rudolf wrote to his parents. 'And then people wonder why the National Socialists get so many votes!' Everything was being cut: wages, pensions, social welfare. For his research for his book, Rudolf paid a visit to the local employment exchange and discovered to his horror that the unemployed husband of their daily help received no more than 16 marks 50 pfennig a week for himself, his wife and their two children. 'They do not mention the fact that she works for us, because then they would get even less.'

By the time the Nazis came to power, in January 1933, *Little Man, What Now?*, the best-seller, was already a runaway success and the Ditzens' money worries were over, for the time being at least. 'It is a story about a marriage and children, with a social background – the fate of a white-collar worker. Not very long, 300 pages at the most,' Rudolf wrote to his parents. To Ernst Rowohlt, his delighted publisher, he explained more fully that the book portrayed the 'little man' and the unemployment crisis, the housing shortage and the shortcomings of the health insurance and social welfare systems. Johannes Pinneberg, the anti-hero, was an accounts clerk, always frightened of losing his job. 'The despair and the love of Johannes Pinneberg, a little white-collar worker, one of millions,' wrote Rowohlt in the publicity material, 'the novel is no novel, it is the life of all of us here and now.' The public could only agree. 'What we need,' the overnight celebrity author wrote to a reader, 'and will eventually achieve, is – above and beyond all parties and ideologies – a Front of "decent people", a Front of people who think in a humane way.' And to another: 'It helps a little to say to people: act decently towards each other . . . I think, for example, that the clerk in the Health Insurance office and who has read the book will be just a little bit nicer to my Pinnebergs.'

'It was five past four. Pinneberg had just checked his watch. He stood, a fair-haired, neatly dressed young man, outside number 24 Rothenbaum Strasse, and waited.' So Rudolf began the tale of this little man, immediately drawing his reader in. The house in Rothenbaum Strasse belonged to Dr Sesame, a gynaecologist, and Johannes Pinneberg was waiting for his girlfriend Emma Morschel who he called Lammchen, little lamb, to find out if she was pregnant and, if so, to try and get an abortion. They were scared stiff. They couldn't begin to afford a child. Pinneberg, the accounts clerk, only earned 180 marks a month. 'That's the way to live,' he thought, looking at the large house as he waited. 'I'm sure that Dr Sesame there has seven rooms. He must earn a packet. What sort of rent would he pay? Two hundred marks? Three hundred? How would I know?'

Lammchen was a shop assistant. She called him Sonny. Finally she came round the corner 'in pleated white skirt and artificial silk blouse, hatless, with her blonde hair blown all about. "Hello, Sonny. I really couldn't make it any earlier. Are you cross?"

'"Not really. But we'll have ages to wait. At least thirty people have gone in since I've been here."'

The reader knew what that meant: everyone was trying to get abortions these days. Inside, Sonny waits while Lammchen is examined by Dr Sesame. 'How beautiful she was! thought Pinneberg yet again; she was the greatest girl in the world, the only one for him.' The reader is waiting as anxiously for the result of the examination as Pinneberg who can hear low voices from the other room. 'Then he winced violently. Never before had he heard that tone from Lammchen. She was saying in a high, clear voice that was almost a shriek – "No, no, no!" And once again, "No!" And then, very softly, but he still heard it: "*Oh Gott.*"' Oh God!

Lammchen was pregnant and Dr Sesame said it was too late to have an abortion. Pinneberg could hardly breathe. Lammchen looked pale with the shock. 'But then she smiled at him, wanly at first, but then the smile spread, becoming wider and wider until it lit up her whole face . . .' What is she thinking, the reader wonders. Lammchen realises she wants the child, and, strong as she is, she's not going to force Sonny to marry her. The bill comes to 15 marks. 'Daylight robbery!' exclaims Pinneberg as they walk away down Rothenbaum Strasse. 'Perhaps your period will start tomorrow. If it does, I'm going to write that man such a letter!' That makes the reader laugh.

They go to the station for Lammchen to catch her train. 'Wait a moment!' Pinneberg suddenly calls out. He storms up the station steps, stands breathless before her and grips her by the shoulders. 'Lammchen!' he says, panting from excitement and lack of air. 'Emma Morschel! Why don't we get married?' The reader is captivated, quite forgetting their own troubles.

They get married, they have their child, Lammchen gives up her job of shop assistant, they struggle. Sonny loses his job, they have to move out of their lodgings into a cheap room in a rough part of town, and finally, into a garden hut on an allotment, like thousands of others. The reader follows Pinneberg's descent from respectable white-collar worker to defeated unemployed man with no collar, no hope and no future. At the end of the novel he stands in front of a large delicatessen, brilliantly illuminated. There's a policeman walking by.

'Move along there!'

'What? Why? Aren't I allowed to . . . ?' He is stammering. He simply doesn't understand.

' "Are you going now?" asked the policeman. "Or shall I . . .?" He had the strap of his rubber truncheon over his wrist. His grip tightened on it. Everyone was staring at Pinneberg. More people stopped to look, a regular crowd of spectators.'

Ach du lieber Gott! thinks the reader. What now?

Lammchen is waiting in the garden hut for Sonny to come back, deeply worried that he's so low he might do something stupid. She has refused the offer of some money from an acquaintance – another of the decent people – telling him money isn't the answer. She explains she goes out sewing for a few marks a day while Sonny stays in the hut looking after their child, who they've nicknamed the Shrimp. 'We can get by, and money isn't what's needed. It's work that would help Sonny, a bit of hope. Money? No.' True, thinks the reader. Very true. Finally Sonny comes back.

'There stood her man, her beloved young man, in the darkness, like a wounded animal, and did not trust himself to come into the light. They had crushed him at last.'

Lammchen chats lightly about this and that, trying to comfort him and get him to come inside, out of the cold: 'The Shrimp kept asking for you all afternoon. He's suddenly saying Daddy instead of Dad-Dad.' But Sonny doesn't move and doesn't speak. Finally she gives up and goes back into the hut, not knowing what else to do. Then: 'Behind her, a far-off voice cried: "Lammchen!" And suddenly the cold had gone, an immeasurably gentle green wave lifted her up and him with her . . . And then they both went into the hut where the Shrimp was sleeping.' The reader sighs and smiles.

'He was one of millions,' wrote Rudolf. 'Ministers made speeches to him, enjoined him to tighten his belt, to make sacrifices, to feel German.' They'd heard it all before. *Little Man, What Now?* was translated into English that same year and, by 1934, was being made into a Hollywood movie. There were Lammchen competitions in the magazines. 'People have said to me: "Why have you no answer to the question 'What Now?'",' wrote Rudolf. 'Lammchen is my answer, I know no better one. Happiness and misery, worries and a child, worries about a child, the ups and downs of life, no more, no less.' That was Rudolf's response to his own life during difficult times: retreat into domesticity. Suse was his Lammchen.

Fabian von Schlabrendorff, still pursuing his law studies in Berlin, had another answer. On 31 March, hardly two months after the Nazis' *Machtergreifung*, a rumour was spreading among his fellow students. Sebastian Haffner, one of the group, had been in the library of the *Kammergericht*, the High Court, when the silence was broken by shouting and doors slamming, followed by jackboots on the stairs. It was the day before the Jewish boycott of 1 April 1933. Sebastian came from a conservative but anti-Nazi family. His best friend was Jewish. Everyone in the library was suddenly tense. The library doors were flung open and an SA troop in their brown shirts marched in. They looked like the kind of guys who delivered beer from the local brewery, Sebastian said. They made their way from desk to desk, weeding out the Jews, including the Presiding Judge. Most of them had already picked up their leather briefcases and quietly slipped away – two months of the Nazi terror regime was enough warning for them, not to mention Hitler's stated aims in *Mein Kampf*. The remaining Jews in the library were ordered to leave, never to return. But one stubborn student refused, insisting on his rights, and he was duly dragged from his desk, beaten and taken off into 'protective custody'. Then the SA went from desk to desk, checking. No one remonstrated. When they came to Sebastian, they asked: 'Are you an Aryan?' To his eternal shame and humiliation, he later admitted to his close friends, he replied, 'Yes.' As he left the building, he realised he'd betrayed his best friend. Everyone hearing the story, including Fabian, knew what he meant, and each wondered what he would have done in Sebastian's place.

Soon after the Jewish boycott of 1 April 1933, Fabian's Jewish civil law teacher, Martin Wolff, was thrown out by the Nazis. It was happening everywhere: doctors, teachers, civil servants, businessmen, all losing their jobs and not knowing where to turn or what to do. Some decided early on that it was time to leave for a new life in England or America or Palestine. Most hung on, waiting to see what would happen, believing such a terror regime could not last and would not be tolerated by the international community. A few of the most courageous went underground to join clandestine organisations like the Red Shock Troop, which distributed leaflets and pamphlets and produced a newspaper illegally from an unknown place. Funded by the Communist Party in exile, it already had some 3,000 members, mostly in Berlin, mostly Communists, but there were some Socialists too. But it didn't last long. By December 1933 most of the leaders had been rounded up by the Gestapo and sent to Dachau.

Dachau was the first official concentration camp, quickly followed by a whole network of camps stretching across the Reich and ultimately into Poland. The first *Kommandant* of Dachau was Theodor Eicke, a one-time Police Commissioner, member of the Nazi Party since 1928 and later of the SS. He'd done a stint in prison for bomb attacks on political opponents, but, with a little help from his friends, managed to escape. Later his extreme violence landed him in a lunatic asylum in Würzburg, straitjacket and all. But by June 1933 *Reichsführer SS* Heinrich Himmler needed to find someone suitably dedicated and brutal to run the new concentration camp, and who better than Eicke?

He was released from the asylum and set to work immediately, formulating Concentration Camp Orders of Discipline, which covered such matters as talking in the toilets, secretly smoking a cigarette or working too slowly, most paragraphs ending with punishments such as indefinite weeks of solitary in the dark with only bread and water, hanging from a tree for a day with hands bound behind the back – his personal favourite – alternatively just a plain hanging or, where necessary, being 'shot on the spot'.

On 1 July 1934, Eicke took a leading role in the culling of the SA Storm Troopers and their leader Ernst Röhm – the so-called Night of the Long Knives – a bloodbath of extreme violence, just to Eicke's liking. So pleased was Himmler with his protégé that he promoted him to SS *Gruppenführer* (Lieutenant General) and made him *Inspekteur der Konzentrazionslager und SS-Wachverbände, SS Totenkopf*, Inspector of all Concentration Camps and the SS Death's Head battalion which ran them, with the distinctive skull and crossbones on their caps and lapels, thus giving Eicke unfettered power over hundreds of thousands of lives.

As things got worse and worse, Fabian decided it was time to get properly organised and make contact with any friends and acquaintances who were reliably anti-Nazi. He'd already sought out Ernst

Niekisch, the editor of the resistance magazine *Widerstand*. Niekisch's house had been searched immediately after the Reichstag fire, but nothing was found because Niekisch took the precaution of hiding most of his incriminating material in the left luggage department at Anhalter railway station. The Gestapo were determined to shut down his magazine *Widerstand*, and were extremely puzzled with orders from on high to leave him and it alone. They didn't know about Niekisch's secret links to the regime and the *Reichswehr*, German Army, since 1926 and their plans to rearm with the help of the Russians, as negotiated through Niekisch's friend Karl Radek who'd gone to Moscow after the war, returning to Germany in 1923 as a delegate of the Communist International.

Fabian didn't know about it either for that matter. All he could see was that, despite Niekische's Communist leanings and strong preference for the Russians above the Western Allies, he appeared to know how to survive the Nazi regime. *Widerstand* continued, without softening its criticism of the regime, until December 1934. And that in spite of the fact that Carl von Ossietzky, editor of *Die Weltbühne*, another courageously outspoken magazine, was sentenced to eighteen months, 'protective custody', in November 1933, for revealing Germany's secret rearmament programme, which was in violation of the Treaty of Versailles. Niekisch wasn't arrested until 1937.

Unlike many of his Communist comrades, Niekisch refused to emigrate. Why not? asked Fabian. Perhaps the people who did had no alternative, was Niekisch's answer. 'Perhaps some with no special political reasons might do it too, just because of the terrible, inhuman circumstances we find ourselves in. But anyone who is politically committed, he has to do everything in his power, even when the most terrible things happen, to show that Hitler is not Germany, and Germany not Hitler.'

That was it of course: Niekisch might be a Communist, but he was also a German nationalist, deeply tied to his *Heimat*, homeland. International Communism wasn't for him. Nor was fleeing. The first terrible thing had already happened to Niekisch, when he and his wife were woken in the middle of the night by the SA banging on his door to arrest him. He was thrown into a Gestapo cellar in Friedrichs Strasse, but then, just as suddenly, let go. The reason: his wife had immediately contacted the *Reichswehr*, German Army, and before they knew it the local Gestapo had received a telephone call. Niekisch, not knowing of his wife's swift action, ran for cover as soon as he was let free. In the early hours of the morning, Fabian heard a loud banging on his door. To his amazement there stood Niekisch, shaken up, asking to be let in. Niekisch rarely left his house these days, let alone in the early hours. Once he knew the *Reichswehr* had stepped in to protect him, Niekisch went home again. And as soon as he'd recovered his courage, he formed his *Bismarck Gesellschaft*, Bismarck Club, a clandestine group of likeminded anti-Nazis from all backgrounds who met secretly at his house, including Fabian.

Later that fateful year of 1933, Fabian found himself in hospital with a serious case of sepsis. His consultant was Sigismund Lauter, a fine man and doctor, short, energetic, elegantly dressed, always cheerful and much loved by his patients. Lauter had a large and beautiful house in Dahlem, a leafy district of Berlin, now, following the Nazi *Machtergreifung*, always full of visitors, all anti-Nazi. Once recovered, Fabian was invited to join the guests. The Gestapo had their eye on Lauter, but they couldn't prove anything – not yet, anyway. Nonetheless, Lauter took the precaution of moving out of his lovely house and into a large apartment on the fashionable Kurfürstendamm, on an upper floor not easily breached or spied upon. Lauter's political views were based on a deep religious conviction. He was a liberal Catholic from Bavaria. The local Protestant pastor in his previous home at Dahlem had been Martin Niemöller, later one of the celebrated resisters of the Nazis. Lauter's view was that when a storm came you had to know how to bend in the wind in order to survive. Then the meadows could flourish all the stronger after the storm was over. But you had to act, not leave your hands idle in your lap.

One day Lauter invited Fabian to join him on a walk across Berlin. Fabian had no idea where they were going, but he couldn't fail to notice that Lauter was often doubling back on his tracks, to make sure they weren't being followed. It was a long walk to the other side of Berlin, and as they walked they talked, safe in the knowledge that no Gestapo spy could be listening in. Like many suspected opponents to the regime, Lauter had noticed strange clicks on his telephone, so now he restricted his phone conversations to domestic matters or coded messages about the weather. On the outskirts of Berlin, they arrived at a hospital run by nuns from the local convent. Lauter gave a password at the entrance, then a nun in her white wimple and long black habit with a heavy crucifix and rosary beads led them through a back courtyard and up some steps to two rooms at the end of a long corridor. Inside sat a middle-aged man, reading. Lauter introduced Fabian, who instantly, and with a sharp sense of shock, recognised the man: Heinrich Brüning, a former Chancellor of Germany during Weimar. Brüning was living like a hermit, Fabian later recalled in his memoir, lying low, hiding from the Nazis. He looked pale and tired. He'd first been an academic and his mind was as active as ever, the conversation quickly turning from polite small-talk to Brüning's passion: politics. He'd been the leader of the Centre Party, now banned along with all the rest. He had no illusions about the brutality of the Nazi regime, and he knew well enough why the 'little man' had turned to them during the economic crisis of the Weimar years over which he'd presided with a series of emergency decrees, not knowing how else to combat the social and political chaos. But he was at a loss now. Fabian got the feeling Brüning had given up.

After that first meeting, he sometimes went to visit the former Chancellor, always enjoying the lively political debate, but never coming up with any answers. Eventually Fabian joined others to convince Brüning that his best bet was to emigrate, which he did the following year, first to Switzerland, then England and finally to America, where he warned constantly of the Nazis' terror regime and their plans for war, to little effect.

Julius Leber was another politician on the run. 'The day will come,' Hoffmann, the Nazi leader in Leber's home town of Lübeck, threatened as early as 1930, 'when we come knocking on your door with the words: "Herr Dr Leber, your time's up!"' Hoffmann's supporters added their penny's worth, spreading the word in Hitler's own style: 'Two hours after our victory Dr Leber will be hanging from a lamp post in the market square!' But it took more than idiot threats to unsettle Julius Leber. He was a big man

in all senses, not easily cowed. When he walked round the streets of Lübeck, most often making for one of his favourite drinking haunts, jacket flapping over a large belly, battered hat awry, people constantly came up to him to have a word or just to shake the great man by the hand. He was one of the leading Social Democrats in the Reichstag and one of its finest speakers – always ready for a fight, by no means only verbal. His answer to the Nazi threats was to remind people it had been just as bad in 1923 when they'd strutted around in their uniforms, swinging their leather truncheons, till the *Reichsbanner* was founded in 1924 with its black, red and gold banner, a multi-party paramilitary organisation to defend the Republic and parliamentary democracy, and to fight extremism, both Left and Right. But then came 1929, the Wall Street Crash throwing the economy into chaos all over again, and out strutted the Nazis once more, marching around singing their victory songs, beating up the workers as usual, Leber accused in the Reichstag, in a rage. He had to shout to be heard over the general uproar.

Leber could shout in many ways and in many places. One of his best platforms was in the pages of the *Lübecker Volksboten*, the local paper tied to the Social Democrats, strongly supported by the Lübeck workers, which he edited from 1921 to January 1933. 'Socialism isn't Party-political as its enemies keep claiming for political reasons. It is fundamental,' he stated in his usual sure way. 'As soon as man could think, he reached for the heights, for freedom. He battled to rise out of darkness, and out of the injustice of his circumstances.'

Again and again, Leber wrote about the scandal of the housing problem and the steep rise in unemployment and the neglected rights of the worker. 'He who provokes the demonstrating worker, let him watch out: he'll get what's coming to him!' he wrote on 27 January 1931. And he warned repeatedly about war. He came from Alsace, but he had chosen to fight on the German not the French side in the last war, he reminded his readers. So he wrote as a patriot. But things could not go on as they were. 'Today the worker stands alone again in the fight for a new political order, alone in the fight against those brutal powers which have brought the people into an abyss of blood and suffering!' he wrote on 30 April 1932, pointing the finger at extremists left and right. 'The workers stand alone, but they know that is also their strength. Because each and every worker knows they can rely always and only on one another.'

Then came the July elections making the Nazis the strongest party in the Reichstag, though not in Lübeck where the Social Democrats remained in control. Leber was up on his feet again warning about the dangers of the starving millions and an impotent government which was sleepwalking into an even worse crisis ahead. Then came the hopeful November elections when the Nazis lost many of the seats they'd gained. 'Hitler's luck has run out,' jeered Leber. Even if Hitler became Chancellor his star would soon wane, he said, because he would face the same social problems as Heinrich Brüning had, and with no better solutions. But by 30 January 1933 it was Leber's luck which had run out, not Hitler's.

On the evening of 31 January, Julius Leber had just returned to Lübeck from Berlin, shocked and outraged at the way Hitler and his cronies had managed, almost behind people's backs, to manoeuvre the Nazis to power. 'Now it's clear for all to see,' he wrote in the *Lübecker Volksboten*. 'We all know this regime's aims. But no one knows what their next move will be. The dangers are terrible. But the German worker is unshaken. We're not scared of these gentlemen. We are determined to carry on the fight!'

He had a temperature and his wife Annedore begged him to stay at home. Yes, yes, said Leber, he'd just hop along to his Trade Union club in Johannis Strasse for a quick grog with friends and then he'd be back in good time. Annedore had heard it all before. At the club he met Otto Passarge, his long-time Social Democrat colleague at the *Lübecker Volksboten*. 'It's very quiet in here tonight,' Leber noted. The Nazis were holding a torchlight victory parade in the centre of town and most people were staying home, heads down. Then the parade – military band blaring, flags waving, flaming torches lighting up the night – came round the corner of Johannis Strasse. Leber went out and joined some SPD colleagues on the street corner, shouting, 'Down with the Nazis!' and 'Freedom!' before they were summarily arrested. All but Leber, who they didn't dare arrest – not yet.

He retreated to the offices of the *Lübecker Volksboten* further down the same street, where he got a telephone call from a comrade warning him not to go home – the cemetery next to his house was teeming with police and SA. So he went back to his Trade Union club for another grog. There Passarge and Willi Rath, both old *Reichsbanner* comrades, tried to persuade him to leave by the back door and go to a safe place for the time being. No, no, said Leber, he wanted to look danger in the eye – at a time like this it was the only way to keep your self-respect and freedom. It was 1am before they managed to get him out, by which time he was fairly drunk.

Some local Nazis and SA caught up with them on the way home. An exchange of insults quickly turned into a fight. The SA were armed and they made for Leber deliberately, attacking him with an iron-tipped truncheon, till he bled profusely. Willi Rath was a hothead and he had a knife on him. Before anyone knew it, he'd lunged at one of the SA men and stabbed him to death. He fled up the street but he was quickly caught and arrested, Leber and Passarge soon after. Once in the cell, Leber really started disturbing the peace, shouting and banging, creating mayhem. When he was let out the following morning he refused to have his wounds seen to in order to prove the seriousness of the attack and that Rath had acted in self-defence. He was only out for one day. By evening he'd been rearrested as an accomplice to a murder and locked up.

As soon as the news got out the Lübeck workers were up in arms and immediately went on strike. Letters and telegrams poured in from all over the country. The SPD, not yet expelled from the Reichstag, demanded his instant release. When nothing happened, the workers went on strike again.

From prison, Leber was persuaded to write an open letter to his supporters, on the understanding that Rath's case would be dealt with fairly. He'd decided to withdraw his complaints against the authorities for the time being, he wrote. The truth would come out in the next few days, so wait in peace with him. He ended the letter with 'Freedom!' During these early days of Nazi rule Leber still believed the justice system was functioning legally, partly because the leader of the Nazi gang was also being held in prison. Leber himself was let out on caution on 13 February, thanks to Annedore's tireless complaints and demands. Leber's exit from prison turned into a triumphal procession. They could hardly open the prison gates, so huge was the cheering crowd. His car had to drive slowly through the streets with the window down so everyone could shake him by the hand. He immediately went into hospital to have his wounds treated. When he came out a week later there were 15,000 people waiting for him on the Burg field. He couldn't speak because his wounds hadn't yet healed, but he was able to call out 'Freiheit!', 'Freedom!' The single word which said everything.

The family went on holiday to the Kochelsee in Bavaria for his recuperation. His friends came to see him, advising him strongly to emigrate. He had no intention of doing that, he countered, calling it an 'odious' idea. He wasn't about to act like a coward in front of the thousands of Lübeck workers who'd supported him through all his political fights. And he wasn't going to deny his family, his wife and two children their German *Heimat*, their home. So back they went to Lübeck for the election of 5 March 1933. They had a *Reichsbanner* guard at the house at all times from then on, because every night the Nazis came shouting in the street outside. They sent their children, Katharina and Matthias, to live with Annedore's parents.

The results in Lübeck were heartening, the Social Democrats retaining control albeit with a reduced majority – a better result than anywhere else in the Reich. When it was time for Leber to return to Berlin to vote in the Enabling Act, Annedore insisted on going with him, too frightened to stay in the house alone. They'd scarcely left before the Nazis broke in. His colleagues in Berlin again advised him to flee. Again he refused. The next day, 23 March, he was arrested in front of the Kroll Opera which was the provisional Reichstag following the fire, and led off in handcuffs to police custody. The Enabling Act that same day was therefore debated without him, no doubt all part of the Nazis' plan.

Annedore, highly alarmed at her husband's disappearance, immediately made enquiries. She didn't find out where he was until the next day. She went straight to the top, demanding to see the President of Police, to no avail. But she did discover that Leber had just left, with a police escort, on his way back to Lübeck for his trial, whereupon she raced to the railway station, and managed to board the one train a day to Lübeck.

'Carefully, I went through the train looking in each compartment. And sure enough, there he was, sitting quiet and relaxed, leaning back, as though it was the most natural thing in the world, in the corner seat, with only one other person: the policeman guarding him,' she wrote in her memoir. 'I slid open the door, like a stranger. A feeling of deep joy raced through me. Like an electric current, I sensed the immediate understanding between us. The policeman told me to leave the compartment. I waited in the corridor, then I tried again. The policeman was of the old school. He let me stay for the whole four-hour journey. In Lübeck station forecourt the prison van was waiting.'

CHAPTER THREE

1933 AND ALL THAT

'A beautiful green Thursday!' wrote Julius Leber from his prison cell at Marstall interrogation centre in Lübeck on 13 April 1933. Not that he could see much past the iron bars except the elm tree in the yard. 'So: forbidden, books and magazines! Forbidden, smoking! Forbidden, to shave! Forbidden, any extra food from home! Is that it? I await further forbiddings, but without getting too worked up about it, after all, everything passes! . . . It's bitter, though, that I can't even have academic books, and that I'm not allowed to write, can't make any notes. Still . . . splendid indifference!'

Perhaps he was thinking about a piece he wrote in the *Lübecker Volksboten* in 1923, that year of political chaos and fighting. 'He who wants to earn the name of politician, he has to have the courage to accept responsibility, and even have the courage, occasionally, to take risks. If you could always know beforehand what was going to happen, then every ass could be a politician. The courage to take on responsibility is what distinguishes the politician from the chap who yaks away at the bar in the local Gasthof.'

For the first three weeks, Leber wasn't allowed any visitors. A frantic Annedore tried to get information about him and permission to see him, to no avail. Finally, she went to see the Lübeck *Reichs Kommissar* Dr Volker, one of the new Nazi appointments. If he had his way, Volker informed her, Dr Leber would be dead already. Count herself lucky! Left to her own devices, she found a rooftop near the prison which looked down on the exercise yard, so she was able to watch Julius walk up and down for an hour every day and check how he looked, which wasn't too bad considering. Best of all, she found one of the prison guards who was an old SPD Social Democrat, and in time they devised a way of smuggling out notes and letters and occasionally even smuggling in a bit of extra food.

In the first days, Leber was still allowed newspapers and books. Annedore sent him Spengler's *Decline of the West*. On 11 April, she was allowed her first and, as it turned out, only visit. After that, all reading material was stopped. It was the Nazi method of trying to break a man: first make some concessions, then take them away. Leber, trying to make light of it, referred to the prison as his 'sanatorium', giving him plenty of time to think. There was certainly plenty to think about: his home, his garden, the children, the war years in the trenches in France where he was gassed, which now caused him some health problems, and the turbulent post-war years when he could see what was coming but could do little to change it. Reflecting on that now, he thought he'd taken life too lightly, and he wished he'd been a better husband to Annedore. But if incarceration made him regret some things, it didn't make him lose his sense of humour. 'I've just discovered that one of the prisoners here has been let free because his wife's been taken to a lunatic asylum,' he wrote to Annedore in one of his smuggled letters. 'It seems the only way. But I can't really do that to you, so I'd better stay sitting here.'

'No newspapers yesterday,' went his journal on 19 April. 'I'm just hanging about, waiting – and it's getting really boring. No post either! Nothing! Not a word from Paulus,' Julius's nickname for Annedore since her 'conversion' to Social Democracy. 'Nor anyone else. Might the so-called regime be getting harsher? The last consolations we had, newspapers and post, now taken away from us?'

He listed his daily timetable:

> 7: get up and tidy cell
> 7.30: bowl of coffee
> 8–12: waiting!
> 12: a midday soup
> 12.30–5: waiting
> 5: bowl of coffee
> 5.30–8: waiting
> 8: lights out

That was when the waiting really started, because Leber rarely managed to sleep before midnight. The next day he admitted to his journal that he'd had some kind of crisis: 'The Devil only knows why! I've been forbidden cigarettes for the last seven days – perhaps that's why.' He had a small table in his cell, and a chair. And some photographs of Annedore and the children. 'I pick them up and look at them a hundred times a day.'

The next day, on 20 April, the outside world was celebrating Hitler's birthday. Leber could hear the cheering from his cell.

'In the last two days the elm has gone completely green,' he wrote on 6 May. 'And the pear tree next to it is in full blossom, a pure joy. Everything is bathed in glorious sunshine. I've just had my free hour, and I walked up and down from one wall to the other, under the sun and the blue sky. There was a dandelion pushing through the cobblestones. I just had to pick it, in all this horror, and stick it in my jacket buttonhole. Even someone who's locked up has to have some connection to these early summer days. Locked up – but not lonely, strangely. I have everyone in here with me who was with me in my freedom.'

A week later, Leber was unexpectedly allowed to write and receive letters again – and given a weekly visit, too. He wrote long letters to Annedore, to fill the time but also to hone his political views, not yet believing it was a crime to express political opinion. 'There I go again, philosophising, Paulus!' he wrote on 23 June. 'But I wanted to clarify for you how I see my political life now.' Still fighting, still planning – though not for much longer.

Julius and Annedore had met in Lübeck in 1927 and got engaged that same year. Annedore's parents were not pleased. Her father, Dr Georg Rosenthal, was the Principal of Lübeck *Gymnasium*. They were respectable middle-class people, politically to the centre. Annedore had been privately educated and went on to study law at Munich University. Now she gave it all up to become a dressmaker in order to stay close to Leber, the left-wing, flamboyant, campaigning editor of the local Social Democrat newspaper, *Lübecker Volksboten*. Who knows where he came from? Alsace, he said, but by all accounts he was illegitimate. His mother had been a housemaid in France, and when she came home pregnant she arrived with a goodly sum of money, presumably donated by the father of the child who, presumably, was the master of the grand house. Perhaps that's where Leber got his cleverness from, Annedore's parents surmised – and his grand manner, mixed with his revolutionary ideas – a dangerous mix. Had the unknown father been Jewish, perhaps? Leber had voted for their citizenship in the Reichstag, where his old enemy Wittern taunted him with his possible Jewishness. He could just as easily accuse Wittern of being a Red Indian, Leber jeered back, to which Wittern replied he was happy to be called an Indian and he'd pay anyone who called him that a *Taler*, but if Leber did the same when called a Jew he'd soon be a poor man. Whatever the truth of it, anyone could see Leber was trouble. But Annedore wouldn't budge. They were married the following year.

Of course, Annedore's parents were right. Leber wasn't a good husband; his two great weaknesses were alcohol and women. Women were always throwing themselves at him, not for his looks since he soon grew into the overweight, untidy man he would remain till prison slimmed him down. No, it was his cleverness, humour and deep political convictions which attracted them, just as they had Annedore. But to her parents' surprise his bad behaviour didn't put Annedore off. It made the marriage difficult, certainly, but she seemed to thrive nevertheless. Soon she was joining him in his Socialist views, supporting him at every turn. Her parents were worried and perplexed. But Julius being Julius, they ended up shifting their political views too, joining the SPD, and later they actively opposed the Nazis.

'Today is 1 May,' Leber wrote in his journal, smuggled out by his loyal SPD guard. It was a single sentence; there was nothing else to say. News got round fast in prison, whispered from cell to cell or during their brief freedom in the exercise yard. Apparently 1 May was now renamed the Day of the German Worker, a national holiday, and in line with their so-called Socialism, the Nazis decreed that employers had to join in the celebrations along with their workers.

Leber could hear it all from his prison cell: another of their parades through the old medieval town and under the famous ancient Burg Tor arch, military bands playing, loudspeakers blaring, crowds singing and cheering, though without the assistance of any Communists or Social Democrats. Most of the Communists in the prison had already been transferred to Fuhlsbüttel, the newly constructed concentration camp outside Lübeck, and now Leber heard that his SPD colleague from Bremen, Alfred Faust, had been arrested on 28 April, along with thousands of other Trade Unionists across the Reich, all despatched to concentration camps or local prisons if the camps weren't ready. On 8 May it was Leber's turn. Without warning two SA men appeared, took him, handcuffed, from his cell, bundled him into a car and drove him to a deserted stretch of farmland outside Lübeck. There they ordered him to get out of the car – which he refused to do. He knew the Nazis' methods too well. He sat there calmly not budging, as he later described it to Annedore, till eventually they gave up. That's the way he avoided the fate of his colleague Feuchenbach who did as ordered and was shot in the back while 'trying to escape'.

Annedore had had bad news: Leber's colleague and friend Bauer at the *Lübecker Volksboten* had committed suicide. The newspaper had been taken over by the Nazis and brought into line politically – *Gleichschaltung*, as they called it.

The quick and easy method of despatching Leber having failed, the Nazis were forced to put him on trial. On 13 May, he wrote to Annedore telling her to get hold of the Hamburg lawyer Dr Herbert Ruscheweyh, an old SPD colleague. Ruscheweyh was optimistic and in fact reasonably satisfied with the outcome: Leber was accused, under article 277, of taking part in a brawl, but the accomplice to murder charge wasn't included. He was sentenced to 20 months in prison with a 50 mark fine. No appeal granted. Leber was downcast. He'd already served almost four months and now another twenty, making two years in all, for a brawl. It never crossed Leber's mind that the sentence was just a formality, with no real meaning at all.

Leber was soon bouncing back. 'The sentence has given me plenty of pause for thought,' he wrote to Annedore on 7 June 1933. 'I'm not that concerned with the punishment itself. Plenty have suffered worse in their fight to make life bearable for those little people with almost no human rights at all. But the absolute stupidity of the sentence, the sheer embarrassment of it, and the injustice of it too – that I find difficult to come to terms with.' With nothing to read he had too much time to think, much like his war years in the trenches, he said. He might not be a free man, but on the whole it was probably better to be free inwardly, with a proud heart, turning to face the future.

'After all, at the moment what could I say to the poor old Lübeck worker except that I can't change anything. As Arndt wrote, they can take your job and position, but they can't take your soul.' He'd found a way of reading through memory, he told her, making his way through old favourites, taking his time. On one rare visit, Annedore brought him some flowers from the garden, picked by Matthias. Leber spent a long time that evening just looking at them as the light faded, thinking about his home, his garden, the children. If you want to join the political fight, you shouldn't have a family, was how he saw it with the benefit of hindsight.

'So now we're outlawed once and for all,' he wrote when the SPD Social Democrats were banned on 22 June with 3,000 prominent members arrested for good measure. Following the intimidation many deputies emigrated, including Otto Wels, which left Leber, locked up in prison, especially disillusioned. 'It's enough to make you lose heart completely.' Sitting alone in his cell, his worst times were when he thought he'd let his family down. And the Lübeck workers. 'But what good would it have done if I'd dragged them into it? Everything was over with our human rights in such a short time,' he wrote to Annedore, the fifth letter in so many days, because, for some unknown reason, he was allowed to write letters again for the time being. 'So there was no other way for me. You know how often I've talked about my worst fears. So I'll have to go through with this tragedy one way or the other. Let's just hope it doesn't turn out to be the tragedy of my life, merely a bad phase.'

In Königsberg, the capital of East Prussia, Fritzi von der Schulenburg was busy putting the Nazis' *Gleichschaltung* into practice, weeding out political suspects from the Civil Service and elsewhere. In March 1933, he'd been promoted to *Regierungsrat,* a senior Civil Service administrative post, as well as the head of the Political Office at the NSDAP *Gauleitung* regional administration. It was Nazi policy to create an alternative system of command, whether local, legal or within the

Reichswehr Army, to run parallel to any existing ones, circumventing them, and answerable only to the Party. The *Land* became the *Gau*, and the old *Oberpräsident* had to deal with the new *Gauleiter* who had the power to 'remove' him at the drop of a hat.

With his double promotion Fritzi, still only 31, became an important influence in the region from one day to the next. He was ready for it, keen to get on with what he saw as the social responsibilities of the post. During the previous year, in the lead-up to the Nazi *Machtergreifung*, he'd gained plenty of experience in regional administration: hospitals, schools, an orphanage, workers in small industries, mills and sawmills, craftsmen, farmers, fishermen, a cement factory, a brewery – all the time battling rising unemployment and bankruptcies. 'His warm heart for everyone in need, and his energetic intervention everywhere he could have an influence earned him the affection of all classes of the population,' wrote Dr Gramasch, his *Landrat* boss, in his final report on Fritzi von der Schulenburg in Heiligenbeil. 'He is open and free with everyone, keen to help, and treating everyone the same.' Gramasch added that his high intelligence and marked talent for administration, his pleasure in his work and sense of responsibility and energy, made him a born *Landrat*. Fritzi was happy in his work. And very happy in his recent marriage to Charlotte too.

But now, in his new role as head of the Political Office in Königsberg, Fritzi's first task was *Gleichschaltung*. He started at the top. Dr Wilhelm Kutscher, the *Oberpräsident* of East Prussia, was well liked and respected, especially by the big landowners Fritzi had clashed with for their iron resistance to social reform. Politically, Kutscher was of the Centre and there was absolutely no chance he would become an NSDAP party member. And he was noticeably slow at *Gleichschaltung*, refusing to move politically unsuitable people from their posts. Admittedly, there weren't always good replacements to be had, and the Old Fighters of the Nazi Party didn't help matters, endlessly petitioning for jobs as mayors and suchlike, demanding to be rewarded for their early Party loyalty. But Kutscher had to go. Fritzi had just the man to replace him: Erich Koch, one of the people who'd persuaded him to join the NSDAP a year before. Fritzi made his recommendation to his boss, Hermann Göring, expecting a smooth transfer. To his surprise Göring wasn't keen. 'I would regret it,' Göring wrote to Hitler on 12 April 1933, 'if the present Oberpräsident Kutscher, who is extremely experienced and enjoys the widespread trust of the East Prussian circle, were replaced by a Party man who is not sufficiently qualified for the post.'

Fritzi suspected the landowners had Göring's ear and decided to act – he wasn't from an old aristocratic Prussian family for nothing. He went straight to Hindenburg to make his case. Still Göring resisted. But in the end, Fritzi triumphed, used to getting his own way and quite happy to make use of the Schulenburg name: Ernst Koch was made *Gauleiter* of East Prussia, amalgamated with the post of *Oberpräsident*.

Now *Gleichschaltung* could proceed apace. Communists, Socialists, Democrats, anyone who wasn't politically aligned to the Nazi Party, were eased out of their posts, either left unemployed or, if they were lucky, deployed elsewhere. An academic Classics teacher in a *Gymnasium* might end up as a form teacher in a local primary school; a renowned doctor might join a surgery in a far-flung village; a civil servant might be lucky to get a transfer to a small town hall somewhere. Jews had mostly already left their posts. The race question was not a part of the job which Fritzi enjoyed. He'd never been anti-semitic, having plenty of Jewish acquaintances, if not friends. But he understood that in this transition period, for this is surely what it was, an active Party member could not pick and chose. Concentrate on the good measures, he told himself – for example, the Erich Koch Foundation, set up largely by himself, to further social reform by encouraging industrialisation in East Prussia, had established hundreds of small industries in the province, to the fury of the big landowners. And keep out of Party politics, he told himself, which, from the earliest days, was riven with conflict and machination.

Fritzi's friend from student days, Rudolf Diels, was a big noise in the local Gestapo now. Close as they were to the Polish border, he was sharp as a knife, catching Socialist and Communist Poles who crept into East Prussia in the night, making trouble. When the East Prussian *Stahlhelm*, the local paramilitary organisation, was incorporated into the SA to the consternation of many, he was quick to arrest the pro-testors. When Koch's chauffeur, an Old Fighter, was sent to prison for street brawling, murder and torching, Diels was happy to turn a blind eye as the SA sprung him from his cell. As to the Jews, Diels could smell them a mile off. For Fritzi this was a mixed bag. He agreed about the danger posed by the Poles and hoped Berlin would give them enough military might to fend off any attacks, but he didn't like the Nazi terror tactics, and he didn't like the hounding of the Jews. 'I imagined much different after the *Machtergreifung* of the NSDAP,' Fritzi admitted in a letter to a friend in November 1933. 'It can't be helped. Gradually one gets clearer and tougher. The idea, in which I believe before and after, will overcome everything.'

It was a case of fighting lesser evils for the greater good. And the greater good was everywhere in evidence during those first years of the Nazi regime, as long as you weren't in prison or a concentration camp. The Focke-Wulf factory in Bremen, manufacturing civil and military aircraft, was a perfect example – a model National Socialist factory. It paid wages above the average, constructed workers' housing estates, offered free lunches, bonuses for good work, a library for self-education and a works newspaper, as well as providing free medical care, social clubs, cultural events, and many sports facilities including football and *Volkerball*, handball, gymnastics, fencing and tennis, sport being fundamental to the Nazi ideology of the Aryan master race. The net result: the workers took a great pride in their factory and their technical and engineering expertise, enthusiastically building their airplanes, especially the new Condor, ready for military deployment by 1939.

Unemployment was high on the Nazis' attack list. To combat it, they instigated a huge programme of public works, building housing and civic facilities and the new motorways – never mind that conditions for the workers were harsh: paid a pittance and housed in rough barracks, and, once enlisted, unable to quit on threat of a stint in a concentration camp. As far as the general public was concerned it got thousands of unemployed off the streets, solving a problem which had completely stumped the Weimar politicians, and it improved law and order as well. As far as the Nazis were concerned, it was a brilliant piece of propaganda with foreign visitors arriving regularly to inspect and admire.

Just as pleasing to the Volk were the Nazis' principles concerning social equality. Expanding the *Reichswehr* army from 100,000 in 1933 to 1.4 million by 1939, the Nazis stated they would change the intake of the officer class, almost exclusively aristocratic in the old Reich, so that by 1936 they constituted no more than 35 per cent. It was a source of pride that in the newly formed SS only two out of every five officers had even passed their final school examinations. Loyalty to Hitler was now the main qualification. As to employers, they were to show respect to their workers, and be seen in the works canteens, not hide away in their large offices, and join in with their workers' leisure activities, their parades and their celebrations.

'The boss gave a talk at one of the last workforce meetings,' reported a worker at a lorry firm employing 4,500, to SOPADE, the Public Opinion Report of the SPD, now exiled in Prague. 'He had hardly been speaking for 10 minutes when Kreisleiter of Franconia, Julius Streicher, who was also present, jumped up onto the speaker's platform and shouted at the boss: "Get off!" and then he began speaking himself. He pointed to those present and, with the agreement of the workforce, explained more or less as follows: "This man is one of the exploiters, he's a typical representative of the capitalist system, against whom we National Socialists have declared war." He gave an extraordinary anti-capitalist speech. The boss had to listen to it as well.'

Best of all for the German worker was the *Kraft durch Freude* movement, 'Strength through Joy'. 'The *Kraft durch Freude* outings are exerting a considerable influence on the community,' another SOPADE for the exiled SPD wrote from southern Bavaria in 1934. 'According to the corroborating reports of everyone concerned, this is a positive achievement by the regime. The popularity of these trips has an even greater effect. Their cheapness is astonishing. Examples: Visits to mountain villages: I met a married couple from Cologne. For an 8 day stay in Frasdorf, including the journey there and back, plus costs and apartment, two people had paid 60 Marks. Otherwise the journey alone with a holiday card would have cost 100 Marks. In any case a worker earning 53 pfennigs an hour cannot manage it on his own.

Again, 1,200 workers from southern Bavaria went to Spitzbergen. The trip lasted 10 days. Inclusive of board, the whole trip cost 76 Marks per person. In all, 900 men from Munich, workers from the town firms and BMW, went on an eight day trip to the Mosel. The trip cost 35 marks per person. The participants got a glass of wine with each midday meal. At one place on the Mosel there was a wine tasting at a public spa, and the participants of the trip were allowed to drink to their hearts' content. You can imagine how enthusiastic the participants were!'

Then there was the *Volkswagen*, the Peoples' Car, and the *Volksempfanger*, the People's Wireless. From now on it wasn't only the wealthy who could afford a car, announced Hitler, with a flourish in 1934, promising a newly built state sponsored factory to produce a basic family car costing only 990 Reichmarks, no more than the price of a motorcycle. It came with a savings plan for the ordinary working man who earned on average 35 marks a week: 'Save only five Reichmarks a week, and own your own car!' it proclaimed, and the Volk flocked to join the scheme – 336,000 of them. Pictures of the prototype revealed a beetle-shaped vehicle, adorned with a swastika-style logo, which could reach 60 kilometres an hour. Naturally, it was only for full citizens of the German Reich. But it turned out to be not financially viable, and was only produced after the war, long after Hitler was dead and gone. The People's Wireless was more successful. It was already for sale by the end of 1933 for 76 Reichmarks, and an even more basic model for 35 Reichmarks, again to be bought in instalments if necessary. Unfortunately, it was so basic that only German and Austrian stations could be heard. This suited Joseph Goebbels perfectly. Perhaps no one told him it was known by the general public as Goebbels' Snout.

The people were key to Nazi success – as Hitler expressed to the General Council on the Economy in September 1933: 'The Volk, you see, are the decisive factor. They must believe in us with such unquestioning trust that, even if an obvious mistake were actually made, they would never dream of the consequences – rather they would swallow defeat like a well-trained army ... a Volk has to be taught how to march through thick and thin with its government, it must be instantly susceptible to every psychological factor, able to be whipped into a frenzy, and be inspired and roused. If this is not possible, then all our efforts will be in vain, we will be forced to surrender.'

Fritzi could only agree. And if some of the means were to be regretted, so be it. His father was made an honorary general in Himmler's newly established SS, his brothers were all enthusiastic members of the Nazi Party, except for Wilhelm, the youngest, who tried to keep out of politics. Only his sister, Tisa, remained firmly opposed and openly Socialist, if not actually Communist. It made for tricky weekends at Tressow even before the Nazi *Machtergreifung*.

The fact is the war had changed everything. Johann Albrecht had come home badly wounded with half his face blown off by a grenade. Wolfi had been a prisoner of war with the French. Their father returned disillusioned, bitter that Ludendorff and the old patriots continued the war long after it was clear Germany could never win. Fritzi came home from Border Patrol flirting with the ideas of Socialism which later turned to National Socialism. As the 1920s turned into the 1930s, there were still happy summer days when the women of the house sat on the terrace together – Tisa, her mother, the two kitchen maids, the cook, her mother's lady's maid Maria, and the two housemaids, all in a circle, bottling peas and beans, stoning cherries, peeling apples, telling stories, singing, laughing. And there were still evenings of lively debate, everyone throwing in their penny's worth: how did all this happen? Who to blame? They sat late into the night in the Yellow Salon, glasses of wine in hand, trying to work it out – how to make Germany great again. The brothers, Wolfi, Heini and Johann Albrecht, but not Fritzi or Wilhelm – calling Tisa their Rosa Luxemburg in so-called jest, with *Mutti* trying to keep the peace.

January 1933 had been the death knell for many things, certainly for Tisa and Fritzi's close relationship. Tisa just couldn't forgive him his Nazi Party membership. At first, she couldn't believe it – Fritzi, her one and only ally in all those years of political debate, always seeing things clearly and honestly and decently, now busy with the terrible *Gleichschaltung*. How could that be? And how was it that his wife, Charlotte, loved by all the family including Tisa, appeared to agree?

Much had happened in Tisa's own life by then: she'd moved to Berlin to continue her art studies, and there she finally found her own crowd. Mostly they were Socialists – artists and writers, people who didn't find her strange and weren't put off by her views, and men who weren't frightened by her forthright manner and her unconventional mode of dress. Through her new friends, she met Hugo Simon, a banker, and his wife, Trude. They lived in the wealthy Neubabelsberg district, in a house filled with modern art acquired for them by their art dealer friend Paul Cassirer – Cezanne watercolours in the dining room, Impressionist oils in the drawing room, a Maillol sculpture in the garden. Everyone came to the Simons' house: politicians, academics, journalists, theatre people, publishers including Rudolf Ditzen's publisher, Ernst Rowohlt, and many artists and writers: Berthold Brecht, Heinrich Mann, Georg Grosz, Max Pechstein, Einstein. They were mostly Social Democrats, some Communists, many pacifists, some Jews. They had international friends and links to international organisations like the Pen Club, and they were against Nationalism of any sort. By the early 1930s they were deeply worried, wondering where it was all leading.

When Tisa's father came to Berlin on business, she felt like an imposter. He still disapproved of her political views which seemed to be moving further and further left and he was suspicious of some of her new friends, yet it didn't stop him acting like a proud father, taking her to meet his old friends. One day, it might be Hindenburg, another it might be the Crown Prince, as old monarchists still called him, on another, Prince Bulow or the Ribbentrops. But his best and most trusted friends were Generals Beck and Fritsch, his comrades from the war years, who shared his own view that Germany should have conceded defeat by 1917, thereby saving hundreds of thousands of lives, including those of the enemy. Of course, Count von der Schulenburg had many old friends in England from his time as military attaché in London, Harold Nicolson among them. Nicolson, like many others, expressed himself impressed by the Nazis' social achievements, especially their tackling of unemployment, an intractable problem affecting England almost as badly as Germany. Sometimes Fritzi would join Tisa and their father when he came to Berlin. Tisa noted how confident he had become, with a wide circle of friends, and she was relieved to see that he was really still the jokey, lively, clever brother he'd always been. But she also noticed that he'd become sharper, hiding his feelings. He'd always been a clever card player, had Fritzi.

At the Simons', Tisa met Fritz Hess. He was 18 years older than her, married and a Jew. Hess's father had been a shoemaker and the family was poor, but Fritz Hess had no intention of staying that way. He started to earn money when he was still at school, buying and selling anything he could lay his hands on. He was built big like his father, and handsome, and he didn't look Jewish. Aged 14, he went to work for an uncle in a textile factory. By the age of 21, he was a partner. People couldn't resist his charm. He travelled everywhere for the business, France, Russia, England, dealing with all the great fashion houses. Like his friends the Simons, he collected paintings: Roger van der Weyden, Cezanne, Renoir, Braque, Daumier. He owned a stable of racehorses and he rode out every morning in the Grunewald woods. He was very sporty and a great admirer of the boxer Hans Schmelling, a frequent visitor to his house in Dahlem. In spite of his wealth though, he was a Social Democrat through and through. Somewhere along the line, he'd married a cousin and they had two children, but the marriage was not a success. By the late 1920s, when he met Tisa, he was a millionaire.

Tisa, young, unconventional, artistic, fiery in her political commitment and aristocratic, was something completely new to Fritz Hess, and as soon as he met her, he wanted to make her his wife. Tisa wasn't sure, but she was 28 by then and she knew that, sooner or later, she would have to marry someone. And who better than Fritz, sharing the same political views as herself, clever, charming, and wealthy too, though this last was more of a hindrance to Tisa who much preferred a modest life. At first she resisted. Why couldn't she be surer? she wondered. When she finally agreed, Fritzi, her brother, went off to Tressow to forewarn their parents. It didn't go down well. Not only was their son-in-law an ardent Social Democrat, he was divorced and a Jew. Not that they had anything against Jews as such, but wasn't it just typical of Tisa to make things more complicated than necessary. On the other hand, she was finally married, and wealthy too.

The trouble was, much as Tisa knew she should be happy in this new life with a charming husband and an elegant life in a beautiful house, she wasn't. She hated the pampered life. She didn't want the 11 servants. She didn't want the chauffeur driven car. She didn't want to ski in St Moritz. She found she couldn't paint. She missed Tressow. She was as puzzled by her reaction as her husband, who loved her and felt he was giving her everything she could want. She felt terrible, hating to hurt him but unable to change. She started wandering the streets of Berlin on foot, drawn to the poorer districts. The artist Käthe Kollwitz, with her harsh studies of the starving poor, was who Tisa admired. She tried to emulate her, but it didn't work.

She was saved from her dilemma by the 1929 Wall Street Crash. Suddenly all Fritz Hess's money disappeared – gone the servants, the chauffeur, the fine paintings, the house. They moved to a small apartment in a poorer district of Berlin, and Tisa couldn't have been happier. Fritz Hess, on the other hand, began to think of leaving Germany altogether. He had contacts everywhere and he was used to hardship and starting over. As the early 1930s polarised the Reich he could feel what was coming, especially for the Jews. By January 1933 and the *Machtergreifung* he was thinking about England. Tisa didn't want to go. She knew times were bad but she didn't want to leave Germany. But then came the Reichstag fire in February when their friend Eduard Fuchs came banging on their door saying the Nazis were arresting every Communist they could find. They hid him for the night and early next morning Fritz drove him to Jüterbog, across the border, out of harm's way. Just in time, they realised, as they watched helplessly as Communist friends, Social Democrats and Jews were arrested, beaten up and despatched to prisons. There would be no more laughing at the SA Brown Shirts – which Tisa and Fritz and their friends had liked to do. Now they saw how completely they'd underestimated their foe. They could hardly believe what was happening. They tried to laugh off their fear, but they too began to dread the sound of hobnailed boots on the stairs. They hated the way people began saluting each other with the Hitler salute, and vowed never to do it themselves. One day, Tisa found four big boys in Hitler Youth uniforms beating up a small Jewish boy in the street outside their apartment. She grabbed them in a fury. 'Is this German? How can you be so cowardly?! Four against one!' They fled.

Matters quickly worsened – so quickly, in fact, that it was hard to keep pace. Almost worst for Tisa was the fact that all her family except Wilhelm remained keen Nazis. How could they? Didn't they see what was happening? One day, their friend, Treviranus, a long-time supporter of Chancellor Brüning in the Reichstag, returned from playing tennis at the Rot-Weiss Club and drove up to his house just in time to see the SA breaking in. Thinking fast, he drove right past and, still in his tennis clothes, drove straight on to the Czechoslovak border. That's the kind of thing that happened all the time these days, Tisa and Fritz told one another, united now in a way they'd never been before. Then came 1 April and the first open hounding of the Jews. Now Fritz was determined to emigrate and he settled firmly for London. He would have gone immediately but he had to wind up his business first, so he didn't manage to leave till November. It took Tisa another six months to arrange domestic matters in Berlin and bid her family goodbye. By spring 1934 she'd joined Fritz in England, together with his son Edgar who was 18, Fritz's daughter having already opted for Palestine. The family of three settled in a small flat in Highgate, north London. Tisa tried to remember the English she'd learned from Vicky, their nurse all those years ago at Tressow. Fritz brushed up his English by reading *The Times*. Edgar enrolled at London University, studying chemistry. When Tisa and Fritz told their new English friends what was happening in Germany, warning them that it would sooner or later lead to war, most of them just laughed.

By 1934 it was becoming clear that the Nazis weren't a short aberrant phase in the Reich's history but were here to stay. For the two-thirds of the population who hadn't voted for them, it was a time to take stock. What to do? Some decided to move their families to distant rural villages, out of harm's way. Others learned to make compromises, to keep themselves and their children safe. Others decided to carry on, donning the mask of co-operation. Some even joined the Nazi Party. Each had their own red line beyond which they would not go. Often it focused on the Hitler salute, that small but dangerous sign of loyalty to the Party and the Führer. The salute had to be executed with the right arm held stiff and high, whenever they entered or left a place of work or entertainment and whenever they passed a member of the SS or SA or a group of Hitler Youth in the street. Keen NSDAP Party members greeted each other with the salute every time they met, be it at the local Gasthof, church or shop. Sebastian Haffner, the law student who felt he'd betrayed his Jewish friend when challenged by the SA in the library, avoided the salute by diving into a dark alley every time he saw a group of Hitler Youth approach. Like most people, he opted for silent resistance. But there were others, by 1934, who opted for something more effective.

The Engelmann family, living in a quiet residential district of Düsseldorf, appalled by what was happening to the Germany they knew and loved, joined a secret network of local resisters, focused round Frau Ney. Everyone in the neighbourhood knew Annie Ney. She and her husband ran the bakery by the tram station. Herr Ney did the baking and Tante Ney, as the young called her, ran the shop and café, selling pastries and tarts and mouth-watering ice-creams, as well as bread – sourdough and rye. Before the Nazis came to power Tante Ney often let the unemployed and poor of the area have a coffee 'on tick', but everyone knew there was no 'tick' about it. Now some of those people were local Nazi officials and they still felt an affection for her, never thinking that this old woman with a bad hip and grey hair might be working against them. Tante Ney, seen here with Bernt's parents, was always cheerful and friendly to everyone, always ready to offer a helping hand. These Nazi bigwigs, flush with new money, might come in and order a whole box of pastries for some occasion or other, and she'd greet them as friendly as could be.

'*Heil Hitler*, Frau Ney!' they'd say, giving a stiff Hitler salute. 'I'd like your largest chocolate cake, if you please!'

'*Guten Tag*, Herr Sturmbannführer,' she'd answer, 'or is it Ober Sturmbannführer now? Not yet? Well, it'll come before you know it, I'm sure. And how about some eclairs? Is it a birthday party? Well let me congratulate you!'

Then she'd pour them both a little glass of Schnapps and clink glasses, chattering away. That was Tante Ney for you.

Bernt noticed that his father had begun to stop by Tante Ney's for a cup of coffee on his way home from work, drinking it not at one of the small marble-topped tables in the front but in the back room of the bakery where they couldn't be heard.

'Here's your ice cream,' Tante Ney said to Bernt one day, taking him by surprise. The shop was busy and he was just hanging around the counter, waiting his turn. She handed him an ice-cream, much larger than his usual one.

'You know the little Wolf girl, Ruth?' she said, between customers.

Of course he knew Ruth. Her father had the small tailor's shop on Tuttlinger Strasse, and that morning some Hitler Youths had thrown a rock into his window, shattering it, and stolen some bolts of cloth as well.

Tante Ney turned to serve another customer: '*Guten Tag, Frau Seiler. Was für ein Wetter haben wir!*' What weather we're having! And then, turning back to Bernt, she said: 'The poor girl had a terrible fright. She sleeps in the back of the shop, you know, they only have the one room . . . And how is Fräulein Bonse these days?'

Fräulein Bonse was a devout Catholic who ran a school exchange programme between Germany and England. Bernt was going himself that year, spending the summer holidays with a family in Yorkshire. He quickly worked out that Tante Ney meant to get Ruth out of the country. Somehow Fräulein Bonse's groups, meeting up at Cologne railway station, always had one or two extra students on board.

'Fräulein Bonse is very well,' he said.

'Good! Tell her to stop by for a coffee today, or tomorrow bright and early. My hip won't let me climb her stairs.'

And off Bernt went on his bicycle to deliver the message.

A few weeks later Bernt's father sent him to Herr Desch's on his way home from school to pick up a suit. Herr Desch was his father's expensive tailor who also specialised in the smartest SS dress uniforms: Bernt didn't like him. He was a member of the SS with a cold, formal manner and a completely expressionless face, like a fish. Fishface. Herr Desch hardly looked at Bernt when he entered the shop, just told him to go into the back room and collect the suit. And there Bernt found Ruth's father, Herr Wolf, and her mother too. They told Bernt that Herr Desch had driven Ruth to Basel himself that morning and she was on her way to America where she had an uncle and aunt. Bernt knew nothing about the Quakers, but it turned out Herr Desch was a Quaker.

When Bernt arrived at Cologne railway station on his way to England that summer, who should be in the background of the crowd of students gathered round Fräulein Bonse but Herr Desch, inscrutable as ever, keeping a quiet eye on the extra children in the group. Apparently he was on one of his regular trips to London to buy the fine woollen cloth for his dress uniforms. As they boarded the train, someone passed Bernt an envelope from Herr Desch. 'Open the first, but not the one inside,' Herr Desch had instructed before moving to First Class. Bernt hid in the toilet and did as he was told. Inside the first envelope he found another addressed to a family not far from the one where he himself was staying in Yorkshire. Quakers again, as it later turned out. He also found an English pound note to cover his expenses – far more than he needed for the bus fare, so the rest, he assumed, was for himself.

Bernt's friends were a mixed bag. His best friend, Kulle came from a devout Catholic family. In his house there was grace before every meal and mass with communion every Sunday. The family wasn't well off, with five mouths to feed, and once the Nazis came to power Kulle's father, a member of the Catholic Centre Party, was terrified he might lose his job at the Post Office. He could only watch as his bosses were 'brought into line' by the *Gleichschaltung* law, and removed from their posts if they resisted, replaced by good Nazis. Once all the other political parties were banned, Kulle's father joined the Nazi Party and told Kulle to join the Hitler Youth. He didn't know what else to do.

Marga's father, on the other hand, was a keen member of the Nazi Party early on.

Marga herself loved all the Nazi razzmatazz: the parades, the military bands, the Führer's birthday celebrations, Harvest Festival, and the *Kraft durch Freude* movement with their entertainments, sports facilities and collective holidays on the Baltic Coast. Soon enough her *Vater* got the promotion he'd been longing for, becoming an associate judge at the district court, replacing a senior colleague who'd been an outspoken Social Democrat. And not long after that, they were able to move into a large apartment in a good area of Düsseldorf, formerly belonging to a wealthy Jewish family.

In contrast, Werner, the only one of their group to go to the local *Volksschule*, elementary school, was the son of a committed Communist. His father worked for the Reich Railways, at the local freight depot, where he had the protection of friends, even some who'd joined the Nazi Party, mostly for their own safety. 'The air's not too good for your asthma today,' one might say to him. 'Why not go to the country for a day or two?' And off he'd go to stay with his sister who had a small farm on the outskirts of Düsseldorf till the current wave of arrests was over.

But none of Bernt's friends was in the same position as Suzanne. She was a beauty. And Jewish. Her parents were wealthy and respected professionals, but soon they were forced to 'retire' from work and had to move from their home. Not long after that Suzanne disappeared from school. A few weeks later she turned up at Cologne railway station in the company of Fräulein Bonse, on her way to a new life in England. But her parents never made it. They took their lives rather than board a freight train for the East.

In Hamburg, Irma Thälmann hardly saw her *Vater* anymore. He'd been transferred to Moabit prison on the outskirts of Berlin, still in solitary confinement, still with an indefinite date of release. He was allowed to exercise for one hour a day in the prison yard, alone. He dressed for it, in jacket, waistcoat and cravat, walking round and round, fast and unbowed. If only they'd moved to Berlin once her father became the leader of the Communists in the Reichstag, thought Irma, then they'd be near him now and able to visit – always assuming visits were allowed. But *Vater* had insisted on staying in Hamburg, with the workers.

How often had Irma attended those strike meetings of the dock workers with her mother, waiting till *Vater*'s rousing speech ended, then waiting again late into the night while he talked to one then another worker about their hardships with no wage coming in, keeping their spirits up, urging them not to abandon the fight against the Capitalists, warning that victory for the Nazis would lead, for certain, to war. When *Mutti* said it was getting too late for Irma, what with school the next morning, he'd tell her to go home ahead of him. He'd come later, accompanied by his security detail as always. 'Rosa,' he'd say, 'these hours with the dock workers are important for me. I learn what's troubling them, and get useful suggestions for my political work. The Party must never lose its link to the worker!'

Before he was arrested *Vater* would sometimes take Irma to the docks or the harbour on a Sunday afternoon, when they'd walk around greeting other families doing the same, looking at the great ocean liners berthed there, ready for their next voyage across the Atlantic Ocean to America and beyond. He'd explain the skill of the small pilot boats, steering the towering liners safely out to the open sea. He'd tell her stories of his own time in America, working like a slave on the farm, exploited, he said, just as badly as the workers in the Reich. Or he'd tell her about the latest goings-on in the Reichstag, talking to her like a grown-up. Irma for her part would tell him about the *Jugendverband* youth movement, which she'd joined, and their bicycle trips into the countryside, their baskets laden with leaflets and pamphlets, encouraging the stricken farm workers to vote Communist in the next election, as they duly did in November 1932. So there was always talk, lots of talk.

Once *Vater* was arrested in March 1933 life was difficult for the family of three, Irma, her mother and her grandfather, trying to make ends meet with no wage coming in. There were small donations from the exiled Communist Party and Rosa found some work as a seamstress, but it was hardly sufficient to cover the rent and food. Life at school had become difficult too, Irma being the known daughter of Ernst Thälmann, leader of the Communists, now locked up in prison and good riddance. The trouble with Irma was that not only was she Thälmann's daughter, she was like him too: stocky and strong, with an iron will. She wouldn't back down for anything or anyone.

'After the Reichstag fire by the worker-murderer Göring in Berlin, life in our school changed immediately. Every morning we had to step up in the wide corridor facing the street, in rows of four, while the hated swastika flag was raised. Everyone passing by outside had to give the same Hitler salute. If we children didn't do it we could be given a beating. Beating was anyway normal now. Brutality was admired. But I wasn't frightened. Days on end I stood in the front row and as the flag was raised I said to anyone listening: "We don't want to sing! We don't want to salute the flag!" The working women passing by clapped. The school principal and other teachers pulled me out of the row and there was always a great commotion. After fourteen days I was forbidden to attend. Because a lot of the Social Democrat children and others began to protest with me.'

Each state in the Reich had its own rules for the way in which the Hitler Greeting had to be executed – all variations on the same theme. 'The Hitler Greeting is also to be used in conversation between teachers and pupils,' went one instruction. 'If the raising of the right arm accompanies a greeting, then it can just be *"Heil Hitler!"* Every day at the beginning of the first lesson the pupils will get up from their places as soon as the teacher enters the class, stand to attention and raise their outstretched arm level with their eyes. The teacher will go to the front of the class and offer the same greeting accompanied by the words *"Heil Hitler!"* The pupils will reply *"Heil Hitler!"*'

Needless to say, Irma refused to salute in class as she did in the schoolyard, and time and again she was beaten for it. Witnessing it daily, her classmates reacted according to their political alignment – or at least that of their parents: the Nazis among them jeered at Irma's stubbornness and stupidity, the rest were amazed at her courage and admired her, though none dared to join her any more. Irma was proud to be standing shoulder to shoulder with her father, the great leader of the German Communists. 'I'll never sing your songs!' she told the school Principal. 'Because my innocent father is in prison.'

The Hitler greeting took hold fast, what with the early successes of the regime, and where that didn't work, forced by threats and beatings. Hitler and Goebbels were both interested in the power of psychology, especially with the young, since youth was the future of the Thousand Year German Reich. 'Total dominance over the Reich' was the aim, but it could only be achieved gradually and pragmatically, once the Volk was fully in the Nazis' power. Propaganda was key. In Hitler's view the masses could be duped about anything, as long as 'the same message was repeated over and over again', and they would 'fall victim more easily to a great lie than to a small one.'

And the place to start was with the education of the young. The school curriculum was changed to reflect Nazi values, academic subjects quickly downgraded. A new-style Geography was introduced giving due emphasis to *Lebensraum*, the need for more land for the coming Greater Reich population, and included the study of the Reich's territory before the Treaty of Versailles. Then there was Racial Biology demonstrating the superiority of the Aryan race. History became Germanic History with special interest in military history, Bismarck and the Germanic myths. And there was sport, always sport. 'We train our youth to use their bodily strength,' proclaimed Hitler at one of the Youth Rallies now held every year at Nuremberg. 'For I tell you, the young man who does not find his way to the place where, in the last resort, the destiny of his Volk will lie, but only studies philosophy and buries his head in books or sits at home by the fire, he is no German youth! I call on you!'

Even Mathematics was used in the service of Nazi ideology: 'A mentally ill person costs the community about 4 Reich Marks per day, a handicapped person 5.50 Reich Marks, a criminal 3.50 Reich Marks. In many cases, a civil servant earns only about 4 Reich Marks, a salaried employee barely 3.50 Reich Marks, and an unskilled worker only 2 Reich Marks. A: show these values in a diagram – according to provisional estimates there are 300,000 mentally ill persons (epileptics etc.) in welfare institutions in Germany. B: What do these cost together per year at a rate of 4 Reich Marks? C: How many marriage loans at 1,000 Reich Marks each – allowing for them not being paid back – could be given out using this money?'

'Our *Gymnasium* was quite an old-fashioned place,' reported a keen member of the Hitler Youth to the local *Ortsgruppenleiter* who was there to check on teachers' political reliability. 'The teachers just didn't understand about leadership mottoes such as "the schooling of character is more important than the schooling of the mind". They pestered us with Latin and Greek instead of teaching us about things we could have used later.' Apparently the Hitler Youths in the class never bothered to do their Caesar translation for homework, saying they had to attend a Hitler Youth meeting instead. And the teachers rarely complained because they were, 'I believe, a little afraid'. This same former pupil was happy to offer an example. 'One day, one of the old teachers screwed up his courage and protested against what was happening. It was immediately reported to the *Gruppenführer* who went to the Headmaster and demanded that this teacher be dismissed. The *Gruppenführer* was only sixteen but as Hitler Youth leader he could not tolerate us being prevented from carrying out our service which was much more important than school work. No one dared argue about this.' By 1936, and after *Gleichschaltung*, 97 per cent of teachers were members of the National Socialist Teachers' Organisation.

Irma, aged 14, had to do one more year at school before she could leave and be free. For First of May the class was told to write an essay about the meaning of the festivity, now renamed a Volk National Holiday. 'The meaning of 1 May is based on a good idea,' wrote Irma. 'For years and years it's been the occasion for workers throughout the world to demonstrate, demanding an 8-hour day, work, bread for their children and against the exploitation of children, and for the freedom of all. Yesterday we heard Hitler's speech in Berlin on our school radio: "We have to eradicate Communism and the Communists!" But that's not possible, because the Communists are the best workers. And if you eradicate them, the German Volk will suffer. My father is a Communist. He is a good father and a good man. I know from him, if we have Socialism in Germany, then everyone will have a job, and we'll have a better and more beautiful land!'

Later that month, *Mutti* finally came back from Berlin. She'd found out where *Vater* was being held after his arrest in March, and had waited weeks just to see him for a few minutes. Years later, Irma wrote it all down in her memoir, quoting her mother.

'He was very calm and considerate,' *Mutti* told Irma and *Grossvater*, sitting at the kitchen table. 'He spoke urgently. But the prison guard interrupted us – no political talk! *Vater* looked him up and down with that small smile we know.'

Irma and *Grossvater* nodded.

'Irma, he sent you his special greeting. He says you must work hard at school to gain the respect of your teachers and school friends.'

Little does he know, thought Irma, but said nothing.

'He tells you to be careful with your health,' Rosa told *Grossvater*, 'because he wants to see you again. His money and keys have been taken from him. He told me to go and see Judge Braun. And Braun sent me to the Karl-Liebknecht-Haus. You can't imagine how I felt, looking at this building in which *Vater* used to work, and now full of those Gestapo criminals. I was sent to one of those worker-murderers. I stood waiting for hours, with a procession of bloodhounds staring at me as they walked past, so I turned my back on them and looked out of the window. The Gestapo official screamed at me to sit on a chair. But I refused. I showed them my contempt.'

Grossvater poured out some coffee and cut some bread. 'Where did you stay?'

'The comrade who brought me from Hamburg took me to people in Schöneberg. A worker family, full of heart. They looked after me, and I could feel their great love for *Vater*. All the comrades I met are courageous in Berlin, full of solidarity. They fight as much as we do in Hamburg.'

In turn, Irma and *Grossvater* told *Mutti* what had been going on at home during the weeks she'd been away. Irma left out most of the trouble she was having at school. But she told her about the swimming baths, how some big BMW girls had caught hold of her legs underwater and threatened her: 'You watch out! If we catch you at your Communist work, you'll soon see what's what!' A woman came to her rescue, Irma said, shouting at the girls. She explained to Irma not to blame the girls: they'd been infected by propaganda and by their parents. 'She told me not to go anywhere on my own. They knew who *Vater* was. They believe all the lies. They've been told *Vater* wants bloody revolution in Germany. And the Reichstag fire was his fault. They're being taught murder, the woman said. And she told me to warn you too *Mutti*, to be careful!'

Mutti shrugged her shoulders. She was just as strong and stubborn as *Vater*. She told Irma that hardship was part of life. 'All the hardship of *Vater*'s childhood has made him the man he is today: his will and his determination to improve the lot of the working man. Many worker children are just as clever as the rich ones. They should become engineers, builders, business owners, just like them.'

Grossvater nodded in agreement. He'd been saying the same all along. As had his friend, Rosa's own father, another old Hamburg worker.

Over the next weeks Rosa wrote letter after letter to the Berlin Gestapo requesting permission for herself and Irma to visit *Vater* during the school holidays. Irma had started shouting out in the night, crying, missing him, and *Mutti* had to wake her. But she didn't comfort her.

'If you don't stop this crying, you'll look terrible,' she said, 'and I won't on any condition take you with me.' That helped. Not long after, permission came through for a visit.

Irma was beside herself with joy and anxiety. The same comrade arrived to accompany them by train to Berlin. In Berlin they went straight from the station to the prison. They had to stay in the waiting room for three hours. There were many other women there too. 'Is my husband still alive?' 'Is my son healthy?' 'Can I take the packet of dirty washing this time?' Hours of talk, but always with care: you never knew who might be listening and denounce you – a spy planted among the women. Rosa had already warned Irma of that before they left Hamburg. So Irma listened but didn't speak. It was a torture. She walked up and down the corridor, waiting, counting the panes of glass in the windows, the cracks in the walls. Each time a name was shouted out she started up, as they all did. Finally a Gestapo official appeared in the doorway and their name was called.

'At first I only saw *Vater*,' Irma wrote, all those years later. 'I wanted to jump into his arms, but there was a table between. He held my hand over the table. I was in such shock I couldn't speak or move. Like a statue. "So, Irma. Don't you want to say good day to me?" he stroked my hand and spoke gently. He and *Mutti* were talking. Sometimes he asked me a question and I answered mechanically, like a doll. Even today I don't really know what we talked about. I only saw the guard standing at the window, always watching *Mutti* and *Vater*, listening to everything. I turned all my hate on him. And that table, separating us. But I remember having to part. And *Mutti* at the door saying, "Come now Irma. Let's go to our friends." On the way home I was upset: "But *Mutti*, I couldn't speak a word. I forgot everything – that terrible building! Isn't it possible to get *Vater* and all the other innocent people out of that prison?" *Mutti* didn't cry. "Yes, Irma. The workers will fight and *Vater* and all the others will finally come home."'

And they took the tram to Schöneberg.

One of the comrades who worked at the Berlin Central Post Office brought some news: apparently there'd been hundreds of letters and cards for Ernst Thälmann for his birthday on 16 April, from the whole of the Reich and from abroad too. Sackfuls. All for him at Moabit prison. During the visit *Mutti* had asked him if he'd received any letters from Hamburg. He knew immediately what that meant. No, only letters from the family, he'd answered, non-committal.

Some time later, Rosa and two of the women in Schöneberg whose husbands were also in prison were allowed another visit. Irma wasn't permitted to go this time so she stayed behind with one of the daughters, cleaning the rooms and preparing a meal for when the three women came back. She didn't show how upset she was, just got on with the work. When the three women hadn't returned by evening the girls started to get worried, wondering if they should go to the Gestapo Headquarters in Prince Albrecht Strasse. Just then the women came back, but without Else, the other girl's mother. 'Don't worry,' said Rosa. 'She'll come. Because we made a statement that we were staying with her in Berlin, since we know no one here.' Later that night she did come home. But some months later, she was arrested for 'illegal activities' and sent to a concentration camp. 'Her husband was murdered by the Nazis,' Irma wrote after the war, now living in East Berlin. 'Else herself came through. And she and *Mutti* are friends to this day.' Irma didn't write what happened to the daughter.

No other prison visit was permitted till October. Then a terrible thing happened. While Rosa was away in Berlin on that visit, *Grossvater* had a stroke. He was rushed to Eilbeck hospital and Irma immediately telegraphed Rosa the news. Rosa got a lawyer and went to Gestapo Headquarters to ask for a few days' leave for Thälmann to visit his dying father. Then she came home, full of hope. In the hospital, she kept reassuring *Grossvater*, 'Ernst is coming. Ernst is coming.' That's all *Grossvater* wanted: to see his son one more time. But his heart gave out before Ernst could come, because the permission for his visit had been deliberately delayed. Rosa had to send *Vater* the news by telegram. If anything could break Thälmann's spirit, this was it: the death of his father who had taught him everything he knew and believed in, and who had stood by him through all the hardship and poverty and the political fight, all his life.

Instead the Gestapo promised Thälmann he could go to Hamburg for the funeral. That turned out to be a lie – another of their little tricks to break him. The funeral at the Hamburg-Ohlsdorf cemetery went ahead without him. But far from being a sad event, it turned out to be a great celebration, attended by hundreds of courageous workers, wrote Irma. In fact, it turned into a workers' demonstration. Plainclothes Gestapo stood at the cemetery gates as the workers streamed past and stood round the edge of the crematorium hall afterwards too.

'Those Bloodhounds!' wrote Irma. 'There were flowers and wreaths piled high, each with their red ribbons and words: "A last greeting for the father of our great leader of the workers Ernst Thälmann!" and "Long live the son of our Volk, Ernst Thälmann!"'

'My dear Irma!' Ernst Thälmann wrote to his daughter later that month, showing, for once, how cast down he was. 'Lonely, isolated and imprisoned, away from everyone, I'm sitting here in these sad hours thinking about your birthday, next Monday. You will understand why I can only send you short and circumspect birthday wishes without any special card, but with my deepest heart and my strongest inner love. The sudden death of your beloved *Grossvater* is hard. Fate which befalls us is full of trials, even for you at your young age. But we nevertheless have to go through these bitter times with courage and bravery. So on this your birthday you will be thinking about your future and your later career. I hope your birthday finds you well and that you can enjoy it in peace. I got *Mutti*'s letter at 10.30 yesterday. I'll answer it separately. I know you were all with me in your thoughts, even though the Gestapo stopped me from attending my dear *Vater*'s funeral. Send *Mutti* my best wishes. And to you once again my best birthday wishes, from my heart, your loving *Vater*.'

CHAPTER FOUR

THE EARLY YEARS OF NAZI RULE

By 1934 the Nazis' *Volksgerichtshof*, the National Socialist People's Court, was up and running. It had always been Hitler's intention to circumvent the established legal system in order to pursue opponents to the regime, and now he could. Circumvention was the key, as it was in so many aspects of the new regime, giving the appearance of legality when in fact it was the opposite. As Hitler had already stated in *Mein Kampf*: 'On the whole my attitude is that one should not hang little thieves and let the big ones roam about freely, but that a German National Court will have to deal with several tens of thousands of organised and responsible criminals of the November 1918 treason, in order to sentence and execute them.'

The 'criminals' were the Social Democrats, Communists and any other opponents of the Nazi regime, and the means of dealing with them was a special court exclusively for acts of treason. The two treasons, *Hoch* and *Landesverat,* the first internal against the state, the second external, a betrayal of country, already existed in German law, but the People's Court ignored any idea of responsibility to the state, replacing it with responsibility exclusively to the Führer. As Joseph Goebbels told the judges selected for their loyalty to Hitler and the Party: the judiciary had to recognise its political task, whether a judgement was just or unjust was unimportant, what mattered was that it fulfilled its purpose, and that purpose was to sentence and imprison or execute opponents to the Nazi regime.

Hitler chose Hans Frank to set up the *Volksgericht,* the People's Court. Frank was a clever lawyer who'd defended hundreds of members of the NSDAP during the fractious Weimar period. He had himself joined the Party in 1923, thereby counting as one of the *Alte Kamaraden,* Old Comrades. Before that he'd been part of the right-wing Freikorps Epp in Bavaria in 1919, fighting the Communists who'd set up their so-called Soviet Republic there. He was still a law student then, but he already knew where his political loyalties lay:

he was an anti-semite who believed the legal system was there to safeguard the racial purity of the Reich as much as to eliminate any elements threatening the Nazi State.

Once the Nazis came to power in 1933, Frank was quickly made Reich Commissioner for the Co-ordination of the Judiciary and for the Renewal of the Legal Order. In other words, the *Gleichschaltung*. He was also made Minister without Portfolio, but he was never part of Hitler's inner circle: there were simply too many things he couldn't agree with. For one thing, he didn't agree with the 'Night of the Long Knives', in early July 1934, when Ernst Röhm, Chief of the SA *Sturmabteilung*, the Storm Troopers, and hundreds of his men were eliminated by the SS, under Heinrich Himmler, and the SD Security Service and Gestapo, under Reinhard Heydrich. For another, he believed in the independence of judges within the judicial system – those in the *Landes* and *Sonder* courts dealing with everything but treason. As head of the National Socialist Jurists Association, he increased the membership to 8,000 – lawyers being as fearful of losing their jobs and livelihoods as anyone else. Much later, once the Nazis had occupied Poland in 1939, Hitler made Frank the Governor-General there. Later still, he was sentenced to death by hanging at the post-war Nuremberg Trials.

The People's Court was inaugurated in April 1934 in Berlin's Prinz Albrecht Strasse, the ceremony attended by numerous dignitaries, though not by Hitler, who hated lawyers all his life. 'I herewith open the National Socialist People's Court,' intoned the Reich Minister of Justice in cap and gown, this followed by the Hitler Salute and a hearty rendering of the Horst Wessel song, by now the virtual national anthem. There were only 12 judges in that first year, but 200 by the end in 1945 – the need to stamp out treason increasing dramatically as time went by. The Court's judges wore the red robes and mortar boards of the judiciary and the structure was like any other criminal court, the suspects prosecuted first by the police and then, if a formal indictment was considered appropriate, by the prosecuting counsel. The sentences ranged from imprisonment, to forced labour in a camp, to death. There were two presidents over the 11-year period of the Court's existence, Otto Georg Theirack till 1942, and then Roland Freisler, the notorious fanatic and racist who, like Frank, considered the Court's main task was to 'purify the Reich'. As such, from the outset the Court was not for Jews, who were racially impure and therefore excluded. Only Aryans.

Hitler's feelings about the Jews, like all other aspects of his ideology, were already clearly stated in *Mein Kampf*. First and foremost, the Reich would become racially pure. The struggle for existence, as Hitler put it, was the struggle of the Aryan master race against the Jew, who was 'vermin' and 'parasitic' and engaged in a Capitalist conspiracy to control the world. The two great enemies of the Nazi State and the Volk were the Jews and the Marxists, the one frequently overlapping with the other. Both had to be exterminated. It was the only solution, and it would lead ultimately and inevitably to war. Total War.

What Hitler and Frank couldn't have anticipated was that as soon as the Court was established it was inundated with people denouncing their neighbours – anyone they held a grudge against for faring better than themselves during Weimar times. They'd heard a neighbour make a joke against the Führer in the local Gasthof, they'd noticed that their son's teacher avoided giving the Hitler salute or that he did it in lacklustre fashion, they suspected meetings were being held by one-time Social Democrats in the local priest's house. As the Hitler Youth and BDM, Band of German Maidens, movement gained increasing hold over the Reich's boys and girls, it was even known for children to denounce their own parents. The Nazis tasked the SA, the secret *Sicherheitsdienst* security branch of Heinrich Himmler's SS, to deal with the avalanche of accusations, along with any other security matters which needed mopping up.

Rudolf Ditzen, like most of his compatriots, hardly noticed the inauguration of the new *Volksgericht*. He was much too busy writing. By 1934, he'd decided fame wasn't such a great thing. Joseph Goebbels, his great fan, kept badgering him to write propaganda material for the NSDAP. All Rudolf could do was delay, saying he was too busy, and hope for the best. He knew as well as anyone that if he didn't make some concessions, the badgering would soon change to something worse. Rudolf couldn't bear to leave Germany, his *Heimat*. Many writers had already left – for France, Switzerland, England or America – Hermann Hesse, Bertolt Brecht, and soon Thomas Mann and Stefan Zweig. Artists and musicians, too. But Rudolf just couldn't do it. Cut off from his home, he knew he'd miss it too much and, even worse, he knew he wouldn't be able to write. His subject, after all, was the little man undergoing all the trials which had beset Germany since the end of the First World War, into the troubled Weimar years, and now on to this, the Nazi era. Rudolf's little man managed to survive by retreating into the bosom of family life. Which is what Rudolf himself decided to do. Hiding, some called it.

When he was briefly arrested by the Nazis at Easter 1933 it wasn't the prison which bothered him – he'd been in prison before and found it quite manageable, peaceful even. A lot better than his stays in lunatic asylums, certainly. No it wasn't the prison cell which bothered him, it was the reason for his being there in the first place. Flush with his new money, the Ditzens had just moved to the village of Berkenbrück on the River Spree, about an hour from Berlin, in the countryside, and not far from his ebullient publisher Ernst Rowohlt. They rented the first floor of a villa owned by an elderly couple called Sponat who'd fallen, like so many, on hard times. There were two bedrooms, a bathroom, a maid's room, a living room, a dining room with a terrace looking out over the river, a study, central heating and a separate entrance. Plus a large garden with fruit trees. Life was good: Suse was pregnant again, and they were happy with the new maid, Marie, who loved Uli, now three years old. The rent was a lot more than Neuenhagen but Rudolf had earned 12,000 Reich Marks in one year alone, so they could easily afford it. They had a phone put in. When Rowohlt offered Rudolf an astonishing 28,000 Reich Marks for his new contract, Rudolf suggested to the Sponats that he buy the house and land off them, allowing them to clear their 15,000 Reich Marks debt. A good deal for both sides, he thought, achieving his and Suse's dream of owning a smallholding. In the end, they settled for a life-long leasehold.

They were aware of their luck and were generous with their money, inviting friends who'd fallen on hard times to stay, and helping some out financially too. 'The sun is shining today and when I look up from my typewriter I can see two arms of the River Spree, boats passing noiselessly by and forest, forest,' wrote Rudolf happily to a friend from his new study. But then one day not long after, out of the blue, the local SA turned up to search the house for, they said, evidence of conspiracy, and carted a protesting Rudolf off to prison. It turned out to be a false denunciation. By none other than the Sponats, good Nazi Party members, who'd planned it as a way of getting the Ditzens out and regaining their home, having already repaid their debt with the Ditzen money.

It was all too much for Rudolf's nerves. He started drinking more and writing less, and smoking like a chimney as always. Rowohlt warned him to take care of himself and of his money which he was spending like water. But there were too many small shocks to the system during those early months of the Nazi regime, starting with the duplicity of the Sponats. Rudolf had hoped to keep his head down, living quietly in the countryside making no trouble for anyone till this threatening Nazi regime was over. As a precaution, he'd torn up his SPD membership card. Suse's brother did the same, though in his case it was only in order to join the Communist Party. But then came the shock of the Writers Union being infiltrated by Nazi Party sympathisers. Rudolf managed to screw up his courage and join the protestors writing a letter to complain at the way writers critical of the Nazis were being excluded. Then came the March 1933 election, when the NSDAP gained 43.9 per cent of the vote thanks to two months of brutal intimidation and imprisonment of Communists and Social Democrats. Then came the shock of Kurt Weil and Berthold Viertel, the composer and director of *Little Man, What Now?* which was being filmed in Berlin. They were both Jews and both wrongly aligned politically, and after the open attack on the Jews on 1 April they fled, lucky to escape with their lives. Rudolf refused to continue collaborating with the film, now under new direction, and he managed to avoid writing short stories and articles approved by Goebbels' new Ministry for Public Enlightenment and Propaganda. But it wasn't easy.

After the burning of 'degenerate' books on 10 May, came *Gleichschaltung* when Rudolf could only watch helpless as friends and colleagues lost their jobs on newspapers and in publishing houses. Then, in June, came the banning of the SPD and the arrest of 3,000 party officials, with many fleeing into exile. And then, when Rudolf tried to get back the 13,000 Reich Marks he'd paid the Sponats, the Nazi Party lawyer they'd engaged informed him he wouldn't get a penny. Worst of all, by far: when Suse gave birth to twins, two little girls, Lore and Edith, Edith was born severely handicapped and died within hours. Rudolf somehow felt he was to blame.

'Quite honestly,' Rudolf wrote to a reader who was perplexed about what to do in the threatening political climate, 'if I knew a way of joining the National Socialist Party at the moment without a lot of fuss, I would do it. Because this is my sincere belief: while one can argue about the details, this is the party which will save Germany from chaos.' Whether he really believed it or whether he was just trying to cover his tracks, fearing another denouncement, who knows? Perhaps it was his way of advising this little man to keep his head down as he himself was doing. The public already had a name for it, an English one: Beefsteak – people who were brown, Nazi, on the outside, and red, anti-Nazi, on the inside. Rudolf certainly knew he couldn't join the NSDAP without a big fuss being made because he was a celebrity now, and he knew too well how Goebbels would make use of it. But he also managed to avoid joining any NSDAP cultural activities. So, in his own small way, Rudolf resisted. Still, it all took its toll.

Ernst Rowohlt, more robust and more daring than Rudolf, helped many of his Jewish authors, inviting them to his home, giving them extra advances for their books, finding them work elsewhere and ultimately helping them to leave the country, using his contacts at the American Embassy. But Rudolf was too scared – he wasn't swashbuckling Rowohlt. In spite of her own sorrows, Suse tried, as always, to steady him, but in June he had another breakdown, ending up in a private clinic in Berlin.

When he came out a few weeks later, he didn't want to go back to Berkenbrück – too many bad memories. Instead, he found them a smallholding in Carwitz, deep in the countryside in Mecklenburg, 'a genuine old farmhouse, very cosy, with electric lighting, stoves, seven rooms and an attic which could easily be converted into two more,' as he wrote to his parents. It had outhouses and some land, which made Suse happy, with wonderful views over a lake and forests. There was no road leading from Carwitz, only a sandy track to Feldberg, the small local town 7 kilometres away, reached by horse and cart, by cycling or plain walking. It had a Gasthof and bakery; otherwise a grocer's and a butcher's van came once a week. Berlin was three hours away, reached by local train from Feldberg to Neustrelitz, and thence by a faster train to the city. It was perfect, far from the temptations of both Berlin and the threats of the Nazi regime. While Suse stayed in a private clinic recovering from the birth of the twins and a thrombosis, Rudolf settled himself into the hotel in Feldberg to oversee the purchase and renovation of the house. Marie came to look after Uli. By October, the house was ready and Suse was sufficiently recovered for them to move in and start family life afresh.

Rudolf was full of good intentions. He would stop drinking and behave better. He would become the husband Suse deserved. She was 'the most wonderful woman in the world', as he wrote to his parents in another of his dutiful letters home, 'who always helps me and is patient with me. I've known for some time now that (she) is the greatest success of my life. Without her I would have collapsed and sunk without trace . . . She has given me the strength and courage to go on working. Marriage is, God knows, not easy but (she) has a tranquillity which is the source of all strength.' He might as well have been talking about Pinneberg's Lammchen. They had the wireless set sent over from Berkenbrück and he bought a gramophone and had another telephone installed. So now he was all set to get back to his next book, which he called his 'prison' book.

As ever, lacking the courage to act, it was through his writing Rudolf managed to make his views felt, speaking of the frightened 'little man' oppressed by the hard times they lived in. And, as ever, the story was based on Rudolf's own experience and his own life. The title of his new book speaks for itself: *Once a Jailbird*. It was a theme close to his heart, one which he'd written about and given talks about too – that prison didn't work, it only made criminals of people who shouldn't have been in prison in the first place but ended up there through some misfortune or other, and then, on release, found there was no support available to help them make a fresh start. Willi Kufalt, Rudolf's little man buffeted and blown off course by a harsh society and ill luck, comes out of prison having done five years for embezzlement and forgery. Now he is having to make a go of life outside.

As he sat writing about Willi in the peace of his new study overlooking the lake and the forest, Rudolf remembered it all: the same crime, the same prison life, the same difficulty of finding his feet in the outside world. Willi lives in a hostel earning a measly wage in a typing bureau (Rudolf knew all about that too). But soon an old crony from prison persuades him to set up his own venture, which inevitably fails, and when he tries to get another job, this time on a local newspaper (Rudolf again) they find out about his criminal record and he's on the skids again. Before he knows it, Willi is back to drinking and back to crime. And then back to prison. At which point, Willi transforms fully into Rudolf, because here Willi finally finds peace and quiet, a certain happiness even. Which rather goes against Rudolf's call, in the rest of the book, for reform of not just the broken prison system, but of society as a whole.

Still, it was a courageous subject to take on. Rudolf knew he'd written a controversial book, what with the ex-con, and an unmarried mother and a homosexual, all sympathetically described. But he thought it was his best book so far and he felt heady with achievement. To compound his courageous act he agreed to employ Dora Preisach, one of Rowohlt's Jewish people who'd lost her job, to come and live with them while she typed the final draft of the book. He didn't mind that *Jailbird* couldn't make as much money as his previous books, times having changed. He knew the subject wouldn't be politically acceptable to the Nazis and he wasn't surprised when Rowholt couldn't find a newspaper to serialise it because most of the editors they knew had left Germany by now, or were, like Rudolf, keeping their heads down, Beefsteak-style, so as not to go against the new Rules of Publication. And once the Nazis quit the League of Nations in October 1933, his foreign sales slowed down too. But Rudolf was a writer first and last. Without it he lost his sanity.

To appease the Ministry for Public Enlightenment and Propaganda, he made a dicey decision: to write a foreword to bring the book more in line with Nazi regulations. Rowohlt advised strongly against it, but Rudolf insisted. It was all very well for robustly healthy Rowohlt to take risks – a man who didn't have to worry about nervous breakdowns and such. The authorities had already asked Rudolf to make certain changes to the next edition of *Little Man, What Now?* so he knew the name of the game: compromise. Taking a deep breath with *Little Man*, he refused to change a Communist character and some sympathetic descriptions of Jews, but he did remove negative references to the NSDAP and the SA. Now, with *Once a Jailbird*, he wrote the foreword without too much soul-searching, having it ready for publication in early 1934. The ridiculous, grotesque and pitiful consequences of the so-called humane justice system, he wrote, were now a thing of the past, thanks to recent changes to society. It wasn't true, he knew, but what else could he do?

To Rowohlt and friends, he admitted he'd decided to 'swallow the bitter pill' because he and his family couldn't bear to leave Germany. The other bitter pill he swallowed was to join the new Writers Union because, without it, there could be no more books. 'The only possible thing would be to emigrate,' he wrote a year later, as things got worse in Nazi Germany. 'But Suse and I both hate the idea, because what after all would we do in a strange country? And we'd have to give up everything we have here in Carwitz – no, it would be too hard.' Thomas Mann, reading *Once a Jailbird* from the safety of exile in Switzerland, put it in a nutshell: 'In order to be published in Germany a book has to disown and deny its humane philosophy in an Introduction.'

The Ditzen family settled quickly into Carwitz. Baby Lore was well, Uli was growing, Marie had left to get married but kept in touch, Suse was busy with their smallholding, Rudolf was busy at his desk. They had a cow for fresh milk, hens for eggs, vegetables from the garden, wood for the stove. They hardly saw anyone except close friends and relations. Winter continued, with snow and sleet and rain. Then came spring and the first leaves on the bare trees. Then the heat of early summer. For days at a time, Rudolf was able to forget what was going on in the rest of the Reich.

On Sunday 27 May 1934, the Ditzens received a visit. It wasn't something Rudolf wanted – in fact he'd already put it off once. But now they came, four young people out for a jaunt, racing along the country lanes of Mecklenburg in an open-topped roadster, off to see Hans Fallada, one of the Reich's most famous authors.

'It was a lovely spring day when we started,' wrote Martha Dodd, 'the chestnut trees all along the roads were glowing, the acacia's wine-sweet fragrance faint in the air.' Martha was the 24-year-old daughter of the recently installed American ambassador to the German Reich. She was very forward in an American sort of way, with a shot-gun marriage to a New York banker already behind her, and a few affairs too. She was hoping to be a writer. With her came Mildred Harnack, another American, from Milwaukee – a very different type, more serious, happily married for four years to her German husband, Arvid, and working as a teacher in the *Abendgymnasium* in Berlin, giving evening classes in English language and literature to mature students. They came with a young man called Ledig, Ernst Rowohlt's son, the person who'd arranged the visit to the reluctant and reclusive author. And another young man, possibly Martha's current boyfriend, Boris Winogradows, a Russian, working at the embassy.

'Mecklenburg is one of the loveliest districts in North Germany, certainly the most beautiful I have ever been in. There is a gentleness to the landscape, in the rolling green hills and bright lakes, a lyricism and poetry in the softness and contour of the land and the water,' wrote Martha, the would-be writer. Finally, after bumping along a bad country lane, they found the village and the 'modest cottage' which was set by a lake and surrounded by a few acres of cultivated land. 'Hans Fallada came out with his buxom, simple wife to meet us. We walked around a little and he described the farming he was doing, his wife proudly showing off her work in the garden.' Fallada was stockily built, blondish hair and charming, with genial features; his wife was plump, blonde, serene, with a peasant face. They had a four-year-old boy and a babe in arms. The wife had prepared a 'wholesome country dinner', after which they went for a walk by the lake, talking of books and life and literature, alternating between German and English. Sitting in the garden afterwards, they took many photographs, 'as is the German custom'. The main photographer would seem to have been the Russian Winogradows, because Rudolf, in tweed jacket and plus-fours, features in most of them, also holding a camera. Martha looks pretty and perky in a stylish beret. Mildred looks wispy blonde, in a light summer frock and loose coat. Ledig mostly hovers on the edge of frame in a dark suit. In the one photograph featuring the tall Russian, presumably taken by Rudolf, he is dressed in a light summer suit and tie and a flat-topped cap. Suse hardly makes an appearance.

'There was a quiet haze of heat spread over the earth, the lakes and hills appeared to be resting softly, and life seemed peaceful,' wrote Martha. 'Their life seemed to be built around their family and their farm. He was isolated from life and happy in his isolation. There was some discussion and though I got the impression he was not and could not be a Nazi – what artist is? – I felt a certain resignation in his attitude.' When they took their leave, they promised to come back.

'But we never went back. This withdrawal from life was Hans Fallada's tragic solution to the problems that might have been troubling his peace. It was a temptation to which he had completely succumbed. And the impression of defeatism he gave us was saddening. Later I heard that he got into trouble on one of his rare visits to Berlin, that he was beaten up by some Storm Troopers and confined to the hospital for a week or two. But he seems to have settled his life in the simple, trivial pattern we saw on his farm, is still writing not very good books, and is for the moment lost to a deeper struggle with life. However he is the one remaining author of recognised talent writing in Germany and one can only watch as time goes on what this intellectual and emotional passivity will do to his talent.'

And back to Berlin they raced in their open-topped roadster, the wind in their hair, the sun on their faces, full of youthful optimism and naivity, the two American women and their German and Russian young men, straight into the arms of the Gestapo spies – though they didn't, as yet, know it.

'Please, my son, don't write anything political,' wrote another of Rowohlt's authors to his son, safe in America. 'It's quite likely that our post could make trouble for us, since most letters are opened. You can't imagine how terrible things are here now, and how, in spite of all precautions, we feel the ground beneath our feet giving way. In our times we have to learn to be deaf and blind, not looking either right or left, showing oneself as little as possible. The denunciations are horrifying . . .'

In Berlin, Fabian von Schlabrendorff was setting off on a visit of his own. In 1934 he was still embarked on his law studies, but more and more of his time was spent seeking out other would-be resisters to the Nazi terror regime, quietly supported by his mother, a dedicated anti-Nazi from the first. Fabian met many fellow resisters in Sigismund Lauter's first-floor elegant apartment on the Kurfürstendamm where

Lauter, his doctor, had moved in order to make it harder for the Gestapo spies to break in. Another of the regular guests was Ernst Rowohlt, who also frequented parties at the American Embassy.

'He was a delightful man, of giant blond Aryan stature and complexion,' described Martha Dodd. 'He had a positively cherubic face, with innocent blue eyes, round, ruddy, plump cheeks and an irrepressible and spluttering humour. He was a tremendous drinker and also a very serious and vital man. He loved life and freedom passionately . . . and spoke bluntly and honestly about any subject that arose . . . he was the type of man who aroused and held the devotion and unswerving loyalty of his subordinates and who could attract anyone by his tremendous energy and intelligence.'

At the other end of the social scale, Fabian made regular clandestine visits to Ernst Niekisch's modest house near the railway station, and to his *Bismarck Gesellschaft*, Bismarck Society, where resisters met regularly – another of those secret places the Gestapo, with all their sniffing-out powers, had not yet discovered. Though you could never be sure. The Gestapo liked to keep a quiet eye on resistance networks, sometimes over many years, in order to arrest the whole group and their families too, in one fell swoop. Everyone knew this and knew what it would mean if they were caught. But Niekisch, so far, and quite beyond the understanding of a young student like Fabian, still enjoyed the confidence of the Nazi regime and the *Reichswehr* Army, because he was the indispensable link to the secret rearmament programme taking place over the border in Russia. Niekisch knew that sooner or later his luck would run out, but meanwhile he went on quite openly publishing his journal, *Widerstand*, which was another great puzzle to young Schlabrendorff. How did he dare? As Niekisch put it: 'Anyone who is committed to politics now has to take on everything, even if it means the worst outcome for oneself in the end, to show History that Hitler and Germany were never one and the same.'

But on this day in 1934 Fabian was journeying further afield, by train, to a region north of Berlin called Hinterpommern, to pay a quiet visit to Ewald von Kleist-Schmenzin. Fabian used to visit Kleist-Schmenzin's country estate as a schoolboy, part of a Weimar scheme for young students to spend time in the countryside, working the fields, getting to know the life and the culture. The young Fabian was instantly impressed by their host, a man of few words but with natural charisma: every word he spoke counted. Kleist-Schmenzin had served in the Great War, and perhaps it was that which instilled into him a deep religious conviction and an inflexible belief in right and wrong. Originally, he'd trained as a lawyer but these days he tended his estate. He loved his forests and his hunting. But he was also active in politics, locally for the time being. He'd been a representative in the Conservative Prussian *Hauptverein* for many years, and when the local farm workers went on strike for better pay and conditions he held out and persuaded other landowners to do the same, preferring to let their fields go to wrack and ruin rather than give in to the workers' demands. What the workers did was wrong as Kleist-Schmenzin saw it, going against the natural order of things. But once the strike ended, he raised their wages, because that was the right thing to do.

At first when the Nazis came to power Kleist-Schmenzin waited to see what their actions rather than their bombastic words would amount to. It soon became clear. As a leading Conservative, he sought a meeting with Hitler and expressed his views, short and clear, with only one result: Hitler saw him as an enemy from that moment on. He also went to see Hindenburg through the good offices of his father-in-law, Oscar von den Osten-Warnitz. The latter had held his peace about the Nazis at first, but once the Jews were attacked by the regime on 1 April he decided to make a stand, openly visiting a local Jewish landowner to express his regrets, and he made a point of doing more business with the local Jewish livestock dealers from then on. When he was called in by the district Nazi *Kreisleiter* and told to desist, he refused, instead returning the Keys of the Town which he'd recently been awarded by a grateful community. It caused a great stir in Neumark. The local SA were despatched to surround Osten-Warnitz's Schloss to force him to hoist the swastika flag. But news got out and, with Hindenburg's help, a local militia got there first, far outnumbering the SA who beat a reluctant retreat.

When the SA arrived at Kleist-Schmenzin's country estate insisting he likewise hoist the swastika flag, he was ready for them, like his father-in-law, with a local militia, and again the SA slunk off. In these early days of the regime the Nazi Party wasn't strong enough nor sure enough of local support to insist. Kleist-Schmenzin knew this, and he knew the power of small everyday acts of resistance. But then came the day when it was decreed that all Protestant churches be amalgamated under one Reich church, bringing them under Nazi rule – and Kleist-Schmenzin made his decision: he would fight them, tooth and nail, to the bitter end.

Which is how it happened that Fabian was paying him a visit. They meant to work together, agreeing with Carl von Ossietzky, pacifist editor of *Die Weltbühne*: 'When someone who opposes the government leaves his country, his words soon sound hollow to those who remain ... To be really effective in combating the contamination of a country's spirit, one must share its entire destiny.' Each resister had his or her own turning point. For Kleist-Schmenzin it was the Nazis' attack on the Churches and on God himself. As for Ossietzky, he was arrested after the Reichstag fire on 27 February 1933 and sent to Oranienburg concentration camp, where he died in 1938, apparently of tuberculosis.

'All the churches are the same,' Hitler announced in one of his private table talks. 'Whichever one you chose, it will not have a future. Not for the Germans, anyway. Italian Fascism may, in the name of God, make its peace with the Church. I will do that too. Why not! It won't stop me eradicating Christianity from Germany, root and branch. You are either a Christian or a German. You can't be both.'

When the Nazis came to power, 62.7 per cent of the population – some 40 million people – belonged to one of the Protestant churches, and 32.4 per cent – some 22 million – to the Catholic Church. After July 1933, only the Catholic Church managed to remain semi-independent of direct Nazi control. The Protestants now had a Reich Bishop, Ludwig Müller. In response, Martin Niemöller, the pastor of Dahlem, set up the *Pasternotbund*, later known as the Confessing Church. By the end of 1933, and in spite of the fact that the Confessing Church was outspokenly anti-Nazi, 6,000 clergymen had joined. There wasn't much the Nazis could do about it, not yet. The public still had to be re-educated, Goebbels willing, but it took time.

In January 1934, Martin Niemöller had asked for a meeting with Hitler, attended by himself and other courageous members of the clergy. And Bishop Müller. In Hitler's study. Göring rushed into the room late, clicking his heels and giving the Hitler salute, then proceeded to read out the transcript of a conversation Niemöller had apparently had with an unknown person. Niemöller tried to think why it sounded familiar. Ah, yes! It was a telephone conversation he'd had that very morning. 'Mein Führer!' Göring continued. 'These people are trying to drive a wedge between yourself and the Reich president!' Hitler started to rage. Niemöller insisted his work had no object but the welfare of the Church, the state and the German people. 'Confine yourself to the Church,' shouted Hitler, 'I'll take care of the German Volk!' As he left, Niemöller tried one last time. 'We too, as Christians and churchmen, have a responsibility towards the German people. That responsibility was entrusted to us by God, and neither you nor anyone in the world has the power to take it from us.' In May 1934, the Confessing Church made a Declaration, repudiating all the 'false teachings' of the Nazis. There was only one Leader and that was Jesus Christ, they stated.

Later Niemöller wrote:

> When the Nazis came for the Communists
> I was silent
> I wasn't a Communist
> When the Nazis came for the Social Democrats
> I was silent
> I wasn't a Social Democrat
> When the Nazis came for the Trade Unionists
> I was silent
> I wasn't a Trade Unionist
> When the Nazis came for the Jews
> I was silent
> I wasn't a Jew
> When the Nazis came for me
> There was no one left
> To protest

The Prussian *Hauptverein* had always had a journal to which Kleist-Schmenzin had often contributed – articles on hunting and the like. But now he contributed in a new way, openly expressing his criticism of the Nazi regime in general and the way it was dealing with the

Churches in particular. He was called in by the authorities again and again, warned that if he persisted there would be trouble. So it was only a matter of time before the SA came to arrest him, which they did on 30 June 1934. But he was alerted by a local man and by the time the SA turned up he'd got his chauffeur to drive him to the small railway station at Bublitz, avoiding the main railway station of Neumark because he knew the SA would be looking for him there once they found he was missing. 'Where's your husband?' they demanded of the Countess. 'How should I know?' she answered. 'I'm not my husband's keeper.' Anyway he wasn't at home, she added, just in case they weren't up on Bible quotations. As soon as they'd gone she sent their forester to stop the chauffeur returning to the Schloss, telling him to hide in the woods for the time being. Then she rang Fabian von Schlabrendorff in Berlin, asking him to find somewhere for her husband to hide.

Ewald von Kleist-Schmenzin made his slow journey to Berlin, taking only local trains and staying one night in a small hotel under a false name. Fabian meanwhile wracked his brains to think of some safe place where his friend could lie low till the crisis was over, because that's how things were in those early days: sporadic. He hit on the perfect solution: Ernst Niekisch. Who would think of looking for a Prussian aristocrat in a Communist's house? Niekisch agreed at once. Fabian took Kleist-Schmenzin to Niekisch's house straight from another small local station. The two men got on immediately, naturally like-minded. Kleist-Schmenzin stayed for several days, then once the coast was clear he went back home. From then on he kept his head down, outwardly at least – another Beefsteak – but he and Niekisch became firm friends and saw each other regularly at meetings of Niekisch's Bismarck Society, to pursue their joint resistance work but also for pleasure, each being a new experience for the other, each amazed to find they had so much in common.

Into the second year of the Nazi regime, people had learned that you had to watch everything you said because there were Gestapo spies everywhere just waiting to turn a 'traitor' in. These were people who'd been neighbours, work colleagues, school friends, relations even, so people lived in constant watchfulness and fear. But that New Year's Eve, the Engelmann family were among friends. They'd gone to stay with friends who ran the best hotel in Westphalia. Bernt was almost fourteen now and allowed to stay up for the festivities. They sat at a large table in the corner of the dining room and after a fine supper a small band started playing waltzes and tangos and foxtrots. Bernt was amused to watch his parents take to the crowded dance floor, and soon the place was humming, people quite forgetting their troubles. At midnight they clinked glasses and wished each other a Happy New Year and the lights were briefly switched off, allowing for the traditional kiss. But when the lights came on again people suddenly fell silent. A heavy, half-drunk man in brown SA uniform and shiny black boots clambered up onto the stage to make a speech. He was the District *Kreisleiter*, who'd previously been a shopkeeper. He spoke in the by now familiar bombastic style of the Nazis, full of nationalistic phrases and slogans, losing his thread. People tried not to laugh. He ended with the usual 'God save our Führer!' and the *'Heil Hitler!'* salute. 'And us from him!' muttered an elderly friend of the hosts, a highly respected local lawyer, seated at their table. Someone must have heard him. A few days later, he was arrested by the Gestapo. The local paper reported that he had been 'unmasked as a dangerous enemy of the state' and 'consigned to a concentration camp'. Not long after, the Engelmanns got a letter from their friends: the man who had suddenly fallen ill at the New Year's Eve festivities fortunately didn't have long to suffer. He was being buried in a private ceremony.

Later that year, Bernt was hanging around in the street in his suburb of Düsseldorf waiting for his friends who were finishing a dancing lesson in the school hall, learning the foxtrot. It was May, the sun was shining, the chestnut trees just coming into leaf and they were off to the cinema to see the latest Dorothea Wieck film. As he waited, Bernt saw Hedwig hurrying towards him, looking distressed. Hedwig had been the family's maid for ten years, since she was seventeen, and throughout Bernt's childhood. It was a sad day for them when she left to marry Klaus, a local carpenter, but they were pleased for her. Klaus was a decent man and a fine craftsman. And a Communist. Now she just said 'Tante Ney', nodding her head in the direction of the bakery. In the privacy of the back room, she told Bernt that Klaus had been arrested a week earlier.

'Why didn't you tell us?' Bernt couldn't believe it.

'I didn't want to get you into trouble,' was Hedwig's simple answer. But now she was desperate.

The Gestapo had arrived at six one morning just as Klaus was setting off for work. His brother was an engine fitter and he'd already been arrested, tortured with pins under his nails then locked in a metal locker, the kind used to hang your day clothes in at work. He was made to stand in the cramped space with hardly any air for twelve hours, that's how the Nazis did it. Now they were both in the new concentration camp in Emsland, outside Düsseldorf. Hedwig didn't know what to do. Bernt promised to tell his parents, though what they could do he didn't know. Then each went their way, Hedwig to try and arrange a visit to Emsland, Bernt to meet his friends.

After the film, they were on the tram going home when a lorry full of men in 'protective custody' came alongside. One of the men leapt from the lorry onto the back of the tram. No one said a word, just made room for him. An old lady silently gave him a handkerchief to wipe the blood off his face. At the next stop, he jumped off and disappeared down an alleyway. And this, all in one day.

One evening over supper, not long after the drama in the tram, Frau Engelmann was telling her husband and Bernt that she'd met Pastor Klotzel in the street that morning, and there'd been something strange about it. He'd looked tired and distracted, saying, as he took his leave, 'Some day we'll see the sun again.' The Engelmanns were not usually church-going people, but soon after the Nazis came to power Frau Engelmann had insisted Bernt attend Pastor Klotzel's confirmation classes, as a show of respect. Because the Pastor, a conservative man, had made his private decision not to disguise his convictions. 'Everyone, even the most simple-minded, can tell right from wrong,' he might say, from the pulpit. The day after their supper conversation the Engelmanns heard Pastor Klotzel had been arrested by the Gestapo for 'misuse of the pulpit' and preaching 'treason'. A few weeks later, they heard he'd 'passed away' in a concentration camp. His young parish curate organised a memorial service. The Englemanns had never seen the church so crowded, Catholics as well as Protestants, many standing outside the church. Bernt spotted Fräulein Bonse, and the Neys too. The young curate delivered a brave sermon then led the congregation singing Luther's rousing hymn 'A Mighty Fortress is Our God', everyone in the church joining in, each with their small act of courage. In the following months, some 2,000 pastors were arrested and consigned to concentration camps, the young curate included.

During 1934, Fritzi von der Schulenburg was still busy putting *Gleichschaltung* into practice in East Prussia, seeing it as the price you had to pay to make Germany great again, divesting the *Heimat* of all dissenting voices. In his view, it was important that the key administrative posts in Königsberg were held by like-minded National Socialists, because there was a lot of unrest in the district, not least from the neighbouring Poles.

But doubts were creeping in.

The first doubt came on 30 June 1934. It was the Night of the Long Knives, when, over a 48-hour period, all those threatening Hitler's leadership within the Nazi Party were murdered. Rumour had it that it was organised by Himmler, Göring, Goebbels and Reinhard Heydrich, the chief of the *Sicherheitsdienst*, already one of the most feared members of Hitler's inner circle, and carried out by the SS and the Gestapo with terrifying brutality. Hundreds were murdered along with Ernst Röhm himself, mainly members of his SA but also any other old enemies, Conservatives and Socialists alike, including the former Chancellor von Schleicher. And Gregor Strasser.

It was a profound shock for Fritzi. Strasser, the man with the Socialist ideas of reform and renewal, had been the main reason he'd joined the Party in the first place. He'd already worried when Strasser resigned as chief of the *Reichs Organisation* Administration in December 1932. 'I must admit, I've really been shaken by the Strasser thing,' he'd written to Charlotte at the time. 'I can't imagine who might replace him in the movement and the building up of the new State.' What was the reason? He'd hoped for Hitler as Reich President and Strasser as Chancellor. And now this. For the first time, he felt personally threatened, because he was a known supporter of Strasser, and all supporters were in danger. It was incredible that things had come to this.

He and Charlotte had been married for 18 months. She was pregnant with their first child. What to do? Like so many others, thinking it over in the dark hours of the night, he decided to go into hiding and retreated with Charlotte to the country house of an old friend, somewhere in Masuren, exact location unknown, till the purge was spent. When he returned to work in Königsberg, he left Charlotte there for safety. He wondered whether it wouldn't be better just to take some distant *Landrat* position for a few years, he wrote to Charlotte on 16 October 1934 – keep his head down. Because everything in the Reich, as he saw it now, was 'fairly depressing'. The essential problem was that 'Everywhere the Party orders the state,' and not the other way round, as it should be. Prussian values were gone, once and for all.

Lately things hadn't been going well with Ernst Koch either – the man Fritzi himself had canvassed Göring about, securing him the post of *Gauleiter* in East Prussia. Once in place, Koch had very quickly abandoned his Strasser Socialist principles and reverted to type. He gave jobs to Old Fighter *Kamaraden* and as soon as possible he got rid of Dr Carl Budding, the *Regierungspräsident* in Marienburg, and Dr Zimmer, the *Landrat* in Stuhm. They were both members of the former Centre party and excellent at their jobs. Both were accused by Koch of treating the local Polish population too softly. Fritzi, critical of Koch's decisions, openly supported the two men. The area was a difficult mix of ethnic Germans, Poles and Jews, he pointed out, and had to be very carefully and diplomatically administered, with fairness and justice. Increasingly in two minds about *Gleichschaltung* now, he tried hard to defend the men, but to no avail. 'Two out of three positions go to Party members who are not up to the job,' he told anyone who would listen. It only served to make Koch and his gang mistrust Count von der Schulenburg, that stuck-up old-style Prussian, even more.

Once the Count started to openly criticise Koch's 'Personal politics', putting the Party above the state and lining his own pockets in the process, Koch demanded Schulenburg's resignation. Apparently he'd proved himself unable to abandon the old Prussian beliefs he'd practised all his life, and 'lately these have become more and more pronounced, leading to decisions which are not in line with National Socialist principles.' By November 1935 Fritzi was transferred to distant Fischhausen, as a modest *Landrat* official, replaced in Königsberg by an old and loyal Nazi Party member.

Fritzi couldn't have been happier. Gone *Gleichschaltung*, gone the Koch cronies, gone Party interference in this small, out-of-the-way place. Now he could get on with administering his region in the way he knew was right, back to the Prussian virtues of efficiency and fairness in work, and modesty and simplicity in personal life. As a first step, he got rid of the second official car. Then he turned a large part of his extensive living quarters into offices or housing for temporary workers, and he insisted on paying for the heating and electricity out of his own pocket. Then he threw himself into the work. Fischhausen was east of the Elbe, far from anywhere else in the Reich, a unique landscape of farms, lakes and sea, early morning mists, hot summers and harsh winters. The people were poor. He quickly set about building up the local economy, getting the *Kreis* finances back into proper order, improving the work and housing conditions of the agricultural workers, building public baths, and getting a cottage industry going, to give the fishermen and their families work to do and money to earn during the long winters. He was soon being praised by his bosses at the Ministry of the Interior, anti-Nazis all, for the quick and visible improvements and for getting on so well with the local community. In spite of Charlotte's protestations, he overworked. By Christmas he was ill with kidney stones. It gave him time to put in writing his protest about what was happening in the Königsberg *Gauleitung*.

From his sickbed, he wrote Erich Koch a letter, on 31 December 1935. 'Most esteemed Gauleiter!' he began, in conventional formal style. 'Since I've heard that you express yourself unclear as to my basic beliefs about National Socialist policies in the region, allow me to clarify . . .'

For a further eight pages, he laid it out for Koch: the necessary alignment between Party and state, the fight against excessive bureaucracy and corruption, the building up of a clean and effective National Socialism, adding: 'You yourself preached this before the *Machtergreifung*, and I was happy to follow you.' It was imperative they held to these precepts, he wrote, or lose the trust and belief of the Volk. He reminded Koch that already in July 1933 he'd written him a letter warning about dangerous developments. The early belief in humility and simplicity was being forgotten. Instead, Koch's name kept appearing concerning byzantine and tasteless acts such as the lavish automobile and chauffeur he'd immediately acquired, against everything National Socialism stood for. Then came the claim that the *Gauleiter*'s official apartment wasn't large enough, so a house surrounded by parkland was bought, pulled down, and completely rebuilt at the shocking cost of 200,000 Reich Marks.

'As I told you at the time, that signified your end as a revolutionary fighter.' The Volk knew about such things, he warned Koch, and they were losing trust. Then came all the jobs he gave to his cronies. Fritzi named one after another, giving chapter and verse. On and on he went about the rights and the wrongs, and about what was needed to build up an effective political administration, which amounted to a lot more than employing people merely for being good sportsmen or Old Fighter *Kamaraden*. This lack of discipline and proper selection was disastrous. The Volk couldn't know the details, but they saw the results, he warned Koch. They saw when someone wasn't up to the job and had been put there for the wrong reasons. They wanted fairness and justice. The result: the Party Political Organisation had lost ground everywhere in the region. They were losing the support of the decent, upright farmer, the ordinary citizen, and the worker, who said 'The Führer is good, but the Party . . .'

Finally Fritzi came to himself: at the beginning he'd only vaguely sensed that something was going wrong, he wrote, but over time the mistakes became clearer and clearer. They would only regain the Volk's trust once they could demonstrate that things had changed. 'The way in which I was, without any consultation and behind my back, sidelined, wasn't a single act, it was part of a whole.' Henceforth he would limit himself exclusively to his work at Fischhausen. As to those who accused him of treason against National Socialism, they should look to themselves. He believed that Koch knew very well how damaging such accusations could be, even when someone was in fact following their conscience, and how difficult it was to answer those accusations. Prussian to the last, Fritz-Dietlof came to the end of his letter with the warning: 'If I come across anyone accusing me of treason, I will see it as an attack on my honour. And I will defend my honour with every means and giving no quarter.' He would be happy, once his health allowed, to repeat all this to Koch in person.

He ended by wishing Koch a good New Year. '*Heil Hitler!* Schulenburg.'

CHAPTER FIVE

HARD TIMES: 1935

Irma Thälmann was 16 in 1935 and no longer attending *Volksschule*, secondary school. Her last day had been 17 March of the previous year. In the old days Communist Youth used to put on a festivity for the school leavers because, not belonging to a Church, they couldn't join in the one held at school. But now that was banned by the Nazis – always referred to as the Fascists or the Bloodhounds in the Thälmann household. *Vater* wrote from prison to say they shouldn't give in but arrange a private festivity at home.

'Early in the morning of 18 March we were amazed,' Irma wrote in her memoir, many years later. The 'we' referred to herself, *Mutti* and *Grossvater*, her mother's father who lived with them now *Vater*'s father had died. 'We were still in bed when the doorbell rang. Many friends, those who hadn't yet been arrested, came with flowers and small presents. On and on they came, all day long: fifty flowers in pots, many more bouquets, all red. I was very pleased, but we all knew it was really for the Party and Ernst Thälmann.' The thing that really pleased Irma was that *Vater* had planned it, by word of mouth all the way from Berlin to Hamburg, from his solitary cell in Moabit prison.

In spite of all the bullying Irma had received at the hands of the Nazi teachers in the school, there were enough decent and fair and courageous ones left to give her a good final report. Her favourite teacher made it his business to get her a place in the local secretarial college, because she already knew what she wanted to be: a secretary in a legal practice so she could help those in prison. But all the other girls came from better-off homes than hers and nearly all were in the BDM, the girls' equivalent of Hitler Youth. They bullied and teased her from the first day, knowing she was the daughter of Ernst Thälmann, and hating her for it. Although she was by far the brightest in the class, they made a point of talking down to her and laughing at her local Hamburg speech. For her part, Irma had no wish to join their stupid conversations at break times – nothing but boys and hairstyles. And then they'd break into one of their Nazi songs, war songs most of them, with Horst Wessel the favourite. And the teachers supported them. *Mutti* told Irma: 'You have to be strong, Irma. Only think of the work.'

The fact was, *Mutti* didn't really understand.

'I want to transfer to the *Haushalts Schule*,' she finally told her one day. 'There are workers' daughters there, that's where I belong.'

She did two years at the Housekeeping College. The History teacher was the same one there as she'd had in the secretarial college. 'Why did you leave?' he asked her one day. 'You were one of the best.'

'Why were you different there?' Irma flared. 'Here you don't dump me in it. There you did it along with all the other teachers.' That shut him up. But of course she knew the answer: he was frightened of losing his job.

Even at the *Haushalts Schule* there was a Fascist bully, predictably the sports teacher, who always tried to make Irma stand in front of the class when they gave the Hitler salute, and every time Irma refused. It was like being back at school. His favourite song was 'Today it's Germany, tomorrow the world'. He used to try and turn the other girls against Irma but it didn't work, because they were workers' daughters. Then he'd lose his temper and shout: 'Just you wait! Your *Vater* and his lot – we'll eradicate them one day!'

One morning the Rector called her into his office. *Mutti* had to go too. When they entered they said, 'Good Morning' and he told them to go out and come in again, this time with the proper greeting, meaning the '*Heil Hitler!*' He was a Nazi of course, or he couldn't have held his senior post. They refused.

'Are you told at home not to give the Hitler salute?' he wanted to know of Irma.

'No.'

'Are you being politically influenced at home?'

'No.'

'Are there any political conversations?'

Irma shrugged. They talked about everything, she said.

'Do your father's comrades visit?'

They had all sorts of friends.

'Do you think the way things are now, under the Third Reich, will ever change?'

What Irma thought was that in the old days this stupid man would never have got the job of Rector. 'Some say yes, some say no.'

When he asked *Mutti*, she said the same.

'Why won't your daughter give the Hitler salute?'

'I can understand it,' *Mutti* replied. 'Her father, who she loves and is innocent, is in prison. I understand her behaviour.'

Irma got her own back on the teacher on Sports Day. In spite of his objections she entered the sprinting race, in the relay team. What's more, she wore her red Pioneer sports outfit. She was told to change her outfit, but she refused. And the team backed her, because they knew they couldn't win without her. Lots of her old friends winked at her when she won. They didn't dare do much else.

Visits to *Vater* were rare and mostly *Mutti* went on her own, permission usually granted for no more than one person at a time, and Berlin being so far away. One day *Mutti* came back defeated and exhausted, quite unlike her usual fighting self. Irma was shocked at how old she suddenly looked. They made her a coffee and she told *Grossvater* and Irma how she'd gone to Moabit, but that *Vater* wasn't there. She'd waited for hours and refused to leave until they told her: he was at Prinz Albrecht Strasse, the Gestapo interrogation centre. She went straight there, threatening public mayhem if they didn't produce him. An SS man in his black uniform and high black boots took her up to a small room with a bare table and two chairs on the top floor of the building. She'd hardly sat down before the door opened and *Vater* staggered in. She nearly fainted. 'In God's name, what have they done to you!' He had teeth missing, a swollen face, blood in the eyes, and he could hardly walk. Gehring, the most infamous torturer at Prinz Albrecht Strasse, had done him over.

'What are you complaining about?' shouted the guard.

'He didn't say anything!' *Mutti* protested, beside herself. 'What have you done to my husband!'

Five minutes later, she was out on the street again. They'd only produced him to prove he was still alive and avoid a revolt. She made her way somehow to the Berlin comrades, who helped her. Thälmann wasn't the only one being tortured by the Bloodhounds at Prinz Albrecht Strasse. Many of their husbands had suffered the same fate. Some had not survived.

Many weeks of worry and fear followed in the Thälmann household in Hamburg, with no news from Berlin. Then one day came a postcard, out of the blue. And it came from Moabit prison. At *Mutti*'s next visit *Vater* managed to tell her a bit about it: Gehring and some other SS bandits had used horse whips, and beaten and punched him for hours, demanding the names and addresses of Communist comrades. It didn't work, he told her with grim satisfaction. On the way back to Moabit prison his minders said, 'Shame you're still alive. But you'll be dead sooner or later. Alive, we won't let you out!' Presumably they wanted him alive a bit longer. 'That it's come to this!' *Vater* was full of hate. 'That the worst elements of our Volk, who are the filth of humanity, now have the power!' He was whispering all this to *Mutti* and the guard got very agitated. 'Quiet! You're not meant to speak of such things. If anyone finds out, I'll be locked up too!' *Vater* challenged him. 'But you old-timers,' he said, 'you who've been here for years, you know what happens here mustn't be hidden and silenced.'

Once news got out of Thälmann's torture, Communists and Socialists everywhere took to the streets, demonstrating: in New York, Paris, Amsterdam, London and Marseilles, as well as in the Reich. Secret delegations were formed and money collected for the families of those in prison. Hundreds of letters were written. *Vater* received none. But he heard about them as, sooner or later, he heard about everything.

As he'd heard about the famous show-trial back in September 1933 – of Georgi Dimitrov and the four other Communists charged with the Reichstag fire – just by listening to the prison guards who could talk of nothing else. It took place with plenty of fanfare at the *Reichsgericht*, the Supreme Court – it being six months before the *Volksgericht*, People's Court, was ready. This meant the proceedings had to be legal – a concern which would never trouble the People's Court. Van der Lubbe, a Dutch Communist charged with actually setting light to the Reichstag, came first. He was quickly sentenced to death by guillotine. Then came the three Bulgarian Communists, Georgi Dimitrov, Vasil Tanev and Blagov Popov – known senior Comintern operatives – said to be the organisers of the fire. And lastly a German, Ernst Torgler. The *Sicherheitsamt* intelligence bureau knew about the Bulgarians and their subversive activities in the Reich, but they failed to get the measure of Dimitrov who turned out to be the head of the Comintern in Western Europe and an extremely astute man. He refused a lawyer and claimed the right to defend himself. Stating his innocence, he protested that he'd served seven months in prison for a crime he didn't commit, five of them in chains. Then he called Göring to the Stand and proceeded to run rings round him, demonstrating to the world that it was the Nazis themselves who had set the Reichstag on fire. The judge had to admit there wasn't enough evidence to convict the men of conspiracy and they were let go, returned to the Soviet Union as soon as possible, which presumably was the reason they were arrested in the first place: to get them out of the Reich. Hitler was in a fury. Determined such a fiasco could never happen again, he hastened the establishment of the *Volksgericht*, People's Court, exclusively for so-called treason. It was up and running by April 1934. In plenty of time for Ernst Thälmann's trial.

'My dearest Rosa!' Thälmann wrote from his prison cell on 10 June 1935. 'Whitsun. It's 5 o'clock. The darkness, the grey, it depresses me so much here. I get up. At the window I draw in the fresh morning air. Through the iron bars of the cell window I can see the blue of the sky. There's still a mist in the air, some white clouds here and there, the morning sun, the Whitsun sun, breaks through. It's shining and glorious. The light falls across half the prison wall blue as a cornflower, the rest is still in a violet shadow. Everywhere is in the deepest silence except for the dawn chorus of the birds. The swallows dip and dive in the blue air, the sunlight catching them. In my depths, I think how small and wearisome is this world – the emptiness of my terrible loneliness. I stand, gripped – silent and motionless. In the distance I hear the sharp echo of a locomotive's whistle. I think of my beloved *Heimat*, so distant now! Whitsun.

'I am overcome by great and unforgettable memories! This is already the third Whitsun when I have to feel and experience this deadening prison world. How long it seems, and then again how fast time passes! When will that happy hour finally come, the Whitsun morning, the morning of golden freedom? A thousand passionate greetings from Moabit to you all, your loving Ernst.'

'*Vater*'s thoughts were often with the great and impressive Whitsun marches of the Red Front Fighters,' wrote Irma. 'The past gave him the strength to bear the heavy present. He was bearing it for the future!'

'Came the day of *Vater*'s court case,' she wrote in her memoir after the war. 'Lawyers and witnesses arrived from the world over. But Göring and Goebbels had learned their lesson from comrade

Dimitroff's case, when their Fascist masks were ripped off. The whole world knew it was Göring and his SA bandits who were behind the Reichstag fire. Dimitroff told them. *Vater* said on one of our prison visits that he'd seen Dimitroff three times in prison. He was amazed at the way he handled himself, there and also during his court case. It made him proud of the strength of the working class – the victory call which came with each of his words. Dimitroff managed to turn the tables and make it a case against the Nazis and the real men behind the fire. *Vater* and all the other prisoners heard about the case because the guards were overflowing with it – couldn't keep their mouths shut. The prisoners took part in the case day by day – just by overhearing the guards talking among themselves.'

Ernst Thälmann was sentenced by the *Volksgericht* on 1 November 1935, according to Para 1 of the Order of the Reich President for the Protection of the Volk and State of 28 February 1933.

'I hereby order that you remain in custody. Grounds: you were working as the leader of the Communist Party of Germany till March 1933. Since you would doubtless continue if let free, it is in the interests of security and order that you be kept in custody.'

Signed, Heydrich.

His custody was indefinite, and in solitary. *Grossvater*, as devastated as *Mutti* and Irma and all the comrades, begged to be allowed a visit next time a permit came through. He was a wonderful man, wrote Irma. Aged 78, he still bicycled into the suburbs of Hamburg, distributing Communist leaflets and pamphlets to the clandestine cells. Somehow he was always cheerful, that was his nature. He was *Vater*'s greatest admirer. Political discussions went on for hours in the Thälmann household. It was like the air they breathed.

Finally, a permit came through. Irma was left alone at home, attending her Housekeeping School. They went by train as usual and *Mutti* said she hadn't seen *Grossvater* so lively and happy in a long time. In Berlin, they stayed with the comrades. Then came the day of the visit to Moabit prison. They had a full hour, who knows why, and they were able to talk quite freely. But on the train back to Hamburg *Grossvater* felt unwell. 'As we left the prison, he was totally broken,' *Mutti* said. 'On the way home he sighed constantly: how can such a thing happen to a man who is so good and clever and strong, imprisoned like that! We need men like him so much now. I won't visit him again. I can't stand it. It'll take years before this Fascist Regime is broken.' The visit was too much for him. He fell ill a few days later and not long after, he died.

After her *Vater*'s trial, in November 1935, Irma was allowed a rare visit. He put on a brave face as always, told her to work hard at her studies, encouraged her to take extra lessons so she could become the legal secretary she wanted to be. And told her about the smuggled packet of cigarettes he'd given to another prisoner he passed in the corridor on his way out to the prison courtyard for his hour of solitary exercise. 'Why?' asked Irma. 'Just to hear him say, "*Guten tag*, Ernst,"' he said. To remind him he was still alive – still Ernst Thälmann.

The final nail in the KPD coffin had been the arrest of its remaining Central Operational Leadership in Berlin in March 1935. They'd been under surveillance since the *Machtergreifung* but until sufficient Communists were in prison and no longer a threat, the Nazis held off picking them up. That October, Wilhelm Pieck, Thälmann's right-hand man who'd fled into exile to Moscow, listed what had happened to the 422 functionaries since January 1933: 219 arrested, 125 forced into emigration, 24 murdered and 42 left the Party. Of the 140 remaining, all but 12 had been arrested at one time or another. Nor did persecution of ordinary members ever let up. In total, over 14,000 were arrested in 1935 alone. Pieck himself had been on the run before fleeing to Moscow, helped by hundreds of unknown Beefsteaks. He didn't return to Germany till the end of the war and the collapse of the Reich.

The solution, the remaining Party officials decided, was to organise small, local cells. These were much harder for the Gestapo to sniff out and were remarkably effective.

By 1939 there were cells in 89 factories in Berlin alone, busily engaged in sabotage large and small. Another activity was the distribution of anti-Nazi literature. The Communist presses were well organised – outside the Reich: Zurich for the South, Prague for Central Germany, Brussels and Amsterdam for the Ruhr, and Copenhagen and Malmö for the North. Political pamphlets and booklets were hidden in innocuous covers, gardening and housework manuals were a favourite, then smuggled across the borders. Once in the Reich, every step for the couriers was dangerous. Yet the Communist presses produced over 600 titles between 1933 and 1944. In 1934, the Nazi authorities seized over a million leaflets, in 1935 even more.

Some of the leaflets were handwritten, such as the one distributed to workers on motorway construction in Bavaria in 1935: 'What has the

Third Reich done for you?' it challenged. 'Slavery and forced labour. Starvation wages and a new unheard-of terror against every worker who does not bow down to these coolie conditions without resistance. Thousands of workers are sitting in concentration camps because they mustered the courage not to die slowly on command. Class comrades! Prove to the Fascist hangmen that the imprisoned comrades are blood of your blood, that victims of Hitler's barbarism are not forgotten. Unite in the Red Help groups and give regular support to those who are in prison and to their families.'

The SPD preferred to keep in contact in less obvious ways, through extensive informal networks of sporting and social clubs which were harder for the Gestapo to detect. Many thrived for years. The Socialist women of Bremen, for example, were already organising communal activities in the local open-air baths and outings by bicycle, hiking or even by steamboat and train, as early as June 1933. Up to 70 women might take part, forming a loose network for exchange of information and secret opposition which spread to other trusted families in the area and workers in the docks and harbour and the local factories. That was during the summer. In the winter months they started meeting at birthday parties, no more than 15 women at a time. Likewise at coffee mornings, when each woman arrived with a cake or tart, or perhaps a bunch of flowers. A woman from the now illegal SPD Party leadership would arrive and give a short talk, with any available news and information, then take questions: how to manage the problems, including financial, of everyday life; how to react to Nazi spies in their street; how to prevent their children joining the Hitler Youth. The solidarity alone was a help. The more courageous women volunteered to distribute anti-Nazi literature, usually produced outside the Reich and smuggled across borders, the main publication being the magazine *Socialist Action*. And SOPADE continued to be active, sending reports of everyday life back in the Reich to the Party in exile.

The Churches also continued to resist, though it was harder for the Protestants, now 'united' under one Reich Church. But many Catholics, first shocked by the Pope's July 1933 Concordat with the Nazis effectively forbidding the Catholic priesthood from any political activity in return for religious freedom for its members, and then angered by the fact that Hitler clearly had no intention of keeping his word, began to demonstrate publicly. Religious festivals and saint days were used as cover, as in Cologne when the 1934 Good Friday

Procession was attended by thousands more than usual.

'On the night of 17 March,' noted the Police Report, 'pilgrims flocked to the meeting point. The procession for the 22.50 departure went on till shortly after midnight, with some 25,000 attending . . . Each parish group carried a large cross in front of it, proceeding to the cathedral, where a devotion was made by Archbishop Schulte. Some Hitler Youth were noted, and the perfect order and discipline. It is noteworthy that the Catholic population of Cologne, in recent times, have banded together strongly. They are taking part in church celebrations and events in numbers of such size that have hardly ever been seen in previous years . . .'

The same happened throughout the Reich. When Nazi officials tried to remove crucifixes from schools in the Saarland in January 1937, the Trier Police reported: '30 or 40 villagers got into the unlocked school on the night of 6 January to hang the crucifix back in its old place. The accused, BA, with the help of a ladder, hung the crucifix up right beside the picture of the Führer, which had been put in the newly assigned place . . . The court at Rhaumen on 9 January 1937 ordered a custodial sentence against BA.'

In Bavaria, the local priests took to greeting parishioners with the traditional '*Gruss Gott!*' instead of the '*Heil Hitler!*' – and on feast days they flew the regional blue and white flag instead of the swastika.

Finally, in 1937, the Pope made his 'With Burning Anxiety' statement, to be read out by all Catholic priests in the Reich to their congregations on Palm Sunday, pointing to the suffering of the Church, the harassment of the Confessors, and that a Führer who 'singles out race, the people of the state, or any other basic element of human social organisation' distorted and falsified the God-given order of things. But only one Catholic Bishop ever served a long prison sentence. It was the rank and file who stood up to the Nazis. Over half of Catholic priests ended up in prisons or concentration camps.

In Düsseldorf, the Engelmann family watched events unfold, increasingly aware that their opposition to the Nazi regime could only be small and local – the big political decisions being way beyond their control. One such had been on 16 March 1935 when Hitler announced to the world that compulsory military service was to be reintroduced in the Reich. Everyone knew it was against the terms of the Treaty of Versailles, yet it was announced with fanfare, in one of Hitler's long speeches, broadcast to every household with a Volk Wireless, and to every factory floor, every office and every school in the Reich. Bernt, now aged 16 and still at his *Gymnasium*, was summoned to listen to it in the school hall, trooping in with all the other boys. Hitler, all fired up, announced he was doing this because he would never countenance anything against German honour and the freedom of the Reich. He wanted 'Nothing but Peace'. There was plenty of cheering in the hall at the end of the speech and then they were given the day off. Walking home with his friend, Kulle, they wondered what would happen next. Kulle's father had joined the Nazi Party because he was too frightened of losing his job and he'd urged Kulle to join the Hitler Youth. Kulle thought this announcement of Hitler's would lead to war, because England and France couldn't allow such a brazen breaking of the terms of the Treaty. But there came only weak protests from Paris and London. Nothing else.

From then on there were two extra hours of 'drill' at school every afternoon. Luckily the man in charge was Herr Dr Konen, nicknamed 'Koko' because of the way he held his head, to one side and looking over his spectacles, when he was telling some boy off, which made him look like a parrot. Koko used the few minutes it took for them to change into their gymnastics outfits to remind them, lacklustre, that they were doing this as their 'Duty to the Fatherland', and as future soldiers in the new *Wehrmacht* army, as it was now called. Then they had to line up in three rows for the examination. After that it was 'Stand easy! Dismissed!' and off they went, either to play football if the weather was good or *Volkerball*, handball, in the gymnasium if not. Koko couldn't have been less interested. Within minutes, he was reading yesterday's newspaper or the *Berliner Illustrierte*. At the end of the session, he dismissed them with a lame Hitler salute. Bernt always admired the way he managed to do it at the same time as waving them off, so you hardly knew which was which. He was no Nazi, Herr Dr Konen.

Bernt's father Herr Engelmann, talking it all over in the privacy of their home, thought Hitler had timed his surprise announcement carefully just before the weekend, because then all the leaders of the Western governments would be off on their country estates, shooting pheasants or fishing trout. And he'd got away with it. So now he knew he could do it again, was Herr Engelmann's opinion.

And he was right, noted Bernt: a year later, almost to the day. It was Friday 6 March 1936 and Bernt's class had football that afternoon, the weather being cold but reasonably clement. On the way home, he was still hot and sweaty from the exertion, so he dropped in at Tante Ney's for an ice-cream. He was just chatting to her when a man, unknown to Bernt, walked in. He was about forty, short, stocky, wearing a thick grey winter coat, scarf, elegant grey Homburg hat, dark grey gloves, boots under galoshes, carrying a furled umbrella and an old-fashioned leather briefcase. In a word, not a local. Bernt got the impression Tante Ney didn't know him either.

'Excuse me,' the man said. 'Am I right in thinking you are Frau Anna Ney?'

'Yes,' she said, dubious.

The man smiled. 'Delighted to meet you, *gnadige Frau*, dear lady.'

Bernt recognised his accent as exactly the same as the announcer on the Swiss radio station his father listened to every night. On the whole his father thought the Swiss station was safer. Their neighbour Frau Metzger had been denounced by some local Nazi for listening to the BBC. They'd let her off with a warning, seeing she was a widow and that her deceased husband had been decorated for bravery in the war. It didn't stop her listening though. She just put a tea cosy over the receiver, she told Bernt's mother. Actually, nothing could stop Frau Metzger from doing what she wanted and thought was right.

'My name is Sprungli,' said the man. 'I've just arrived from Basel. Your brother asked me to drop by and send you his good wishes.'

Tante Ney was slightly less suspicious. Her brother did indeed live in Basel, whence he'd gone three years earlier to escape the Nazis because he was a card-carrying Communist. Tante Ney's own opinion on the Communists was given to the Engelmanns one evening in the privacy of their home. 'I'm against Communism,' she stated. 'I'm for people believing in God and respecting every religion. I also approve of private possessions, not communal like the Communists – at least if you've earned it yourself through hard work. But today I'd help any Communist on the run from the Nazis. After all, my brother Jupp is a Communist. Just lucky he escaped to Switzerland in time!'

Now she looked more carefully at Herr Sprungli, if indeed that was his real name. Bernt hung around eating his ice-cream, watching closely. The little shop and café was full, but no one else seemed to be taking any notice, all caught up in their own conversations. Tante Ney offered the stranger a cup of coffee and a piece of cake, which he took at the counter.

'How is my brother? We haven't heard from him for a long time.'

'He's well.'

'Are you travelling through?'

'I am. I only stopped here briefly to give you his good wishes. And to have a quick look at your mantle clock. Your brother told me it was a valuable piece with a beautiful chime, made by Ernest Borel of Geneva. I know those clocks well. Have you already had it repaired?'

Bernt was all ears.

'No,' said Tante Ney, still unsure. You never knew . . .

'Well, maybe my little visit is well-timed then,' said Herr Sprungli. 'You see, I'm a watchmaker. Your brother told me the clock was in your little holiday house in Meerbusch, which isn't far, is it?'

'About twenty minutes by tram,' said Tante Ney, reassured now. 'What else did my brother say, Herr Sprungli?'

'He also sent your husband his good wishes. "Griesgen" he called him!' Herr Sprungli laughed. But Griesgen was indeed Herr Ney's nickname, because of his thick head of grey hair. 'He told me to ask Griesgen if he still wore the tie he gave him for his birthday, the blue one with the silver crowns.'

That did it. 'Could you repair the clock?'

'Well, I'm in a bit of a hurry, but I could probably spare a few days. A job like that takes time you know.'

Tante Ney understood he needed somewhere out-of-the-way to stay for a while. So did Bernt, listening hard and taking his time over the ice-cream.

'The tram leaves in twelve minutes,' she said. 'I'll get you some food to take with you. And we'll come and join you for a meal after Mass on Sunday.' Then she turned to Bernt. She knew he'd heard everything. 'Wait here for me,' she told him over her shoulder, already making her way out back to the kitchen and her husband.

Herr Sprungli busied himself with his coffee and cake. Bernt hung around, keeping his ice-cream going.

Five minutes later she was back with a wicker basket which she handed over to Bernt. 'You can show Herr Sprungli the way can't you?'

'Of course.' The tram stop was just up the road from the bakery.

'Tell him to get in after you, in the second half of the tram,' she whispered.

'Where are the keys?'

'In the basket. Now hurry up!'

In fact, there was no need to tell Herr Sprungli how to do these things – he did it automatically. When the tram got to Meerbusch he got out after Bernt, waited for any other travellers to disperse, then followed him to the country lane leading to the little house. As he walked, Bernt wondered who Herr Sprungli really was. There'd been an item in the newspaper that a courier from Moscow was on the loose. Could he be a courier? He didn't look it. He looked more like a country doctor. So who was he, and what was he up to? One thing was certain: he wasn't a watchmaker. Apart from anything else, the Neys' clock didn't need mending.

They got to the house via the back garden so no neighbour would see them. Herr Sprungli waited on the terrace while Bernt went round to the front to open the door. He often went to the house so no one would be surprised to see him. Once inside, he led Herr Sprungli round the house: 'Here's the kitchen, here's the bathroom, here's the telephone, the spare bedroom's on the first floor.' Then he unpacked the wicker basket for him: rice, noodles, sausage, cake, cigarettes. They hardly spoke.

Bernt was about to leave when Herr Sprungli asked: 'Do you happen to have an upper window in your house which looks out over the Rhine?'

Bernt couldn't have been more surprised. But he realised Herr Sprungli had been watching him closely and must have decided to trust him. 'We don't live on the Rhine.'

Then he remembered Fräulein Bonse, the one who ran the school exchange programme which always had a few extra young people on the list. 'But I know someone who does,' he said, adding, 'she's a friend of Frau Ney. Her windows look out over the Oberkasseler Bridge.'

'Can you tell her to keep a watch over the bridge early tomorrow morning?'

'Well, yes . . .'

Could he ask Herr Sprungli a question now? Bernt wondered. 'What should I tell her to look out for?'

'Soldiers,' answered Herr Sprungli. 'Columns of soldiers, armaments, military vehicles, tanks. At about 5 o'clock.'

Bernt was shocked. 'Is it war?'

'Could be,' answered Herr Sprungli.

'But we're on the left bank, in the demilitarised zone.'

Herr Sprungli said nothing.

'If Hitler orders the Wehrmacht to march in, the English and the French will stop him.'

'Let's hope so.'

'Or there could be civil war here against the Nazis.'

'Who knows,' answered Herr Sprungli. 'Anyway, we have to be prepared.'

It struck Bernt that they weren't the only people Herr Sprungli had visited. Everywhere along the Rhine – Cologne, Bonn, Duisburg, Wesel, Remagen, Koblenz, Ludwigshafen and Karlsruhe – everywhere where there were bridges across the Rhine there would be observers, put there by Herr Sprungli. And they would broadcast the news, should there be any, to the world.

Bernt went back to Tante Ney and, in the back room, told her and Griesgen what had happened.

'*Lieber Gott!*' Tante Ney looked appalled. 'Does that mean war?'

When Bernt went to bed that night he set his alarm clock for 4.30 the next morning and had his bicycle ready in the hallway. By five o'clock, he was standing on the Lueg Alley, next to the Oberkessler Bridge. And sure enough, first he heard them in the distance, then on they came: marching columns of infantry, about 500 of them, with motorcycle out-riders, military vehicles, lorries, even a field kitchen! As news got round, more and more people came to line the road, mostly in silence, a few cheering. An SA man in his brown uniform near Bernt shouted '*Heil! Heil!*' and gave the Hitler salute. But he stopped when so few joined him. The Catholic Rhineland wasn't one of the Nazis' strongholds.

In school that morning, no one talked of anything else. Many thought it a fine thing, getting their own rightful territory back from the French. During the morning break, the boys were summoned to the school hall to listen to Hitler's broadcast: 'In the interest of the most basic human rights of the Volk to protect its own borders and its own defences, the Reich government has today reinstated in full the sovereignty of the demilitarised zone of the Rhineland.' After which could be heard the minutes-long 'Heil! Heil! Heil!' of the 600 Nazi officials gathered to listen to Hitler's speech, their boots stamping the parquet flooring. Bernt could remember one sentence from the long speech: 'We make no further demands for territory in Europe. Germany will never break the terms of Peace!' Then the triumphant School Principal, giving the Hitler salute from the stage, gave the boys the rest of the day off.

The Engelmann household was tense during the next few days, waiting to see what would happen. Herr Engelmann was constantly listening to the radio broadcasts, Swiss and BBC as well as the Reich. On the Sunday afternoon, before leaving to have coffee and cake with some close friends they could trust, he noted that the British government had called everyone back from their country weekends for an emergency meeting of the House, something which had not happened in the last hundred years. 'But they won't do anything,' he added. 'Neither the English nor the French! All the while, it would the perfect opportunity to put an end to this terrible Nazi regime, without too much sacrifice. They'll come to regret it, that they didn't intervene strongly now.'

Years later, Bernt, doing some research in the archives for his memoir of those times, found that Hitler had instructed the Wehrmacht to retreat immediately if the English and French intervened with military force. General Jodl, at his Nuremberg trial in 1946, confirmed that even if it had just been the French military who intervened, they would have been forced to retreat. Hitler's translator, Paul Schmidt, also confirmed: 'The 48 hours after the occupation of the Rhineland were the most nerve-wracking of my life. Had the French intervened, we'd have had to retreat in shame, because our own military might, in those days, was nowhere near strong enough to withstand them.'

Everything hung on a knife's edge that weekend, wrote Bernt. The lack of action by the English and French gave Hitler a greater victory than he could ever have hoped, and a new popularity, even among those who might have joined the opposition. Because there was a great deal of discontent among the population during that winter of 1935–6, due to the low wages and higher and higher prices of everyday goods. Hitler had taken another gamble, and it worked. Three weeks later, after a massive propaganda campaign, the Nazi leadership held a plebiscite in which every citizen had to vote. 'Did they agree with the Reinstatement of the Honour of the German Volk and the Regaining of full Sovereignty of the Reich?' they were asked. On Sunday 29 March 1936, shortly before midnight, for maximum dramatic effect, Joseph Goebbels announced the result: 99 per cent of the German Volk had voted for Adolf Hitler and the NSDAP!

By now Julius Leber, the Social Democrat politician, had been incarcerated for three years. The ebullient champion of the Lübeck worker with his large belly and large lust for life wrote to his wife Annedore from Wolfenbuttel prison, whence he'd been transferred after some loyal Lübeck supporters, aided by the former SPD prison guard, tried to spring him from the local prison. He was 'fairly indifferent' to the conditions in his new surroundings, he said. That was Leber all over: he made a point of not caring – he wasn't minded to do the Nazis the favour. The man who'd once been a leading member of the Social Democrats in the Reichstag, the most charismatic one, brilliant in debating his point, using humour and scorn to win the argument, and not past having a good fist fight either, sat in prison and worked out that it might take up to five years to get rid of the Nazis. And that he, Julius Leber, meant to be part of it. In March 1935, he was due to be released in weeks and he couldn't wait to get back to the fight.

But it wasn't easy for Annedore. Wolfenbuttel was near Braunschweig in Lower Saxony, and it meant she had to travel five hours, every six weeks or so to visit him, and that visit often lasting no more than half an hour. She wondered whether she should move to Berlin with the two children, which was nearer, but her seamstress business was going well, and her ailing mother needed her in Lübeck. Her father had fallen ill after losing his school job through *Gleichschaltung*, and died not long after. Leber felt guilty that he couldn't comfort Annedore more, stuck in prison as he was. In fact, his life in Wolfenbuttel was better than it had been in Marstall, his Lübeck prison. He had a job in the prison library, he wrote to Annedore, and he was able to read a lot.

But their relationship was suffering, he knew. There was never enough time to talk, and Annedore's life was too hard. Time and again in his letters to her he counted the days when he'd be out. Now that the end was in sight he allowed himself the luxury of remembering old friends, asking Annedore about them, pleased to hear they were managing to get by. As he himself meant to do. He knew it would be difficult at the beginning. What job could he do? How could he earn a living?

He told Annedore to get hold of 'Dar' by which he meant Gustav Dahrendorf, an SPD Reichstag colleague he'd known and trusted in Weimar times. Dahrendorf was ten years younger than Julius Leber and his greatest admirer. He'd been arrested after the *Machtergreifung* along with everyone else but let out after a few weeks and, for the time being at least, merely kept under surveillance. After his release he'd made his way to Berlin, and, natural entrepreneur that he was, he soon had an extremely successful oil and coal business. Which is why Julius told Annedore to get hold of him: to find him a job. Dahrendorf did manage to find him a job, with a Dutch oil firm in Amsterdam. Julius was delighted and immediately got a Dutch dictionary out of the library, determined to teach himself enough of the language to do business.

'Only now is it becoming clear to me,' he wrote to Annedore from Wolfenbuttel, 'as my inner tension begins to relax, how lightly I've managed to take my prison sentence, and mean to go on taking lightly in the coming months. I feel stronger than ever, and I firmly believe life has still got tasks for me. How often, in my thoughts, am I in our garden, among the flowers and the shrubs and under the old trees by the greenhouse. This garden which probably won't be mine any more in the future. Still, the world is large and wide, and everywhere there is beauty, wherever there is fight and the love of mankind.' Julius was heady with the thought of his approaching freedom.

On 17 March 1935 he wrote Annedore a last letter before his release. He'd had a discussion with a Braunschweig Police official about his plans. 'On his question, how did I see my future, I could only say it was uncertain. But I had some contacts in the oil business, which might have possibilities, as long as no one made difficulties for me.' Apparently the official wondered if Leber might like to leave the country. 'Only in the event of finding no solution for me and my family here,' Leber had answered. Also he'd need a travel permit. The official thought that might be a possibility but he couldn't promise. He left the meeting full of hope, he wrote. He was less sure about going to Amsterdam now. Could he be a salesman, he wondered?

Then, just as he was making his final plans, he was told he wasn't to be released after all, but taken into '*Schutzhaft*', protective custody, to Esterwegen concentration camp. It was the Nazis' favourite trick: have a date for release from prison, then take it away at the last minute and send the enemy to a concentration camp instead. It was aimed to be a crippling blow, so crippling it could even work on Julius Leber.

'You found my last letter too short,' he wrote to Annedore from Esterwegen on 31 July 1935. 'Me too. But what is there to write about? Everyday matters are of no interest. It's always the same. And the thing which interests you most, my state of mind, well, that's just fine, as ever.'

But Annedore knew different. Her husband was changed. Thinner – surely a good thing? he joked. Less ebullient. The weather made several appearances in his letters now. And he had to ask her to use a typewriter because the camp censor complained he couldn't read her handwriting. To add insult to injury: the authorities sent him a bill for 1,336 Reich Marks to cover the 'cost' of his previous prison stay. The Nazis were confiscating bank accounts and property wherever they could, from fleeing Jews and opponents of the regime alike, but this was pure spite. It added to Annedore's mounting debts, because she was still paying off the costs of Julius's court case. In April 1936 she had to write to Lübeck County Court to beg for a delay. In addition, she was helping out with Jutta Busch, who was Julius's illegitimate child. 'If you move to Berlin,' Julius wrote, 'don't take Alex with you.' Alex was their sheepdog. Julius said the city wouldn't suit him.

He'd been sentenced to a further two years. 'Fate is powerful, accept it,' was his way of dealing with it, adding 'but man is more powerful, as long he doesn't let himself be rattled by it.' He didn't forget the children's birthdays, or Christmas, nor his and Annedore's wedding anniversary. By May 1936, he was only allowed to write letters twice a month. And no more packets of food or presents. By August, Esterwegen was being shut down – too close to the Berlin Olympic Games perhaps – and Leber was transferred to the newly built Sachsenhausen concentration camp. The first three months were in the Zellen Bau, a single-storey building with 80 isolation cells, reserved for those who'd committed the greatest crimes against the Reich. It was terrible. There was no looking out of the cell window at the blue sky now, because the Zellen Bau was surrounded by a high wall to hide it, even from the other inmates of the camp. Annedore heard nothing from him for the first four weeks. When she finally got a letter his handwriting was wavering. 'No chair, no table, no work, no exercise, no warm food, no bed cover, no bed,' he wrote. He slept on the bare floor. He didn't tell her about the beatings.

But news got out, as always, appearing in a SOPADE report. Otto Wels, reading it in exile, wrote to an SPD colleague in Brussels on 8 July 1936: 'Among all the horrors listed in this Report, the most distressing and shocking concern our colleague Dr Julius Leber. When we first read it we thought we'd publish it in full, to show the world, once again, how matters really stand in the Land of the Olympics regarding human rights and human dignity.' They decided against it because they knew from experience that such information had little impact and might in fact make matters worse for Leber. Instead Wels suggested a leading English politician might make contact with Major General von Fritsch, one of the secret opponents of the Nazi regime. Annedore found, on one of her rare visits once Julius was in the main camp, back in the land of the living, that he was in low spirits and close to defeat. He, predictably, denied it all.

'Christmas lies before us,' he wrote to Annedore on 31 December 1936, 'and this the fourth Christmas I'm separated from you. Fate has it in for us, but it's not too bad. Hard tests and emergencies hammer the inner man into shape. It teaches him a clarity about himself, and a judgement. No time in a man's life is lost time, other than the times he lets slip by with stupid and senseless thought. Is that relevant to our four years of separation? No! because they have formed us, and we're no longer the people we used to be. Fate's path, which has demanded this, doesn't only wound us, it presents us with a gift.'

Otto Wels was right about the 1936 Berlin Olympics. All traces of the terror regime, whether 'Jews Keep Out!' signs in the shop windows or rumours about concentration camps, were forbidden for the duration – replaced by a benign regime bent on nothing more than providing an arena to celebrate the excellence of sport, showing the German Reich willing to 'co-operate in large international projects designed to further universal Peace,' as Goebbels put it. Volk and foreigners alike flocked to the Games during those sixteen days in August 1936, thrilled by the spectacle and awed by the sheer technological achievement of the Nazi regime. Forgotten the recent Nuremberg Laws for the

Protection of German Blood and German Honour, forbidding marriage between Aryans and Jews. Forgotten the thousands of Jewish bank accounts which had subsequently been seized and the hundreds of Jewish teachers dismissed. Forgotten the burning of 'degenerate' books. Forgotten the hounding of Communists and Social Democrats. Forgotten the banning of the Trade Unions, the freedom of the press, and the independence of the Churches.

Few saw it for what it really was: a massive propaganda campaign orchestrated by Joseph Goebbels to demonstrate to the world the superiority of the Aryan master race. The Swiss Workers Federation of Gymnastics and Sport was one of the few dissenters: 'Our members would like to open the eyes of public opinion to the dangerous totalitarian and racist politics of the Third Reich,' it put on record. They'd met German workers who told them about the intimidation and imprisonment of any opponents to the regime. 'To take part in the Games is to work with the Nazi propaganda game. Hitler wants to use the Berlin Games to prove to the world the superiority of the Aryan Race.'

The Swiss Olympic Committee begged to disagree, accusing the Workers Federation of being 'Reds', a comment which neatly summed up the real battle going on in Europe at the time: between those supporting the Capitalist and, in some countries, Fascist system, and those supporting the Communist. A few countries engaged in some soul-searching, but finally joined the 53 countries who decided to take part in the Games, Switzerland included.

First came the Youth Games, when 92,000 Hitler Youths and garlanded BDM, Band of German Maidens, members, all in white, paraded with their military bands and flags and performed their precision athletics. On the following day, 1 August, came the Opening Ceremony, choreographed to the last detail by Joseph Goebbels and masterfully captured on film by Leni Riefenstahl, the ambitious film director, using all sorts of new technical tricks, such as cameramen on roller-skates, and including plenty of close-ups of handsome, blond Aryan athletes, to the strains of Richard Wagner. At 3.18 precisely the motorcade bearing Hitler in his black Mercedes set off on its route along Wilhelm Strasse and Unter den Linden, 45-feet-high swastikas, flags and banners on either side, with the Führer standing in his open-topped car saluting the one million people lining the streets, held back by 40,000 Storm Troopers. *Er kommt! Er kommt!* He's coming! He's coming!' blared hundreds of loudspeakers, whipping the crowds up into a frenzy.

The Führer arrived at the Amphitheatre at 4pm exactly. The stadium held 100,000. The entrance was flanked by two towering and heroic statues of Aryan heroes holding horses. Hitler entered to a fanfare of trumpets followed by the German National Anthem and the Horst Wessel song, the anthem of the Nazis. On his procession across the green swathe, he was presented with a bouquet of flowers by a small girl in a white dress with a garland of flowers on her blonde head. After the Hoisting of the Flag and more triumphal music from the Olympic Symphony Orchestra, guns were fired and hundreds of white doves of Peace, in fact pigeons, were released into the air. At 5.20 the athlete bearing the Olympic torch entered the Amphitheatre. He, too, was Aryan blond, chosen for his looks rather than his athletic prowess, which was negligible. He was the last of hundreds of athletes, running a kilometre each, from Athens to Delphi, Salonika, Sofia, Belgrade, Budapest, Vienna, Prague, Dresden and on to Berlin – a reinvention of an ancient tradition which had, in fact, never existed.

Then the Olympic teams of the nations entered the Amphitheatre, with the French team reportedly extending their right arm in a quasi-Hitler salute. There were 1,800 journalists from 59 countries to cover the Games, plus 125 accredited photographers. Radio broadcasts blared across Europe and the Reich, controlled by a switchboard directly below the Führer's own box, 20 metres long. Cinema news-reels reached the globe. There were three electronic cameras, an early experiment in television broadcasting, relaying the Games three times a day into twenty public television salons in Berlin, Potsdam and Leipzig, filmed from the top of a lorry which held a dark room inside so the footage could be developed within minutes. Hitler left the Amphitheatre to the strains of Handel's *Messiah*: 'And He shall Reign for Ever and Ever'. The only thing Goebbels wasn't able to control was the weather. 'Heavy clouds and some showers. Moderate winds w/ sw. 19°C,' reported the Reich Weather Service. Nor Jesse Owens, the 'negro' American athlete, who won four gold medals including the 100 metres and the 200 metres, both.

'German sport has only one task,' wrote Joseph Goebbels, the man with the club foot, in his diary, 'to strengthen the character of the German people, imbuing it with the fighting spirit and steadfast cama-raderie necessary in the struggle for its existence.'

What he meant by 'the struggle for existence' was made clear in a
SOPADE report from Bavaria: 'The way in which Youth is prepared
today for the coming war can be seen clearly once again in the end
of year celebrations in X. In the largest room in the town which was
decorated for the celebration, around 130 boys and as many girls
who had just finished their eighth year at school were assembled . . .
Over the stage, in big lettering, stood: WE ARE BORN TO DIE FOR
GERMANY. In his talk, reported by one of the boys who was not
named, the School Principal emphasised that "we must give our faithful heart to the Führer, and, since he is Germany's liberator and greatest hero, that our whole life belongs to him. In the fight for the final
freedom of all Germans, even Youth may not shy away from offering
itself up selflessly." Then came the History of the German Nation, plus
the Treaty of Versailles etc. At the end, there was the Oath: And if it
must be, we know why: We are born to die for Germany.'

In December 1936 came The Hitler Youth Law, stating the Hitler
Youth Organisation was to prepare 'the entire German Youth for its

further duties'. By now the membership had increased from 107,956 in 1932 to over 6 million. Once 90 per cent of pupils of a school had joined the Hitler Youth, it was allowed to fly its own Hitler Youth flag. 'In my great educative work, I am beginning with the young,' Hitler announced in one of his famous talks. 'We older ones are used up. Yes, we are old already. We are rotten to the marrow. We have no unrestrained instincts left. We are bearing the burden of a humiliating past and have in our blood the recollection of serfdom and servility. But my magnificent youngsters! Are there finer ones anywhere in the world? Look at these young men and boys! What material! With them I can make a new world. My teaching is hard. Weakness has to be knocked out of them. A violently active, dominating, intrepid, brutal youth – that is what I am after. Strong and handsome must my young men be. I will have them fully trained in all physical exercises. I intend to have an athletic Youth – that is the first and chief thing. I will have no intellectual training. Knowledge is ruin to my young men. But one thing they must learn – self-command! They shall learn to overcome fear of death, under the severest tests.'

Joseph Goebbels was well pleased. After the stunning success of the Berlin Olympic Games he threw one of his fancy parties. Martha Dodd, the daughter of the American Ambassador who had gone with her friend, Mildred, and two young men to visit the famous author Hans Fallada, was one of the guests.

'Göring and Goebbels have the custom of giving annual parties for the diplomatic corps, journalists, government people, stray visitors, and a scattering of Berlin society, and it is noticed that neither of them appears at the party of the other,' she wrote in her memoir written in 1939, from the safety of America.

'One party that Goebbels gave, after a lavish circus-fair entertainment given by his enemy, surpassed anything in elaborateness I had yet attended in Berlin. Several thousand people were invited to an evening dinner, reception and ballet on an island on one of the beautiful lakes near Berlin. The guests crossed from the mainland on a bridge thrown across the water and held fast by men in boats along the sides. On the island were innumerable lanes through the trees and hills, necklaced overhead with many-coloured little lanterns and lined with young page girls in tights. In an open space, tables were laid and a stage set for dancing. Overhead were lanterns and, in the huge dark trees were tremendous artificial butterflies lighted from within. The tables were elaborately set with many wine glasses and an endless course dinner which included all the expensive delicacies.

'Towards the end of dinner there were fireworks on a grandiose scale, ending in a terrific roar and red explosion that called to mind the bombardment of a war scene. The suggestion was so clear that most of the diplomats at our table commented on it and were deeply offended, believing the whole thing a badly designed threat in the worst sort of taste. Later we were served with ballet girls and a sort of revue. We didn't stay until the end, but took an inconspicuous leave after saying goodbye to the smiling, vivacious, well-pleased host. Göring did not put in an appearance.

'There was so much gossip among the simple people of Berlin about the cost of this tremendous festival – with so much bitter comment on their own living conditions and so many questions as to where the money collected through the *Winter Hilfe*, Winter Aid, went – the Nazis became somewhat apologetic. A few days later it was announced that on Sunday the island would be open, with the same decorations, for the German people to visit and disport themselves on.'

Goebbels was on a high. As he'd written in his diary on 7 August 1936: 'After the Olympics we'll get ruthless. Then there will be some shooting.'

CHAPTER SIX

THE NAZIS TIGHTEN THE SCREW

As time went on, Rudolf Ditzen found it harder and harder to refuse Joseph Goebbels' demands for stories and articles promoting the values and virtues of the Nazi regime. Unlike Leni Riefenstahl, that most biddable of collaborators busy editing her film of the 1936 Olympic Games, Rudolf, time and again, had found excuses not to collaborate with the Minister of Propaganda and Public Enlightenment. Now he started writing children's stories to bring the money in, along with his usual output of short stories and novels. But it took its toll. With each new demand from the Ministry the self-confessed coward had to screw up his courage to refuse, each time knowing that sooner or later his luck would run out. Meanwhile, he made some compromises, kept his head down, and held his breath. There were frequent moments of despair when he thought he couldn't write anymore, because he couldn't write without the Nazi authorities interfering and threatening.

But he did go on writing and he did go on compromising, because without writing, he couldn't live. Luckily the reading public still loved their Hans Fallada. His latest novel *Once We Had a Child* sold 17,000 copies in the first three weeks. 'The title says it all,' Rudolf wrote to his sister Margareta, referring to the loss of their own child, for which he blamed himself, and the stresses of the past weeks.

The book was a new departure for Rudolf: less dialogue, more description and an anti-hero even less likeable than the weak-willed Pinneberg. This was Johannes Gantschow, a farmer in a long line of farmers on the island of Rugen, living in a remote farmhouse with his alcoholic father. Gantschow is hard-working but bloody-minded. He won't join the Labour movement and people are frightened of him – his moodiness and his rages. When he returns to the island, after trying his hand at a job on the mainland, he marries Elise, a local school teacher. His alcoholic father has died, so they move into the old farmhouse and restore it. But Gantschow treats Elise badly and finally he leaves her for Christiane, his childhood sweetheart, the daughter of the local Count. Elise, in despair, sets light to the farmhouse, razing it to the ground. Christiane gets pregnant, but the child dies soon after birth. Finally she leaves Gantschow and returns to her husband. At the end of the novel, Gantschow is left on his own.

How did Rudolf get away with such a bleak tale?

For the reader, the answer lay in the writing. Rudolf's narrator tells the story with such sharp humour and realism that the reader is fascinated by Gantschow, flaws and all, horrified one minute and laughing the next. Human folly, they say to themselves, shaking their heads. They can only agree with Gantschow when he finally blames himself and sees the loss of the baby and Christiane as a kind of punishment.

'He understood everything,' wrote Rudolf, sitting at his desk in Carwitz. 'He had never loved her. He had never loved another human being on this earth, he had only ever loved himself, and now it was too late.' Rudolf's narrator agrees: 'For God's sake, it was just. If stupidity and coarseness were to go unpunished, what would become of this world, what sort of world would it be? There could be no doubt that he had been stupid and coarse. It had all turned out as it should. It was exactly right.' That was the last sentence of the novel.

'There are few things I'm so proud of as these last few lines,' Rudolf wrote to his sister. By which he meant that he'd managed to state his true belief and a coded message to the reader: don't let coarseness and stupidity go unpunished or what sort of world would it be? Yes, he'd said what he wanted to say, and they'd read it.

But the Nazis at the Ministry of Propaganda and Enlightenment were not fooled, even though some saw it as a novel in the 'Blood and Soil' tradition. The reviews in the newspapers were predictably lukewarm: 'Once we had a Hans Fallada,' joked one wit. Another wrote that it wasn't the kind of book needed 'these days'. Tightening the screws, the Ministry now recommended all copies of his previous novel, *Little Man, What Now?* be withdrawn from public libraries. And they warned Rudolf about his Swedish publisher: be aware, the man was an active anti-Nazi. Then they put pressure on him to accept the chairmanship of the new Writers' Union, under Nazi control. He screwed up his courage and refused. 'I just stood up and said they had better choose someone else, that my nomination would not be approved by the leadership since I was a completely "undesirable writer",' he wrote to his parents, adding: 'I have nothing to hide and I am not going to keep my eyes shut. Nobody is forced to like my books and, anyway, Rowohlt is quite right: if you make concessions to *those* people, they'll really stick the knife in.' Brave words. But not for long.

Ernst Rowohlt, Rudolf's loyal and patient publisher, was lending him money now that sales were down. So were Rudolf's parents. Where did all the money go, for heaven's sake? Into the renovated house at Carwitz, into Suse's smallholding, into cigarettes, into a heavy tax bill and, increasingly, back into drinking. Rowohlt, keen drinker and high liver that he was, warned Rudolf to take care. Stop spending all that money. Stop drinking. They both knew the difference between them: Rudolf was too highly strung for that sort of life – always in danger of another breakdown. Rowohlt was as robust as they come – tough enough even to resist the Nazis, 'lending' his struggling out-of-favour authors money, finding new jobs for his former Jewish employees and arranging for those on the run to flee the country. And keeping in touch with other anti-Nazis at Sigismund Lauter's apartment in the Kurfürstendamm – the same Lauter who was Fabian von Schlabrendorff's doctor and now hosted secret meetings to find ways of fighting the Nazi regime which they had all underestimated so badly in the early years.

'I was introduced to one of the most picturesque and active publishers German literary life has ever had,' as the young American Martha Dodd wrote in her memoir of those times. 'Before Hitler, Ernst Rowohlt published most of the important and talented writers of Germany – many of them radicals, some Communists, others liberals and pacifists. He also published several of the best contemporary American writers, including Wolfe, Hemingway and Faulkner. He was a delightful man, of giant blond Aryan stature and complexion. He had a positively cherubic face, with innocent blue eyes, round, ruddy, plump cheeks and an irrepressible and spluttering humour. When I first arrived he was learning English and spoke very badly with a strong accent, but so amusingly and with such obvious delight in his mistakes and his attempts to right them, that his bubbling, stumbling, lisping jargon was a positive joy to listen to. Rowohlt was a tremendous drinker and also a very serious and vital man. He loved life and freedom passionately, was tremendously proud of his past record, and spoke bluntly and honestly about any subject that arose.'

Dora Preisach, the woman forced to quit her job with Rowohlt because she was a Jew, came for Easter, pleased to get away from the terrors of Berlin. The Nuremberg Laws for the Protection of German

Blood and German Honour had taken away her German citizenship and forbade her marrying or having sexual relationships with an Aryan German. What future was there for her in Nazi Germany? Rudolf and Suse offered her a full-time job as their housekeeper but she told them she'd decided to emigrate to Israel. Rowohlt came on a visit and told Rudolf not to hurry with his next novel and to try and calm down. He could see Rudolf was getting into one of his states again. Suse looked after her nervy husband like a nurse, as she always did. But nothing worked.

'I can no longer write what I want to write,' Rudolf wrote to his sister.

'I really enjoy writing stories but you can only tell a good story by giving free rein to it, without thinking about the audience and so on. So I can't write anymore.' That, for Rudolf, was the end. By May, he was suffering a complete nervous breakdown. Suse was terrified that this time he was actually going mad. When Rowohlt visited him in the Berlin clinic he was so shocked at his condition, he got him transferred immediately to the Charite Hospital and into the care of the psychiatrist Professor Karl Bonhoeffer, the father of Dietrich Bonhoeffer who would later be executed by the Nazis, along with his brother, Klaus, and two of his brothers-in-law.

When Rudolf finally got back to Carwitz, he swore not to touch another drop of alcohol. And he started writing again, sitting at his old typewriter, looking out of the window at the landscape he loved, chain-smoking, dreaming up another tale, one which could get past the fiends at the Reich Literary Chamber. He thought he might get away with a story set in the past, a sort of fairy-tale, with hidden meaning about decent values for those who cared to see. It was titled *Old Heart Goes A-Journeying*, and for the first time in months Rudolf felt alive again. Suse's smallholding was making some money now – bottling fruit, selling vegetables, rearing pigs – the children were over their mumps, he was teaching them English in his spare time and playing with them in the afternoons, as he loved to do. He employed Dora Preisach to type the manuscript. Rowohlt managed to get 10,000 Reich Marks for the serialisation of the book in the *Berliner Illustrierte* magazine and he also pulled off a deal for Rudolf to write a film script for 4,000 Reich Marks. Everything was on the up again. Until the editor from the *Berliner Illustrierte* arrived in Carwitz demanding changes to the text. When Rudolf greeted the man at the door, he didn't give

the full Hitler salute – it was one of the small principles he was still
holding to through thick and thin. But it didn't go unnoticed and it
didn't help the editing. The handicapped character in the tale had to
go. So did the one with epilepsy. And he had to write another of his
compromising Introductions. Rudolf bowed to the inevitable.

Worse, much worse, was that Uli, now aged 5, caught meningitis
that Easter 1936, and was rushed to hospital in Berlin. When Rudolf
went to visit him it was enough to plunge him straight back into a
depression. Then the *Volksgesundheit*, the Nazi medical journal,
wrote a threatening review of *Old Heart Goes A-Journeying*. They
strongly objected to Hans Fallada's favourable depiction of Herr
Doktor Kimmknirsch, one of Rudolf's 'decent' men, who treats his
patients with respect and as he thinks fit. 'We are not willing to let
someone whom we generously permit to continue to earn a living in
Germany upset our rebuilding of the German Nation. Herr Fallada
would do well to note this for future reference,' it wrote, adding that a
doctor like Kimmknirsch 'in our National Socialist opinion no longer
has any place in Germany'. Reconstruction would soon include euthanasia for people like Rudolf's handicapped characters, and doctors
who didn't agree would find themselves faced with *Gleichschaltung*,
forcing them to give up their jobs and find employment elsewhere.
Or not at all.

As the Nazis got into their 'shooting' stride following the success
of the Berlin Olympics, the terror regime tightened its grip on the
Reich and started to threaten their opponents more viciously. Heinrich
Himmler became Chief of Police as well as *Reichsführer* SS. The Nazis
sent troops to fight on Franco's side in the Spanish Civil War. Now even
robust Ernst Rowohlt began to lose heart. Martha Dodd, meeting him
at another American Embassy party, was shocked at the change in this
once ebullient man: 'His firm has been taken over by the Nazi Party;
he has been forced to submission in a more or less minor role in the
publishing house and is a broken and tragic figure. He was the type of
man who aroused and held the devotion and unswerving loyalty of his
subordinates and who could attract anyone by his tremendous energy
and intelligence. In his house in the early days one could find the last
remains of independent literary thought collectively gathered in Berlin.
Now it is a different story.'

Rudolf's solution, now that Uli was back home and recovering, was
the same as usual: get writing. He sat down at his old typewriter and

began a novel set in 1923, the year of hyperinflation during the chaos of the Weimar period following the crushing terms of the Treaty of Versailles. The Nazis were always keen on criticism of Weimar, reckoned Rudolf, so he felt reasonably safe. After all, it didn't stop him writing a novel about the little people, battered this way and that by fate and ill-fortune – his subject first and last. And if the book never saw the light of day, so be it. So he wrote and wrote, keeping off the drink, smoking like a chimney. He wrote in a frenzy, convinced it would anyway 'end up in a drawer', inventing furiously as he went along. Characters, stories, Berlin, a country estate in East Prussia, a prison, an elegant house in Dahlem, a lodging house in a back courtyard, good people, bad people, little men, big men, all battling to survive the desperate times. By the time he finished, *Wolf Among Wolves* was 1,200 pages long. 'I was once again gripped by the old familiar passion; I wrote without looking up, nor did I look round either – neither to the left, nor to the right.'

The year 1936 ended badly in the Ditzen household. Hubert Rader who worked for Suse in the smallholding and was loved by the whole family, especially the children, was called up for military service. It was agreed that he'd spend every leave with them, but it wasn't the same. Now they only had one odd-jobber to help out with the smallholding and the pigs, and only one maid to help Suse with the household. They sold their horse and cart and planned to sell their one cow too. They spent a quiet and alcohol-free Christmas with Suse's mother.

The next year wasn't any better. In February, Rudolf was called up for eight weeks' military service. In the event he was saved by his evident ill-health, but it was enough to rattle his nerves again. In April, his father died. They spent a week in Leipzig arranging the funeral and supporting Rudolf's grieving mother. At home the smallholding wasn't making enough money and there wasn't enough from Rudolf's writing either, what with all the bad publicity and censorship. One friend was forced to divorce his wife because she was half-Jewish, another was threatened with sterilisation because he was diagnosed as schizophrenic. Some of Rudolf's children's stories were removed from school libraries. His nerves in shreds, Rudolf temporarily fell out with Rowohlt because he refused to pay back a loan. Should they leave Carwitz? they wondered again and again. Many of the villagers were hostile, some denouncing them as anti-Nazis. Perhaps they should emigrate? But how would Rudolf earn a living, seeing as he couldn't write anywhere other than in his beloved North Germany. And where, anyway, would they go?

Instead, Rudolf wrote and wrote, well into 1937, banging out the story of Wolfgang Pagel, a drifting, gambling young man still trying to find his place in the world since serving as a second lieutenant in the war, and Petra Ledig, his pregnant girlfriend – another of Rudolf's sweet, strong, decent young women who shine through a vast cast of characters tumbling unbidden out of Rudolf's fevered imagination, but always based in gritty reality. This sprawling tale is divided into 7 Parts and 56 Chapters, each chapter again divided into several sections, jumping from one tale to the next, but never losing sight of the main thread nor the main story of Wolfgang and Petra. Part One alone is over 300 pages long and takes place during a single 24 hours.

'A word to the reader,' wrote Rudolf in a Preface once the book had, luckily, been taken on by Rowohlt. 'The author has been reproached by some readers of his novel *Once We Had a Child* for making his hero, Johannes Gantschow, such a brute. He has read this complaint with some astonishment, for as he wanted to portray a brutal man he could not depict a kind one. To avoid similar complaints the author warns in this Preface (which can be glanced through in a moment at any bookstore) that *Wolf Among Wolves* deals with sinful, weak, sensual, erring, unstable men, the children of an age disjointed, mad and sick. All in all, it is a book for those who are, in every sense, adult.'

Turning back to his typewriter, he wrote: 'A girl and man were sleeping on a narrow iron bed. The girl's head rested in the crook of her right arm, her mouth, softly breathing, was half open; her face bore a pouting and anxious expression – that of a child who cannot understand why it is sad. She lay turned away from the man, who slept on his back in a state of utter exhaustion, his arms loose. Tiny beads of sweat stood out on his forehead and in the roots of his curly fair hair; the handsome defiant face looked somewhat vacant. In spite of the open window the room was very hot, and the pair slept without blanket or covering. This is Berlin, Georgenkirch Strasse, third courtyard, fourth floor, July 1923, at six o'clock in the morning. The dollar stands for the moment at 414,000 marks.'

Like thousands of others in Berlin in 1923, Wolfgang and Petra live in one room in a dingy lodging house. He has no job, and whenever he manages to scrounge some money he quickly loses it at the gambling tables. Petra, the illegitimate daughter of a harsh woman who turned her out as soon as she was old enough to fend for herself, has been forced into prostitution. And this, in fact, is how the two meet: on the dingy dirty streets of Berlin. '"By the way, my name is Wolfgang Pagel," he said with a little bow. "Pleased to meet you," she replied in the correct manner. "Mine is Petra Ledig." He laughed: "Come on, little one. I shall call you Peter."'

The reader is immediately captivated, thrilled to be in familiar Hans Fallada territory, hoping against hope that all will turn out well in the end.

'Out of the dark well of the courtyard the smells from a hundred lodgings drifted into their sleep. A hundred noises, faint as yet, entered the open window where a dingy curtain hung motionless.' How well the reader knew that world, living it day by day, struggling with the same desperate circumstances as Wolfgang and Petra. Petra calls him Wolf. He is the Wolf among Wolves, eat or be eaten. She loves him but she knows he's not ready to become a father, he must first 'become a man'. Will he manage it? By Chapter Five he's still a long way off. He's trying to borrow money from an old school friend who has made a fortune in dubious ways, but refuses to lend him the money. Humiliated, Wolfgang wanders the streets. And here, out of the blue, comes one of Rudolf's 'decent' people: Liesbeth, a young woman who sees his plight, feels for him and invites him to her house in the wealthy district of Dahlem, just to help him out. She takes him into the kitchen and tells the cheerful cook to give him something to eat.

'He had never seen such a kitchen. It was large as a dance hall, white, silver, copper-red, its saucepans a dull black.' He was sitting at 'a long, snow-white dining table and comfortable white chairs. Yes, there was even a fireplace of beautiful red bricks.' Waiting for his food, he feels like a beggar. 'He stared into vacancy. He hadn't a bad brain; he had ideas, but he had gone to seed and he was lazy, he didn't want to pursue a thought to its logical conclusion. Why should he? I'm like that and I'll stay like it. Wolfgang Pagel for ever!' The stout house-keeper comes in and gives him hardly a glance. Then an elderly liveried manservant comes in. 'May I offer you something to drink?' he asks Wolfgang. The cook, kitchen maid, everyone, Wolfgang notices, are all well-spoken and pleasant. There are still such places, he realises: beautiful homes belonging to decent people.

'The door opened and in came a little girl, the daughter of the house, ten or twelve years old, bright and cheerful.' At first she doesn't notice him sitting there. Then she bids him a polite good day. Wolfgang feels he has to make some conversation, so he asks her age and about her school. 'He felt lower and more miserable than ever before those serious eyes.' She didn't go to school, she answered. 'I'm blind. Papa is also blind. But Papa used to be able to see. I have never been able to, at all. Mama can see. But she says she would prefer not to, as she never knows what Papa and I feel like. We wouldn't let her though.'

Little by little, over several hundred pages, Wolfgang comes to understand that he has to take courage and do something about his life. 'I used to think courage meant standing up straight when a shell exploded and taking your share of the shrapnel. Now I know that's mere stupidity and bravado; courage means keeping going when something becomes completely unbearable.' Petra supports him through it all. Finally Wolf escapes the Wolves and takes a job as a manager on a country estate in East Prussia, just like Rudolf himself. He makes a success of it, then comes back to Berlin to take up his medical studies, now bent on helping his fellow human beings. 'Once he had been merely lovable – then he became worthy of love,' wrote Rudolf to the joy of his readers, showing them that their fate lay in their own hands and in private domestic happiness, even as their public life became more and more unbearable. The book ends where it began. It is a year later and Wolfgang and Petra are in bed again, but now 'everything has changed', even the currency, which has finally stabilised.

'The young wife smiles – at life, at her husband, at happiness . . . It is not a happiness dependent on external things; it rests in herself as the kernel in the nut. A woman who loves and knows herself to be loved feels the happiness which is always with her as a blessed whispering in her ear – drowning the noise of the day – the tranquil happiness which has nothing more to desire. She hears the man breathing; then, softer and faster, that of the child. Gently the white curtains stir. Everything has quite changed. She puts out the light. Good, good night!'

Rudolf felt as happy as Petra. Even happier when Rowohlt came to say he'd read it and loved it and would publish it, paying him an advance of 10,000 Reich Marks. Franz Hessel, a former employee, would proofread it, unofficially, since Hessel was Jewish. *Wolf Among Wolves* was published in September 1937 and sold out in weeks. Within months it had been translated into English, somewhat abbreviated. Only Margaret Mitchell's *Gone with the Wind* was a bigger bestseller that year. Rudolf was able to employ a full-time housekeeper

again, Frau Ellenberg. Sophie came back to look after the children and
help Suse, who was suffering from an ulcer. Even Hubert Rader came
back for a long leave, bringing his niece with him for further help in
the house. 'It is now so wonderful here that it makes my heart glad
and dispels any thoughts we ever had of selling Carwitz,' Rudolf wrote
to his mother. 'Here we are and here we are going to stay.' Everything
had quite changed.

Except that Rudolf had chosen to write a story acceptable to the
Nazis, happy ending and all. And his Preface was forced to include
the inevitable compromise, to make sure the book got past the censors
at the Reich Literary Chamber: 'While not aiming at photographic
likeness, the author wishes to picture a time that is both recent and yet
entirely eclipsed. It behoves the rescued not altogether to forget past
danger, but, remembering it, to appreciate doubly the happy issue.'
In 1937, the Nazis had yet to do their worst, nevertheless the 'happy
issue' was the Nazi terror regime. Their newspaper the *Volkischer
Beobachter* gave the book high praise for showing how Fascism had
saved Germany from the hyperinflation and mass unemployment of
the Weimar period. 'A terrific book!' wrote Goebbels in his diary on
31 January 1938. 'That fellow has real talent!'

In East Prussia, Fritzi von der Schulenburg was a puzzle to his friends –
was he pro-Nazi or not? By 1937 he was still employed as the *Landrat*
civil servant administering Fischhausen, in spite of his loud, and
some said not too clever and rather naive criticism of Erich Koch, the
region's *Gauleiter*. Even after Gregor Strasser, the man Schulenburg
had revered in the National Socialist movement, was murdered, he
still continued to work alongside the Party. It was odd. Everyone knew
Koch had engineered Schulenburg's transfer out of Königsberg to distant Fischhausen, fed up with his high-handed Prussian aritstocrat's
ideals about the state's duty to the Volk and whatnot. Who did he
think he was, asked Koch? Things were different now. You didn't
need to come from some grand Prussian family to become *Gauleiter* –
you didn't even need a specially good education. All you needed now
was unquestioning loyalty to the Führer, which Koch certainly had,
being an Old Fighter. And Old Fighter *Kamaraden* stuck together. He
employed more and more of them in his *Gauleitung*, as mayors and
suchlike, surrounding himself with loyal Nazi Party members – only
to have Fritzi complain to his friends in high places in Berlin that they

were not qualified for the job and should never have been employed in the first place. Then Schulenburg started accusing Koch personally of corruption and favouritism. At which point Koch got him transferred to distant Fischhausen, far up on the East Prussian coast, with poor agriculture and an impoverished fishing industry. Teach him some loyalty.

Schulenburg promptly started showing his true, high-handed colours again: getting rid of the second official car, converting almost half his *Landrat* residence into work rooms for local people, setting up the *Heimwerk Samland* cottage industry to give the unemployed fishermen work during the winters – carpentry and wood-carving for the men, weaving for the women – and spending large sums of money on local amenities such as new paths and walkways. He even turned one of his cellars over to a *Wein Stube*, a social club with beer and wine. He appeared not to understand that the important word in National Socialism was National, not Social. Koch decided to turn a blind eye for the time being. The bigwigs in Berlin said they needed a good administrator in the district, it being so poor and under-developed, and so many administrators arrested by now.

Fritzi couldn't have been happier. Now, finally, he was able to do some good in the proper Prussian way, and without interference. He instigated the monthly *Landrat* day, visiting the district's villages in turn, arriving early in the morning and staying till late, listening to the villagers' news and worries, taking note, promising to do something wherever possible.

'When Schulenburg appeared in the village square in his car,' the whole village turned up,' remembered his friend Klaus von der Groeben, one of the 'high-ups' working at the Ministry of the Interior in Berlin, 'men, women, children, to see him and tell him what was happening in their village, or what had been achieved since his last visit: how many fish they'd caught, who was ill, who had died, a baby born, a cow calved, a boy been naughty, a couple moved to Pillau or Königsberg, or even Hamburg or Essen. It was rarely about administrative matters, mostly queries, wishes and news of a personal nature. The *Landrat* would surely have an answer for them, or some advice. He was a young man, but they still looked on him like a father. They brought him small presents like children: an especially large fish, two gulls' eggs, a pot of honey. He knew how to talk to them all, high or low, educated or not. He made suggestions, perhaps about the upbringing of a child, or to a wife about a drinker husband. The deciding thing though was that they felt he answered them not only with his head, but with his heart.'

The very first thing Fritzi did when he arrived in Fischhausen was to make sure his predecessor, *Landrat* Nuade, got a job in Quedlinburg, a district even more cut-off than Fischhausen – but at least a job. *Gleichschaltung* is what caught Nuade out, because he hadn't been minded to hide his distaste of the Nazis. Fritzi wasn't bothered about all that. Nuade was a decent man and he was happy to pull strings with his friends in the Reich Ministry of the Interior and make sure Nuade wasn't punished for his political views.

Once he got into his stride in Fischhausen, Fritzi canvassed these same friends for a massive increase in his *Landrat* budget, because he had even bigger plans now: first and foremost to build terraced housing for the workers, each with a small garden. Then he shut off the cliff-top walk every Sunday and feast day for the villagers to use, infuriating local landowners. Then he employed the architect Hans Hopp to build a promenade along the seafront. How did he get away with it? Hans Hopp was a suspected Communist. But by the summer there was a souvenir shop selling models of ships carved by the men and shawls knitted by the women during the winter. And a new factory for the fishing industry at Pillau.

Fritzi worked day and night, which didn't leave much time for family life. Charlotte had two children to look after now, two daughters, Fredeke and Leveke Christiane, known as Schuschu and Beba, and perhaps she would have liked to see more of her husband, but she knew how he was – how powerful his Prussian sense of duty, how much he battled with his conscience over his position within the NSDAP, how determined he was to rid it of those bad elements as represented by Erich Koch – and how hopeful he still was that the movement would in time grow and prosper and that good men with modern ideas would overcome the others.

But was it just bad individuals? Or was it the movement as a whole which was brutal and corrupt? Those were the questions plaguing Charlotte's husband during the Fischhausen years.

It didn't stop him being the exuberant heart of any party they gave – and there were many, as his friends and colleagues remembered. Alongside his seriousness, Fritzi also had an infectious *joie de vivre*: he loved music, he loved to sing, he loved wine. And he loved to dance.

Summer parties in the garden of the Schulenburgs' official residence went on late into the shimmering East Prussian night. With the old friends came new local ones, some NSDAP members included. And every Sunday there were walks with Charlotte and the children by the silent, lonely lakes or along the coast and the white dunes with the sea beyond. Sometimes Fritzi and Charlotte went travelling on their own, leaving the children in the care of the children's nurse – once to the island of Reichenau on the Lake of Constance, visiting the South German Baroque churches on the way, another to visit their friends, the Hardenbergs, in Litauen. And every year there was military service, which Fritz-Dietlof, the impractical intellectual, undertook with as much enthusiasm as he could muster.

In June 1936 there was a family tragedy. Wilhelm, the youngest, now in his late twenties, was killed in a car accident. Wilhelm had been a lieutenant in the 9th Infantry Regiment in Potsdam – the regiment which later numbered many who plotted to assassinate Hitler. The funeral was at Tressow, the family home, with full military honours. Graf von der Schulenburg's old friend from the war years, Major General von Fritsch, attended. The coffin was draped with the regimental flag. As it was lowered into the grave, they sang *Ich hatte einen Kamarade*, 'Once I Had a Soldier Comrade', and then the hymn *Lob den Herren*, 'Praise to Thee the King of Heaven', was played by the regimental Music Corps.

Wilhelm and his sister Tisa had been the only ones in the family who were not members of the NSDAP. Tisa couldn't go to the funeral, being married to a Jew and living in England. She was devastated by the news. 'This beautiful, shining, effervescent, best-loved boy,' as she described him in her memoirs. She and Fritz Hess were in their cottage in Walberswick on the Suffolk coast when the telegram with the news of Wilhelm's death arrived. They still had their flat in Highgate, but weekends were mostly spent in Suffolk.

By all appearances they were adjusting well to their new life. Fritz, the excellent businessman, had managed to get some money out through Holland as soon as the Nazis came to power in January 1933 and was investing it cleverly. Tisa took up her painting again. Fritz's son was continuing his studies at London University. His daughter was settled in Israel. Tisa's English, remembered from childhood, was better now. Fritz learned his from listening to the BBC and reading *The Times*. By 1936, they had an interesting group of friends including

Victor Gollancz, the publisher, who was introduced to them by Ernst Freud, the son of Sigmund, who had left Austria early, unlike his parents who couldn't bear to leave until the last minute. It was architect Ernst who found them the cottage in Walberswick and renovated it for them. It was in a wild and unspoilt area with sweeping beaches and sand dunes not unlike East Prussia. Many artists chose to live and work there and Tisa was soon one of them.

So why wasn't she happy? She missed Mecklenburg. She missed her family. She spent hours daydreaming of Tressow: the lake, the forests, the fading evening light, the distant sound of her parents' voices from the terrace. She wanted . . . What did she want? She hardly knew herself. All she knew was: she should have been happy with Fritz who loved her and was a good and clever man. But she wasn't. She took to walking around the slums in the East End of London, astonished to find that the poverty and unemployment was almost as bad there as in Germany. But they were different, these people. Less bitter, less political altogether. Perhaps because they'd won the war. Though what kind of winning was that?

It was the same in Durham among the coalminers, where she went in search of, what? Again she didn't know. She sketched the miners and their families in the style of Käthe Kollwitz, who knew how to capture misery and deprivation like no other artist Tisa knew. She made new northern working-class friends. She did voluntary work. But nothing helped. Tisa didn't know what was wrong. She only knew she wanted to go home. But she couldn't. Even when Wilhelm died, she couldn't. Because she was the Jew Fritz Hess's wife.

Instead she travelled to Denmark to meet her mother who travelled there by ship from Lübeck. They hadn't seen each other in almost three years. At first it was wonderful, if sad. But then all the old problems came back: her mother and the rest of the family were still putting their faith in the Nazi Party. Even Fritzi, asked Tisa? Of course, said her mother. He's the *Landrat* in Fischhausen, didn't you know? Yes, she knew, but still . . . And was Tisa happy in London with her Fritz? *Mutti* wanted to know. Tisa couldn't give a clear answer. Really, she'd always been the odd one out, thought her mother. The awkward one. Nothing had changed apparently. Both were in tears as the ship left Copenhagen bound home for the Reich, *Mutti* waving from the deck above, Tisa waving up from the quayside below.

But something changed for Tisa after her brother's death. At first she didn't realise it and tried to carry on. She made some new friends – members of the Artists International Association, all open anti-Fascists: Duncan Grant, Vanessa and Clive Bell, Barbara Hepworth, Ben Nicolson, Henry Moore. They sent an ambulance to the Spanish Civil War. Tisa went to one of their meetings and stood up and talked about what was happening in Germany, even talking about her own family's sympathies. Unlike many of her other English friends, these new ones listened and took her warnings seriously. But what could they do? It helped her nevertheless and, after that, she often went to their meetings. And she went back to Durham.

By then it was December and bitterly cold. The coalminers lived in tiny terraced houses, two-up two-down, for a family of six or seven, with no heating save a small coal fire, a privy outside in the backyard, and hardly enough money to feed their families. The unemployed hung about the street corners, freezing. Many were homeless, living in hostels which closed from 10 till 6 – men who had fought for their country in the war. Men who had been her former enemies and who, she saw, were no different to the homeless and disillusioned men in her own country. She joined a house full of social activists and volunteered at the Spennymoor Settlement, giving art lessons and financial support. Once she was allowed down a coalmine. It was shocking – a half-hour trek to the coalface, bent double, water dripping everywhere and the miners standing in it as they worked, crouching, in semi-darkness, with no helmets, wielding their pickaxes. There were many accidents and no insurance. And when the miners emerged at the end of a ten-hour shift, faces black, the day was almost over. In winter, it was already dark. Their only consolation, as Tisa saw it, was their evenings in the working men's clubs. And the drink. And all this while the owners of the pits lived like lords. It was hard to countenance. But at least it wasn't a terror regime as in Nazi Germany – you could be a Communist or a Jew in 1930s Britain without ending up in a concentration camp. Or dead.

Fritz listened to her shocking tales, but he was less concerned, partly because he was more conservative politically than Tisa but mostly because he was so grateful that, as a Jew, he'd found a home and safety in England. And that he was able to make a living for the family again. Really, he couldn't understand Tisa and her discontent. She felt trapped, she said. But trapped by what? Freedom? Finally she decided to go into psychoanalysis, to save their marriage. And to work out what she called her hidden drives and longings. But nothing helped.

Back in the Reich, Fritzi wrote to Charlotte: 'Koch has lately been complaining about me again, saying my post wouldn't last long. He'll probably try to push through a transfer.' But, try as he might, Koch couldn't get rid of him – he was too good an administrator and too well protected by the Reich Ministry of the Interior – secret anti-Nazis, all. And when he was finally transferred, in July 1937, it was by way of a promotion, as Deputy President of Police in Berlin. Why on earth did he accept the post, some of his friends asked themselves. Some thought they knew the answer: Fritzi's friends in high places at the Ministry, including Klaus von der Groeben, had pulled strings to get him there, and Klaus was surely an anti-Nazi, gathering other opponents of the regime around him. So, who knows . . . ?

For Fritzi, leaving Fischhausen was hard. The worst was telling his people in the villages – the ones who brought him presents like children, deep with gratitude and love for this man who'd arrived from nowhere and had immediately set about making their harsh lives better. They could hardly believe he was leaving them to their fate. Nor could he. But by the end of July 1937 Fritzi was back in Berlin, presenting himself at the Ministry of the Interior, ready to take up his new post.

'The departure from East Prussia has hit me harder than anything I've ever had to do,' he wrote on 1 August 1937 to Charlotte who was left behind with the children while he looked for an apartment. 'It felt as though this land was being wrenched powerfully away from me, causing me anger and pain.'

But Klaus von der Groeben, his old friend from the Königberg times who shared Fritzi's admiration of Georg Strasser, needed him. 'Among his many gifts,' wrote Klaus after the war, and long after Fritzi's terrible end, 'perhaps the most important one was his powerful influence over people. He was able to gather a new circle of devotees round him wherever he went, and whatever the task. And this without abandoning loyalty to his old friends. It was hard to put your finger on it, the secret of this charisma. Middling in height, a not especially striking appearance apart from the scar on his cheek, with an easy, relaxed manner, you might not notice him – till he began to speak, eyes lit up, in that quiet, but immediately powerful way of his.'

Fritzi's chief was Wolf-Heinrich Graf von Helldorf Paroli. At first he wasn't sure of him. Helldorf Paroli was notorious for his high-living and his many affairs. There was nothing of the Prussian aesthete about him. Yet they got on famously. 'At first he didn't want me, but his other suggestions for the post were rejected,' Fritzi wrote to Charlotte, 'but after our first meeting we found we agreed on all the most important matters. He makes a clever, jokey impression. And in his position at the Ministry he is the complete, energetic man of state. I can't yet see what really lies hidden behind this, but outwardly he makes an open and direct impression. I think we'll be able to work together.'

Fritzi quickly set about bringing some order and clarity to his post, reforming the administration, including the personnel. By February 1938, he had produced a memo about the language used by the administrators: it needed to be more intelligible to the ordinary citizen. 'Express yourself in short sentences. Avoid unnecessary high-flown sentences. Avoid wooden German and the official language of bureaucracy.'

By March 1938, he was giving a lecture to the officials at the Ministry. It was titled 'The Prussian Inheritance of the National Socialist State'. It went on for over 20 pages. Many thought you had to choose between their Prussian Inheritance and National Socialism, he began, but that wasn't the case. A well-functioning state rested on order and clarity. Finances had to be transparent. Corruption banished, Duty and Honour exercised. Frederick the Great, Luther, the Prussian Army – everything was brought into the argument. The war, followed by virtual civil war had been their undoing, he said. While the Army had held on to its Prussian inheritance, it was all but lost to officialdom and the state. The original idea of National Socialism was to make the Volk the meaning and basis of everything in a new Socialism. Hitler in *Mein Kampf* already referred to the Prussian values of National Socialism. He quoted Joseph Goebbels in his speech of April 1932: 'The idea to which we hold fast is Prussian. Our aims are, in more modern form, those of Frederick the Great and Bismarck. The Volk wants us to reinstate these Prussian values.' We have to find room for the spiritual, Fritzi added, for religion and for responsibility, 'God help us.' National Socialism and Prussian values were not opposites. National Socialism was merely the political expression of these same ideas in modern form. He ended by quoting Moltke: 'We will not retreat! We are Prussians!'

Fritzi wasn't the only one. The remaining members of the Communist Party in Germany did not retreat either, as a report by the State Police Office to Darmstadt's Gestapo office about the funeral of a Communist shows. 'Concerning: Communist demonstration on the occasion of the burial of Adam Schaefer from Mainz-Kostheim who was a prisoner in protective custody in Dachau. The investigations into the above affair have so far discovered: on 24 March 1937 Adam Schaefer was shot by an SS guard whom he attacked. At the expressed wish of the parents, the corpse was transferred to Mainz-Kostheim, where the funeral took place on 29 March 1937. Even before the corpse had arrived, the rumour around Mainz-Kostheim was that Schaefer had not been shot but beaten to death, and that this was the reason the parents refused to open the coffin. About 800 people were present. About 40 per cent were known former associates and members of the SPD and the Centre; perhaps 60 per cent were former Communists. Participants appeared from far removed suburbs and even Mainz itself. The Communists stood pretty much together during the ceremony at the graveside. After the end of the religious ceremonies, M appeared out of the ranks of his likeminded comrades, about 2 metres from the graveside. From here he threw a wreath on to the grave with the words "Rest in Peace". His whole demeanour in carrying out this action was such that everyone had to recognise the symbolic purpose behind it. The big turnout at the funeral and the laying of the wreath for all to see should be taken as proof that the KPD is not dead, but rather continues to exist illegally. As a result, M was immediately taken into protective custody.'

Julius Leber, the great Social Democrat, had been imprisoned by the Nazis for four years now, since March 1933 – first in the local prison in his home town of Lübeck, latterly in Sachsenhausen concentration camp. 'Christmas is coming,' he'd written to his beloved Annedore from Sachsenhausen on 21 December 1936. Fate had been hard on them, he conceded, but he could put up with it: it had made him stronger; it had changed them both; it was a gift as well as a wound. This was Leber being Leber: he wasn't about to admit defeat. But by the beginning of May 1937, with his release in sight, he was writing in a different tone. 'Believe me, my joy and expectation are no less than yours. My thoughts go round and round in the same circle: Hope of our reunion.' He was careful not to hope too much, because he'd been promised release once before, only to have it whipped away at the last minute.

But he was finally let out on 5 May 1937 – most probably so the local Gestapo could watch his movements and track other Social Democrat anti-Nazi activists. For some, a few months in a concentration camp was enough to break them, leaving them frightened of everything. Not

Julius Leber. The years had changed him, he admitted, but they had not broken him nor intimidated him. As soon as he was free, he went back to fighting the Nazi regime in any way he could. Annedore, his devoted wife, didn't stop him. She knew it wouldn't get her anywhere.

Leber's local newspaper, *Lübecker Volksboten*, had long since been taken over by the Nazis, so that wasn't available to him. Instead he set about secretly making contact with old friends and Socialist comrades, always bearing in mind he'd be under surveillance from now on. Still, reckoned Leber, they couldn't watch him all the time. Like most other active resisters he quickly learned the skills of deception, jumping on trams and trains at the last minute, doubling back, wearing disguises, joining spurious 'clubs' which were a cover for something else, never using the telephone for anything important, and always looking out for informers.

'There are in every village, in every countryside, in every city, a network of paid Gestapo agents posing as officials of one sort or another, most of the time posing as secret enemies of Fascism,' wrote Martha Dodd, safely back in America. 'In one small factory town one man, known to be a town official, got the word around among the workers that he was sympathetic to the Loyalist cause in Spain. After a week or so of penetrating into workers' homes and sympathies he drew up a secret petition for financial aid to the Spanish. He got over fifty signatures before someone caught him out and warned the workers. But these fifty names were off the payroll of the factory and could soon be found on the concentration camp roll-call. Let it be stated very clearly that whenever real opposition is located, no matter where, the technique of the Gestapo is always the same: liquidation.'

This might have been news to the American public, but it was old news for Julius Leber. Carefully, he set about contacting Social Democrat comrades who were still in the fight – the same fight he'd always stood for, before, during and after his incarceration: the fight for social justice for the worker and a fair and democratic political system. 'You either have to rule, or you have to stand in unequivocal opposition. If you don't have the responsibility to do the first properly, and if you don't have the courage for the second, therein lies the biggest mistake any politician or political party can commit,' as he'd written in the days when there was still a free press in Germany. Incarceration by the Nazis didn't stop him.

'Thoughts on the Banning of German Social Democracy' was the title of his seventy-page paper written in prison and smuggled out section by section by Annedore and her helpful prison guard. In it Leber conceded that Social Democracy as an organisation was dead, but did that mean the belief in it was dead too? There followed a detailed history of Germany's plight following the disastrous Treaty of Versailles, then the virtual civil war of Weimar. Finally his key point: a warning that National Socialism was a different kind of animal altogether, not concerned with the rational, nor with the usual political theories. The engine driving National Socialism was Will and Power, pure and simple. It tore up every other political theory. The result: the people were profoundly confused by the loss of their ideals. So it was the Socialist politicians' duty to make sure they would eventually have a better future, based on the Rule of Law and Freedom.

Now that he was free again, Leber meant to pick up where he left off four years earlier.

While Julius was still in Sachsenhausen, Annedore had moved from Lübeck to Berlin. She needed to make a better living for herself and the children, Katharina and Matthias, something difficult in her old home town where everyone knew Leber. Also, thinking ahead to her husband's release, she knew he would be able to hide more easily in Berlin. They had support: her brother lived in Berlin, as did many former SPD colleagues and friends, all trying to get by as best they could.

In Berlin, she quickly found work as a seamstress. One of her clients was Lina Dahrendorf, the wife of Gustav, Leber's SPD colleague from Weimar times, who had been arrested for three months following the *Machtergreifung* in 1933. Dahrendorf was a brilliant businessman and now had a top job at Preussag, the oil and coal company, so the Nazis were minded to leave him alone, desperate to keep their Volk as warm and content as possible during the snow and ice of winter. And Gustav Dahrendorf was very good at keeping his head down, a Beefsteak of the first order.

Annedore was already secretly in touch with many of the old SPD resisters in Berlin by the time her husband was released from Sachsenhausen in May 1937. Dahrendorf was their first visitor on the second day of Leber's release. He was shocked at the sight of his old mentor – the big belly and the exuberant manner replaced by a thin, haggard man, trying his best to adjust to his new life of freedom. Leber said his children had barely recognised him, but he tried not to think or talk about his worst times – in solitary for weeks on end, sometimes without bed, chair, table, exercise or warm food, often beaten – and to concentrate instead on the future. 'The four years of incarceration have left their mark,' Dahrendorf noted, 'but he's bodily and spiritually unbroken.'

Annedore was pleased to note that the old friendship between the two former Social Democrat politicians was 'fully re-established, and they determined to keep in close contact'. The 'close contact' was their joint resistance work, which began there and then, and continued for seven years till 1944 when they both appeared before the Nazis' *Volksgericht*, People's Court.

Dahrendorf was surprised how well informed Julius Leber was, even after all those years of incarceration. Leber just laughed. 'You think news doesn't reach the concentration camps? Wrong. The Sachsenhausen information lines are very effective.' Moscow, London, Germany, news came in from all over the place. There was nothing the Nazis could do about it.

'When I was first in prison, I told Annedore I'd give them five years,' said Leber. 'I reckoned I'd be inside for two. Then two more years waiting at the ready. In the fifth year, if the Nazis were still in power, I'd have to take action. Now look!'

Leber could say anything to Dahrendorf. The two men trusted each other completely. They agreed on all the major points: that Weimar had needed reform, certainly, but not extinction; that the Social Democrats had to bear some of the blame – too stuck in their old ways and not prepared to reach out to others on the Left, including the Communists; that a democratic two-party system was the best, as in England, based on majority rule. And that politics needed big personalities and good leaders. As far as Dahrendorf was concerned that was Julius Leber.

As Annedore recalled that first meeting of old friends in her memoir, she noted that they also agreed on that day that a coup against the Nazi Regime was the only solution. But first they had to prepare a fully functioning alternative government and administration to step in and rule the moment they ousted the Nazis. A coup was only the first step. So they started to make lists of politically reliable people. They agreed that Ludwig Beck, the highly respected general from the war years, now Chief of Army General Staff, was key. But how to contact him? Before he left the Lebers that evening, Dahrendorf gave his friend the names of two SPD resisters who were already making some progress: Ernst von Harnack and Ludwig Schwamb. And he agreed to find Leber a job in the coal business.

Ernst von Harnack was the brother of Arvid, Martha Dodd's friend. The family was middle class, cultured, with friends who were writers, musicians, former politicians and academics. Ernst had studied law and fought in the war till 1916 when he was gazetted out due to extreme exhaustion. His decision to resist stemmed from those years in the trenches when he met, for the first time, the ordinary working man, and developed a strong social conscience. After the war, he joined the SPD and worked in local administration. Like Dahrendorf, he was arrested for a few weeks after the *Machtergreifung*, just to frighten him off. Once he was let out, he started a small textile business which he used effectively as a cover for his political activity.

Ludwig Schwamb had a similar story: a lawyer in Mainz, he'd also served in the war, also joined the Social Democrats, also been arrested by the Nazis in 1933 and had also made his way into business after release, in his case working in the Konrad Tack shoe factory, also in Berlin. Oil, coal, textiles, shoe factories were all essential businesses to keep the Nazi regime's economy going – and all excellent covers for resistance work.

During the first year of his freedom, Leber kept his head down, contacting no one from his old home town of Lübeck, leading a quiet, anonymous domestic life, causing no trouble. Annedore earned the family money working as a seamstress. She didn't complain that there were still debts to pay from the old law case. Nor even about the maintenance Leber had to pay for an illegitimate daughter – carelessly conceived in those heady, distant days when he was the great politician, but not the great husband. She was happy to support him while he sat tight, reading his books, preparing for future action.

So for a good year, Leber did nothing. The Gestapo agents probably concluded that four years of brutal imprisonment had done their work. But just as in Sachsenhausen, Leber was getting all the news, gathering information, making plans: he knew what he was up against. War and extermination was what the Nazis stood for and always had. Hitler had written it all in *Mein Kampf,* way back in 1923: 'Now that I realised the Jews were the leaders of the Social Democrats, scales, as it were, began to fall from my eyes.' Jews, Social Democrats and Communists all had to be incarcerated, or better still, killed outright. 'Liquidated,' as Martha Dodd put it. 'What do figures matter now?' Goebbels wrote in March 1933 after the Reichstag election results which showed that their brutal terror tactics were winning. 'We are the Masters in the Reich and in Prussia now.' It was the last election the Nazis ever held.

Julius Leber, in Lübeck prison by then, could only watch as the Nazis stepped up their preparations for war, starting with the Army. From August 1934 every officer and foot soldier had to swear the Oath, binding him to the Führer. 'I swear by God this Holy Oath, that I will render unconditional obedience to the Führer of the Reich, Adolf Hitler, commander of the Armed Forces, and that, as a brave soldier, I will be ready at any time to stake my life for this Oath.' By 1936, after his successful gamble to take back the occupied territory in the Rhineland, Hitler was noting: 'First: the German army must be ready for action within four years. Second: the German economy must be ready for war within four years.' By then, the membership of the Hitler Youth was over six million. 'We are born to die for Germany', as their banners proclaimed. The figures hadn't surprised Leber. He knew that any family which failed to send their sons to the Hitler Youth would be threatened and punished. But it didn't stop them holding their own views. They might attend bodily, to avoid trouble, but how they felt spiritually was a different matter altogether.

Ludwig Schwamb became a close family friend, loved by the Leber children. He was 'a rare friend, during bad as well as good times,' wrote Annedore in her memoir. 'Where his friend stood, so stood he. When his friend was in danger, so was he.' Meanwhile, Ernst von Harnack came up with a clever idea: in 1937, he volunteered for the job of tending the war graves in Berlin. The man in overall charge of the cemeteries was General Ludwig Beck. They all knew you couldn't achieve a coup d'état without the support of the *Wehrmacht*. Harnack was soon having meetings with Beck, by no means all of them about the war cemeteries.

CHAPTER SEVEN

TURNING POINT: 1938

'Do you ever think about that beautiful night when I was allowed to go with all of you?' Irma Thälmann asked *Vater* on one of her rare prison visits. She was thinking of the Communist Party gathering in Hamburg for the 1930 election which she was allowed to attend, provided she held *Mutti*'s hand throughout. *Vater* had suddenly appeared right in the middle of the crowd, to wild cheers and shouts of '*Teddy! Teddy! Teddy ist hier!* Teddy's here!' because, once again, Thälmann and his security detail had outwitted the Nazi bloodhounds. He'd arrived at 10pm, late after another gathering elsewhere, but everyone had waited and waited, just to hear the great man talk.

'In the Ernst Merk Hall? Yes, Irma, we'll never forget that.' It seemed such a long time ago. Well, it was such a long time ago. And yet . . . 'Those thousands of people who were there with us, they still think the same way today as they did then.'

Ernst Thälmann knew that for a fact because, in spite of his solitary confinement, just like Leber, he was well informed about the outside world. The Communists had very effective secret lines of communication, as the Social Democrats did, reaching all the prisons and concentration camps. So he knew about the continued resistance of the workers in the shipyards of Hamburg and Kiel, especially the time, in March 1936, when 5,000 at Bloehm and Voss had walked out of the Führer's speech being relayed in the main building, and 6,000 more at Germania-Werft had openly heckled another broadcast, even though they knew they were being watched, only to be beaten up and arrested by the Storm Troopers as soon as they left the shipyard gates.

Mostly they talked about the past during those prison visits. But, quietly inserted in conversations about their glorious memories and the weather, Irma and Rosa passed on vital information about the continuing Communist resistance. Mostly they spoke in code, mentioning no names. Sometimes they were lucky with the prison guard. But then they were especially careful, not to get that guard into trouble.

They were two of a kind, father and daughter, fighters both of them.

'You are the only child of a man who has dedicated his life to the Workers' Movement. You have to lead your life to show that, as my daughter, you are worthy of this,' *Vater* wrote to Irma on her 16th birthday. Even then, locked up in prison, Thälmann couldn't stop teaching his daughter how to fight for the cause, and Irma, in turn, responded with the deepest respect and conviction. 'Soon the responsibilities which such a life demands will get greater for you, and in fighting them you will find out the strengths and the weaknesses in your character,' he continued. 'The highest task in this battle is and remains the way you handle yourself, and your basic attitude to the task. Without that there is no improvement, no going forward to something better. That's an ancient law. Keep a deep respect for your mother's wisdom. All the impressions which will come your way – try to understand and deal with them, and bring them into your feelings and thoughts. In my youth the smallest experiences often shaped the path I took.'

He reminded Irma to read Goethe and Schiller, and to allow herself to feel passionately about those ideas which appealed to her. This was important, he wrote, otherwise, where would one find the strength to do battle and to understand others? 'I can't be beside you, to advise you and lead you,' he ended, 'but I am always with you in spirit, watching over you as you go your way. Your *Vater*.'

'My dear *Vater*!' Irma wrote back. She'd recently been allowed a short prison visit, but had found it a kind of torture, to have him sitting there before her, 'larger than life', only to go back to Hamburg alone, without him. 'You said you were concerned that I was becoming too serious. *Vater*, believe me, these years filled with worry have affected me. They've taught me to love you deeply, but also to deeply feel your hard fate . . . How much longer will they rob you of your freedom, and me of my *Vater*? These thoughts are what make my young life so serious.' She ended by telling him that seeing him had nevertheless given her hope that he might soon be allowed home. And she sent him passionate greetings from *Mutti* and herself. 'With strong, true love, your child, Irma.'

When Irma left school, she had wanted to become a legal secretary, to help those in prison. But she hated the secretarial college, so she ended up transferring to the *Haushalts Schule* and finished her studies there. But once she left, she couldn't get a job. She tried not to talk too much to *Vater* about it. He had enough troubles of his own.

'After I'd finished my Housekeeping studies I first applied for a job with a legal firm,' Irma wrote later in her memoir of those times. 'The lawyer refused, he was too frightened. In all of Hamburg, there was no legal office which would employ me. I tried everywhere. To be without work was hard. I tried other jobs, but the daughter of Ernst Thälmann wasn't wanted. When I went to the Employment Bureau everyone knew who I was and waved me away: "We've got nothing for you." Every day I read the job advertisements in papers. Sometimes I almost got it – till I had to give my name. Then they became icy. Other employees in the office whispered amongst themselves, stared at me, left their work for minutes on end. Hate and opposition only grew in me. But I also got some secret friendly looks, a few whispered good luck wishes as I left the firm, downhearted. It was especially bitter because I knew how much *Vater* wanted me to have a good job, together with other young people. He always went silent when I told him how I'd gone everywhere in vain.'

'The biggest enemy of every people lies in their own country,' *Vater* reminded Irma, quoting Karl Liebknecht. 'The main enemy of the German Volk is in Germany itself: German Imperialism, the party of war.' And he told her to go on learning, even if she couldn't find a job. Hadn't he himself been self-taught, once he got back from the war and saw how things stood in his own country – virtual civil war as it was. The only way forward, he'd told his Communist colleagues, was to learn. Read. Study. Make notes. Be informed. Passion alone could achieve nothing. All during Irma's childhood she saw him, head down at the kitchen table, reading, making notes, educating himself. And now, here he was, confined to a small cell, with nothing but a bed, a chair and a table and all the time in the world to think. And do nothing.

Sometimes *Vater* was allowed reading material, sometimes not. You never knew. Sometimes he got post, sometimes not; sometimes he was allowed to write a letter home, sometimes not. 'Your deep feeling for my situation, which is our joint, rich experience, became so alive through your letter, it made me happier than I've been for a long time,' he wrote to his wife Rosa in January 1937. 'The prison guard has just locked my cell, and deadly silence surrounds me. I look out of the barred window and think of my beloved *Heimat*, Hamburg. Now come the hours of thinking and wrestling. My path ahead is known to me, however hard it will be. My cell window and my own unshakeable conviction will see me through. The daily humiliations and deprivations are terrible. But this fight is my fate.'

Two months later he was allowed another letter. This time he wrote to Irma as well as Rosa. It was the 3rd of March. 'Today I've spent exactly four years in the harshest, almost indescribable isola-tion of unbroken solitary confinement, cut off from the daily life of the German Volk, separated from the real world by the iron bars of my cell window . . . Sometimes I've been shaken by it to the depths of my heart. Hard times and bitter ones lie behind me. To which are added the other blows of fate which have befallen me: the death of my beloved, unforgettable father, which shook me profoundly, and the death of my father-in-law who I'd come to love – made all the worse by the fact that I couldn't be present at their funerals to honour them. Is it possible to bear all this without hope of any effective result? It was my consolation, through all this, my dear Rosa, to know that you were still well. So you can imagine how disturbed I was by the news you gave me during your last visit.'

Poor Ernst. Poor Irma. Along with all their other troubles they now had the added worry of Rosa's health.

There must have been a good prison guard at Moabit, a secret Beefsteak, who smuggled Ernst's next letter out, because it came only three weeks later. 'My dearest Rosa!' he wrote, 'the 27 March is the day of your 47th birthday! The fifth birthday which you are celebrating without me. Fate has it that we can't share it together in our *Heimat*. But my silent thoughts will be even closer to you on this day, and my longing for you all the stronger. Only someone who knows about longing can understand how much suffering it causes me. My birthday present to you is this letter . . . You and I have shared everything in the past, be it something hard or something joyful.

'The story of our marriage started in Kaiser times, carried through the war, and then the whole Weimar period, and is now living through the harshest blows of fate. One thing you and I know: our life is nour-ished by inner riches, but also by our many-sided experiences which we have shared over these years. But they were never separate from daily life and the life of our working Volk, in the swift current of life, which is where we ourselves learned to swim . . . In a marriage where the wife is the equal fighting partner of the husband, as it is with us, every blow of fate can be conquered, because to experience such happiness, just to have even glimpsed it, is already a very great thing . . .'

The letter went on for many more pages. Their child had grown into someone of great inner strength, he wrote, because of the happiness and health of their marriage. How lucky they were with Irma! Sometimes he wandered through the streets of his childhood in his mind – the years before he knew what lay ahead. This year spring had come late. Last year the lilac already had leaves, this year only buds, longing for the warmth and power of the sun. He couldn't give her a bouquet of lilac for her birthday as he used to, but he enclosed three beautiful autumn leaves which he'd kept – his thanks to her for everything.

He ended with some lines of Goethe, remembered by heart:

> *Ja, in der Ferne fuhlt sich die Macht,*
> *wenn zwei sich redlich lieben,*
> *drum bin ich in des Kerkers nacht,*
> *auch noch lebendig geblieben.*
> *Und wenn mir fast das Herz bricht,*
> *so ruf mir nur: Vergiss mein nicht!*
> *Da komm ich wieder ins Leben!*

> Yes, from afar you can feel the power
> when two people truly love each other,
> this is why in the darkness of prison
> I have been able to stay alive.
> And when my heart almost breaks
> just call out to me: Do not forget me!
> And so I come back to life!

'In thankful and unforgettable love, I send you passionate and deep greetings, your loving Ernst.'

The good news: there was no mention of Rosa's health. Presumably that danger, at least, had passed.

Five months later, on 13 August 1937, Ernst Thälmann was suddenly transferred from Moabit prison in Berlin to another in Hanover. Who knows why. Probably because Thälmann, with his charismatic personality and deep convictions, was beginning to win round some of the prison guards. Watching him day after day, they couldn't but be impressed by the dignified way he conducted himself in his isolation. If he had a book, he sat and read. If he had pen and paper, he sat and wrote. If he had none, he sat and looked out at the sky beyond the small cell window. Was it blue? Was it raining? Could he hear a bird? Were the leaves falling from the tree beyond the prison wall? On his daily exercise in the prison yard he always walked firmly, neatly dressed in jacket and waistcoat and necktie, shoes clean, quite alone except for the prison guard, with the prison rising high behind him, four tiers of cells, filled mostly with political prisoners, watching the great man as he strode round and round. For the rest of the twenty-four hours, whenever he had a chance, he quietly set about teaching the Beefsteak prison guards about workers' rights and the danger of a coming war, always with a smile, never with resentment or hate. He followed Lenin in this, who taught that you can't win politics by hate. 'This hate,' wrote Lenin, 'makes people blind. It takes away the possibility to think clearly and work out one's own strategy.' That's why he himself was prepared to work with the Social Democrats, *Vater* told Irma.

She didn't need him to tell her; she knew most of his speeches by heart: 'We call on the Social Democrat worker to stand shoulder to shoulder with us in our fight,' as he'd declared in 1925 and repeated many times since. 'We make this offer of unity in honest brotherly friendship. We hold out our hand to them. We stand beside them in our common daily needs. We never forget, not for one minute, that they are our class brothers who suffer and are oppressed just as we are, and all German workers.' He must have known it was unrealistic to expect the Social Democrats to trust the Communists. And looking back from his cell to 1933, he knew very well it wasn't only the failure of the right-wing parties to stop 'the little corporal', as Hindenburg liked to call Hitler. It was the fatal lack of unity on the Left. But he never gave up, because he was Ernst Thälmann, and he knew the eyes of the world were on him.

Why didn't the Nazis just execute *Vater*, wondered Irma and Rosa again and again. They'd executed so many of the Communist leaders. Only Wilhelm Pieck was still alive, organising small cells of resistance in factories and local districts from his exile in Moscow. But they knew the answer: *Vater* was too popular, too dangerous. And the world was watching. On 24 August 1935 the *News Chronicle* of London had reported: 'The appalling case of Thälmann is not only his long incarceration without trial, but the shocking lies the Nazis use to try and excuse it . . . One thing Herr Hitler and his colleagues should know: Thälmann's treatment at his future trial will be followed in detail throughout the world with the very greatest interest. Because, in the eyes of the world, it is not only Herr Thälmann who will be standing trial.'

When no trial materialised, that too was noted.

'Free Ernst Thälmann!' Wilhelm Pieck had written on thousands of leaflets distributed throughout Germany for the great leader's 50th birthday. 'We the German Communists have the special holy duty, in our own country, to prepare and carry out the destruction of Hitler Fascism. On this day a million people throughout the world demand: "Ernst Thälmann must go free! The fight to free Ernst Thälmann is the fight for peace against the war-mongers! Forwards the cause of the worker!"'

But by 1937, the Nazi terror regime was gaining a tighter and tighter grip on Germany and they were less inclined to play safe. It had indeed come to the authorities' notice that some of the prison guards were falling under Thälmann's spell, and there was a rumour that a Communist cell was planning to break him from prison. Moabit was no longer a secure place to incarcerate him. That summer he was transferred to Hanover.

The first Irma and Rosa knew of it was when they saw two Gestapo hanging around in the street opposite their apartment, keeping watch. They weren't hard to spot. Minutes later they forced their way into the apartment and ordered them to hand over *Vater*'s letters. 'You'll get nothing from me,' said Rosa the Fighter. Whereupon they turned the apartment upside down, all the cupboards and drawers, and took every letter and every postcard they could find. It was heart-breaking, because Irma and Rosa read those letters again and again, lingering over every sentence. For Irma, it was an added tragedy because it had been *Vater*'s way of guiding her and bringing her up – from his prison cell. The only consolation: some of the more compromising letters were hidden elsewhere, with the comrades. A few days later, the Police called *Mutti* in. They had intercepted a letter from *Vater*, sent from Hanover. From now on, as and when there was a letter, Frau Thälmann could come to the police station to read it, but not take it away. Irma and Rosa were amazed that they went to such lengths. Why? As with so many things under the Nazi regime, there was no logic to it. As for *Vater*, once he heard the letters could only be read in the police station, he said that was it: he wouldn't write any more. It didn't of course include the letters smuggled out from time to time by a Beefsteak prison guard. There was nothing the Gestapo could do about that.

Nor could they stop Thälmann making contact with the world outside. 'There is a real danger that Hitler will force a war against the Soviet Union at any cost, which would be terrible for Germany,' Thälmann wrote to a Communist colleague in August 1938, to be distributed to the Communist cells. 'The war would probably last a long time, and Germany will become a total war zone. If war breaks out, we in Germany have only one possibility to prevent the annihilation and destruction of Germany: the elimination of the war-criminal Hitler by the German Volk.' To Rosa he wrote: 'Courage, my dear Rosa, today more than ever ... in these hours, courage and inner strength are the priceless means to strengthen the human will, and our own strength. That you are blest with such a hopeful courage fills me with joy and lightens my fate.'

Fabian von Schlabrendorff, another determined resister of the Nazi regime, was a practising lawyer by 1938. But his undercover work continued as before. First he'd sought out Ernst Niekisch, the man with the most unexpected contacts, including Russians. Then there was his doctor, Sigismund Lauter, who regularly held 'soirées' in his elegant apartment on the Kurfürstendamm as a cover for resisters, and who'd taken Fabian to meet the former Chancellor of Weimar Germany, Heinrich Brüning, hiding out from the Nazis in a convent in a Berlin back street. Perhaps most important of all, there was Ewald von Kleist-Schmenzin, the man Fabian had admired since his youth when he used to visit the Schmenzin country estate in Pommern, and who'd had to disappear for a while due to his anti-Nazi views, too openly expressed.

It was Fabian who'd found him a hiding place with Ernst Niekisch – a nice touch, since who would think of looking for an old Prussian aristocrat in the house of a proto-Communist? And who would have thought the two men would become such close friends, opposites as they were? But they did, working together to fight the Nazi regime to the last, whatever the cost. In fact it soon cost Niekisch his freedom. Because by 1937 the Nazis no longer had need of him for his liaison work with the Russians concerning their secret rearmament programme. Having won the gamble to take back the Rhineland from French occupation, they were happy to rearm more openly now. So Niekisch was summarily arrested and imprisoned, indefinitely.

In March 1938, Fabian contacted Kleist-Schmenzin again, as a matter of urgency. The Nazis had been planning the *Anschluss*, annexation, of Austria, ever since the early 1920s. Hitler, being Austrian, took it personally. Now he'd summoned Kurt von Schuschnigg, the Austrian Chancellor, to his alpine retreat at Berchtesgaden. Schuschnigg was no fan of the Nazis and their brutal methods, so he could see the way the wind was blowing: threats, not discussion. There were three generals present at the meeting – a clear sign that if he didn't agree to Hitler's demands they'd take Austria by force. Schuschnigg protested. Hitler ranted. Schuschnigg wavered, remembering how the Nazis had assassinated Engelbert Dollfuss, the previous Austrian Chancellor.

Eventually he offered a compromise: they'd hold a plebiscite: the Austrian Volk should decide whether they wanted to remain independent or preferred to unify with Germany. Hitler appeared to agree. But as soon as the plebiscite was announced the Austrian Nazis and their SS went into action, attacking Jews and anti-Nazis, spreading terror, marching through the streets tearing down the Austrian flag and replacing it with their swastika.

Sunday 13 March was the agreed date for the plebiscite. Hitler had no intention of taking part. At dawn on Saturday 12 March, German troops marched across the border into Austria, to 'restore order'. The Gestapo, SS and SD security followed in the Army's wake, arresting 76,000 citizens, including Schuschnigg, and despatched them to Dachau. Of those, 35,000 were eventually executed at Mauthausen, Austria's newly built concentration camp. By 10 April, Hitler was ready to hold the plebiscite, which the Nazis won hands down.

'I believe that it was God's will to send a boy forth from this land to the Reich, to let him grow to manhood, to raise him to be the Führer of the Nation, that he might lead his Homeland into the Reich,' Hitler announced on the wireless that day, broadcast into every school, office, factory floor and public institution. 'There is a higher providence, and we are nothing but its tools.' The next day Jews were made to wipe Schuschnigg's election slogans for Independence off the walls and scrub the pavements, with crowds of Austrian Nazis gathered to watch and jeer for the benefit of the newsreels, orchestrated, as ever,

by Dr Goebbels, to be shown in cinemas throughout the newly formed
Greater German Reich and beyond.

Watching these events closely, Fabian knew that time was running
out. He urgently needed to meet Kleist-Schmenzin, because Fabian
knew he was one of the few men who would not only see the situation
clearly for what it was, but would also be prepared to take action.
'When he walked into a room he always stood out. People listened
when he spoke. He wasn't the kind of man who formed an opinion
after the event, like so many,' wrote Fabian. 'He formed it right then,
at the very beginning, and spoke about it openly and with clarity.'

So, one evening Fabian made his way through the streets of Berlin
to Sigismund Lauter's soirée in the Kurfürstendamm, taking a circui-
tous route and waiting below for some time before going up, to make
sure he wasn't being followed. He reckoned Kleist-Schmenzin would
be there, being a regular along with many other resisters to the Nazi
regime, including Ernst Rowohlt, Rudolf Ditzen's publisher. Kleist-
Schmenzin spent more and more time in Berlin these days. His wife
had recently died of scarlet fever, caught from one of the children. It
was a terrible loss, but it made him even more determined to fight the
Nazi regime.

By 1938, the Nazis were happy to openly unleash their brutality
against any opponent of the regime, large or small. A month before
the *Anschluss*, they'd engineered the public humiliation and resignation of Werner von Fritsch, Commander-in-Chief of the Army. Fritsch
had remained in the severely reduced *Reichswehr* after the Treaty of
Versailles, and was heavily involved in the secret rearmament programme with the Russians during the 1920s. When the Nazis first
came to power he was a keen supporter, disillusioned by the chaos of
Weimar democracy. But as the Nazis and their SS became increasingly
brutal and increasingly powerful, threatening the independence of the
Reichswehr by creating their own parallel military system, he soon
became disillusioned. Fabian, searching for like-minded resisters, had
gone to see him in June 1934. Fritsch agreed privately that Hitler and
his gang were a danger to Germany, but he wasn't prepared to take
decisive action. 'He was a decent enough man,' wrote Fabian later,
'but basically a subaltern who did as he was told.'

Then came the secret Hossbach Conference of 1937 where Hitler
announced his intention to go to war with Russia as soon as the Reich
and *Reichswehr*, now renamed the *Wehrmacht*, were ready – another

two years off. Fritsch was appalled and made little secret of it, nor of his hatred of Heinrich Himmler's SS. The last thing Fritsch and the army generals wanted was war – let alone with Russia. Hitler's solution was to remove those who wouldn't submit, and replace them with others loyal to the Nazi regime. Fritsch, a confirmed bachelor and professional soldier to his fingertips, was accused of homosexuality. Once the *Anschluss* with Austria was effected, he was completely exonerated by an Army Honour Court. But by then it was too late.

'It is absolutely essential for you, as well as everyone in a responsible position, to understand the vital importance of the internal battleground, which in case of war will mean life or death for us,' Himmler told the generals at OKW Army High Command in summer 1937, speaking of the enemy within. 'We must have more concentration camps. At the beginning of the war, mass arrests on an unprecedented scale will be necessary. Many political prisoners will have to be shot out of hand. Utter ruthlessness is essential. Any way in which we neglect the internal battlefield will lead to catastrophe.'

Secret though the Hossbach Conference might have been, news of it soon leaked out, along with Hitler and Himmler's plans for dealing with the 'internal battleground' – all soon up for discussion at Lauter's soirées. Fabian was fully informed and fully involved. Discussing the situation late into the night, they agreed that what they needed was help from outside of Germany. The Nazi terror regime was too powerful for them to act alone. Luckily, one of the regular attendees at Lauter's was the English journalist Ian Colvin, foreign correspondent in Berlin for the *News Chronicle* since 1937.

'You do not believe this is the end, do you?' Kleist-Schmenzin confronted Colvin one evening, referring to the *Anschluss*. 'Hitler has his plans against France, Holland, Belgium, Denmark, Russia, against England and the new world. Mad? Yes, he is mad, but he is in command of his faculties. Now let us think of the situation as it is at present. Czechoslovakia is the next step . . .'

Colvin, remembering that evening, described Kleist-Schmenzin as a conservative landowner from Pomerania, 'a short greying figure with hard eyes and precise gestures', who was knowingly risking his life by speaking to Colvin in such a direct and open way. He told Colvin the resisters needed England to intervene, to say 'no' to Hitler – and mean it. Then, and only then, could the opponents of the Nazi regime attempt a coup d'état. But without England's support they could do nothing.

'One thing I know for certain,' said Kleist-Schmenzin. 'If England says "no", if only through diplomatic channels, the adventure must be put off. Hitler has admitted this, and what he fears *wie die Pest*, like the plague, is that England will caution him. For then he must give way, and that will be a grave blow to his prestige in Germany. Tell your friends in London that we cannot make war yet. The army has few reservists and no reserves of material. The people are against war. The fortifications in the West are not even half completed. The Nazis bluff. Their bluff carries them far, but in the end there is only one possibility, defeat. Do not publish anything I tell you, but let them know in England that the General Staff needs a sheet anchor. The British Government alone can throw it to them by a firmly spoken word.'

He was right about the German people. And it wasn't only war they were against.

'Our general impression is: among the bulk of the people dislike of the regime is steadily growing, and while it will probably not show itself in open opposition, the Nazi Party are conscious that they no longer have the bulk of the people behind them,' reported an English employee of Hambros Bank in Berlin to the Foreign Office in London – one of the many informants contacting the Permanent Secretary Sir Robert Vansittart and his colleagues in that year – churchmen, academics, journalists, army officers, diplomats.

'In Berlin the best opinion is that Hitler has made up his mind for war if it is necessary in order to get back his Sudetens,' wrote William Shirer, the American correspondent, in his diary on 9 September 1938. 'I doubt it for two reasons: first, the German army is not ready; secondly, the people are dead against war. The radio has been saying all day that Great Britain has told Germany she will fight if Czechoslovakia is invaded. Perhaps so. But you cannot forget *The Times* leader of three days ago inviting the Czechs to become a more "homogenous state" by handing the Sudetens over to Germany.'

Facades had to be maintained at all times, a diplomat at the British Consulate reported. 'Nazi skill in the use of terror consists precisely in the fact that, while everyone knows and must know that barbaric terror is applied, they are nevertheless kept in ignorance as to where, when and on whom. An atmosphere of secret horror is thus created.' Christabel Bielenberg, an Englishwoman married to German lawyer Peter Bielenberg and a close friend of Adam von Trott who was active in the 20 July plot, reported how the conversation immediately changed when a stranger arrived at one of their 'wives tea parties', everyone suddenly talking about domestic matters, with no criticism of the Nazi regime. They all knew about Frau Solf who had invited a new friend to one of her social 'events', who turned out to be a Gestapo agent. They were all arrested within days, many of them executed.

Kleist-Schmenzin was already in contact with many other secret resisters. Firstly with diplomats at the German Foreign Office in the Wilhelm Strasse under State Secretary Baron Ernst von Weizsäcker who was in regular secret contact with Vansittart at the Foreign Office in London. Then at the *Abwehr*, the Military Intelligence Department at the Reich War Office under Admiral Wilhelm Canaris, especially its counter-espionage section under General Hans Paul Oster, which was a hotbed of resistance. And also with Ulrich von Hassell, the great diplomat who'd been German Ambassador to Rome till 1938, when he was sacked by Hitler's new Foreign Minister von Ribbentrop, for being politically suspect. Most important of all, Kleist-Schmenzin was in contact with General Ludwig Beck, Chief of General Staff.

Beck, like Fritsch, had first been a supporter of the new Nazi regime, again due to the debilitating and humiliating terms of the Treaty of Versailles and the chaos of the Weimar years which followed. But by 1934 he was becoming disillusioned. Hitler had appointed himself Commander-in-Chief and now required all officers and soldiers to swear an oath of loyalty to himself, the Hitler Oath, so bypassing the traditional power structure of the *Reichswehr*. By 1935, the *Reichswehr* had been replaced by the new *Wehrmacht*, again under Hitler. And by 1938, the *Wehrmacht*, *Kriegsmarine* and *Luftwaffe* all came under the *Oberkommando*, OKW or High Command, sealing Hitler's total control over the German armed forces.

Watching these developments, Beck had secretly begun to build up his own intelligence network, making contact with other resisters, finally convinced that

only a coup d'état could remove Hitler from power. For this, he needed the Army to work with civilian resisters, because a coup could only be successful if there was a fully operating alternative government waiting in the wings, ready to take over. The key figure for that was Carl Goerdeler, an economist by training, the Mayor of Leipzig and Reich Commissioner for Price Control in the early years of the Nazi regime. Time and again, Goerdeler had tried to warn Hitler of the dangers of inflation due to the massive expense of the secret rearmament, pointing out that what the Volk really needed was housing and food. Time and again, he warned about the institutionalised corruption. It fell on deaf ears. He resigned in 1935, keeping only his post as Mayor of Leipzig. Then came the removal of the statue of Mendelsohn in Leipzig by the Nazis, because Mendelsohn was a Jew. Goerdeler had already openly criticised the Nazi boycott of Jewish shops and businesses on 1 April 1933, but the Mendelsohn statue somehow crystallised for Goerdeler, deeply religious and conservative, where he stood. He resigned in March 1937. General Beck resigned a year later. From then on both men were intent on removing Hitler from power. But how?

It was agreed by the Beck/Goerdeler group, as with the Lauter group, that a coup couldn't be successful without intervention by the British, hopefully backed up by the French. A terror regime such as Nazism could not be defeated from within alone – as they'd each found out for themselves over the past five years. It was too powerful, too brutal, and what help was anyone once they were locked up in prison, or in a concentration camp or plain dead? They needed an emissary to go to London. They decided on Ewald von Kleist-Schmenzin.

'A Herr von Kleist' was coming by air to London on 18 August, Sir Nevile Henderson, British Ambassador in Berlin, telegraphed Foreign Secretary of State Viscount Halifax in London on 16 August 1938. He was coming as an emissary of the moderates on the General Staff. His mission: 'to obtain material with which to convince the Chancellor (of Germany) of the strong probability of Great Britain intervening should Germany take violent action against Czechoslovakia.' Sir Nevile understood 'Herr von Kleist' carried introductions to 'leading politicians'. In his view 'it would be unwise for him to be received in official quarters'. Herr von Kleist intended to see Churchill and Lord Lloyd. 'The German War Office approved the purpose of his (secret) visit . . . He should not be rebuffed.'

There had been many telegraphs from Sir Nevile Henderson to Viscount Halifax since July, all about the dangerous developments in the Czechoslovakia situation: Hitler was on the march again, intent on incorporating the Sudetenland region with its large population of ethnic Germans into the Greater German Reich. Henderson's inform-ers 'confirm my opinion that the Germans, apart from a section of extremists, are just as afraid of war as anybody else – or even more so,' he wrote on 26 July. And again on 6 August: 'For what my opinion is worth, the last thing the Germans want is serious trouble, or to be involved in a general war. The German military have not that object at all.' Adding, 'I believe that if we really showed our teeth, Hitler would not dare to make war today . . .' By 8 August, there was more urgency: 'My dear Secretary of State,' he wrote. 'I have written you many letters and I sometimes fear that I repeat myself too much. The omens of the storm are rolling up in Germany . . . I still cling to my belief that Hitler wants a peaceful solution . . .' His was not a strong voice. And Lord Halifax was busy elsewhere.

'The Foreign Secretary said he was very lazy and disliked work,' wrote Lord Halifax's Private Secretary when Halifax first took on the job. 'Could he hunt on Saturdays? I said there was a lot of work, but much of it could be done at home or in the train.' Halifax was Master of the Middleton Hounds and liked to travel up to Yorkshire Friday afternoons. It wasn't easy to get hold of him over the weekend.

Finally Halifax had agreed to write a formal memorandum, to be communicated to His Majesty's Ambassador in Berlin, for transmis-sion to Herr Hitler. It was headed 'Foreign Office 11 August 1938', and after some diplomatic preamble came to the need for interna-tional appeasement and the fact that: 'measures to bring about such an appeasement of the international situation are hindered by the Czechoslovakia question . . . This has been shaken recently by the behaviour of the German press, which, as it seems to us, has been going out of its way to whip up public opinion to a state of dangerous exasperation over every incident occurring either in Czechoslovakia or on the frontier . . . On top of this, and following upon the decision to complete the system of western fortifications in the shortest possible time, comes the news that it is intended to bring an unusual number of formations of the German Army up to war strength . . .'

Viscount Halifax appeared not to understand that the many incidents in the Sudetenland region of Czechoslovakia and on its borders with Germany were whipped up by the Nazis themselves, merely using their press for propaganda purposes. As for Herr Hitler, he didn't even bother to respond.

Ian Colvin wasn't impressed. 'Sir Nevile Henderson was an emotional man. Tall, lean, fastidiously dressed, he had the outward points of a British diplomat but without any inner strength. His staff complained of him that he showed a bullying temper to his subordinates . . . His main theme was that German aims were limited.'

Colvin had admired Henderson's predecessor Sir Eric Phipps, a man of much stronger character, and, unlike Sir Nevile, not at all in favour of appeasement – which was doubtless why Viscount Halifax replaced him, despatching him off to Paris instead. 'Sir Nevile Henderson is a national danger in Berlin,' warned Vansittart in London. But no one listened. Instead, Chamberlain resolved to replace Vansittart as soon as possible with Sir Alexander Cadogan. 'I fear he is writing a paper,' wrote Cadogan about Vansittart in his diary. 'I only hope it won't be another in his usual German-scare style.'

By August, Ian Colvin and his anti-Nazi friends, seeing little hope of any positive action from Great Britain, had taken some action of their own, because they not only knew the Nazis meant to invade Czechoslovakia, they knew the date as well. They'd been given it by General Ludwig Beck. On 16 July, Beck had written a final memo to von Brauchitsch, Commander of the *Wehrmacht* army: 'Forcible military advance by Germany against Czechoslovakia would lead to immediate military intervention against us by France and thereupon also by England, and lead automatically to a European war or World War, and end in general catastrophe for Germany.'

On the same day, he added a second memo: 'Final decisions about the continuity of the Vaterland are at stake here. History will burden these leaders with blood guilt if they fail to act . . . If in such a situation their advice and warnings fail to find a hearing, then they have the right and duty to the Volk and to history to resign from their offices. If they act with a united will, execution of an act of war is impossible. Thereby they will have saved their Vaterland from the worst, from ruin. Exceptional times require exceptional actions. Other upright men in responsible positions of state outside the armed forces will join the military men on their course.' Following his own advice, Beck resigned in August.

His main hope still rested, against all the evidence, with Britain's intervention.

It was decided that Colvin should write a warning report enclosed in a letter to a sympathetic acquaintance in England, Lord Lloyd, to be passed on to Sir Robert Vansittart at the Foreign Office, and thence to Lord Halifax.

'The Abwehr of the War Ministry believes that a war would be disastrous for Germany,' Colvin wrote. 'It has therefore asked a good friend of mine to go to London and see whether he cannot find material to support the theory that Great Britain will intervene (they bother less about France). He is a courageous and upright gentleman although suspect to the Nazis. I think that pains should be taken to supply him with support for his opinions.'

He included the date of the planned invasion of the Sudetenland: 28 September 1938.

The first person Ewald von Kleist-Schmenzin went to see when he arrived in London on 18 August 1938, after dropping off his suitcases at the Park Lane Hotel, was Sir Robert Vansittart. They didn't meet at the Foreign Office but in a private place nearby. Herr von Kleist arrived at 4 o'clock, as Vansittart later wrote in his notes of their conversation – the notes to be passed on to Lord Halifax and thence to Neville Chamberlain. 'Herr von Kleist said I was one of the few people to whom he could speak freely,' he wrote, adding that von Kleist had opened the conversation 'with utmost frankness and gravity,' and that what he said coincided 'with a great deal of information I have (already) given you.'

'Do you mean extreme danger?' Vansittart had asked von Kleist.

'No. I mean complete certainty,' answered von Kleist.

He went on to explain that Hitler alone was the great danger – with plenty of encouragement from Herr von Ribbentrop, the German Ambassador to London, who kept telling him 'when it comes to the showdown neither France nor England will do anything'. Herr von Kleist added that all the Generals in the German Army who were his friends knew it, and they *alone* knew it for a certainty. And they knew the date.

'Do you mean *all* the Generals?' Vansittart found that hard to believe.

'Yes. They are all dead against the war, but they will not have the power to stop it unless they get encouragement and help from outside.'

'What is the date?'

'Why, of course you know it!' von Kleist had laughed. 'Anyhow, your Prime Minister knows it.' The Nazis would wait till after the Nuremberg Party Day, he said. 'After 27 September it will be too late.'

Von Kleist said there were two means of stopping it: first to convince Hitler that the British Government wasn't bluffing. Second, 'a very great part of the country is sick of the present regime, and even a part that is not sick of it is terribly alarmed at the prospect of war . . . I wish that one of your leading statesmen would make a speech which would appeal to this element in Germany, emphasising the horrors of war and the inevitable general catastrophe to which it would lead.'

Vansittart ended his notes with: 'Herr von Kleist is seeing Mr Winston Churchill tomorrow. He does not wish to have any contact with people influential in the press. He says if Hitler carries the day and plunges the country into war, he will anyhow be one of the first to be killed, and he has anyhow come out of the country with a rope round his neck to stake his last chance of life on preventing the adventure . . . He said he had come over here to give the warning that we were no longer in danger of war but in the presence of the certainty of it, and to risk his own existence in doing so. He added there was no prospect whatever of a reasonable policy being followed in Germany so long as Hitler was at the head of affairs, but if war was avoided, it would be the prelude to the end of the regime and a nascence of a Germany with whom we could deal. Von Kleist added that it was his friends in the Army who had facilitated his coming to London.' Herr von Kleist was returning to Germany on Tuesday.

The next day Ewald von Kleist-Schmenzin travelled down to Chartwell for a secret meeting with Winston Churchill. He got straight to the point as usual: an attack on Czechoslovakia would happen after the Nazi Nuremberg Party Congress and before the end of September. Nobody in Germany wanted war except Hitler. But among the

Generals 'there was extreme dread of facing Hitler personally on account of his fury and his power'.

Churchill assured von Kleist that the British public would fight, but only if necessary, and stressed that those who thought as he did were 'anti-Nazi and anti-war, not anti-German.'

Some gesture was necessary, said von Kleist. Everything possible had to be done to encourage the Generals, who were the only ones who could stop the war. There could be a new government in place within 48 hours. Churchill expressed himself prepared to give 'cordial support to strengthen a peaceful regime'. He agreed to write a letter which Kleist-Schmenzin could show the Generals.

The letter was dated 19 August 1938. 'My dear Sir,' Churchill began. 'I have welcomed you here as one who is ready to run risks to preserve the peace of Europe.' He was sure that if the Nazis crossed the frontier with Czechoslovakia it would mean a renewal of war. 'Such a war, once started, would be fought out like the last, to the bitter end, and one must consider not what might happen in the first few months, but where we would all be at the end of the third or fourth year.' The British would be weaker at first, but not for long.

'As I feel you should have a definite message to take to your friends in Germany who wish to see peace preserved and who look forward to a great Europe in which England, France and Germany will be working together for the prosperity of the wage-earning masses, I have communicated with Lord Halifax . . .' He ended by expressing his wish for a peaceful and friendly solution and 'true reunion of our two countries'. He posted the letter, using the diplomatic bag, to Kleist-Schmenzin c/o the British Embassy in Berlin.

On the same day, 19 August, Neville Chamberlain wrote to Lord Halifax, having heard from Lord Lloyd and Lord Hutchinson of Montrose, another friend of the resisters, about Kleist-Schmenzin's visit. 'I take it von Kleist is violently anti-Hitler and is extremely anxious to stir up his friends in Germany to make an attempt at its overthrow.' It reminded him of the (failed) Jacobite rebellion, he wrote, and he felt they should 'discount a good deal of what he says'. However, it did leave him feeling 'uneasy'. Should they call for Henderson and then make some warning gesture regarding Czechoslovakia? They could meet and decide on 29 August.

'Let me know what you think, Yours ever, N. Chamberlain.'

A few days later, Fabian von Schlabrendorff was called to the British

Embassy in Berlin to collect the letter, addressed to Kleist-Schmenzin, and keep it safe till he arrived back in Berlin. After his visit to London, Kleist-Schmenzin had returned to his estate in Pommern, and Sir Neville thought it unwise to post the letter on to him, knowing the dangers of the Nazi postal system. Fabian personally handed the letter to Kleist-Schmenzin some days later when he came to Berlin. Kleist-Schmenzin took the letter to Admiral Canaris at the *Abwehr* and to Herr von Weizsäcker at the Foreign Ministry in the Wilhelm Strasse. By 6 September, an extract of the letter was circulated to a chosen few. Kleist-Schmenzin, realist to the last, didn't hold out much hope. But the Generals were encouraged, and attended a secret meeting organised by General Hans Oster of the *Abwehr* to discuss the details of the coup d'état and the new government to follow.

Hans Oster was a man of many parts. He was known as the most elegant officer in Berlin, slim, athletic in build, with clever, clear blue eyes. He was a great horseman, much admired for the way he sat on a horse, and could be seen riding out every day in the Tiergarten. Unlike many of his fellow officers, when he went out and about in society he dressed in civilian clothes, not in uniform. On those occasions he was full of lively conversation, but when it came to politics he became extremely discreet. Behind his desk in his office at the *Abwehr* hung a motto: An eagle doesn't catch flies. People could make of that what they would, but Fabian Schlabrendorff, who came to know him well, understood that it described Oster himself, who had absolutely no time for small, unimportant matters, like flies. He used his whole cleverness and skill, every day, to fight the Nazi regime and he was soon the leader of the resisters in the *Abwehr* and beyond. His Chief, Wilhelm Canaris, knew what he was up to and supported it, but was rarely prepared to come out in the open, knowing that he was only of use if he stayed alive. He'd been quietly opposing the Nazi regime since 1934, making contact with other early resisters once it became clear how matters really stood, but he was careful not to put his head above the parapet. Except when helping those fleeing the regime, including Jews, to escape across the Swiss border where the *Abwehr* had several useful contacts.

After Kleist-Schmenzin's trip to London and the meeting Hans Oster organised as a result, nothing more of any significance transpired from London. Until 29 September, when Neville Chamberlain flew to Germany to sign the Munich Agreement, along with Eduard

Deladier, the French Prime Minister, recognising Germany's right to annex the Sudetenland, provided Hitler agreed not to invade the rest of Czechoslovakia, and not provoke a war with Great Britain and France. Hitler happily agreed. Chamberlain returned to London waving his piece of paper, 'Peace for our Time', for the benefit of the waiting press.

'A total and unmitigated defeat,' stormed Churchill. 'This is only the beginning of the reckoning. This is only the first sip, the first fore-taste of a bitter cup which will be proffered to us year by year unless, by a supreme recovery of moral health and martial vigour, we arise again and take our stand for freedom as in the olden time.'

Not long after the Munich Agreement was signed, Churchill made a broadcast to America. 'If the risks of war which were run by France and Britain at the last moment had been boldly faced in good time, and plain declaration made, how different would our prospects be today,' he warned. 'This would have been an opportunity for all peace-loving and moderate forces in Germany, together with the Chiefs of the German Army, to make a great effort to re-establish something like sane and civilised conditions in their country . . . A whole population of a great country – amiable, good-hearted, peace-loving people – [has been] gripped by the neck and by the hair by a tyrant bent on war.'

Hitler couldn't believe his luck. He had gambled again, bluffed again and got away with it again. It was incredible really that the British put their faith in a mere signature. What was a signature after all? By 1 October, German troops were crossing the border into the Sudetenland, closely followed by the SS and the SA to mop up any troublemakers.

'International atmosphere stormy,' wrote the former diplomat Ulrich von Hassell on a train from Berlin to Weimar as his first entry in a secret diary which he decided to keep to record events as they unfolded, now that the die was cast. 'At home there is growing despondency under the weight of Party rule and fear of war. Hitler's speeches are all demagogic, delivered in ranting tones.'

By October, back at his desk in his study in his house at Ebenhausen near Munich, he noted: 'Rintelen (military attaché) said Hitler was very angry with the generals who had, all too impudently, expressed their views on our inability to wage a world war. He is demanding their dismissal.' Then, in November, another horror: 'I am writing under the crushing emotions evoked by the vile persecution of the

Jews after the murder of von Rath . . . Goebbels has seldom won so little credence for any assertion as when he said that a spontaneous outbreak of anger among the people had caused the outrages and that they were stopped after a few hours . . . As a matter of a fact there is no doubt that we are dealing with an officially organised anti-Jewish riot which broke out at the same hour of the night all over Germany! Truly a disgrace!'

The first Bernt Engelmann knew of Kristallnacht on 9 November 1938 was the sound of broken glass and the splintering of wood from downstairs in his apartment block in his suburban district of Düsseldorf. He'd stayed up late to listen to the 11 o'clock news on the BBC, turned down low so none of their neighbours could hear and denounce him.

His mother had gone to bed. His father was away somewhere on business. Bernt turned off the wireless set and went out onto the landing to look down the stairwell. A group of Hitler Youths led by two SA men were trashing the ground floor apartment belonging to a family of Jews. A young girl was in the hall screaming. Her parents were out apparently. Bernt's mother, appearing on the stairs in her dressing gown, took the girl upstairs and told Bernt to go and intercept the parents. She tried to ring Fräulein Bonse, the local woman who'd helped so many Jewish children escape from Düsseldorf, putting them on the train to England. But there was no answer. Bernt raced into the street and found the parents barely a block away, hurrying home. 'Don't go to your apartment,' he warned them. The woman was screaming that she had to go to their daughter. 'She's safe with us,' Bernt told her. But where to take the parents? Did they know anyone?

'Only the friends we've just been visiting,' said the husband.

'Are they Aryans?' Bernt found himself asking.

They were. Together they raced back to the friends' apartment and rang the bell. The friends took them in without a word.

On the way back home, Bernt passed several other scenes of destruction. He could hardly believe what he was seeing. In Fischer Strasse, a crowd was gathered outside the large house on the corner. There was broken glass everywhere and noise and screaming. Then a shot. Then a body fell out of an upper window and landed with a thud on the pavement. It was Dr Lichtenstein. 'Those damn thugs!' said a man in the crowd, and no one disagreed.

Back in his own apartment he told his mother what he'd seen, in hushed tones so as not to distress the young girl. 'Your parents are safe with their friends,' he assured her. Then he went down into the hall where he kept his bicycle. 'Be careful,' warned his mother. But Bernt wanted to go to the centre of town to see for himself what was happening.

There he found all the Jewish stores had been smashed and plundered – the streets full of scattered merchandise: fur coats, shoes, china, pieces of furniture. Everywhere there were people struggling with suitcases, whether they were fleeing Jews or plunderers was hard to tell. In the distance, he could see the Kasernen Strasse synagogue in flames. In Stern Strasse, he came across a mother and child cowering in a dark doorway. He offered to help them, but the woman was rigid with fear.

'Do you have a place to stay?'

'No more.'

They weren't far from Herr Desch's tailor's shop, and Bernt knew Herr and Frau Desch lived in the apartment above. Perhaps they could take them in, at least for the night. All the way there he had to reassure the woman that she would be safe as long as she went with him, though he had no idea if it was true or not. He found the block and rang the bell. It was 2am, but he heard Herr Desch's cautious voice on the other side of the door.

'*Wer is das?* Who is it?'

When he opened the door, Bernt saw Herr Desch was fully dressed. He merely nodded and took them in, locking the door behind them, then led them into his workroom. There were people everywhere, lying and sitting, and not a murmur.

'It's a bit crowded in here,' said Herr Desch, 'but the back room is better. There's milk and hot tea in the kitchen. My wife and Fräulein Bonse are upstairs with the injured. The doctor's here.'

The British Consul in Frankfurt reported back to the Foreign Office in London that the Nazi Party was out of touch with the majority of the German people: 'The action against the Jews has aroused passionate resentment and compassion not only among members of the Christian churches, in the army, and the civil service, but (among) all classes of society; it may even bring about a split in the Party itself.'

If the Engelmann family needed a final warning, Kristallnacht was it. The Nazis' Nuremberg Racial Laws of 15 September 1935 had already alerted them to the dangers: Herr Engelmann's family on his father's side was Jewish. There were two Nuremberg Laws, the first

'For the Protection of German Blood and German Honour' forbidding marriage or sexual relations between Germans and Jews, the second 'The Reich Citizen Law' stating that only pure Germans could have Reich citizenship, the rest to be state subjects with no citizens' rights. Herr Engelmann's Jewish grandparents on one side of the family were enough to put him in danger of both.

Bernt was 19 by now and had left school the previous year. His father's import/export firm did a lot of business with England. During the next few days, father, mother and son sat round their dining table to discuss what could be done, and swiftly came to the decision to emigrate. To England. Herr Engelmann would go ahead, find somewhere to live, set himself up in business with the help of friends, and Bernt and his mother would follow later. Meanwhile Bernt (right), recently back from the obligatory months of Reich Labour Service on a farm, decided to volunteer for the Luftwaffe.

'Are you mad?' asked his friend Kulle.

'Hardly a matter of choice, is it?'

Since 1935 all young men in Nazi Germany had to do a year's military service.

'We can either wait to be conscripted, or volunteer early. I'm volunteering. That way I'll have some say in where I'm sent and in what section.'

'But don't you realise war is coming?'

'Yes. But not yet.'

Kulle couldn't believe what he was hearing. Bernt would soon be able to emigrate – unlike himself who didn't have the means.

In fact, Bernt had another reason as well: it would be easier for *Vater* to get the necessary emigration papers if his son showed himself to be a keen volunteer.

Bernt's friend Werner was having a bad time. His father, the Vice President of Police in Berlin, had been arrested at Easter 1935. Two Gestapo men in leather coats and armed with pistols had arrived early one morning and turned the two-roomed apartment in their back courtyard block upside down looking for evidence. They found nothing. All his *Vater*'s papers and pamphlets were wrapped in wax paper, as instructed by the local Communist cell, and hidden under a wood pile in the garden. But his father was arrested anyway. He was sentenced by the *Volksgericht*, People's Court, to two years in the local Fehlsbuttel concentration camp for 'conspiracy to commit treason'.

Werner, as a result, lost his apprenticeship for 'political unreliability' because he was his father's son. His *Vater* had always had a good job with the Reich railways at the freight depot, but now there was no money coming in to feed the family of five. The tiny sum they received from the Welfare Bureau didn't even cover the rent. His mother took a cleaning job and Werner delivered newspapers until he eventually found another apprenticeship with a printer. On the surface it was a model Nazi business, but there were no Nazis, only Social Democrats and ex-union members. The printing trade had always been a special case, employing skilled workers, unionised and politically aware. Werner's *Meister*, boss, gave him a day off every six weeks to visit his father. The visit lasted twenty minutes and left them both desolate. His father was released that year, 1938, but he returned home a broken man, his hair completely white.

By December 1938 Bernt was stationed at his garrison town in Westphalia, undergoing wireless communication training with the Luftwaffe. His father was in England trying to make a new life for his family. His mother, still in Düsseldorf, was continuing with her small acts of resistance, helping Tante Ney and Fräulein Bonse.

Time passed quickly during training. Bernt found he enjoyed learning about wireless communication. He even enjoyed aspects of military life – the healthy outdoors, the comradeship. The only thing he had to be careful of was choosing who to talk to about the way things really stood in Nazi Germany. But that wasn't too difficult. A few quiet remarks, a nod, a glance, and that was usually enough. You could spot the real Nazis, the former stars of the Hitler Youth, a mile off.

In July 1939, Bernt had two weeks' leave. After he'd spent time with his mother and various relations he went to see Tante Ney at the bakery. She greeted him like a long-lost son and treated him to a slice of her husband's special *Schwarzwalder* cake, though how Herr Ney laid hands on the ingredients Bernt couldn't imagine – probably an old customer of Frau Ney's, now in a position of some power in the local Nazi hierarchy. Tante Ney was still active in her resistance to the Nazi regime, still undetected, though she had to be more and more careful these days. Then he went to see Herr Desch. Bernt found him in his workroom, tailoring another fine SS uniform, pins in mouth, white chalk to hand. Fish-face, as Bernt used to privately call him, actually smiled when he saw him.

'What you need, *Junge*, young man, is a dress uniform,' said Herr Desch.

'A dress uniform?'

A mannekin in the shop window was wearing one – dark blue, very smart, very expensive. But why did Bernt need one? Only the keenest recruits, former Hitler Youths, ever bothered to have one of those.

'Exactly,' said Herr Desch. He was already measuring Bernt up. 'Wireless communication is it?' he asked.

Bernt explained a bit about it, and why he'd volunteered.

'Very sensible,' agreed Herr Desch. 'And how fortuitous. You must go and visit Fräulein Bonse. She has acquired a short-wave transmitter, but she doesn't know how to operate it. You can teach her.'

'However did she get it?'

Herr Desch just smiled.

Fräulein Bonse turned out to be a natural – very quick to learn Morse code, and quick to work out a simple code, based, as they decided, on a Heine poem. Fräulein Bonse's English school exchanges had been stopped by the authorities now, so she needed another route out of Nazi Germany for her charges. Düsseldorf was only 30 kilometres from the Dutch border. There was a fine villa on the German side belonging to a wealthy couple, fervent anti-Nazis, which she used as a safe house. A Catholic priest, Pfarrer Vincent, accompanied the children across the border and into the hands of Dutch friends and accomplices, usually at night. But it all needed careful co-ordination – hence the need for a wireless set.

When Bernt met up with his old friend Kulle, he told him he was brushing up his English during his free time at the army garrison, because once his military service was finished, in the coming December, he meant to go to England to study.

Kulle wasn't optimistic. 'If you're lucky,' he said. 'I can almost smell war in the air.'

Kulle was right. By September, Germany was at war and Bernt Engelmann was in the Luftwaffe.

CHAPTER EIGHT

THE ROAD TO WAR: 1939

Fritz-Dietlof von der Schulenburg was opaque – to all but his closest friends.

'Fritzi had many friends, one might almost say, disciples. But not all of them understood him,' said one of the close friends later. 'To most of them he appeared extremely complicated and opaque. There were some who thought he wasn't up to much: first he was one of those students who belonged to a duelling fraternity, then he was "the Red Count", then he was the Nazi, then he was the anti-Nazi. His supporters called him "the eternal rebel". Who was the real Fritzi? I think I knew him well enough to say, yes, he was a rebel. But he wasn't that because he was a stubborn man, destructive or inconsequent, but because, through his unusually sharp and creative understanding, he always followed his instinct, always held the line. This line was old-Prussian, in Fritzi's own way, having nothing to do with Imperialism or Junkerdom. It was something he was completely conscious of, to the extent he even gave lectures on it from time to time.'

Other close friends agreed: Fritzi only opened up in intimate circles, but then he debated his ideas with passion. 'He never posed, but he did increasingly wear a mask, due to the times we lived in. Sometimes he played the world-weary aristocrat, the arrogant man – and in fact he could be drily sarcastic as well as humorous. He hated opportunists. But he was never reactionary, always modern and forward-looking. He was a good listener and a great talker: Socialism, religion, poetry, modern town-planning, the need for human rights, all spoken with a certain irony and self-mockery. But he was deadly earnest underneath. It was strange, the power he held over people, the charisma. Because, strictly speaking, he wasn't a handsome man, with his balding head, sticking-out ears, large, crooked nose, energetic chin, the scar, and the pale, clever eyes, constantly changing in expression.'

And often the monocle. And his careless dress. 'I look like a country priest, don't I?' he'd say, laughing at himself.

By 1939, Fritzi had been in his new post of Vice President of Police in Berlin for eighteen months. His former Chief, the corrupt *Gauleiter* of East Prussia, Erich Koch, who'd worked tirelessly to get him transferred, had expected the stuck-up, high-minded Schulenburg to be sidelined as a lowly *Referent* in some community even more isolated than Fischhausen had been. Instead, he'd been promoted. It was beyond belief, thought Koch, and really made you wonder what was going on. Where was loyalty to the Führer? Where the commitment to the Nazi regime? Koch thought he knew the answer: all those friends in high places, those patronising Prussians, that's what rescued Graf von der Schulenburg. But just wait. They'd catch up with him sooner or later.

Koch was right: it was two old friends, Hellmuth von Wedelstadt and Klaus von der Groeben, both working in the Ministry of the Interior, both secret anti-Nazis, who made sure Fritzi got the job. The Secretary of State, Wilhelm Stuckart, was easily persuaded. He still referred to Schulenburg's 1933 memorandum 'Reform of the Bureaucracy' as one of the great expositions. And Fritzi's boss, Graf von Helldorf Paroli, had soon been eating out of his hand, in spite of their differences, the one a notorious high-liver engaging in endless love affairs, the other a Prussian aesthete, happily married with their fourth child on the way. Fritzi's only problem had been leaving the people of Fischhausen, the hardest thing he'd ever had to do as he confided to his wife Charlotte, because he loved them and they loved him. But there was work to do in Berlin, and not all of it official.

Originally Fritzi's disillusionment with the Nazi regime had concentrated on individuals like Koch. But he was increasingly aware that it wasn't just the individuals who were brutal and corrupt, it was the whole system. At first he was minded to fight it from within, working for good against evil by example, as he had in Fischhausen. As late as March 1938, he was still trying, giving a lecture entitled 'The Prussian Inheritance and National Socialism' in which he argued, not for the first time, that the two should not be seen as mutually exclusive. He warned that a well-run state was ruled by respecting its people, with proper responsibility, and not by force. Everyone was equal before the Law. 'No one today can claim that the state is the lean and strong shape which the Volk need in their fight for life,' he ended. 'No! The big tasks still stand before us.'

Hitler wasn't interested in Fritzi's 'big tasks'. As far as he was concerned the Civil Service was nothing but an irritation and a hindrance to his grand plans. He despised bureaucrats. The future administrators of the Greater German Reich wouldn't be 'dry nit-picking pen-pushers' but men who could 'hold a pistol loose and at the ready.' Pistols had always to be at the ready. As Hitler put it in one of his private 'table talks' in 1932: 'We are obliged to depopulate, as part of our mission of preserving the German Volk. We shall have to develop a technique of depopulation. If you ask me what I mean by depopulation, I mean the removal of entire racial units. And that is what I intend to carry out – that, roughly, is my task. Nature is cruel, therefore, we too, may be cruel. If I can send the flower of the German nation into the hell of war without the smallest pity for the spilling of precious German blood, then surely I have the right to remove millions of an inferior race that breeds like vermin!'

Fritzi stepped up his criticisms at a session of the Reich Price Commission in Stuttgart. 'We are not living under normal circumstances but at a time when powerful forces oppose one another and have to be challenged,' he said. 'This can't happen without showing strength not weakness. It requires, from each and every one of us, courage and a sense of responsibility, not cowardice and ducking under the parapet. When someone criticises you, fight back! When someone tries to undermine you, speak up!'

But was it enough? The Fritsch affair had shaken Fritzi almost as much as the early cold-blooded murder of Gregor Strasser, his mentor within the NSDAP. He knew that General Ludwig Beck, a family friend, had resigned and was quietly making contact with other resisters, planning a coup d'état. Beck was seeking out civilian as well as military resisters, because there was no point orchestrating a coup without having an alternative government ready in the wings, fully prepared to take over. Beck was working with Carl Goerdeler, the former mayor of Leipzig, pulling strings wherever they could, manoeuvring Nazi resisters into key positions. The main stumbling block, as far as Beck and Goerdeler were concerned, was the lack of support from England, because without their intervention the Nazi regime was too brutal and powerful to overthrow. Fritzi, finally accepting that there was no hope of the regime following the Prussian example of responsible government, went to see General von Witzleben, another secret anti-Nazi and the man chosen to be the Commander in Chief of the *Wehrmacht* in a new post-Nazi Germany. Privately, he let Witzleben know that, in the event of an intervention by the Army, the Berlin Police would be at their service.

In March, Hitler took the rest of Czechoslovakia with hardly a murmur of protest from England or France. 'The radio reports Slovakia has declared its "Independence". There goes the remains of Czechoslovakia,' wrote William Shirer in his diary on 14 March. And on the next day: 'The German army has occupied Bohemia and Moravia, and Hitler, in a cheap theatrical gesture from the Hradshin Castle in Prague, has proclaimed their annexation to the Third Reich. It is almost banal to record his breaking another solemn treaty. But since I was personally present at Munich, I cannot help recalling how Chamberlain said it not only had saved the peace but had really saved Czechoslovakia.' And ten days later: 'Madrid surrendered yesterday, the rest of Republican Spain today. Franco's butchery will be terrible.' Franco and Hitler hand in brutal hand together.

Finally, on 31 March, Chamberlain stood up in the House of Commons to announce a complete change in British foreign policy: Britain would go to the aid of Poland if Polish independence were threatened. Hitler took the opportunity to rant and to threaten. 'Just as Hitler began his broadcast,' Shirer wrote, 'an order came through from the RRG control room where I was standing by, to stop the broadcast from getting abroad. I protested vehemently to the Germans about cutting us off once Hitler had begun to speak. But orders were explicit. They came from Hitler himself, just before he started speaking. The speech was also not being broadcast directly in Germany, but only from recordings later. You can always edit recordings.' All he wanted was peace, was Hitler's line.

On 19 May 1939, Fritzi's father, Graf von der Schulenburg, died. He was still a member of the SS, so Hitler insisted on a state funeral to take place in Potsdam, with full military honours. Hitler, Himmler and all the top brass Nazis attended, making a great show of it, with the Führer walking solemnly behind the coffin, and Brauchitsch, the Army Commander in Chief, giving the funeral oration. Afterwards Hitler personally offered his condolences to members of the Schulenburg family, shaking each by the hand, Fritzi included. Caught on camera, Fritzi is standing smartly to attention, wearing his army reservist's uniform. Who knows what he was thinking? His mask was fully in place by then. There was really no telling whether he was a Nazi or an anti-Nazi. Except that, for the burial at Tressow, he refused to fit in with Himmler's plans, insisting on a traditional religious ceremony at the graveside, against all Nazi objections to Christian rituals. It meant taking on his brothers, but Fritzi, the great card player, brought out his winning ace: the Christian burial had been *Vater*'s own wish, on his deathbed and spoken to Fritzi alone. He made a point of bringing the Army pastor with him from Potsdam to conduct the service, just in case. In the presence of hundreds of mourners, the grand and the humble alike, the pastor blessed the coffin, and then the Army Music Corps played the traditional hymn, *Ich bete an die Macht der Liebe, die sich in Jesus offenbart*, 'I pray to the Power of Love, which is Embodied in Jesus', as the coffin was lowered into the ground. Fritzi chose it in spite of Hitler and Himmler, who strongly disapproved and no doubt took note.

Tisa, the awkward Schulenburg sister, wasn't present at the state funeral, only at the private burial at Tressow. She'd flown over from London, her first time back in Germany since 1934. Even when brother Wilhelm died in 1936 she'd only come as far as Denmark to briefly meet and console her mother. If she had gone on to Germany the Nazis might have arrested her, because she was married to a Jew, Fritz Hess – which is why they'd left Germany in the first place. After the Nuremberg Laws, the only way Tisa could live in Germany was if she divorced her husband. That was highly ironic because, as it happened, Tisa was getting a divorce anyway. The marriage wasn't working – perhaps it never really had. She knew it was her fault. Fritz Hess did everything to try and make her happy. But she felt trapped. She didn't know why. In London she started psychoanalysis, encouraged by their friends the Freuds, but nothing seemed to help. The only time she was really happy was when she was up in Durham with the workers at the Settlement, helping those living in desperate poverty – the miners, the unemployed, the women trying to feed their starving families. Then came news from Germany of Kristallnacht. Fritz Hess managed to get his parents out of the Reich to London, but not his sister and her husband who both later perished in the Holocaust.

And there was Tisa, living in relative ease in England, miserable. And hating herself for it. Until one day a letter arrived from her mother saying that *Vater* was seriously ill – dying in fact. 'When are you coming home?' *Mama* wrote. At first Tisa didn't know what to do. She was crying, driving her car, a spoilt woman in a fur coat as she herself described it, crying like a child, missing home, missing Tressow. Her divorce had just come through. But go home? To a family who were all Nazis? How could she? She had her own small house in Suffolk now, not far from their cottage at Walberswick, and she had many good friends, all asking 'Will there be war?' as though she might know. *Gott im Himmel!* In February 1939, she went alone on a holiday to the Cornish coast, walking the high cliffs in wild isolation, trying to work things out. Finally she steeled herself and applied for a passport. By Easter, she was back in Germany, in the sanatorium, sitting at her father's bedside.

She stayed in the local Gasthof, astonished to find herself back in Germany, eating the same *Bratwurst* sausages, drinking the same Pilsner beer, hearing the same, dear old language, and the same dear old tunes, played um-pa-pa style by a small dance band. And having the same fierce rows with her brothers. Her father was on morphine now, but it didn't stop him dominating the conversation, alert as always: 'What's the man with the umbrella doing?' he asked, meaning Chamberlain. How should she know? 'What's going to happen?' he added. 'Won't all the harm we've done to the Jews come back to revenge us?' He was never anti-semitic, her *Vater*.

Life is a terrible mix, thought Tisa, sitting at *Vater*'s bedside, gazing out of the window. May was such a beautiful month – the wheat fields green, the fruit trees pink with blossom, the dark forests pierced by sharp sunlight, the farmsteads busy with milking cows and children playing and dogs barking. *Heimat*, home. It transpired Himmler was paying the fees at the sanatorium for SS *Obergruppenführer* Schulenburg. And for two SS personal carers as well. It made Tisa sick. Like it made her sick to watch her brothers in their black uniforms strutting about with pride at such an honour.

Yet in the midst of the anger and the shame came a moment of pure joy: Fritzi arrived from Berlin to stay in the same Gasthof as Tisa. It was the first time brother and sister had been together since the day she left Germany for England. Then he'd been a Nazi – not like his brothers but a Nazi nevertheless – dazzled by Gregor Strasser's so-called Socialism. But now, sitting in the darkened empty dining room of the Gasthof late at night, he told her he was part of the Opposition to the Nazis and had been for some time. She could hardly believe it. But she knew that once committed Fritzi would make no compromises. She almost cried for joy and relief. He was her Fritzi after all. She had him back. After all these years, she had her childhood friend and partner back. 'All the distance between us fell away,' she wrote in her memoir. 'We were tied together, as we were as children.'

'The only solution may be to assassinate Hitler,' said Fritzi. 'A coup d'état is not enough. Go back to England. I'm not alone in the plot. Soon everything will change here. Then you can come back to Germany again, in safety.' He'd always had a fanatical side, thought Tisa – once embarked on something, he never gave up.

'Don't breathe a word. Or we both lose our lives,' he warned. He didn't need to say it, Tisa already knew.

General Beck, *Vater*'s old friend, was staying at the same Gasthof. He and Fritzi had their secret night-time conversations, alone. Tisa went to bed and never said a word.

'Come and visit us in Berlin after the funeral,' Fritzi said.

The next day Tisa was sitting alone at *Vater*'s bedside. Night was falling when he suddenly woke with a moment of clarity.

'Why did you divorce Hess?' he asked, out of the blue. 'He was such a good man.' Tisa was so shocked she didn't know what to say.

'That one of my children is a leftie doesn't matter to me. But you have to make peace with your brothers. Politics isn't important to me anymore.' Tisa asked his blessing and that he forgive her. He died that night.

After the burial, she went to visit Fritzi and Charlotte in Berlin. They were living in a small house on the edge of the Grunewald forest, with only one maid, Klara, to help out. They had three children now, the last a baby boy called Fritz; Charlotte was pregnant with their fourth. They were still deeply in love, as Tisa saw at once. She recognised it with a sharp pang: this could never be for her.

The next day Wolfi arrived. It was awkward, but Tisa did her best to fulfil *Vater*'s last wish and keep the peace – until the matter of the will was discussed. Then all was lost. The brothers had decided to divide the inheritance equally among the four remaining siblings, making no distinction because Tisa was a girl.

'But you have to sign, here,' said Wolfi, pushing a document across the dining table to Tisa, 'swearing your loyalty to Hitler.'

Tisa flatly refused. She was beside herself. 'In that case I don't want the money!'

Wolfi was exasperated. 'Why *im Gottes Willen* not? Typical!'

'Don't you know, Wolfi: these are the methods of the concentration camps! Sign here and we'll let you out, they say. Don't sign, and you stay in.'

Wolfi turned to Fritzi for support. Fritzi agreed wholeheartedly with Wolfi. Tisa left the next day for England.

By August, Fritzi had been 'transferred' from his job as Vice President of Police in Berlin to Breslau in Silesia, on the border with Poland. Someone somewhere no longer trusted Schulenburg. His new post was as the representative of Joseph Wagner, the *Ober President*. Perhaps he should have felt thwarted. Instead he was elated. 'Flew over my region of Silesia in brightest sunshine,' he wrote to Charlotte, who remained in Berlin for the time being. 'In the afternoon I was installed by Wagner who listed the responsibilities of my new position as Vice-Oberpresident, which pleased me. Then he spoke about the necessary harmony between the Party and the state. In the evening there was a buffet with beer. All in all, a very comradely atmosphere with no unpleasantries. All the officials say that Silesia is a place where they can serve freely, without too much interference. I think, in spite of our difficult times, things will go well here.' Politics or no politics, Fritzi was back where he belonged.

Back in Berlin, General Beck and Carl Goerdeler were still trying to find ways to persuade the British, at this late hour, to intervene and help them crush Hitler and the Nazis. Even the threat of war seemed not to influence Chamberlain and the appeasers in his government. After his return from England in September 1938, Kleist-Schmenzin had been cast down. He held no false hopes and sank into despair. All he could see ahead was catastrophe. Beck and Goerdeler decided to send another emissary. But who?

A suggestion came from Ian Colvin, the English journalist. Colvin had been the liaison for Kleist-Schmenzin to go to London and he was shocked at how despondent the man was on his return. He realised the appeasers in the British government had done their usual diplomatic trick of sounding sympathetic, promising to look into the matter, and then doing nothing. He thought it a terrible mistake. And he was appalled that Chamberlain and his clique seemed oblivious to the fact that Kleist-Schmenzin and many others – churchmen, academics, businessmen – had risked their lives making the trip to England. As far as Colvin could tell, only Churchill and Vansittart at the Foreign Office had taken Kleist-Schmenzin at his word. But by now Vansittart had been moved sideways, replaced by Cadogan, one of Chamberlain's men. Just as Ambassador Phipps in Berlin had been replaced by Henderson. 'He sends minutes to the Secretary of State, snarling at some of Sir Nicholas Henderson's telegrams, which Halifax gloomily hands back to me,' wrote Cadogan in his diary about Vansittart. 'I keep them for two or three days and then send them back to Halifax saying, "I'm very stupid. I can't remember what you told me to do about this." He looks unutterably sad and says, "I think we might burn it now."'

One evening Colvin and Kleist-Schmenzin met in the Casino Gesellschaft Club, the oldest in Berlin, in Bendler Strasse, right opposite the Reich War Ministry. A whole section of senior civil servants, bankers, retired army officers, nobility, lawyers and businessmen used to meet there. Most were anti-Nazis, many of them Beefsteaks of necessity. They took care in conversation, but on the whole they could talk freely there. Colvin and Kleist-Schmenzin found themselves a table in a far corner of the main *Saal*. Colvin had heard Beck was searching for another emissary to London. He had an idea: what did Kleist-Schmenzin think of Fabian von Schlabrendorff?

Kleist-Schmenzin had known Fabian since he was a schoolboy visiting his country estate in Pommern. He knew he was a committed anti-Nazi, active in the Opposition since the very beginning. But he was young. Was he experienced enough? Colvin thought Fabian was committed enough and serious enough for a man twice his age, and suggested Kleist-Schmenzin put him forward when he next had a meeting with General Beck.

By mid-June 1939, Fabian was sitting in the elegant drawing room of Lord Lloyd's house in London. Fabian was recently married and he'd brought his wife, Luitgarde, with him, partly for cover, partly for the fun. There was no point talking to Chamberlain, Lord Lloyd said. Go straight to Churchill. The next morning Fabian and Luitgarde made their way by trolley bus to Charing Cross Station, a young couple on a sight-seeing trip to England, and took the train down to Chartwell. They found Churchill busy in his garden, building a wall like any bricklayer, in a boiler suit. He was shorter than Fabian expected, and corpulent, but fairly cracking with energy and determination.

'I have never in my life encountered a bigger personality,' Fabian wrote later. 'He immediately put down his trowel and greeted us very naturally. Then he went inside to change.' Before luncheon Churchill talked mostly to Luitgarde, who was a Bismarck, which fascinated him. Over luncheon he talked about his visits to Germany, pre-Nazi era, and about naval manoeuvres during the First World War. After the meal they went back into the drawing room, just the two men, and sat on a huge sofa under a portrait of Marlborough. The butler brought Churchill a double whisky. Fabian had a tomato juice, which didn't impress Churchill one bit. He lit a fat cigar then turned to the reason for Fabian's visit.

'His whole instinct was towards the matter in hand,' wrote Fabian in his memoir. 'He was only concerned with the important things, never the small ones. He went straight to the heart of the subject. He asked lots of questions. When I asked a question he remonstrated: no, I'm the one who asks the questions! When I repeated all the dangers Hitler posed, to us but also to England, he waved it away with "I know all that already." He was a risk-taker, suspicious of all ideology. He was a master of words and expression. Not an academic – more than that: an artist. England was ready to go to war, he said, if it was unavoidable. The British were a strong people.'

He puffed at his cigar. 'We might lose at the beginning, but end up the victor.'

'I'm not a Nazi,' Fabian found himself protesting. 'I'm a patriot.'

'As am I!' replied Churchill. It shot out of him 'like a pistol' Fabian wrote.

Fabian went back to the beginning: 'But how can we avoid war? Even now? Given Hitler wants it.'

Again and again they came back to it.

'Only power impresses Hitler,' Fabian said. 'Can you threaten with your Navy?'

Churchill shook his head. 'The current government wouldn't countenance it. They continue to hope for peace, making one concession after another. So we will have war.' They sat in silence for a while, contemplating it.

'You should have kept your monarchy after the war,' said Churchill. 'How strong is the Opposition within your Army?'

Fabian hesitated. Churchill smiled and shook his head.

When Fabian and Luitgarde got back to Berlin, Fabian went to report back to the small circle surrounding General Beck. They heard it, downcast.

In mid-August 1939, there was a family wedding. Luitgarde tried on her gown and hat and long gloves, laughing because the gown was getting tight. She was pregnant with their first child. At the wedding, Fabian met for the first time a distant cousin, Gerd von Tresckow. He was a tall, burly man. He'd been in the war, wounded many times, and was highly decorated. He had a small country estate, but little money. Once the German army was enlarged again, breaking the terms of the Treaty of Versailles, he joined it as an officer. He had few qualms about it. The Treaty had been so draconian. He was a direct man, with no side to him, extremely well-educated and well-read, with a good sense of humour. Once he was your friend you could rely on him, even in the most extreme circumstances – a quality Fabian was to experience many times in the coming years. He hated the Nazis, and was dangerously open about it. He had that touch of bravura about him.

'My brother Henning wants to speak to you,' he said, coming up to Fabian without any sort of introduction. 'He's at our country estate in Wartenburg. I know you were in London in June and spoke to all sorts of high-ups.' He gave Fabian the address and the time he was expected, and then he was gone. Fabian travelled to Wartenburg the next day.

Henning von Tresckow was waiting for him when the butler brought him in. He was tall like his brother, but slimmer, with bright intelligent eyes and a strong handshake, dressed in civilian clothes. He was 38 at the time, and had left school early to fight in the war, joining the Prussian First Infantry in 1917. He was an admirer of the English, the language and the idea of the 'gentleman', but not uncritically. After the war, he'd been apprenticed to a Jewish banker. He was soon promoted, finishing up in the Stock Exchange. But he always remained in contact with the Jewish banker and, after 1933, he helped him and his family to emigrate. By then Tresckow had re-joined the *Reichswehr*, the limited army allowed by Versailles, into Infantry Regiment 9 in Potsdam, nicknamed the *Graf 9* regiment because it was so full of Counts and other aristocracy. Then he went on to officer training in the *Kriegsschule*, the Military War College, run along similar lines to Sandhurst in England, where he passed out First of his year.

By 1933 he was a *Generalstabsoffizier*, officer on the General Staff, greeting the new Nazi regime with cautious enthusiasm. Like everyone else, he still smarted under the terms of the Treaty of Versailles and the chaos of Weimar which followed, and like many of his fellow officers, he was keen to reclaim the so-called Polish corridor, lost to Germany after the war. In Potsdam he served under General Ludwig Beck and Werner von Fritsch, admiring them both. But he was soon disenchanted with Hitler and the Nazi Party. Their humiliation of Fritsch confirmed his worst fears and he became an active member of the Opposition, once and for all. By then he'd married Erika, the daughter of von Falkenhayn, the Prussian Minister of War. All this Tresckow told Fabian openly, by way of background. Then he moved swiftly on to the matter in hand. 'Hitler wants war,' he said. 'And that will be the death of Germany.'

Fabian saw that there was nothing he could tell Tresckow. He was a man who, once decided, never wavered. The thing he couldn't and wouldn't countenance was illusions and indecision. 'It's not enough to see a situation. You have to act. And wear a mask, and lie if necessary. If you want to topple a tyranny you have to be prepared to arm yourself and fight. Hitler is like all madmen. He only knows one thing: All or Nothing.'

It was a long time since anyone had talked so openly about it with Fabian. And with such single-minded determination. Tresckow left him in no doubt that he would fight it out to the very last. He was disgusted with the collaboration of Müller and the bishops and all those academics, doctors and lawyers who'd swiftly replaced the Jews and political resisters who'd lost their jobs through *Gleichschaltung*. Not to mention industrialists like Krupp and Siemens who funded the Nazi Party and were now busily producing armaments for the coming war.

'So tell me about your trip to England. Will they step in to avert war?'

'If Chamberlain is replaced by Churchill, then yes. He's the only one who can stop Hitler. He knows Hitler means war. But now . . .'

Henning von Tresckow thought it over. 'So, no, in fact.'

'Churchill will go to war if necessary, whatever it costs, and see it through,' said Fabian. 'He told me so. His main hope is America.'

'Then it's war.' Henning von Tresckow, the man with no illusions, was thinking what it meant for Germany. 'We'll have early successes. But that will just give the enemy time to strengthen and concentrate.' For Tresckow the British were already the enemy, noted Fabian. 'Finally the Americans will come in, just as they did in the last war.'

They parted with a nod. Each knew they had two enemies now. And each knew the only solution to both was to get rid of Hitler, by any means – whatever the dangers.

'Among the upper classes the Gestapo supervision is just as vigorous and ruthless if somewhat more subtle than in the working-class population,' wrote Martha Dodd, now safely back in America. 'But let it be stated very clearly that whenever real opposition is located, no matter where, the technique of the Gestapo is always the same: liquidation. *Agents provocateurs* are even more numerous among the so-called leisure class. I have told how professors, intellectuals, artists and scientists are no longer able to carry on free and animated conversations. Small business men in cities and the bourgeoisie in general must be careful not to sell goods to Jews or mix with people not wholeheartedly behind Hitler. Our concern about telephones and dictaphones when we were at the Embassy in Berlin is an illustration of the complicated and subtle sort of espionage which is always at work even in the diplomatic corps itself. Of our servants there was not one before whom we could speak openly.'

There was no reason why Martha Dodd should know, but by 1939 there were hundreds of thousands of servants and workers of every sort, increasingly disillusioned at the higher and higher cost of living and frightened by the brutality of the terror regime, who were fighting the Nazis in small ways and large. The Reich, re-arming in preparation for war, was in short supply of skilled workmen – craftsmen, engineers, chemists – which gave them more power than previously. Slow work and absenteeism were endemic. As to the former Communists, those still at large, they fought on regardless, as they had even before the Nazi *Machtergreifung*.

Between 1933 and 1939, tens of thousands had been arrested and incarcerated in concentration camps. Hundreds were 'shot while trying to escape' or sentenced to death by the *Volksgericht*. Some 10,000 had fled and emigrated. Yet they managed to establish clandestine cells of resistance in numerous armaments factories, sabotaging production and infiltrating the workforce. They had also instigated a new role of Instructor – agents who moved around the Reich addressing the cells here and there, bringing news of other cells, and the deliberations and motions of the International Communist Conferences held in Brussels in 1935 and Bern in 1939, as well as news from the Party's Central Committee in Russia. Some Instructors were already in exile, slipping over the borders in the dead of night. Others were Beefsteaks, living regular lives in the Reich.

'There have been complaints for several months about inadequate production at the armaments firm of Middle German Steelworks in Groeditz, district Grossenhain, which has a workforce of about 6,000 people,' went a Report from the Dresden Police to the local Gestapo on 29 June 1939. 'Absence from work and sickness is very high, up to 1,200 workers temporarily missing. In several cases damage to machinery caused suspicion of sabotage. Since October 1938, the Gestapo has become involved in about fifty cases. Two former Communists were arrested at the start of June, Karl Albert, lathe operator, born 8 January 1907, former member of the Red Sport Unit, punished in 1933 on account of Communist activity. And Ernst Rudolf, machine fitter, born 26 October 1914. An Imprisonment Order against both has been issued by a lawyer. Another six workers had to be arrested on account of similar actions. They admitted having been stirred up by the above. According to my conclusions, the situation is no isolated phenomenon. It will become more serious as the possibility of war comes ever more into consideration.'

It was happening everywhere. In Hamburg Irma and Rosa Thälmann had to be careful, knowing they were being watched, but it didn't stop them. They were good at all the methods of subterfuge by now: doubling back, jumping on trams at the last minute, hiding in dark alleyways. There was a secret and as yet undetected meeting place in the Hamburg docks for a large group of active resisters to the Nazi regime, many of them ex-Communists, at widow Kopke's bar.

Widow Kopke was not unlike Tante Ney in Düsseldorff – an old lady who was friendly to everyone, including those new high-ups of the local NSDAP who'd once been the desperado unemployed she'd helped out with a free drink here and a word of encouragement there. At the centre of the group at widow Kopke's was Alma Stobbe, a young woman as courageous and tough in her way as Irma Thälmann. Alma had joined the Communist Party in 1931, aged 17. She worked at a local factory and joined the RUO, Red Union Opposition, which went underground after the Reichstag Fire in 1933 when Communists everywhere feared for their lives. They organised themselves into twenty-one committees in different districts of Hamburg, started an underground newspaper distributed secretly by couriers, collected monthly dues, pasted leaflets on walls at night, helped Jews and other political runaways across the border into Denmark, and continued their acts of sabotage in the factories and the docks and the shipyards. Back in 1934, after all the arrests and executions, they still had 7,000 members – heart and soul followers of their charismatic leader Ernst Thälmann.

They all knew what would happen if they were caught. 'In March of last year several new personalities in the Communist Party formed an alliance. The five men are: Walter Hochmut, Albert Bennies, Griegat, Gauert and Grosse,' went a local Gestapo report. 'These five men, all intelligent and resolute, succeeded in creating an underground Party apparatus within three months. When we closed in on them about four weeks ago, even we had no idea of the dimensions of the organi- sation.' In the next three months, 800 more were arrested and tortured in the notorious Gestapo interrogation cellar at City Hall before being incarcerated in Fuhlsbüttel Concentration Camp. Or simply executed in one way or another.

By 1939, Alma was living with Dagobert Biermann, a machinist in the shipyard. She'd met him in 1936 when he'd come to see her about 'mailing' an important message to Copenhagen. They used to go to the fish market together on Sunday mornings, then take a walk along the river Elbe, 'meeting' people on the way, because by then the RUO had been replaced by less formal resistance groups, on a smaller scale, all loosely connected. Dagobert managed to get jobs for many com- rades saying they were specialists in this or that. His brother-in-law was a barge captain who learned about the huge armament shipments to Spain. They organised a network of longshoremen and railroad workers to collect and disseminate the information. Workers sabo- taged the warships and fighter planes being built by Blohm and Voss. Others sabotaged the factories producing rifle ammunition. Leaflets appeared all over Hamburg: 'No weapons for Franco!', 'Down with Hitler and Franco!' Thousands of shipyard workers read them before they could be removed. Stickers appeared on doors and windows of underground trains and buses, warehouses and factory gates, on beer bottles even, for the workers at Blohm and Voss. Money collections in factories, right under the bosses' noses, were for 'funeral wreaths' or a 'marriage'. Most of those on 'errands' were women and children, often on bicycles.

Alma went about her 'errands' with a shopping bag, dropping in on the lending library on Lübecker Chaussee which had a mimeograph machine. 'I'm here for the romances you put aside for my grand-mother,' she'd say, placing the packet of leaflets in her shopping bag. Resistance activity in Hamburg was so extensive and nefarious, it was impossible for the local Gestapo to stop it. On those rare occasions when Irma and Rosa were allowed a prison visit to Thälmann, still in solitary confinement after six years, they were able to convey in coded language how strong the resistance in Hamburg still was, in spite of all Gestapo efforts. And not only in Hamburg.

Everyone in Communist circles knew about Artur Goeritz, Stefan Lovasz and Joseph Seidel, all ex-KPD members, who'd finally been executed, by guillotine, in June 1938, after three years of incarceration and torture at the infamous Plötzensee prison where hanging by meat hooks became a method of execution for those the Nazis hated most. For special 'guests' the Gestapo preferred to keep them alive for a while, in order to torture them, as an act of pure revenge and as a terrifying warning to others. The three men had all been workers at the Dornier armaments factory in Friedrichshafen, resisting the Nazi regime with acts of sabotage and by passing information of Hitler's secret rearmament programme at the underground munitions factory at Celle to the outside world via the Central Committee of the KPD, now based in Switzerland. They had documents and photographs, and a courier too, a young member called Liselotte Hermann who came from a large family of resisters. Liselotte was setting off on her 'student trip' to Switzerland when she was denounced. All four were arrested and sentenced to death for high treason by the *Volksgericht*.

Resistance to the terror regime came less from the lower middle classes, those who'd voted in their droves for the Nazis in 1933. But higher up the social scale it was becoming as active as it was among former Communist and Social Democrat workers.

It began later than the workers' resistance, but once begun, it became key. In Berlin, a highly effective group were gathered round Harro Schulz-Boysen, working in the Reich Air Ministry, and Arvid Harnack, working in the Reich Ministry of Economics, later named *Die Rote Kapelle*, the Red Orchestra. Arvid was the brother of Ernst, Julius Leber's friend and colleague, and he was married to Mildred, the American friend of Martha Dodd who'd gone to visit Hans Fallada in Carwitz all those years ago. Arvid and Mildred had met at Wisconsin University and married there before deciding to return to Germany for Arvid's work in 1929. Both were intellectual Marxists, surrounded by like-minded friends: academics, artists, writers, journalists. Once in Berlin, Mildred found work as a lecturer in English literature at the university. Through Mildred, the group had access to the First Secretary at the American embassy, Donald Heath, passing on vital information about Hitler's rearmament programme and preparations for war. Harro Schulz-Boysen had meanwhile joined the Nazi Party in order to operate more effectively – another Beefsteak – and could be seen walking around the Reich Air Ministry in full Luftwaffe uniform.

Mildred's husband Arvid was in touch with a businessman called Graudenz who had dealings with an air force engineer, passing information to a Russian known only as 'Erdmann', regarding German armaments and airplane production, warning England and Russia of planned attacks in the East, commando projects behind the lines, and new weapons being produced, as well as the location of industrial sites and industrial production. 'As far as I could gather,' a witness later confirmed, 'the extent of the treason was greater than was actually discovered. The value of the information given to the Russians cannot be overestimated. Its effects on the train of military events must have been significant.' The Red Orchestra, loosely structured and connected to many smaller Opposition groups, involved some 400 active resisters. Based in Berlin, but reaching far beyond, it was still undiscovered by the Gestapo in 1939, at the outbreak of war. Resisters had learned their lesson: no more large organisations.

By 1939 Julius and Annedore Leber were also living in Berlin, Annedore still working as a seamstress, Leber now running his small coal business, arranged for him by his old friend and political colleague Gustav Dahrendorf. During his time in prison and Sachsenhausen concentration camp, Leber had learned, as he put it, to know himself better, to admit his weaknesses, and judge himself more harshly than he had in happier times – before 1933, when he'd hardly judged himself at all in fact, wandering around his home town of Lübeck, the great leader of the Social Democrats, larger than life, greeted by one and all, with plenty of women among them. And plenty of drink too. But now – gone the ebullience, gone the optimism, gone the ample girth and hearty laugh – though not gone the spirit. Nor the fight. Nor the love of his wife. 'My greatest happiness and consolation,' he'd written to Annedore from prison, 'are to think of my family, and my Lübeck workers.' He signed off as usual: 'your old Julius.' Sometimes adding, 'always was, and will be.'

After he'd finally been let out of Sachsenhausen in May 1937, 'changed but not bowed', as Dahrendorf confirmed, Leber was careful to cultivate the appearance of one who'd learned his lesson, avoiding any political activity which could only end him back in Sachsenhausen. He wasn't likely to forget those first weeks in prison in Lübeck in the spring of 1933 – weeks when he still believed there was a rule of law in Germany and he'd soon be let out again. In those far-off innocent times when hope was still alive, he thought it was merely a matter of putting up with the irritations of his everyday life and waiting, just waiting. But by February 1934, he was in Wolfenbuttel prison. Then Esterwegen concetration camp, after a false promise of release was snatched away at the last minute. Then, finally, after hearing nothing from Annedore for weeks, nor she from him, in September 1936, it was on to Sachsenhausen.

Esterwegen was a hell on earth, as recalled by Ernst Niekisch, the former editor of the *Widerstand* journal, door-stepped by Fabian Schlabrendorff in his search for other opponents to the newly 'elected' Nazi regime. 'It was barbaric,' Niekisch wrote later. 'The prisoners were battered till they bled, pushed to the very edge of what a human being can bear. They had to do the most meaningless work, all day long: quick march from one side of the yard to the other, carrying gravel from here to there and back again. If they fell from exhaustion they were ordered to get up again at gunpoint. Young totally immature lads, uneducated former Hitler Youths, now SS, were given free rein. Incredible things: clergymen told to build churches out of human shit. The former SPD Reichstag delegate Herr Doktor Leber was ordered to eat it.'

No, Leber wouldn't, couldn't, go through all that again. Or so the Berlin Gestapo thought. Big man, loud-mouth Leber, *Liebling*, darling, of the has-been Social Democrats, had finally learned his lesson. And anyone watching the Leber family would certainly only see a modest bourgeois family life: mother working, father at home reading and writing and recovering, children off to school. Holidays were spent on the Baltic coast. Sundays were spent quietly. When they saw friends it was just family friends. When they wrote letters, they were just about family matters: the children's schooling, the weather, a small birthday party they'd held for Annedore.

But Leber hadn't changed his views – not at all. 'The Will to Power is no more than a slogan. It only achieves content and meaning through the courage to act, and the courage to take responsibility with all its consequences,' he'd written years earlier and still believed, even after all the torture and humiliation.

'To pursue a fight which has already been won, well, any ass can do that. Those who wait for such a situation wait in vain, like a good old soldier waiting for nine tenths of his life. So in the end he can only console himself with the fact that, although he made few mistakes, he made even fewer advances. He who wants to make real progress has to take power. And if you want power you also have to have the courage to make some mistakes. Only, you have to be clear: to make a mistake might mean you find yourself in danger. But you have to be prepared for that: to sacrifice your life if necessary. If you have that confidence in yourself and your political convictions, then go to it! Fight! If it works, good! If not, you have to take the consequences. You either have to rule or stand in outright, active, Opposition!'

Leber was quietly reading and writing and plotting at home in Berlin-Zehlendorf, a district of Berlin full of erstwhile Social Democrats, all moved there from their home towns to get away from the place where they were too well known, and disappear like ghosts in Berlin. The Leber family could never have managed financially if they hadn't been helped by secret donations from the SPD Party in exile, these days based in Paris. And by friends like Schwamb, still in work. Ludwig Schwamb's apartment was also in Berlin-Zehlendorf. Why shouldn't he go and visit friends and neighbours? How could the Gestapo keep a watch on everyone, every moment of the day and night? Especially now that war loomed.

Once Leber was ready to go out and about again, it was at Ludwig Schwamb's that he met Wilhelm Leuschner, the great Trade Unionist, and Carlo Mierendorff, the political theorist – two key men in a growing network of resisters, both potential members of a new post-Nazi government. They had known each other since the late 1920s, both members of the *Reichsbanner*, the organisation formed to defend the Weimar Republic from undemocratic forces. It had more than three million members, mostly Trade Unionists and Social Democrats, when it was banned by the Nazis in 1933 along with all Trade Unions and political parties save the NSDAP. But Leuschner and Mierendorff continued to work together in secret, and soon enough they'd teamed up with Schwamb and Harnack, and thence with others.

In early 1939, there was a meeting at Harnack's apartment with Leuschner and members of another loose group of resisters which included Gustav Noske who had been Weimar's first Minister of Defence and later *Oberpresident* of Hanover, till he was relieved of his duties in 1933. Klaus Bonhoeffer was there too – a lawyer with Deutsche Lufthansa, a job which provided an excellent cover for his resistance activities, allowing him many trips abroad. Klaus was the son of Karl Bonhoeffer, the neurologist and resister, and the brother of Dietrich, the theologian, who'd stood up so courageously to Hitler back in 1933 when the Protestant church was being forcibly brought into line under Bishop Müller. At the meeting they agreed, once again, that links had to be made to the *Wehrmacht*, without whom there could be no coup d'état – or even an assassination if necessary, though many resisters, including Bonhoeffer, felt they couldn't support the taking of life. Annedore noted that Schwamb, delightful man that he was, found conspiracy very hard. It went against his nature.

The group made a list of sympathetic senior army officers and thought General Alexander von Falkenhausen might be persuaded to join the cause. Others had in fact already approached Falkenhausen, a friend of Carl Goerdeler and General von Witzleben. But who should go? They chose Julius Leber, the strongest of their group and already their natural leader. Leber met Falkenhausen at a secret location. In vain. Falkenhausen was happy to listen to 'the old Social Democrat' and his opinions on what needed to be done about Hitler's dictatorship and the coming war. But he wasn't prepared to take part in any coup d'état.

By 1939, Dahrendorf had fulfilled his promise and set Leber up in a small coal business in Berlin-Schöneberg. 'Two small rooms in the little house by Schöneberg station,' wrote Theodor Heuss, another secret resister, 'between the coal mountains of Meyer and Co – a true resisters' club. Sometimes the bell at the outer door tinkled, so then Leber had to go into the front room to deal with a customer. But in the back room, sitting about on old chairs and stools, there was passionate political talk and planning.' They needed a democratic system along English two-party lines, decided by majority rule, with the SPD the foremost party on the Left. Above all they needed a strong, charismatic leader to galvanise the Volk. The kind of leader the Communists had in Ernst Thälmann. And that meant Julius Leber. But time was running out. Their iron rule: talk to no one. Everyone knew what would happen if they were caught.

Time was running out in all senses for the Volk of the Reich. But especially for the Jews. By early 1939, the Domestic Situations Required columns in *The Times* of London, coming at the front of the newspaper after Births, Marriages and Deaths and before The Law Reports and Sporting News, were filled with advertisements from desperate people looking for jobs of any sort to escape the Reich and find a place of safety. 'Married Couple, still in Austria, 45 and 42, good at any work, skilled, good cooking, experienced in all household duties, speaking English, must leave Vienna end of month, urgently seeking post,' was typical. Typical too that children were never mentioned – presumably left behind in the Reich, hidden by courageous friends and neighbours.

Luckily the life of an English country house in those heady pre-war days required endless servants, inside and out: housemaids, parlour maids, ladies' maids, laundry maids, between maids, kitchen and scullery maids, housekeepers and cooks – all to be found in the lengthening columns of *The Times*, some calling themselves German, others Jewish, others non-Aryan. 'Housekeeper, German Jewish, 27, well versed in all household duties, fond of children, speaks English, seeks post as housekeeper.' There was another long list for men: butlers, valets, gardeners, chauffeurs, hall boys, footmen, handymen, farm workers. 'German Jewish butler requires position in private household. Prepared to do any work. Excellent credentials. Still in Berlin.' Some offered to pay their own fares. Some advertisements appeared in the columns again and again. Local applicants took to pointing out they were English or Scottish, for those employers who weren't keen on Jews.

Rumbling anti-Semitism was a fact of life everywhere, but nothing to compare with the German Reich where the Nazi terror regime was designed as a fully fledged Racial State from the start. The purity of the Nation and its Volk was the ideology underpinning everything else in Hitler's Reich, including the upcoming war. The Nazis' twin enemies were the Communists and Socialists on the one hand and the racially subhuman, *Untermensch*, on the other – often fatefully combined in the Jew. While the officers of the SS were busy breeding the racially pure Aryan race in Himmler's new *Lebensborn*, Fount of Life, homes, Jews were hounded into ghettos and thence to concentration camps, finally to the extermination camps. The two went hand in hand.

'The ideal German should be: as blond as Hitler, as tall as Goebbels, and as slim as Göring,' was a joke passed around the bars and Gasthofs when no one was listening.

Part and parcel of the same ideology was the policy of euthanasia, the compulsory killing of the mentally and physically handicapped, instigated in 1939 on Hitler's personal order. It was meant to be done in secret but news soon filtered out, causing religious and moral outrage, as expressed in a letter from the Bishop of Limburg to the Reich Minister of Justice:

'Perhaps eight kilometers from Limburg, on a hill directly above the little town of Hadamar, there is an institution which used to serve a variety of purposes. It has been converted as a place in which, according to popular opinion, euthanasia has been carried out for months – well known throughout the government district of Wiesbaden, because death certificates are sent from a registry in Hadamar to the home districts concerned. Buses with increasing numbers of victims arrive in Hadamar several times a week. School children in the area know these vehicles and say: "Here comes the murder box again." The people of Hadamar watch the smoke rising from the chimney and are upset by the constant thought of the poor victims. This is especially so whenever they are troubled by unpleasant smells after the wind changes direction. Children taunt each other: "Watch out! You're not very clever, you'll end up in the Hadamar baking ovens!" All God-fearing people feel this extermination of the helpless is an almighty crime. Officials of the Gestapo are trying, as one hears, to suppress talk about what is going on at Hadamar with severe threats. The conviction is multiplied by the bitter knowledge that the talk is banned by threat, but the actions themselves are not prosecuted under law.'

Some 150,000 'unworthy of life' were murdered over the next two years, until the order was rescinded in 1941, due to public outrage. But it didn't stop other methods of purification of the Aryan race: 400,000 so-called carriers of hereditary defects were sterilized. Some 10,000 homosexuals were murdered and thousands more incarcerated and castrated. Female foreign workers, transported into the Reich from the newly occupied territories, were forced to have abortions.

For some, personally affected, this was when they finally felt compelled to take action. 'If you hear strange things about me, don't think that I have changed,' wrote a secret resister, Kurt Gerstein, to a family member. 'Please tell that to the Church President as well. I shouldn't like him to think badly of me. I have joined the SS, and now, at times, I talk their language. I do this for two reasons: the collapse is coming. This is absolutely certain. There will be a Day of Judgement. When that moment comes, these ruthless desperados will do all they can to get rid of anyone left whom they regard as their enemy. At that point, help from outside will be useless. Help then can only possibly come from a person who can suppress orders or deliver them in garbled form. That is where I come in. The second reason is that I am on the trail of so many crimes! My aunt was killed at Hadamar. I want to know where and by whom the orders for these murders were given!'

Another secret and lone resister was a carpenter from Wurttenberg in Southern Germany called Georg Elser. The product of a harsh and impoverished childhood during the chaotic Weimar years, Elser decided there was no other solution, after six years of terror and now the certainty of war, than to assassinate Hitler and as many of the upper echelons of the NSDAP as possible. Elser had voted for the Communists because he felt they were the only party to defend workers' rights, but he never joined the Party. Above all, he was a loner, tough and clever. A time bomb seemed the best solution to Elser. Knowing the extreme dangers, he told no one. He was a highly skilled worker and he planned everything down to the last detail. Once it was announced in the newspapers that the Führer would make his speech at the Bürgerbräu beer hall in Munich on 8 November 1939 as usual, to honour the so-called martyrs of the Beer Hall Putsch, Elser got to work. Several high-ups of the Nazi Party including Himmler and Göring and Hess were due to be present.

By now, Elser was living in lodgings in Königsbrunn in southern Germany and working at the local Waldenamier armaments factory where he had access to fuses and detonators. He'd previously worked at a clock factory, so he knew all about timers. He made his first trip to

Munich and the Bürgerbräu the previous year, on 8 November 1938, just checking where Hitler stood to make his speech to the assembled Party faithful. Thereafter he made several more trips, checking the speaker's platform, then making his sketches and calculations back in his lodging house later. There was a pillar behind the platform and Elser, the skilled carpenter, saw how he could access it from the gallery above, then make a cavity in it for the bomb.

By August 1939 he'd moved to lodgings in Munich and become a regular at the beer hall, arriving shortly before closing time, then hiding out in the gallery for the night, working hard. First he made a secret trapdoor for access to the platform below, then he made the cavity in the pillar. He left every morning at 6.30 when the beer hall opened, by a rear door, carrying his work bag like any other labourer. Except this work bag contained rubble along with the tools of the trade.

On the night of 7 November, Elser set the timer for 9.20pm the following night – about half way through the Führer's speech. Then he went to the railway station and took the train to Friedrichshafen on the Lake of Constance, planning to cross the border into Switzerland the next day. From the safety of Switzerland, he would write a letter to the Reich authorities admitting responsibility, and making it absolutely clear that he'd acted entirely alone, so no one else would be incriminated.

The bomb went off at 9.20 exactly as planned. But the weather on 8 November was foggy and Hitler wanted to make it back to Berlin in time, so he cut the speech short and he and his entourage left early. The ceiling and a large part of the wall completely collapsed. Seven people were killed, sixty-three injured, many seriously. Hitler was totally oblivious of the matter till he reached Berlin. Elser was picked up at the Swiss border and found to be carrying bomb-making tools in his suitcase. It was pure bad luck. He was transferred to the Gestapo Headquarters in Prinz Albrecht Strasse in Berlin and underwent five days of interrogation and torture. Throughout he insisted he'd wanted to assassinate the NSDAP leadership to avoid the bloodshed of the coming war which he'd thought was unavoidable since autumn 1938.

Elser's entire family was rounded up and held in Moabit prison – the same prison which had held Ernst Thälmann before he was transferred to Hanover. It was clear the family knew nothing of Elser's plot. Before they were let go, they were brought to Gestapo Headquarters,

face to face with their relation. 'His face was swollen black and blue. His eyes were bulging out of their sockets,' as one described later. As to Elser himself, he disappeared into the bowels of Prinz Albrecht Strasse to endure years and years of torture before finally being executed on 8 April 1945 in Dachau Concentration Camp, during the very last days of the war.

'All Germany is talking about the attempt on Hitler's life at Bürgerbräu,' wrote the former diplomat Ulrich von Hassell, sitting at his desk in his house at Ebenhausen. 'The press is quite unable to cover up the fact that there is absolutely no "fanatical indignation" as described by official propaganda. Rather, an astounding indifference and many people quite openly express regret that the explosion was delayed.'

Hassell had been dismissed from his post as German Ambassador to Rome by a suspicious Ribbentrop in 1938. Once 'freed' he quickly made contact with other resisters, including Beck and Goerdeler. And he started his diary, determined to leave a record of the Nazi terror regime. 'Yesterday it was announced that the would-be assassin had been caught. An astonishingly frank man whose attitude is puzzling,' he added a week later. It was hard to tell fact from fiction and lies in the newspapers these days. Goebbels had a field day. It was a gift from heaven for the propaganda machine. Elser had not acted alone, they said, but in collaboration with the British Secret Service. As to the Führer – his escape had been a God-given 'Act of Providence,' Hitler announced in a wireless broadcast to the Volk.

Meanwhile the great Führer was preparing to take the Reich into war. On 23 August 1939 Foreign Minister von Ribbentrop and Russian Foreign Minister Molotov had signed the Nazi–Soviet Pact, ostensibly a Non-Aggression pact, but effectively agreeing to carve up Poland between them once the moment arrived. It threw everyone and everything into confusion, not least the leadership of the KPD German Communist Party. Surely Stalin didn't want to become an ally of the

Fascist Hitler? What could it mean? What could they do?

'The German working people, and especially the German workers, must support the peace policy of the Soviet Union,' announced the German Communist Secretariat two days later, on 25 August, totally confused. 'They must place themselves at the side of all peoples which are oppressed and threatened by the Nazis, and must now take up the fight as never before, to ensure that peace in the spirit of the Pact which has just been concluded between the Soviet Union and Germany is also made with Poland and Romania, with France and England . . .'

Five days later, Hitler was demanding the return of the Polish Corridor and Silesia which had been taken by the Treaty of Versailles. On 1 September, Germany invaded Poland. 'Few people on the streets,' wrote Hassell in his diary. 'Only official enthusiasm over the closing of the border.'

On 3 September England and France finally understood that Hitler's protestations of peace were nothing but lies, and declared war on Germany.

CHAPTER NINE

INTO THE DARKNESS

The year 1940 began badly for Rudolf Ditzen. And that was before even thinking about the war. The truth of it was that Rudolf, the best-selling author Hans Fallada, had been making one compromise after another with the Nazi authorities, ever since his friend and publisher and constant support Ernst Rowohlt was dismissed by the Reich Literary Chamber in July 1938 for his 'non-aligned' political views. Rowohlt had joined the NSDAP in 1937 as a means of protecting his authors and staff, but it hadn't worked. No one was fooled. His business was taken over by the 'approved' Deutsche Verlags Anstalt, and he was given a post as consultant – till the end of the year. From then on Rowohlt's only link to the business was his son, Ledig, the young man who had accompanied Martha Dodd, Mildred Harnack and their Russian Embassy friend to visit Rudolf Ditzen in Carwitz back in 1934. Ledig and Rowohlt had used Martha and the American Embassy as an escape route for some of their Jewish friends, but now that Martha was back in the United States, that was closed to them. Still, Ledig had managed to hold on to his job, becoming yet another Beefsteak. He had to accept a Nazi party member as joint-managing director and he had to sign his letters with a '*Heil Hitler!*' but he decided to put up with it. Rowohlt's wife was Brazilian, so, reluctantly, he'd decided to emigrate. It was the obvious solution to his insoluble situation. But it left Rudolf a nervous wreck.

He'd already conceded some small compromises before the terrible news struck – including a new introduction to *Wolf Among Wolves* reminding the reader that the bad old times were over thanks to the new Nazi regime, which earned him great praise from Joseph Goebbels who called it 'a terrific book!' Rowohlt had warned against the compromise, but Rudolf thought it a manageable price to pay for the fact that he didn't have to make any serious changes to the text itself – which was the only thing that really mattered to him. The result was that *Wolf Among Wolves* was another best-seller for Hans

Fallada, and the 'approved' Tobias Film Company promptly offered him a contract to write another book, this time 'dealing with the fate of a German family from 1914 to 1933'. It was titled *Iron Gustav*, to be made into a film starring Emil Jannings, a favourite with the cinema going public, which immediately got the go-ahead from the Ministry of Propaganda and Public Enlightenment, quickly followed by another offer for a film of his story *Old Heart Goes A-Journeying*. Things were looking up, felt Rudolf, as yet blissfully unaware that his protector Rowohlt would soon be gone.

He wrote *Iron Gustav* like a train, racing through the story of Gustav Hackendahl as though his life depended on it, which, to an extent, it did. Hackendahl was based on an old carriage driver in Berlin, known to everyone for his indomitable character and iron will. 'Perhaps it was the grey mare, old Hackendahls' favourite, demanding its feed by dragging the halter chain through the manger ring and pawing the floor of its stable,' Fallada the great story-teller began, 'perhaps it was the dawn replacing the moon, the light of earliest morning breaking over Berlin, which had awakened the old man. Possibly, however, it was neither the dawn nor his favourite grey that awakened him at twenty past three on the morning of 29 June 1914, but something quite different . . .'

And there Fallada had them, his readers, back in 1914, during the last weeks of peace before the war which ruined all their lives, wondering already what that 'something different' might be to wake old Hackendahl at twenty past three in the morning with dawn just breaking. They soon found out: beloved as he was by his customers, Hackendahl wasn't so loved by his children, five of them, two girls, three boys. Iron Gustav was a tyrant at home, the reason all five had their troubles later in the story. 'The *Vater*, he held the power, the threat over the whole Hackendahl family. *Vater*: that meant giving orders, judging, laying down the law, to beat and bellow every will out of us – It's his fault!' Yes, this was going to be a good read.

Within weeks, Else Bakonyi had arrived at Carwitz to type out the manuscript. She was another of Rowohlt's rescue jobs – a successful journalist who found herself unemployed after 1933 because her husband was Jewish. Together they worked to finish the book in record time, Rudolf pacing up and down his bureau, chain-smoking as he dictated the final draft, Else banging out the paragraphs on the typewriter, racing to keep up. But in his haste Rudolf clean forgot the deal made with the Reich Ministry of Propaganda and Enlightenment and ended the story in 1928 not 1933. Was it naivety? Or stubbornness? Or did he think he could get away with it because he was a best-selling author? One way or the other, it didn't work.

When Rudolf went to meet the people from the Tobias Film Company in Berlin, they informed him that Reich Minister Goebbels liked the book in general but insisted on one major alteration: the story had to continue till 1933 as originally agreed and cover the rise of the NSDAP. It was an awful shock, made a thousand times worse by Rowohlt's dismissal from the Reich Literary Chamber and subsequent emigration to Brazil.

Rudolf tried hard to get out of it, but he was no match for Goebbels. So he made his big concession to the Nazi authorities: Heinz Hackendahl, the good son who'd lost his job as a bank clerk and become one of the millions of unemployed during the bad days of Weimar, joined the NSDAP Party, his father Gustav became a Nazi sympathiser, and Eric, the bad son who'd turned to crime, became a Communist. 'This month is marked in black in my diary,' wrote Rudolf later. 'The world filled me with loathing, but I loathed myself even more for what I was doing.' And all in vain. Alfred Rosenberg, the racial ideologue of the Nazi Party, let it be known he didn't like the book and nor did he like Hans Fallada. Never had. The reviews were poor and the book was soon removed from the bookshops. Both film projects were cancelled. Defeated and wracked by bad nerves, Rudolf agreed to write a foreword for a new edition of *Farmers, Functionaries and Fireworks*, saying that wrong had been done on all sides, not just to his decent little people.

Rudolf had always admitted he was a coward. It was his need to write, and to keep on writing for his sanity, which made him especially vulnerable to the demands of the Reich Literary Chamber. 'It's one thing to sit at your writing desk creating your own world, quite another to then go out into the real world and be a man there. These are two quite different things,' he wrote later. 'I personally only felt all right when I could sit in the quiet, in the countryside, out of the storm, with sheets of clean, white paper lying before me.' Without that, his life and health fell to pieces. So he held to his routine through thick and thin: every morning at 7.15 he came from his bureau to the kitchen for his coffee, irritated if Suse was a minute late to prepare it. He'd already been up and writing for two or three hours by then. At 7.45 it was back to his writing desk. What he hated above all was *brummelei*, messing about, wasting time – probably because he'd done so much of it during his misspent youth he'd say, with one of his crooked smiles.

For the first and only time in his life, Rudolf seriously thought of emigrating. Rowohlt was on his way to Brazil, their old friend, Lore Soldin was on her way to England with her children, and Franz Hessel and Paul Mayer, both former employees of Rowohlt's, were on their way to Paris and Mexico respectively. Rudolf's publishers in London, Putnam, arranged a ship to pick up the Ditzen family in Hamburg and bring them back to England, keen to help their best-selling author. Rudolf and Suse started sorting out their possessions and packing up, telling the villagers at Carwitz they were going to stay with Suse's family in Hamburg for a while. The children, Uli and Lore, chose their favourite toys and books. They were all ready to leave when Rudolf said he wanted one last walk, a last goodbye, and set off up their country road.

He was gone a long time. When he came back, he told Suse to unpack. He couldn't do it. He couldn't leave Germany. He couldn't leave Carwitz. He couldn't write in another country – he'd lose his fragile health and sanity. He knew what it meant, he said: from now on he would have to limit himself to children's stories and popular novels and short stories – the sort which wouldn't offend anyone. He told himself that the one thing he wouldn't do was actively write for the Nazis. Suse started unpacking.

Ledig, engaged in his own compromises, reassured Rudolf that there was an insatiable hunger for light-hearted books. In those times of national crisis, with war on the horizon, the Volk wanted escape above all else. Rudolf soon came up with an idea for a long, light-hearted novel, judiciously set some time before the Nazi period. It was still about his favourite subject – the decent little people struggling to survive – but it had a simple theme: a couple who unexpectedly inherit seven million marks. Referring back to his biggest best-seller, it was titled *Little Man – Big Man, Roles Reversed* and had a heartening message for difficult times: money doesn't make you happy. When it was serialised in a women's magazine, the editors insisted the title was changed to 'Heavens! We've inherited a Castle!'

Still, it kept Rudolf satisfactorily engaged for some months, and life returned to an even keel for a time. They owned a car by then, a Ford, and Suse had passed her driving test so there was no more going

to Feldberg by cart or bicycle to get provisions. Their smallholding
was doing well, with a new woodshed, a smokehouse for their annual
pig slaughter and sausage making, and some beehives introduced
by Hubert Rader, returned from his military service and now living
with them permanently at Carwitz, much to the children's joy. There
was plentiful fruit from the fruit trees, vegetables from the enlarged
vegetable garden, and eggs from the henhouse. Suse was always busy
with cropping and pickling and preserving. Rudolf was busy with
his writing, banging out acceptable material, earning a steady 1,200
marks a month – which is what the average factory worker earned in a
year. Uli went back to school in Berlin, living with the Burlage family,
Rudolf's doctor and friend, during term time. Lore had an operation
for tonsillitis. They bought a wooden punt for their lake. And Suse
was pregnant again. Family and close friends came to visit. Little else.
What else could anyone want?

    Except that in March 1939 Hitler had broken another promise
and marched into the rest of Czechoslovakia without a blink. It was
a severe blow to Rudolf because, along with most of the German
Volk, he'd believed Hitler when he promised, after annexing the
Sudetenland, this was the last of his territorial claims. Unsettled, he
began work on a new novel, *The Unloved Man* – the kind of popular
story which could be serialised in the *Berliner Illustrierte* magazine.

Then came the Non-Aggression Pact with Soviet Russia. What was going on? Rudolf kept his head in the sand and wrote a short story – a harmless *Boy's Own* type story – for the Hitler Youth magazine. He knew he was on a slippery slope, but what could he do? Humiliatingly, reviews of his work remained lukewarm because the Reich Literary Chamber refused to include him in their list of top authors. Fallada was good, they stated with breath-taking superiority, but not that good. And then, blow of all blows, when rationing was introduced in August 1939 because of Hitler's massive expenditure on armaments and raw materials for the coming war, Rudolf found his writing paper was rationed too. Only the top 'approved' authors could get as much paper as they wanted.

There was no peace ahead, not for Rudolf, nor for the Volk. By 1 September 1939 German troops had invaded Poland – Hitler claiming they'd been forced to it by the Poles who were creating mayhem and terror across the border, which even Rudolf, intent on living in cloud cuckoo-land, could not believe. He and Suse drove to Berlin in a rush to bring Uli home before it was too late. Once home, they tended the harvest, stacked the hay, built an air-raid shelter in the cellar and Rudolf bought another bicycle knowing that petrol would be scarce, so no point relying on the car now. Hubert Rader was called up. Rudolf could only hope and pray the same wouldn't happen to him. Not to mention his anxiety about Suse's pregnancy, remembering the last time. He was smoking like a chimney, drinking and not sleeping. In November, he had another nervous collapse, ending up in Burlage's clinic again.

Nothing seemed to be happening on the war front, except to poor old Poland. Britain and France had declared war on Germany on 3 September, quickly joined by Australia, New Zealand, South Africa and Canada, followed by the 'phoney war' when everyone waited to see what might happen next, all the while using the time to rearm as fast as possible. The Reich Film Chamber contacted Rudolf, knowing escapist cinema was the best remedy to keep the Volk happy in frightening times – and who better to write a film script than Hans Fallada? They commissioned a light, romantic story about a young German man who returns to the Reich from America and falls in love with an 'ordinary girl' to be played by Zarah Leander, the most popular film star of the day. They assured Rudolf there was no political content – except that the 'ordinary girl' and her family had to be National

Socialists. The fee would be 20,000 marks. Rudolf wrote *This Heart Which Belongs to You* in less than three weeks and was paid another 5,000 marks for script revisions. Rudolf had capitulated and hated himself for it.

In January 1940, he and Suse decided to remove Uli from his school in Berlin for good.

By now the Nazi authorities had given up all interest in schooling, disliking traditional academic education and concerned only to prepare their youth for war. Thousands of teachers had lost their jobs through *Gleichschaltung* – those who'd been Social Democrats and Communists. Thousands were in concentration camps. Thousands more were being called up. The rest hardly bothered to teach. Lessons were non-existent at Uli's school, as the Burlages were able to confirm. Only a few *Gymnasiums* managed to hold out against the Nazi authorities, and one, as luck would have it, was a boarding school at Templin, twenty-five kilometres from Carwitz. It was a bitter winter that year, snow piled high, icicles hanging from the eaves of the house, the lake frozen, the country roads impassable. Undeterred, Rudolf and Suse set out by horse-drawn sledge to visit the school. It took them three-and-a-half hours.

Rudolf took Uli to his new school in April. Suse was staying with the Burlages in Berlin awaiting the birth of their child – a boy who they named Achim. By the end of April Ledig was called up, joining some three million new army recruits on standby for Hitler's next gamble. On 10 May, the *Deutsche Rundfunk* radio station triumphantly announced the German attack on France. Like everyone else in the Reich who possessed a Volks Radio, Rudolf and Suse listened to the unfolding events day by day, hour by hour. The newspapers were full of it. It was incredible.

It only took six weeks for France to fall, along with Belgium, Luxemburg, Holland and Norway. By 14 June, German troops were goose-stepping through Paris. The British, led by Winston Churchill after Chamberlain's resignation as Prime Minister on 10 May, had come to France's aid, but to no avail. The BEF, British Expeditionary Force, had to evacuate Dunkirk in a humiliating retreat. Hitler was triumphant. The tide had completely turned in Germany's favour. The Volk were jubilant – even some of the more sceptical ones. To think, only a year earlier, things were looking so bleak for the Reich – people fed up with the rising cost of basic food and clothing, longer working hours, lower and lower weekly wages, and always the fear of war. Now, on 21 June, here was the Führer in the Forest of Compiegne, on the very spot of Germany's humiliation in 1918, insisting that the exact same railway carriage in which they'd been forced to sign the Armistice be brought from the local museum and set up for the signing of the new Armistice – how gratifying that was! The Führer even insisted on sitting in the same chair as General Foch had used in 1918. A nice photo opportunity. Those milk-livered French! No fight, no pride! *Unglaublich!* Unbelievable. Who were the Masters now! England was next. 'So, we're marching! Yes, we're marching! Yes, we're marching a-gainst Eng-a-land!' went a new marching song specially composed for the coming invasion.

As to Poland – that summer 1940, Reinhard Heydrich, Chief of Security Police and *Reichsführer SS* Himmler's right-hand man, sent Kurt Daluege, Chief of Police, a report about the failing working relationship between the *Wehrmacht* officers and the SS: 'In all previous actions, by virtue of a special command from the Führer, Special Police action groups were acting alongside the advancing troops. In accordance with preparatory work, they carried out significant blows systematically against those elements which were inimical to the Reich, by means of imprisonment, confiscation, and securing the most important political material. Cooperation was generally good with the troops below staff level, but in many cases a fundamentally different view developed among the senior military commanders over basic questions about fighting the enemies of the state. This view, which for the most part developed out of lack of knowledge of the ideological position of the enemy, caused friction as well as giving orders running counter to the political activity which was being carried out by *Reichsführer* SS Himmler in accordance with the orders of the Führer and of General Field Marshal Göring.'

The reason for this report: by July 1940 the SS special action groups, known as *Einsatzgruppen*, were acting quite separately from the *Wehrmacht* Army in Poland, in parallel to it but not of it. Their main target: the liquidation of the Polish leadership.

'Wolff told me about a telegram from Schulenburg covering his conversation with Potemkin,' Ulrich von Hassell wrote in his diary on 11 January 1940, referring to the Ambassador who was Fritzi's cousin. Hassell was still busy collating information and organising opposition from his home in Ebenhausen. 'The latter said that thousands of Poles and Jews were constantly trying to cross the border. They were shot down in droves by the SS ... This bestiality has become absolutely intolerable.'

'I wish to have a population which is racially impeccable and am content if a *Gauleiter* can report it in ten years' time,' wrote Hitler to Albert Foster, the *Gauleiter* of the new *Gau* of Wartenburg. 'You yourself are such an old National Socialist that you know that one drop of false blood which comes into an individual's veins can never be removed.'

Hans Frank, the new Governor General of occupied Poland and Himmler's man on the spot, thought the simplest methods were often the best. 'We can only talk of these things in the most intimate circles,' he told a meeting of Police Chiefs in Cracow in May 1940. 'The Führer told me we must liquidate those people whom we have discovered form the leadership of Poland; all those who follow in their footsteps must be arrested and then got rid of after an appropriate period. We do not need to burden the Reich organisation of the German policy with that. We don't need to bother to cart these people off to concentration camps in the Reich because then we would only have trouble and unnecessary correspondence with their relatives. Instead we will finish things off here. We will do it in the simplest way.' By the end of the war six million Poles had been 'liquidated' one way or another.

Poles and Jews, subhuman joint enemies of the master race.

Goebbels, sky-high on the unbelievable success of German conquests in Poland and then France – greater than he could ever have imagined – decided the time was ripe to commission a film from one of his favourite film directors, Fritz Hippler. The Volk were ready for it now he reckoned. It was titled *Der Ewige Jude*, the Eternal Jew. 'Wherever rats appear,' began the narration to terrifying images of rats scurrying around in dark corners, scavenging, 'they bring ruin by destroying mankind's foods and foodstuffs. In this way they spread disease, plague, leprosy, typhoid, fever, cholera, dysentery and so on. They are cunning, cowardly and cruel, and are found mostly in large packs, just like the Jews among human beings.' The Jews were spreading like rats through Europe, and thence to the entire world. They were responsible for most of international crime and 98 per cent of prostitution. They bagged all the best jobs and earned all the money. 'Under the leadership of Adolf Hitler, Germany has raised the battle flag against the eternal Jew,' the film ended on a rousing note. 'The eternal law of nature, to keep one's race pure, is the legacy which the National Socialist Movement bequeaths to the German Volk for all time.'

The film was in the cinemas by November 1940. It appealed to the very worst element in German society. In Carwitz the Nazi mayor, who had never liked the Ditzens, envying them their privileged life and knowing full well what their political beliefs really were, felt he had the upper hand now and could finally get his own back. He denounced the Ditzens for employing too many staff, buying too much wood and not selling enough of their market garden produce. By July, Rudolf was back in Burlage's clinic. The strain of it all was affecting his marriage. When he came home Suse had the unenviable task of policing his drinking and his pills. Their only hope: that the war would be over soon – before Christmas as people liked to believe, what with the speedy invasions of Poland and France, and the uselessness of the Allies. The Ditzens started making plans to leave Carwitz as soon as it was over and move back to Berlin.

But then the RAF started bombing German cities. The Ditzens gave a 14-year-old boy evacuee from Duisburg a home for a while. Soon Suse's sister and brother-in-law arrived as well, to get away from the bombing raids on Hamburg. Rudolf's mother decided she was too old to travel so stayed alone in Celle. Hubert Rader arrived for three weeks' leave, just in time to help with the last of the harvesting. The *Wiener Illustrierte* was serialising Rudolf's *The Unloved Man*, but they weren't paying him anything like as much as in former times. Rudolf had another nervous crisis and ended up in Burlage's clinic again. He got home in time for Christmas but spent most of the time in bed. The only good thing that happened – an amazing thing in fact and quite out of the blue – was a telephone call from Ernst Rowohlt on New Year's Eve. From Berlin! It turned out he'd come home because he was expecting 'the imminent collapse of the Hitler regime', at which point he intended 'to start publishing again'. And to be frank, life in general and his marriage in particular weren't working out in Brazil. He came to stay at Carwitz for a few days and told them about his plans.

Rudolf was in a bad state again, mainly because a new edition of *Little Man, What Now?* only ran to 10,000 copies, due to the restrictions on paper, earning him less than he required for day-to-day living. On the other hand, this time he managed to fight the authorities' request to remove all references to Nazis, Communists and Jews, only conceding a new typeface, 'Antiqua', which the Reich Literary Chamber had designated the official typeface of the Reich. Ledig, somehow released from his stint of military service, had managed to swing that small victory for him.

'How did you and *Vater* meet?' Irma Thälmann, now 18, asked her *Mutti* one evening as they sat in their flat in Hamburg. Of course Ernst and Rosa had met through the Communist Party, she didn't really have to ask.

'We were always busy,' said Rosa, remembering those early years of their marriage. '*Vater* did something for the Party every evening. When he came back from the docks or some other place, he washed, ate something, rested a while, then started his day again: read the newspapers, studied, prepared a speech, till late at night. He often forgot our wedding day. Didn't even remember which day it was.'

Irma laughed. Typical *Vater*.

'But I always had some small present to give him, once he came to bed,' added *Mutti*, looking a bit embarrassed.

Mutti didn't talk about the past often, especially romantic stuff, but this time she did, sitting opposite Irma at the kitchen table, drinking a cup of *ersatz* coffee – made from acorns apparently – just the two of them, because *Vater* was still in prison and the two grandfathers were both dead.

It was quiet in the kitchen with the wood fire burning. A fearfully cold winter, even the docks frozen over. Since rationing had been brought in food was more scarce, the costs rising. Bread, flour, potatoes, meat, sausages, sugar, jam, lard, milk, cheese, tea, *ersatz* coffee, soap, washing powder, coal, coke, textiles, shoes, leather, tobacco, all rationed – if you could get them at all. Rosa and Irma never bought new clothes, just mended the old ones again and again. And knitted, as and when they could get hold of some wool – but more often by unravelling an old jumper which had so many holes it wasn't worth mending. Without the financial donations of the KPD in exile, they could never have managed, wrote Irma in her memoir.

But this particular anniversary *Vater* hadn't forgotten. It was amazing. He'd been transferred from Moabit prison in Berlin to Hanover by then. And they'd allowed a rare prison visit for *Mutti*, only *Mutti* – perhaps because it was their 25th wedding anniversary, who knows?

All sorts of strange things went on in those days. It just depended who happened to be on the spot at the time, making the decision. Perhaps there was a Beefsteak high up in the Hanover prison administration. Prison officials were harder to get hold of these days, so many had been called up for the invasion of Poland.

So *Mutti* had taken the train to Hanover, and this time it was she who got the surprise: *Vater* had been allowed to buy a few flowers and some twigs of fir. He'd made a wreath and cut out a colourful number 25. There was a vase of flowers on table. He'd smartened up his clothes. And he was in high good humour when she arrived. Rosa couldn't remember feeling so happy in a long time. He told her how grateful he was for those 25 years – how she'd been his finest comrade and friend. It was such a joyful visit.

'My life was enriched by *Vater*,' she told Irma that evening. 'He was my life's companion. He still is. I thank him. Through him I learned everything.'

In one of his letters to *Mutti*, he wrote: 'We never lived separate from the life of our working people. We studied among and through them, and learned to swim in the current of life. You learn throughout life!' That's how it was for Ernst and Rosa Thälmann. And for Irma too.

'The prison visits to *Vater* in Moabit and later in Hanover were always very tense, for *Mutti* and me, but especially so for *Vater*,' Irma recalled later. 'The Gestapo officials, Heller, Suffenplan and Opitz, who took turns watching us, always made provocative comments, taxing *Vater* with political questions. For example, they called the *Anschluss* with Austria a "glorious freedom" and a "return home to the Reich". *Vater* answered: "You'll bring them into line just as you have us, trampling over every democratic right and feeling, robbing them for your German capitalism, drawing them into war, just like in the Balkans and Czechoslovakia." Suffenplan was ready with an answer: "Not at all," he said. "We don't want war. Our Führer is for peace and Socialism." *Vater* laughed sharply: "Socialism is for peace, not war. Socialism doesn't allow for workers of one country fighting workers of another. Nor arresting and locking up those who are fight-ing for their own freedoms. Locking up thousands of people, is that freedom? Is that Socialism?" Then he listed all the things the Fascists were doing in preparation for war.' He was right of course, wrote Irma. And now here they were, embroiled in a war on two fronts:

Poland and France. All funded by Krupp and Thyssen and all.

'After the Fascist army marched into Poland *Vater*'s Gestapo offi-cials were enchanted. He told them: "Poland is only a first step to the invasion of the Soviet Union. I know your plans. But Stalin won't let himself be put off by you!" During my first visit after the invasion of the Soviet Union, the Gestapo man Heller jeered: "We're doing a *blitzkrieg* against the Russians. We'll be in Moscow in no time. Then even you will have to admit the superiority of our Aryan Volk. It's all over with Stalin!" *Vater* replied: "Stalin will break Hitler's neck!" The Gestapo lot just laughed. *Vater* went on: "Your Fascist army will come to grief in the Soviet Union. The Soviets freed their people in 1917. Not one child, or woman, or farmer, or worker would want to live in a land of Capitalists and Hitler Fascists. The whole Soviet Union will fight, till the country is free. Your *blitzkrieg* in the Soviet Union will end with your destruction. You wouldn't be so confident if you knew the Soviet worker, if you knew how a Volk lives which is free from Capitalism and its lackeys. In the Soviet Union each and every man has a lot to lose. Because the whole land belongs to the Volk. The people are free and rich, and the will of the People rules. What has the German Volk by comparison? Prisons and concentration camps. A few warmongers rule the people."'

'One word always led to the next,' wrote Irma. 'I used to tremble when it got going, but I was always happy to hear my father's strong answers. I was thrilled and proud. And I despised these Hitler lackeys. It was awful how these German Fascists talked about the Russians once they'd invaded: "They live in dark holes. These Russians are dirty. They're happy to be freed by us. We bring them culture." To me they'd say, "In Russia they call women like you hyenas. But we'll soon get rid of them!" Sometimes during these visits, I thought *Vater* would jump at them. In anger he'd say: "All your talk! But when you went to school – I imagine you did – you just learned how to repress the Volk. You have no love for your own German Volk, only your own wellbeing – that's your real concern."'

Perhaps he shouldn't have provoked them. But then, he was Ernst Thälmann, leader of the German Communists. Why wouldn't he speak out? It wasn't really a war of nations, he pointed out to his warders, just as he had in all his speeches from the earliest years. No, it was a war of the Capitalist bourgeoisie against the worker. Everywhere. 'Terrible that it's come to this! The worst elements of our Volk, who are the Filth of Humankind, now have the power. They can hound and whip impotent people who love their country and Volk, for fighting against war and Fascism,' is how he saw it – and held to it for the rest of his life. But Irma and Rosa were always frightened for *Vater* after those prison visits and the way he insisted on speaking out. What did they do to him afterwards, those Bloodhounds? They'd seen the evidence once, in Prinz Albrecht Strasse, way back in 1934, when he'd shuffled into the room with his teeth knocked out, face swollen and eyes filled with blood. Irma and Rosa lay awake at night, worrying about it.

But Thälmann knew the fight was still on – and that gave him strength. Throughout his time in prison, eleven years of it in all, and all of it in isolation, news of continuing Communist opposition to the Nazi regime seeped in through the cell bars. Which is in fact more or less how it was: two soldiers on flak duty at the prison in Hanover were Beefsteaks and former KPD members. They played their part well, expressing all manner of racial and war-like opinions, but they were secretly loyal to the great Thälmann, their Teddy, now in their care, and for whom they were prepared to risk everything. They devised a clever information route, via semaphore. It was a pleasing solution, given all three men had worked as Hamburg seamen at one time or another. Whenever the men had flak duty on the roof of the prison, and as soon as he was left alone in his cell by his prison guards, Ernst Thälmann would go to the barred cell window and start signalling them. And they signalled back. Amazing it was, how much information he got that way about the great and terrible events going on in the outside world – starting with Poland, later France, and then the invasion of Russia. He heard about the continued arrests of KPD comrades. And he knew all about the concentration camps. In fact, there was little Ernst Thälmann didn't know about. The signalling took time of course, but then he had all the time in the world.

And there were the prison visits, sporadic and rare and only for the wife and the daughter, but still – much, much better than nothing. In time, once she knew the Hanover routines, Irma smuggled in two small black slates and some chalk, hidden inside the most private parts of her clothing. A listening device had been installed in *Vater*'s cell by then, the prison guards making a big point about their generous decision to no longer sit in on the visits. Which fooled no one. Irma and her *Vater* both knew the Gestapo hoped to glean some information about Communist activity that they hadn't managed to get out of Thälmann with their beatings and torture. So whilst they chatted about domestic matters – the cost of food, news of friends and relations, the cold winter, the wet spring, the hot summer – they quietly wrote on their slates, wiping the words off as soon as they'd been read. 'I've got a link to the soldiers who do flak duty on the roof,' *Vater* wrote one day. 'These soldiers are fighting the Hitler system, courageously.' Then he added, because he couldn't resist the old slogans: 'Hitler will come and go, but the German Volk and state will remain.' For her part, Irma prepared her sentences carefully beforehand, short and simple, giving *Vater* news about those comrades who'd been arrested, those tortured, those sent to concentration camps, those executed. And those who were still, incredibly, surviving and fighting the regime, including an astonishing number, women as well as men, employed in armaments factories who had formed clandestine cells, sabotaging the works – apparently with great success.

'The Instructors are still getting through,' she wrote on her slate one day before quickly rubbing it off. *Vater* knew all about the Instructors – the decentralised system introduced in 1937 to oppose the regime, making it harder for the Gestapo spies to detect. These days the Instructors came across the borders from their various exiles, in the dead of night, risking their lives, on a ten-day tour of their sections – Stuttgart, Munich, Karlsruhe, Berlin – visiting the cells, passing on information from the exiled leadership, giving talks on subjects like 'Party policy and methods', offering practical advice on clandestine work. There were pamphlets to distribute and leaflets to post. Radio

Moscow had German-language programmes, as did the BBC, but the reception was bad and, if caught, it meant certain death. There were active cells in hundreds of factories, many including former SPD members – six Siemens factories in Berlin alone, producing essential electrical and engineering products for the war effort – all sabotaged. Some cell members even managed to get positions on their works' councils and the administration of the Nazi Labour Front which had replaced the Trade Unions.

In addition, more and more former KPD members, those too old to fight, were getting jobs in the prisons, some even in concentration camps – all of them happily swearing undying loyalty to the Führer. There were agents and counter-agents. Many had been hardened by fighting in the Spanish Civil war – 5,000 of them, of whom only 2,000 ever made it back home. Paris and Amsterdam were good centres of KPD activity, Amsterdam especially where the International Mineworkers Federation was jointly run by Franz Vogt, former SPD, and Wilhelm Knochel, former KPD. Disruption of coal-mining output was a highly effective blow against the German war effort. Why, after all, did Hitler need to get to the Ukraine? For the coal and the oil.

'I always said: work closely with the SPD,' *Vater* Thälmann wrote on his slate.

Irma knew. 'When the workers unite, they succeed.' It was always politics with Irma and her *Vater*. It was the way they expressed their love for one another.

'Like the War Economy Decree of September 39,' scribbled Irma.

The Decree was meant to put the economy on a war footing: no more fringe benefits, no more overtime, no more paid holidays, less wages, longer hours. No more workers' rights. It didn't last long. There was a great wave of indignation, followed by an ominous fall in production. The Decree was quickly withdrawn. That same September leaflets had appeared on the seats of trams in Berlin. 'I call on the Youth of the world: only the overthrow of Hitler and his band of warmongers can bring peace.' It was signed 'Communist Youth League'. Within days Heinz Kapelle, a former KPD member leading a group of sixty young Communists who'd already done two years in a concentration camp, was arrested. He was routinely tortured during 'intensive interrogation', then finally executed in July 1941.

With so many arrested, in concentration camps, or fighting at the Eastern or Western Fronts, manpower was an increasing problem for the Nazis. Years later, long after the war, one worker, Marie Jalowicz Simon, sat down with her son and recorded 77 tapes of how it was then. Marie was Jewish and 18 years old in 1940. Her mother had died of cancer two years earlier. Her father had lost his law practice and been refused a visa to Palestine. They lived in two rooms in a derelict district of Berlin, scraping a living. By 1940 the Jewish population of Berlin, once a vibrant 163,000, was down to 75,000. They were forbidden to attend Aryan schools, theatres, cinemas, share public transport, use the same shops or even park benches, and within a year they were forced to wear a yellow star.

But the Nazis needed workers for their factories. So, in 1940, Marie was called up as forced labour with 200 other young Jewish women into the Siemens armaments factory in the Spandau district of Berlin. The days were long – 12 hours, plus travel, paid 20 marks a week, barely enough to live on after rent and fares and the 'voluntary' donations to Nazi causes like Winter Aid – but at least she was earning a wage. Many of the overseers at the factory were Nazis. Marie soon realised that 'the same Aryan German who hated the rich Jew from the big house like poison had nothing against starving young girls who worked hard, just as he worked hard himself.' There were rows and rows of work benches on the vast factory floor, six girls at each, operating the lathes. It was hard, noisy, monotonous labour. They had to use their hips to operate the lathes, hour after hour, with no leather aprons to protect them. Fluid ran constantly over the metal which had to be mopped up off the floor with cloths. But therein lay a secret: the cloths were excellent for hiding messages, taking them from workbench to workbench. Marie's supervisor was Max Schulz, an ethnic German from Upper Silesia and a devout Roman Catholic. His priest told him to treat his underlings fairly, like a good Christian. He was a fine tool setter but he had problems filling in the columns listing the number of screws each worker produced, because he could read but he couldn't write. Marie helped him, taking the ledgers wrapped in oil cloths to the toilets and filling in the columns for him.

There was an extremely effective sabotage ring in the Siemens factory run by former Communists and Social Democrats working together. Marie was soon one of them. But first she had to learn the technical expertise: understanding the tolerance value of a product – a nut had a tolerance of no more than a fraction of a millimetre so the internal thread had to be cut as narrowly as possible but not so narrow as to be detected by the superintendent who sat at a high desk in the middle of the floor, overseeing and inspecting everything. At the same time, in another department, the screw for the nut was made as wide as possible. The parts passed their quality control tests separately, but later they wouldn't fit together. One of the organising saboteurs, a tool setter called Hermann, former SPD, started to engage the good-hearted but simple Max Schultz, in conversation during their break-times, explaining things to him in an easy way, and in time persuaded him to join the sabotage ring. 'But stay in the Party,' Hermann warned Schultz. Thus Schultz became a most useful source of inside information. The ring worked extremely well and was never exposed.

Catholic Poles were another source of manpower – shipped to the Reich as industrial and agricultural forced labour. An indignant report from the *Ortsgruppenleiter* to the *Kreisleiter* at Kaiserslautern in February described a local problem: 'On Sunday 18 February 1940 in his church the Catholic priest of Schallodenbach, Father Seitz, told the parents of the village to stop their children doing things to these people from Poland – that is to say, swearing at them. The mother of the priest after the service gathered these Poles around her in front of the church and chatted with them – as much as was possible. They then took the Poles into the priest's house where they served them coffee, according to their own admission. Only in the evening did the Poles return to their bosses. I request that this matter be followed up.' The result: Father Seitz was taken in for Gestapo interrogation. Soon after, a telex arrived in the Gestapo office: 'Concerning local priest Friedrich Seitz, born 28 Jan 1905 in Mayen. The *Reichsführer* SS Himmler has ordered that the priest Friedrich Seitz be taken into protective custody. I request that news of the internment be relayed.'

By early 1940, Bernt Engelmann was stationed in the far north of the Reich, on the isolated island of Sylt close to the Danish border. His ploy of volunteering early for the Luftwaffe had worked beautifully. He'd gone off for training straight after completing his months of Labour Service leaving his mother alone in a small apartment in Berlin – a new one which she'd moved to after Bernt's father had emigrated to England to escape the Nazis. The plan was for *Mutti* to join him later. As for Bernt, by the time war broke out he was a fully-fledged private in a communications unit of the Luftwaffe, attached to one of the *Wehrmacht* regiments.

One evening in February, Bernt and his friend Erwin were sitting in the deserted Fisherman's bar as usual, just passing the time. They'd met in barracks during training and quickly became friends, easily spotting the like-minded: Erwin's father had done a stint in 'protective custody' in 1933 in the infamous Kemna concentration camp outside their home town of Wupperthal – a private concern, because there hadn't as yet been enough time for the Nazi regime to build their own. Once he was let out – all fingers on both hands broken – he was done for. But Erwin managed to volunteer for the Luftwaffe, just like Bernt. He'd been an electrician and now he was head of their unit, a team of four, in charge of a Mobile Radio Car. It was perfect. Except that their fourth member, the driver of the car, called Barczustowski, was a card-carrying Nazi.

In the bar, Bernt and Erwin were discussing ways of getting extra leave. They didn't have to watch their backs as they talked because the place was completely empty, it being a cold and dark night. And the owner had made it quite clear where he stood politically, favouring those who shared his views. The way he worked it out: if they didn't come in with a keen '*Heil Hitler!*' and didn't toast their 'beloved Führer', they were sound. He hated Hitler. But you'd never know.

'You have to do it like Hitler,' Erwin the corporal told Bernt the private. 'You have to lie big – lots of lies, not just one.'

In point of fact, it wasn't that difficult to get extra leave. First, there was nothing doing on the Isle of Sylt – just hundreds of enlisted Luftwaffe, naval personnel, army reservists, administrators, you-name-it, all hanging around waiting for orders while the 'phoney war' dragged on. Second, their Commanding Officer, Major Zobel, had been an academic at a university before being called up – a naturalist whose only interest appeared to be bird-watching in the sand dunes. As long as his men behaved themselves, he really didn't care.

'What do you make of the Double Doctor?' Bernt was referring to a new recruit to their Unit, a scientist with two doctorates.

'I think he's fine,' said Erwin. 'But let's see.'

The other new recruit they called Little Hans, because he was so tall. He had a degree in meteorology. Erwin thought he was fine too. So that just left bloody Barczustowski.

Once the bar was completely empty, the owner came over with some whisky, 'washed up on shore' as he liked to say – namely, smuggled in from the Danish island of Romo. Erwin's preferred toast was always 'to the final victory', by which he didn't mean Germany.

A week or so later Bernt and Erwin were playing chess with the Double Doctor in the Strand Café, a slightly superior place to the Fisherman's bar, but not much. Inge, the owner's daughter, was behind the counter, attracting all the soldiers' attention because she was the only reasonably pretty girl left on the island, most of the local population having left once war was declared. It was getting late when Little Hans came to join them.

'There's someone asking after you,' he told Bernt. The unknown man was having dinner in the one and only hotel left open on the island, the Hotel Hamburg, chatting away with the proprietor. The mystery was how did the man ever get permission to visit the island, which was strictly off-limits to civilians? Little Hans handed over a business card. Could Bernt please pay the man a visit, either this evening or in the morning, since he was leaving by noon? 'Bespoke Tailor. Finest fabrics and Superior Workmanship,' read the card. It was Herr Desch.

Bernt went straight to the dining room in the Hotel Hamburg and found the two men laughing away, talking like old friends. The proprietor was asking: would Herr Desch like to take the measurements for the new suit now, or might they just have another drink first? Herr Desch looked up and spotted Bernt making his way hesitantly between the tables of the dining room. Privates were not normally seen in there.

'Ah! Here's my nephew!' said Herr Desch, greeting Bernt warmly.

'Hello Onkel Hubert!' Hans rallied jovially. He couldn't imagine how he suddenly remembered that Herr Desch's first name was Hubert.

Onkel Hubert turned back to the proprietor. No, no! No need for coupons, between friends. And the best of it was he still had access to the finest English cloth, even now they were at war! Ha ha. A good joke, that one. The proprietor was paying Herr Desch with some cases of the finest French wines. Another good joke.

Bernt couldn't work out how on earth Herr Desch had managed to get onto the island in the first place. But it turned out one of his oldest customers was stationed there and had just been promoted to Vice Admiral and needed a new uniform. No one seemed to question how unlikely it was that a tailor be fetched all the way from Düsseldorf, as though there weren't any tailors closer by. Presumably the unknown vice-Admiral was a 'friend' of Herr Desch's, surmised Hans.

'And it's just lucky I'm here,' continued Onkel Hubert, 'because your Onkel Erich has decided to give up his legal practice and go back on active duty, now the war is on. You know how patriotic he is. After all, he's a Major in the reserves.'

Of course Bernt knew. His 'Onkel' Erich was a friend of the family and of Herr Desch's too apparently – a Jewish lawyer who'd gone underground soon after 1933, assuming a new identity, which had worked quite well for some time because 'Onkel' Erich was a consummate actor. Always had been. Presumably the Gestapo were onto him now. But how could he get a posting here on Sylt? And wouldn't people think it a bit odd that Bernt had not one but two 'Onkels' turn up? Later Bernt worked out that the Vice Admiral was going to put in a word.

'This place is full of units of every sort as far as I can see,' said Herr Desch once they were alone, 'endless administrative posts of one sort or another. Must be a job for Major von Elkan somewhere.' So he was Major von Elkan now, was he? Well, well.

Herr Desch asked Bernt about his own duties on the island, taking careful note.

'Not much doing,' said Bernt. 'We track all aeroplanes entering our North Sea airspace and keep in radio contact with other local radio stations. If there's any danger we have to alert the flak batteries. Nothing's really happened so far but Erwin decided we should issue alerts regularly, just to keep everyone happy – and because we get one mark a day for it, sometimes some cigarettes and coffee or chocolate too. It's called Combat Duty Supplements.'

Herr Desch laughed. Really old Fish-face was in high good humour, thought Bernt. And even more so once he heard how the owner of the Fisherman's bar smuggled whisky from the Danish island of Romo. 'Just the place for Major von Elkan,' he said.

About a month later, Bernt ran into Major Zobel in the corridor of their barracks. Bernt was just coming off night duty, Major Zobel was just off for an early morning swim, wearing a short red and white striped bathrobe over his nightshirt.

'You're related to Major von Elkan, I hear,' he said, in passing.

'Well, distantly,' Bernt replied, rather taken aback.

'Sends you his best wishes. We played chess last night. Nice fellow,' said Major Zobel before disappearing down the corridor for his swim.

Later that day Bernt rang the Hotel Hamburg, pretty sure that's where 'Onkel' Erich would be staying.

'Of course,' said the switchboard operator. 'Let me connect you with his office.'

'Planning Bureau,' came a clipped military voice. 'Major von Elkan speaking.'

Was nun! Whatever next!

As it happened, the plan to get 'Onkel' Erich across the Danish border didn't work out, because the Germans occupied Denmark in April 1940, encountering hardly any resistance because the Danes were taken completely by surprise. Norway had a little more time to organise and fought hard, but ultimately suffered the same fate.

Major von Elkan found himself suddenly called away from the Isle of Sylt, much to Major Zobel's distress. He liked their chess games. Later, whilst doing research for his memoir, Bernt found out 'Onkel' Erich had acquired a new set of false documents, no doubt with Herr Desch's help, and lived for some time in Berlin, fully registered with the police under the name of Erich von Elkan, Major, retired. Later still, he surfaced as a down-and-out in a working-class district of Berlin, local dialect and all. Apparently, he survived the war, outwitting them all.

A few weeks later, Bernt and Erwin were summoned to a meeting with Colonel Kessler, their regimental Commander. He appreciated their vigilance and zeal, he said with a certain sarcasm. But all these night alerts had to stop. Erwin tried to account for them by explaining that they'd been fine-tuning the aircraft reporting system. It didn't work.

'Dismissed!'

'And, by the way,' the Colonel added just as they were leaving. 'One of your team will have to transfer to Norway, to the new aircraft warning centre in Drontheim. They need a trained wireless operator.'

Erwin consulted with Major Zobel who happily took his advice. And that was the end of Barczustowski. He was soon replaced by a new young recruit, Jens Kroger, aged 20, a keen fan of Duke Ellington, Tommy Dorsey and Gene Krupa.

'Better check him out first,' said Erwin, knowing there were Gestapo plants everywhere, even on the Isle of Sylt. But Krupa, as they were soon calling him, checked out just fine. He'd opted for Communications because with a good receiver you could pick up jazz concerts, sometimes even from Carnegie Hall. He'd played percussion in a band until the Nazis designated jazz 'degenerate', and he arrived with a phonograph and some jazz records, knowing it was *verboten* but considering it worth taking the risk.

Krupa was part of the so-called Swing Youth – or had been until he was called up. 'The dance music was all English and American,' went an official report from a Gestapo plant who attended an illegal Swing festival in Hamburg in early 1940, judging that some 600 young people were present. 'Only Swing dancing and Jitterbugging took place. At the entrance to the hall the words "Swing prohibited" had been altered to "Swing requested". The participants accompanied the dances and songs, without exception, by singing the English words. Indeed, throughout the evening they attempted to only speak English or, at some tables, French. The dancers were an appalling sight. None of the couples danced normally; there was only Swing of the worst sort. Sometimes two boys danced with one girl; sometimes several couples formed a circle, linking arms and jumping, slapping hands, even rubbing the backs of their heads together; and then, bent double, with the top half of the body hanging down, long hair flopping into the face, they dragged themselves round practically on their knees. The band played wilder and wilder pieces. None of the band was sitting down any longer, they all "jitterbugged" on the stage like wild creatures. Several boys could be observed dancing together, always with two cigarettes in the mouth, one in each corner . . .'

Krupa turned out to be a good driver, which was just as well, because on 4 May 1940 their communications unit was given the order to leave Sylt that same night. For France. To somewhere called St Pol near Dunkirk, according to Major Zobel, on the coast in Northern France apparently, near the Belgian border. So the five of them, Bernt, Erwin, the Double Doctor, Little Hans and Krupa set off in their new eight-cylinder Horch Mobile Radio Car, heavy-hearted, knowing the 'phoney war' was over now and the real war had begun.

The German *Wehrmacht* had marched into France with hardly a hitch. The soldiers were told to treat the locals politely – France was being occupied, not fought. The French would have their own government, Vichy, further south. Think of them as collaborators, not enemies. Except for the Kommies, of course. And the Jews.

On 5 June, the Horch Radio Car was parked in the village square of St-Pol-sur-Mer – their third St Pol so far. Krupa was exhausted. He'd been driving all night, this way and that, lost, constantly blocked by blown-up bridges and flooded roads. Which St Pol had Major Zobel meant? It was three weeks since they'd left Sylt. They'd lost wireless contact with their regiment which was – who knows where? And there were no German troops in sight, only an endless stream of French refugees, trudging, rather suspiciously, in the same direction as they were driving. And French prisoners of war, about a thousand of them, lying in a meadow in the sun. They told Erwin and Bernt they reckoned they were the lucky ones – out of the war, and still alive. True enough, thought Erwin and Bernt.

It was early morning in St-Pol-sur-Mer and the five musketeers were starving. A small café was just opening on the other side of the square. Bernt, the French-speaker, walked across and asked if there was any chance of some breakfast. Coffee and croissants? Eggs perhaps? The proprietor looked surprised.

'How come you lot are still here?' he asked, not especially friendly.

Bernt didn't know what to make of that. He offered the man a cigarette from a pack they'd bought somewhere on the way, hoping to help breakfast negotiations along.

'I thought you Tommies had all left!'

Lieber Gott! Good God! The man thought they were Tommies. Understandable, perhaps, since their Luftwaffe Communications uniforms were nondescript grey, and their caps had no badges or insignia, quite unlike the regular *Wehrmacht* uniform.

Bernt took out a 50-franc note and handed it to him. 'Breakfast?'

'You're stuck now,' said the proprietor, taking the money. 'The evacuation's over. The Germans will be here by noon, latest.'

'Do you have any eggs?'

'You can sit here, outside,' he said, indicating a round iron table and chairs.

After breakfast they set off for Dunkirk. The road was like Armageddon: burning tanks, abandoned vehicles, streets blasted, villages blown up. Dunkirk, once they reached it, was bombed to smithereens. The beaches were like a deserted battlefield, everything left lying in the sand: wrecked army trucks, crates of munitions, whole field kitchens, thousands of dead Tommies.

Bernt couldn't believe it. The British Army had gone down. Defeated. Erwin disagreed. They'd fight back, *nur warten*, wait and see. Victory for England! *Vive* Churchill! The Double Doctor agreed with Erwin. He'd just made wireless contact with Major Zobel. 'No. The Brits rescued most of them. And some Frenchies as well.' They gave a quiet thumbs up.

'Major Zobel sends his congratulations. He says he's proud of us! And that we're to get moving again. Immediately. Southwards.'

CHAPTER TEN

A WAR ON TWO FRONTS

Hitler launched Operation Barbarossa, the invasion of the Soviet Union, at dawn on 22 June 1941, attacking his three worst enemies – the Communists, the Jews and those *Untermenschen*, the subhuman Slavs who resisted him – all in one fine sweep. It is a moot point whether Stalin was taken completely by surprise, as German propaganda had it. But that night 153 divisions of 3 million *Wehrmacht* troops crossed the border, along with 3,500 Panzer tanks, backed up by 5,000 Luftwaffe planes. Army Group North, under General Field Marshal Leeb, struck north, towards Leningrad. Army Group Centre, under General Field Marshal Bock, struck out for Moscow, and Army Group South, under General Field Marshal von Rundstedt, struck south, making for the huge reserves of oil, wheat and coal, all by now desperately needed in the Reich. That first day 1,200 Russian planes were destroyed. The following weeks were a success so great, it took even the *Wehrmacht* by surprise: 600 miles of territory conquered along a 1,000-mile front, three million prisoners captured. The flat land of the Western Soviet Union was ideal for the German Panzer, charging ahead in the bright June sunshine, followed by jubilant troops singing their Nazi marching songs. Stalin's army was no match for them, not least because it was still suffering from Stalin's most recent purges. And in the wake of the *Wehrmacht* came Himmler's SS *Einsatzgruppen*, systematically exterminating Hitler's three worst enemies as they went.

Fabian von Schlabrendorff had joined the *Wehrmacht* army as soon as war was declared. What else could he do? He'd already tried everything – gone to England to plead with Winston Churchill to intervene to remove Hitler before war was declared, plotted and schemed with Ernst Niekisch, former editor of the *Widerstand* journal, now serving life in prison, and with Ewald Kleist von Schmenzin on his country estate in Pommern, as well as Hans Oster and Wilhelm Canaris at the *Abwehr*, the German military intelligence, and numerous others. All to no avail. The only way to defeat Hitler and the

Nazis, now that they were at war, was to join the *Wehrmacht*. Only army officers stood a chance of organising a coup against Hitler – and then keeping the peace afterwards, preventing civil war breaking out in the Reich once a new regime was established. Meanwhile the *Wehrmacht* was the safest place to hide from the Gestapo. Better to die on the battlefield than in 'protective custody'.

He wasn't the only one. Thousands of young men were relieved to join the *Wehrmacht* rather than endure the hardships and risks of the Nazi terror regime. The male members of a clandestine resistance group at Munich University known as the White Rose were nearly all serving in the *Wehrmacht* by 1940. Hans Scholl and his sister, Sophie, were among the leaders of the group, distributing pamphlets and an underground newspaper and putting up posters around the university in the dead of night. Each time Hans and his comrades came back on leave from first Poland then Russia they had worse and worse stories to report on the crimes being committed in the Reich's name by the SS *Einsatzgruppen*. They printed leaflets detailing the crimes, copying hundreds on a duplicating machine and using couriers to distribute them throughout southern Germany.

'Since the conquest of Poland three hundred thousand Jews have been murdered in that country in the most bestial way,' went one leaflet. 'Why do the German people behave so apathetically in the face of these abominable crimes, crimes so unworthy of the human race?' Another called for 'sabotage in armaments plants and war industries, sabotage at all gatherings, rallies, public ceremonies, and organisations of the National Socialist Party, sabotage in all areas of science and scholarship which further the continuation of war – whether in universities, technical schools, laboratories, research institutes, or technical bureaus.'

They always knew it couldn't last. By February 1943 the Gestapo had tracked them down and arrested the leaders. Dr Roland Freisler, the notorious judge of the Nazis' *Volksgericht*, flew down especially from Berlin to Munich to preside over the trial. Sophie arrived in court on crutches, her face badly bruised. Still, she challenged him: 'You know the war is lost!' All the other members of the group showed evidence of severe torture. When it was Hans's turn to speak, he pleaded for the life of his sister, knowing his own life was already over. 'Shut your mouth! Shut your mouth!' Freisler screamed in his high-pitched voice. They were all sentenced to death by guillotine. The Scholl parents were allowed a few minutes with their two children before the execution. 'You will go down in history,' their father told them, in tears. 'There is another justice than this!'

So Fabian had good reason to disappear into the army on 1 September 1939, into Infantry Regiment 230 in Brandenburg, bound for the Western Front. Their Commander was Prince Oskar of Prussia, the exiled Kaiser's second youngest son, a strong and active leader as it turned out. By May 1940, the regiment was crossing the border into Lorraine. They encountered little resistance. Fabian couldn't understand it. What were the French thinking of? Why didn't they fight to defend their country? Perhaps it hadn't dawned on Fabian that the last thing the French wanted was another war. Nor that many of those on the Right actively welcomed the Germans in their fight against Communism. One way or the other, the German Volk were jubilant at the astonishingly swift victory over their former enemy. At last some revenge for Versailles. The troops had their new marching song: 'So we're marching! Yes we're marching! *Nach Eng-e-land!*' because England was next.

'Dear Yorck,' wrote Helmuth von Moltke, one of the diarist Ulrich von Hassell's co-conspirators, to his cousin Peter Yorck von Wartenburg on 17 June 1940, about the conquest of France. 'We must today reckon with having to live through a triumph of evil and, whereas we had steeled ourselves to face any amount of pain and misery, we must now prepare to do something which is far worse, namely to keep our heads above water amid a flood of public good fortune, self-satisfaction and prosperity. I want to use this letter to link it to a conversation I had with you and Schulenburg a fortnight ago. You will perhaps recollect the wager. Schulenburg was ready to bet that within ten years a state would have come into existence of which we could fully approve. I was ready to maintain the opposite of this proposition.'

The Schulenburg to whom Moltke was referring was Fritzi. All three, Moltke, Yorck and Schulenburg, were part of a group of resisters loosely gathered round General Ludwig Beck who had resigned from the army in protest in 1938, and Carl Goerdeler, the former Mayor of Leipzig. All were cast down by Germany's early victories. It made their plans for a coup much more difficult. Only Fritzi remained optimistic, saying it might take longer now, but sooner or later, they'd win.

By early 1941, Fabian had been transferred to Posnan in Western Poland – by personal request of Henning von Tresckow, now First

General Staff Officer with the 228 Infantry Division – to be Tresckow's adjutant. Fabian and Henning had kept in close contact since their first meeting at Henning's family estate back in the summer of 1939. Henning had talked about everything then, holding nothing back, each man trusting the other completely, knowing they shared the same aim – to rid the Reich of Hitler and the Nazi terror regime. A professional soldier with the *Wehrmacht*, Henning had been among the first wave of troops into Poland. At first, he'd been glad. Still smarting from the harsh terms of the Treaty of Versailles, he was especially keen to reclaim the Polish Corridor. But when he saw what the SS *Einsatzgruppen* were up to, he changed his mind. 'War is madness,' he told Fabian. 'Hitler is the key. He's the cancer. We have to bring him down – if necessary, by assassination.' Fabian, implacable opponent of the Nazi regime from the first, was shocked. But he'd already heard the same from Ewald von Kleist Schmenzin and Ernst Niekisch, two similarly uncompromising and realistic men.

'He's preparing to invade Russia, you know that don't you?' Henning was talking to Fabian in his usual forthright manner, full of energy.
Though he was a military man through and
through, he was unconventional with it. Tall and scholarly looking, with a high forehead and receding hair, some thought him a bit too ironical and high-handed. But not his men, who admired him and trusted him. He didn't take anything too seriously, did Tresckow, least of all himself.

'What happened to the invasion of England?'

'Never serious,' said Henning.

Fabian was younger than Henning, and not at all experienced in matters of war. Henning, by contrast, had been in the army since 1924. *Junge*, young man, that's how Henning saw Fabian von Schlabrendorff. But he saw his single-mindedness too, and he knew he could rely on him to do whatever was required. It was why he requested Schlabrendorff be transferred to him in the first place. Colleagues were surprised. Schlabrendorff was only a lowly Lieutenant in the Reserves – a civilian really, a lawyer, and a bit high-minded and stand-offish with it. But Henning always got his way they said, laughing.

'Read *Mein Kampf*, Junge. It's all there. And now this terrible success in Poland and France . . .'

'Why take the risk of invading Poland?'

'Ideology. *Lebensraum.* Extermination of the Slav and the capitalist Jew. You know all that.'

Fabian knew it in theory, Henning knew it in fact. Henning couldn't forget what he'd witnessed in Poland. Nor the Night of the Long Knives back in 1934. Nor the hounding of the Jews at *Kristallnacht*. So he wasn't surprised when he heard about Hitler's meeting with junior army officers, mostly new recruits from the Hitler Youth, on 30 March 1941, in preparation for Barbarossa. 'The Soviet Kommissars are the bearers of ideologies directly opposed to National Socialism,' Hitler said, 'therefore the Kommissars will be liquidated.' Stalin had never signed the Hague Convention, he reminded his listeners, so the Russian civilian didn't have the protection of international law. 'The struggle is one of ideologies and racial differences and will have to be conducted with unprecedented, unmerciful and unrelenting harshness.' For those with qualms the great Führer added, 'All officers have to rid themselves of obsolete ideologies. I know that the necessity of these methods of making war is beyond the comprehension of your generals, but I insist that my orders be executed without contradiction!'

Tresckow and Schlabrendorff were attached to Army Group Centre. Their Commander was General Fedor von Bock – a decent enough man. Tresckow was intent on gaining some influence over him before the invasion of Russia. If anyone could do it, it was Henning.

'These early successes – they won't last,' Henning told Fabian. 'Once we invade Russia it'll be Napoleon all over again. Wait and see. Great advances, but not great enough to beat the Russian winter. Don't these people read their history?'

'They don't read anything.'

Then off they went to another lecture by one of the Party hacks, giving them all the idiot racial propaganda. Henning managed to avoid most of them, but you had to attend some to avoid suspicion. Fabian, being a lowly lieutenant, had no choice.

'Dear Herr Stalin,' Hitler wrote on 14 May 1941, 'I am writing this letter at the moment of having finally concluded that it will be impossible to achieve a lasting peace in Europe, not for us, not for future generations, without the final shattering of England and her destruction as a state.' To this purpose, he explained, he had placed 'a large number of my troops, about 80 divisions, on the borders of the Soviet Union. This possibly gave rise to rumours now circulating of a likely military conflict between us . . . I assure you, on my honour, that this is not the case . . . By approximately June 15–20 I plan to begin a massive transfer of troops to the West from your borders. I continue to hope for our meeting in July. Yours sincerely, Adolf Hitler.'

Five weeks later, on the night of 21/22 June, he launched Operation Barbarossa. It was preceded by a *Führer Befehl* Order: Russian troops to be shot on the spot. Take no prisoners of war.

'Gersdorff, remember this moment,' Tresckow told Major Rudolf Freiherr von Gersdorff, another secret conspirator at Army Group Centre. 'If we don't manage to persuade the Field Marshal to do everything in his power to have this Führer Order taken back, then Germany will have lost, once and for all, her Honour. A hundred years from now, that will still be so. And they won't just blame Hitler. It'll be you and me too. And our wives, and our children, and the boy in the street playing with his ball. Everyone.'

They went straight to Bock. 'Tell Hitler to take it back!' shouted Tresckow. 'This Order will be our downfall!'

He had direct access to Bock because Bock was his uncle. 'You have to fly to Hitler today, and what's more, with Rundstedt and Leeb too. I've already been in contact with them and prepared your plane. You have to tell him: you promised you wouldn't implicate regular troops in any war crimes. You have broken your promise with this Order.'

Bock made a lame protest. He was a vain and ambitious man. And he knew as well as anyone that Hitler wouldn't listen, not to him, not to anyone, and that he himself would be dismissed instead, if not outright arrested.

Henning von Tresckow saw how things were and knew he'd have to act without his uncle's help from now on. Fabian von Schlabrendorff was one of the last to join a group of trusted conspirators he was gathering around him for decisive action, whatever the cost. He'd already managed to place two of his old friends, Lieutenant Heinrich Graf von Lehndorff and Major Hans Graf von Hardenberg, as adjutants to Bock. Then came Major Gersdorff and Berndt von Kleist, an old *Kamarad* who'd been in the Great War with him and shared the same horror of what the Nazis were doing to the Germany they loved. The newcomer, Schlabrendorff, was to act as unofficial 'courier' between the plotters at Army Group Centre and those back in the *Heimat* – the

Beck/Goerdeler group, and the group at the Foreign Office in the Wilhelm Strasse, and Hans Oster and Canaris at the *Abwehr*.

So across the border into the Soviet Union Henning von Tresckow and Fabian von Schlabrendorff marched and fought on the night of 22 June 1941, along with the rest of Army Group Centre and Guderian's elite Panzer regiment – with the *Einsatzgruppen* torching and exterminating in their wake, stringing up partisans and local district Kommissars in village squares from telegraph poles and trees by way of warning. There were already partisans hiding out in the villages and woodlands, blowing up railway tracks and the enemy's munitions stores and depots and poisoning the water in German army barracks – hardened fighters, including women – though nothing like as many as later when they made life pure hell for the German troops. Apparently one of the most feared leaders was a man called Voss, a German Communist who'd slipped out of the Reich and into Russia after the Reichstag fire arrests. *Unglaublich!* Unbelievable, thought the German foot soldier, that a German like themselves could be joining the Russian partisans. Treason, it was!

As predicted, the three Army Groups – Centre, North and South – made astonishing and sweeping progress at first. Who knows whether it was because Stalin was really taken by surprise or merely biding his time? But by mid-July Army Group Centre was already at Borissow, near Orsha, making for Smolensk and thence to Moscow. Minsk had already capitulated. In spite of the *Führer Befehl* Order to shoot Russian troops on the spot, they had taken some 700,000 Russian prisoners of war, the *Wehrmacht* Generals refusing to break the international terms of warfare.

Hitler was beside himself. He decided to visit Borissow and give Bock a piece of his raging mind. He arrived by plane, travelling the four kilometres from the airfield to the HQ in a heavily guarded fleet of cars specially transported from Poland. The great Führer trusted no one. He stayed no longer than it took to berate Bock for not being a true *Fleischerhund*, Bloodhound, who was baulking him at every turn. Bock had been against him ever since the retaking of the Rhineland, Hitler shouted and raged, right up to the conquest of France and beyond. Bock had better watch out! And with that, Hitler, the only true *Fleischerhund*, got back into his fleet of cars, surrounded by his SS personal bodyguard – 6 feet tall, black uniforms, shiny jackboots – and sped off back to the Führer plane. Fabian heard all about it afterwards from Henning in the privacy of his rooms. It was *lächer-lich*, ridiculous, funny even, except that it was so deadly serious.

That same July 1941 Stalin announced his scorched earth policy – torching everything which might be of use to the advancing Germans as his Russian troops retreated in order to regroup and counter-attack, on three Fronts as it turned out, and led by their top generals, including the formidable Zhukov. Incredibly, they managed to take 80 per cent of their munitions industry and war machinery with them, leaving almost nothing for the Germans. Tresckow knew this. So did most of the Generals.

'He's playing warlord again,' wrote General Halder, another secret resister and Chief of General Staff in Berlin, in his private diary, about the Führer, 'and bothering us with such absurd ideas that he's risking everything our wonderful operations have so far won. Unlike the French, the Russians won't just run away when they've been tactically defeated. Every other day now I have to go over to him (Hitler). Hours of gibberish, and the outcome is there's only one man who understands how to wage wars.' Halder told von Brauchitsch, Commander-in-Chief, and von Rundstedt, Commander of Army Group South, and some other generals he knew were secret anti-Nazis. But no one else. It was too dangerous. The trouble was, once power got into the wrong hands, into a terror regime and dictatorship, there was not much anyone could do about it. Unless they were prepared to give up their lives for it.

Then came Führer Order 33. Instead of marching on Moscow before winter set in, Army Group Centre was to detour and take Kiev and Smolensk first, and capture the Ukraine's vast reserves of oil and corn. And coal. Had the Führer gone completely mad? Commander-in-Chief Brauchitsch tried to argue it out with Hitler. In vain. Next, Halder and Bock and Guderian requested a meeting with the Führer. They explained, with respect, the problem: quite simply, it couldn't be done – there were no proper roads, the railways were being blown up, the troops were exhausted, it took at least a week for reinforcements and spare parts to arrive from the Reich or Poland. Unless Moscow was taken before winter, it would not be taken at all. The Führer raged at their impertinence and disloyalty. Guderian asked, not for the first time, to be allowed some weeks of leave to recuperate. It was refused and they were dismissed. Henning von Tresckow, waiting in the wings, joined them for a secret meeting later that day. What on earth were they to do? It was a long, tortuous meeting, with no decisive outcome. Except for Henning who knew the only solution: Hitler had to be eliminated, one way or another.

He despatched Fabian to make urgent contact with the civilian resisters and conspirators back in the Reich. Army officers knew they were the only ones who could effect a coup or assassination, but the civilians – former politicians, diplomats, civil servants, police and economists – were the ones who had to be fully prepared to immediately form a new, democratic government if civil war in Germany was to be avoided. There were some surprising names on Fabian's list, including Johannes Popitz, former Prussian Finance Minister and member of the Nazi Party, and Arthur Nebe, a feared SS Gestapo chief.

At the beginning of October 1941, Fabian arrived at Ulrich von Hassell's country house at Ebenhausen near Munich. It was beautiful, he noted, as befitted a former grand diplomat – great Chinese vases and a Chinese gong in the lofty entrance hall, a Madonna and Child by Rogier van der Weyden above the fireplace in the drawing room, and a library filled with hundreds of leather-bound books, including a first edition of Dante.

'A few days ago Sch(labendorff) reserve lieutenant and lawyer, turned up,' wrote Hassell in his secret diary on 4 October 1941, using only code-names. 'He was sent by his task-masters to find out whether opposition here in the *Heimat* was crystallizing, to be able to assure them that "one" was ready to act. He came to me through Burgers (Guttenberg) to obtain information on the foreign situation. A very sensible man, but his comments reveal the naivety with which the Josephs (generals) are approaching this problem. Among other things he asked if there were any guarantee that Britain would make peace soon after a change of regime was effected. I told him there were no such guarantees and that there could be none. Were it otherwise any cobbler's apprentice could overthrow the regime.

'I could guarantee him something different: 1. that, even if England and America were rock bottom, Hitler would *never* get a peace deal, and 2. that only a decent Germany would have a chance of making a peace, which would be an acceptable one. Moreover, the case for a regime change was *our* business, a business we alone could decide, not our opponents. This S seemed to understand. He repeated that he thought we would broker a peace immediately after the regime change. I had to disabuse him of that illusion too.'

Naive Schlabrendorff and Hassell, the old diplomat, talked on. When Fabian left, Hassell noted that the visit had been most encouraging, because for the first time he had concrete evidence that an initiative was being taken *over there* by the army officers. But he had to warn Schlabrendorff that a 'dirty' time was unavoidable after the event, when the disillusioned Volk would still believe that Hitler had had victory snatched from him by the conspirators, and that a peace deal would not be forthcoming. It was the old dilemma: if one waited till the outcome of the war was clear to everyone, then the chance of brokering a good peace was lost. The outlook was *in any event* bad, but in that event, it was terrible.

The first snowfall in Russia came mid-October 1941. The German troops weren't ready: they had no proper winter clothing, reduced to stuffing newspaper in their boots to try and keep warm. Their Panzers, so effective across the flat dry land in summer, got stuck in the mud and snow and sank in the treacherous areas of marshland. Horses drowned. Some men too. Spare parts took even longer to arrive now, and there was an extreme shortage of petrol. By early November the Russian winter had set in, just as Stalin expected, and Army Groups North, Centre and South, far from making progress, were having to dig in, and finally to retreat to safer positions. Equipment and vehicles froze up. The troops were warned not to touch any metal or their skin would tear off. There were 100,000 cases of frostbite. Dysentery was rife. Sentries died at their posts, fallen asleep, frozen like statues. German casualties were running at 3,000 a day. By December the temperature had fallen to minus 35 degrees Celsius. The Führer had a new medal struck for his heroes at the Eastern Front. The heroes were soon calling it The Order of the Frozen Meat.

Back in the Reich, Goebbels was working double time on his lies and propaganda. 'Never before in our history has the Reich found itself in such a favourable position,' he told a gathering of SA leaders on 15 October, his statement duly reported in the newspapers. 'On our side stand all the factors that guarantee victory: ingenious leadership, the best armed forces, powerful weaponry potential; no more problems with food supplies in the Reich (all that Ukrainian wheat), also an unassailable economy. The enemy has undertaken in his confusion a hopeless attack against the German soul, against which the national leadership has shielded its people. The war against the Soviet Union is indeed decided, but it is not yet ended. Any danger from the East is finally struck down thanks to the Führer's commanding artistry, our brave soldiers, and the unshakable *Heimat*.'

'Decided, but not yet ended.' For those who could see their way through the gobbledygook and read between the lines, it was nothing but bad news. The rest of the Volk hung on in desperate hope, against all the evidence, with the lists of the fallen heroes on the Eastern Front – their sons, and husbands and fathers – growing longer and longer.

In Münster, Catholic Bishop Galen spoke out. From the pulpit. 'Repeatedly and even very recently we have seen the Gestapo arrest highly ranked and innocent people without a court judgement or a defence, to deprive them of their freedom and put them in prison. My dear Christians, the imprisonment of many blameless people, the emptying of the abbeys, the eviction of innocent people of the cloth, our brothers and sisters, compel me to remind you today of the old truth: Justice is a fundamental right. Justice is the basic foundation of our State. The right to life, the inviolability of freedom, is an essential part of the moral order within society. We demand justice. If this call remains unheard and the reign of justice is not reinstated, the German people and the German Reich will perish in spite of the great victories, in spite of the bravery of our soldiers; it will perish because of internal rot and decay.' Bishop Galen had already protested publicly about the Nazi policy of euthanasia which had resulted in 70,000 deaths in the last year alone. And he'd protested about the Nazis' racial policies. But they couldn't touch him because he was too powerful to arrest. Just yet. In the meantime, he was placed under house arrest.

Rundstedt resigned on 30 November. Guderian was dismissed three weeks later, though subsequently reinstated. On 7 December came the shocking news of the Japanese attack on Pearl Harbor in Hawaii. Hitler declared war on America. Churchill in England did a victory jig and poured himself another whisky. On 19 December the Führer dismissed Brauchitsch, the Commander-in-Chief, replacing him with the only man who knew how to lead an army and conduct a war: himself.

Goebbels went into action again, as reported in the *Frankfurter Zeitung* on 14 December 1941, a newspaper read by the educated German. 'The Russian winter has made it almost impossible for quite some time to launch extensive offensive operations in the East. Every day the enemy tries again and again to push against the German lines at many points or to break through, using the cover of fog, the advantage of night, and all their weaponry. However, our soldiers bloodily beat back the Bolsheviks' reinforced attacks using at times tanks, heavy artillery, and airplanes. By the way, for now and for yet awhile it will not be the possession of this or that piece of land that is crucial, but only the fact that the enemy, as weather conditions and terrain permit, is under the gun and suffers heavy losses of men, weapons and equipment. The important thing is not obtaining or maintaining any particular place or point, but the occupation of wide positions favourable for tactical reasons or for the quartering of troops.'

Fabian was waiting in the anteroom of the blockhouse in Army Group Centre's HQ where Henning and the two other officers, Hardenberg and Lehndorff, had requested a meeting with Field Marshall von Bock. At first all was quiet. Fabian could hear because the door had been left ajar. Bock was agreeing that the situation on the Eastern Front had now changed dramatically. Henning was combative.

'So what's your suggestion then?' countered Bock, his irritated uncle. Cool-headed, Henning replied: 'There is only one way: we have to assassinate Hitler.'

Bock started to shout: 'How dare you! I won't listen to this!' and marched out, straight past Fabian hovering in the anteroom and into the freezing air beyond. He wasn't ready to hear it yet, the remaining three agreed. He was a career army officer, had sworn his oath of loyalty to the Führer and all the rest of it. But sooner or later . . .

Fabian and Henning walked back to Henning's billet together, through deep snow. Beautiful it would have been under any other circumstances.

'History will demand it of us,' Henning said. 'He who acts too late will be found wanting. Civilians can't do it. They have no idea. We in the army have to do it.'

'Will the Field Marshal be a danger to us now?' Fabian was worried.

'Not he,' said Henning. 'I know Bock. He wouldn't go that far. He wouldn't put another officer under the knife. Anyway, it would be putting himself in danger.'

Fabian could see that. And he trusted Henning's opinion completely. As a young officer at Potsdam, Henning had been told he would either end up Commander-in-Chief or a revolutionary executed on the scaffold. Apparently, he'd chosen the scaffold. When he was told to shoot his first Russian Kommissar, he'd refused point-blank. The news spread like wildfire. There was no turning back after that.

'You'll see,' said Henning about his uncle. 'He'll lose his post soon.'
And he did.

By the autumn of 1941, Fritz-Dietlof von der Schulenburg, husband of
Charlotte, father of Schuschu, Beba, Fritz and Puppi, was also in the
Wehrmacht – the Reserve Army, in his case – and for much the same
reasons as everyone else. Fritzi had decided long ago that the only
way to rid his beloved Germany of Hitler was from within, as part
of the regime. It was the only way to have the necessary information,
power and access to do the deed – whether by coup or assassination.
Complicated man that he was, Fritzi was also proud of Germany's
successes in the war so far, especially the war against France, the old
enemy. In effect, by 1941, he had two enemies: the Nazis at home and,
now they were at war, the Allies abroad.

His father and younger brother Wilhelm were both dead. His own
life, Fritzi knew, was in danger, both from the looming war and from
his plotting to rid Germany of Hitler and the Nazis. His thoughts
turned to God. 'I want my children to be brought up with a deep
and personal sense of religion,' he wrote to Charlotte, who stayed in
Breslau with their four children, the youngest just a baby. 'I only came
to it myself in mid-life, and only lately, but clear as the bells tolling in
our garrison church in Potsdam. Can we spare them all that wasted
time? Probably not. But we can plant the feeling of it so deeply in
them, that it can come to them with clarity later in life. I myself am
at a turning point in my life, asking myself questions about Good and
Evil, and then, about how *Mama* would answer, as always coming to
the right conclusions.'

At first, he had remained in his administrative job in Kattowitz, the
centre of a new district of Poland, now part of the Greater German
Reich. He still believed his best course of action was to remain within
the system for the time being, doing his best for the people. To this end,
he gathered a group of like-minded officials round him, organising
the local Poles who were effectively slave labour for the Reich. Fritzi
was minded to see they were fairly treated, thereby setting himself in
direct conflict with the local SS and Gestapo. When the Polish workers
caused trouble with acts of sabotage and refusing to work, Fritzi saw
it as an administrative problem, getting the leaders transferred to the
region of Poland known as the General Government. The local SS saw

it as part of a racial struggle for existence, requiring immediate action by summary execution. The situation was even worse for the local Jewish community, and here too Fritzi tried to mitigate against the regime's worst crimes.

One of Fritzi's *Landrats*, Dr Seifarth, later recalled that it was in Poland that Schulenburg determined Hitler had to be assassinated, at whatever cost. '*Pestbeule*', Black Death, is how he now referred to the Nazis in private. He knew that if they suspected he was working against the regime he would lose his job, if not his life. He was able to get away with it for the time being because he was fully supported by Joseph Wagner, the President of Silesia. However, by summer 1940, the Nazis had dismissed Wagner from his post, and Fritzi soon after.

Fritzi's first doubts about the Nazi terror regime had begun early in 1934, after Strasser's murder, growing after Fritsche's dismissal in 1938. He was part of a group of friends known as the *Grafenkreis*, the circle of Counts – all anti-Nazis. They included his old friends Peter Graf von Yorck, Nicholas Graf Üxküll and Caesar von Hofacker, who was later his main source of information in France. And through them, he met Adam von Trott zu Solz.

Trott was well-known in England. He'd been a Rhodes scholar at Oxford University in 1931 and made many close friends there, including David Astor. He was a vocal opponent of the Nazi regime from the start and, like many others with British connections, he made several visits to England during the 1930s, helped by Astor who had friends in high places, trying to alert the British government to the dangers and begging for intervention, explaining, as did all the other secret envoys, that without outside intervention the opponents to the regime within Germany could never succeed. And that, ultimately, it was in Britain's self-interest to intervene, because Hitler meant war. Like the rest, Trott's pleas fell on deaf ears because most British, remembering the Great War, wanted to avoid conflict at all costs.

Trott's friends urged him to stay in England, safe from the Nazi regime, but he refused. 'I belong to this society,' he told David Astor, 'and I must take responsibility for it. It is my duty.' The only people who had any chance of success were those close enough to the Führer to get past the massive security surrounding him, he explained. Contrary to the impression given by Goebbels' newsreels, Hitler spent most of his time in the heavily fortified Berghof at Berchtesgaden and, once war began, he rarely went to the Front. Trott made the decision to join the Nazi Party, knowing full well that the British would conclude he wasn't to be trusted. 'But he had to do it,' said David Astor. 'He had to have a cover.' He had to wear a mask. There were secret resisters everywhere, Trott assured him. 'There is still another Germany.' He was a member of the Kreisau group, gathered around Helmut von Moltke. And it was probably Trott who introduced Fritzi Schulenburg to them. Fritzi's first recorded attendance at one of the Kreisau Circle meetings dates from summer 1940.

Fritzi's solution once he lost his post in Kattowitz was to volunteer for the Front. 'I feel truly freed!' he wrote in early June 1940 to Charlotte. 'It's a good feeling, to have completed my duty and now be able to turn to a different one. The whole Polish *Wust* lies behind me, thrown off and gone.'

His first posting with the Reserve Army was at Potsdam, training recruits. By July he was off to France, to an HQ near Meursault. By August he was in Potsdam again. By the end of September he was back in France, in Paris, Reims and then in Brussels. It was the perfect opportunity to make contact with other anti-Nazis. It only took a few minutes to establish who was for or who was against and who was sitting on the fence – though you always had to be careful of Gestapo plants. In Brussels Fritzi met Alexander Freiherr von Falkenhausen, the military commander of northern France and Belgium, a close friend of Carl Goerdeler and Field Marshal Erwin von Witzleben, now commander of the 1st Army on the Western Front. All were already plotting to remove Hitler. But in 1940, most still hoped to achieve it by a coup, stopping short of an assassination.

Fritzi's temperament was different: he suspected assassination might be the only way. In France that summer, he met a young officer, Axel von dem Bussche, who became a fast friend and in due course, godfather to Fritzi and Charlotte's sixth and last child, Adelheid, known as Neiti. As they got deeper into conversation Fritzi worked hard on Axel to join the conspirators. These brutal actions against the local Polish resisters and the Jews weren't isolated events, he explained to Axel, who was only 22 and finding the whole thing overwhelming. It was part and parcel of the system. Brutality and murder were political acts for the Nazis, not the sporadic act of evil individuals.

By November Fritzi was in hospital with jaundice. By early 1941 he was back in Potsdam and Berlin. Then it was Poland. 'You think too much of me,' he wrote to Charlotte on 19 April 1941 from his billet in the Warthengau, that area of Poland annexed by the Germans in September 1939. 'Basically I'm just a poor, bending reed, blown about by the wind. Just now, during this period of waiting and hanging about, it's clearer and clearer to me how little one can do about the great events of History on which hangs the fate of each and every one of us. You yourself are inextricably bound up in it, because you have devoted yourself to me. I know what a mountain of responsibility I drag around with me, but there's no weight I would rather carry. And still, I have to go my stumbling way. And I'm profoundly happy and thankful to have you at my side, in your unwavering, sure way.'

At the end of May, Fritzi's regiment was on the march. He couldn't wait for action now. 'Last night we went on manoeuvres and this afternoon I was able to bathe in a small river and sun myself on the riverbank,' he wrote to Charlotte on 1 June 1941, happy as a child. 'We slept on straw, which suited us very well. It was in an old orphanage, very poor and dirty. It always strikes at my heart to see children looking so pale and wide-eyed forlorn.'

He was disgusted to see that Party folk, who'd been nobodies in earlier times, were staying in the best houses of the town, while they, the soldiers, bedded down in the dirt. He'd heard news of his old foe, Erich Koch. Apparently, he now inhabited the castle which used to belong to the Princes Radziwill. He'd had it rebuilt by hundreds of slave workers and furnished with priceless antique furniture. Koch let it be known that it wasn't for 'personal' but for Party use. Everyone knew that was a lie. 'Why do all this right in the middle of war, when the Volk has to go without even the most basic materials and foodstuffs?'

There was a lot of hanging about. When he wrote to Charlotte on 18 June his thoughts were turning darker, to his children and their possible futures without him.

'At the heart of their upbringing has to be a belief in God, his All-Mighty power and guidance,' he wrote, trusting Charlotte to fulfil his wishes. 'Tell them to listen to their conscience, because if they listen carefully it will show them the right way. They need to learn that even in the best people, light and darkness resides, and that they have to make right decisions anew every single day. Teach them to put their heart and soul into every activity they undertake, do nothing by halves, without real passion, merely superficially. And I want my children to learn a craft, so they discover the art of working by hand, with proper concentration. Teach them to know the difference between matters of real importance, and not be led astray by the unimportant ones.'

And so on he went – for two more long pages: teach them not to lie, to respect others, to see good in people wherever possible, like good Christians. Show them beauty. Take them on great travels and wanderings, but without ever losing their roots. They should spend some time on the land. Tressow must remain their true home. Teach them to love and respect their bodies and make them strong. To enjoy the lighter moments in life. To become simple, clear-sighted people, like the best Schulenburgs, and always to speak their opinions, but without arrogance. Tell them that he would remain bound tightly to them in a deep love, wherever life took him. He wrote like a man who knew he had an appointment with death.

Three days later Fritzi was marching across the border with the Reserve Army as part of Operation Barbarossa. He wrote a diary during his first days in Russia, from 20 June to 11 November 1941, the early pages full of zest and curiosity. Prussian Fritzi couldn't help but be thrilled at the speed of the German advance into Soviet Russia – the long night marches, life under canvas, field kitchens, the camaraderie. On rest days, there was time for reading and writing. Later, he even had time to pay a visit to old friends in other regiments like Axel von dem Bussche and Carl-Hans Graf von Hardenberg. The regiment was making for Minsk and the great Dnieper River. The roads were strewn with abandoned tanks, lorries, canons, rifles, stinking dead horses and men – sure signs of the Russian army in an all-out retreat, he noted with some satisfaction. But as the weeks passed, he found himself impressed by the enemy's toughness and bravery, and quickly concluded that this adventure was not going to be a *Spaziergang*, an afternoon stroll. When their *Hauptmann* gave a talk to the battalion, assuring them that they'd be home with their mothers by Christmas, he wasn't impressed. He thought the best they could hope for was peace by 1942. And then, perhaps, a new Europe could emerge, neither dominated by Soviet Communism nor 'parasitic' Capitalism. Fritzi, Prussian aristocrat with Socialist leanings, was keeping his fingers crossed.

By October, they were on the road to Smolensk. The weather was changing. The troops had experienced a Russian breakthrough and their first defeat. They were quickly demoralised, Fritzi noted, because they'd been fed on Nazi propaganda which spoke of nothing but victory. They were wet and exhausted, suffering from a plague of lice and the horror of the swamps and marshes in that district. By early November, Fritzi was recalled to Berlin to take up a post at the Ministry of the Interior. Travelling by official car to the airfield at Smolensk in a heavy snowstorm he passed a column of his old battalion, trudging along. Their faces were hollow and drawn, their uniforms in disarray. But there they were, marching steadfastly, and Fritzi felt moved and proud of them.

In Smolensk, he met Henning von Tresckow. And Field Marshal von Bock. He wasn't impressed by Bock, but he was by Tresckow, who quickly disabused him of the idea that the war might be over soon. Once back in Berlin, he met Ulrich von Hassell who had expressed himself keen to have contact with the younger group of conspirators. Because Hassell had heard many of them were more left-leaning than the older ones – less hampered by tradition.

'I was always afraid we had too little contact with younger circles,' wrote Hassell in his diary on 21 December 1941. 'Now it has happened. First of all I had a long talk with Saler (Trott) during which he was passionate that any semblance of "reactionary attitudes", "gentlemen's club", militarism, and so on, should be avoided'. They discussed who might take up positions in the future, post-Nazi government. Saler suggested Niemöller as future Chancellor, or perhaps Popitz, the former Prussian Foreign Minister and another active anti-Nazi.

'Afterwards I met the alert, cultured Blum (Peter von Yorck) who expressed similar sentiments,' continued Hassell. 'Finally, at his suggestion, I went to see Geissler (Popitz) again. There I met Hellmann (Moltke), Saler (Trott) and Burger (Guttenberg). All four, under Saler's (Trott's) leadership, set to work on me furiously. On the day of my departure from Geissler's (Popitz) Dortmund (Schulenburg) arrived and hammered away at the same theme. Of the five young men he is easily the most sharp-minded and politically aware, but also the most prejudiced against the Crown Prince.'

From the first there was a split among the conspirators – the older generation more traditional and conservative, the younger generation more open to the need for an entirely new society based on Socialist ideas of greater equality and proper respect for the workers. Many, especially those around Moltke at Kreisau, could not countenance an assassination – the taking of life. Others like Schulenburg argued that while a coup might be preferable, assassination could and should not be ruled out. All through 1942, in their separate groups, they argued it out. They made lists of members for the new government and wrote long papers on political theory. But they couldn't solve that intractable problem – coup or assassination? How, anyway, could the assassins gain access to the Führer? There were three separate rings of security round each of the Führer's HQs. Everyone knew he hardly left his Wolf's Lair HQ at Rastenberg in East Prussia or his Berghof hideaway at Berchtesgaden these days. He hardly ever visited the Front. On the rare occasions that the Führer appeared in public, the venue and timing were changed at the last minute. And the appearances usually lasted less than an hour – just enough time for Goebbels and his film team to prepare a newsreel for the Volk to admire in their local cinemas later.

The Russian winter had brought the German onslaught to a complete standstill. Once spring came there were some territorial gains, but by 1942 the three Russian armies were a match for the Germans, defending their Motherland with a ferocity which took the German troops by surprise. They hadn't reckoned with the *Untermensch* Slavs being such fierce fighters. It was terrifying to see a line of the T34 tanks, more basic but much hardier than the German Panzer, rumbling towards them – the only solution: to curl up in a foxhole and let the tank roll over you, then two minutes later throw your grenade at it before it turned and rumbled back to crush you. Or to see wave upon wave of Russian troops, women as well as men, charging at you, only the first wave armed, the next wave picking up the guns left lying on the ground by the dead. They charged and they fell. They charged again and fell again. It was really *unglaublich*, incredible.

Fritzi did a few months in Berlin before returning to the Front with Army Group South under Field Marshall Eric von Manstein to the Crimea in June 1942. He found the officers living a life of some ease at their HQ near Sebastopol. The food was good, so was the wine. There were plenty of cigarettes and cigars. And real coffee. He was shocked. And even more so by rumours about the behaviour of the SS, who were doing their worst – effectively an alternative army with alternative officers and commanders, much like the alternative Civil Service back in the Reich, manned by Nazi Party members.

Fritzi's job at Army Group South was to write reports and check the foreign press. He noted that the Ukrainians wanted to be free of Soviet Russia, but to have their independence, not to become slaves of yet another dictatorship. In secret, he was deputed to try and get Manstein on side for the planned coup or assassination. At first he was impressed by the Field Marshal – a soldier through and through, and by no means an admirer of Hitler. But in time he found that Manstein was all words and no action. There was no getting him on side. He was what Fritzi, the idealist, hated most: an opportunist.

Fritzi was a man divided, fighting for his country on the one hand, and against the Nazis on the other. The German *Wehrmacht* was in much the same dilemma: an order went out to the troops from the Generals to treat the Russian people correctly, with no plundering, on pain of severe punishment, but the Führer ordered them to shoot Russian POWs and partisans on the spot. Although Fritzi's regiment progressed mainly across country and rarely entered a town, he couldn't fail to see some of the atrocities perpetrated by the SS *Einsatzgruppen* which followed in the wake of the *Wehrmacht* – women as well as men strung up from lamp posts and trees, villages torched, Jews rounded up for extermination.

He lived two lives: the one as a decent patriot German, the other as a resister to the Nazi terror regime, making contact with other plotters wherever he went. He knew the dangers. In November 1942, on his way back to Berlin from the Eastern Front, he called in on Graf von Hardenberg, the brother of Carl-Hans, known by his friends as Ali. It was his 40th birthday. That evening at the festivities, Fritzi recited one of his favourite Stefan George poems. Ali found him in the hall afterwards, in tears. 'Ali, pray for Charlotte and the children, that they don't do anything to them! My head will surely roll,' he said. When Hardenberg protested, Fritzi countered: 'Ach, Ali. That just shows you don't know them!'

Meanwhile Henning von Tresckow (centre) and Fabian von Schlabrendorff (far right) at Army Group Centre were working hard on General Günther von Kluge, the replacement Commander after the dismissal of Henning's uncle General von Bock. Kluge was a supporter of the conspirators, but not to the extent of joining in any action. '*Kinder, Kinder!*' he liked to say. 'Children, children! I'm with you!' But he didn't actually do anything. The trouble was, Kluge had accepted half a million Reich Marks from Hitler as a 60th birthday gift, or, as Henning put it, a bribe. And Henning being Henning, he'd confronted Kluge with it, accusing him of corruption. That didn't go down well. On the other hand, it gave him a certain hold over Kluge.

So when Carl Goerdeler wanted to visit Army Group Centre as part of his continued efforts to find supporters for the coup, Kluge found it hard to refuse. Goerdeler duly arrived in November 1942 and, impressive and persuasive man that he was, he soon had Kluge convinced of the need to join the conspirators – until Goerdeler left, after which Kluge soon reverted to type. The best Henning von Tresckow could get Kluge to do was turn a blind eye. And to agree to invite Hitler on one of his rare visits to the Eastern Front, saying that the brave troops needed to see their Führer, thus giving the conspiring army officers a chance to take a shot at him. Kluge was like the moon, thought Fabian. He had no light of his own. He needed Henning's sun.

'A bad month lies behind us,' wrote Hassell on 20 December 1942 in his secret diary at Ebenhausen, the home which Fabian von Schlabrendorff had visited in October 1941. As usual he wrote on tiny scraps of paper, wrapped in oil cloth hidden in a Ridgeways Pure China Tea caddy, then buried in woodland behind his garden. 'The double breakthrough by Russians at Stalingrad encircling one and a half armies has been kept secret,' he wrote. A senior officer of the Luftwaffe had told him about it, as well as the imminent mobilisation of schoolboys for flak duty. The Gestapo had paid him a visit by way of warning, but K (Weizsacker at the Foreign Office) had reassured him he'd heard nothing dangerous. Nachbarn (General Waldersee) had reported from Stalingrad about the insane commands coming from above. 'Continual, indescribable mass murder of the Jews. SS men patrol the ghettos after curfew with automatic pistols and shoot anybody who is still out and about, including children playing in the streets who unhappily forgot the time . . . Groscurth, as Chief of Staff, remonstrated against the order to kill thousands of children. He was given a severe dressing down by Reichenau and a disciplinary transfer. Endless fruitless discussions with Geissler (Popitz), Pfaff (Goerdeler) and so on. You see disaster coming closer and closer, but find no means of putting a stop to it. The radical Leftists are beginning to get strong. I had a very satisfactory exchange of ideas with the younger group – for example Droysen (Peter Count Yorck), Neffen (Hans Bernd von Haeften) and S (Trott) at Dagmar's (Countess Dohna).'

Henning von Tresckow and his group of conspirators at Army Group Centre believed that General Ludwig Beck was the man to lead the post-war government. Beck was living quietly in retirement in Berlin. They needed to contact him. Henning was already in contact with Hans Oster at the *Abwehr*, and through Oster it was arranged that the go-between, Fabian von Schlabrendorff, would go to Berlin and meet Karl Guttenberg, another conspirator, who would drive him to Beck's house, not far from his own in the Goethe Strasse in Lichterfelde.

They waited till after dark. Beck himself opened the door. Beck's wife had died several years earlier and he lived in the house with his daughter and a housekeeper. He was an army officer top to toe, Fabian noted, even now, in retirement and in civilian clothing. He made it clear he wasn't pleased to see them – it was too late, and even after dark, it was a risk. But Guttenberg had brought a fine bottle of wine, a Kleinod, one of Beck's favourites. That helped. It was hard to get good wine these days. They went into the drawing room, Beck opened the bottle and they sat down. Then they went to it, holding nothing back. Fabian brought greetings from Army Group Centre, especially Henning von Tresckow and Schultze-Buttger who'd been Beck's adjutant when he was Chief of General Staff. Beck sent his greetings back. Then it was on to coups and assassinations and post-war government.

After that Fabian became a regular visitor to the Beck household whenever he was on an 'errand' to Berlin – always at night. Together they watched events unfold, like a *Götterdämmerung*. Beck expected Stalingrad to fall. He thought that, along with the British army's successes at El Alamein, catastrophe was not far off. Fabian told Beck that Tresckow thought it imperative to try and make a deal with the British as soon as possible. They discussed it back and forth. Sometimes Carl

Goerdeler joined them, sometimes others.

Then came Stalingrad. Talk to any German soldier after the war – those who survived their time in Russia as prisoners of war, which was less than a third – and they'd tell you they knew the war was lost after Stalingrad. It was only the civilian back home in the *Heimat*, suffering worse and worse Allied bombing raids, who still believed in victory. How could they know that Hitler, their Führer and Supreme Commander of the *Wehrmacht*, preferred to let millions die, whether fighting the war on two Fronts or fighting the bombers at home, rather than surrender. The Goebbels propaganda machine told them again and again that victory was in their grasp. Wasn't that the whole art of propaganda, he and Hitler had agreed way back in the glorious 1930s? Repetition. Big lies, not small. You couldn't get much bigger than Stalingrad.

'The battle in and around Stalingrad found its end today at 4 o'clock,' wrote Friedrich Kellner, another secret diarist, on 2 February 1943. 'The drama is over! The Sixth Army under General Field Marshal von Paulus no longer exists. More than 300,000 men are dead or in captivity.'

The Hitler Youth magazine didn't agree. 'The homeland will never know the likes of the heroic behaviour of the fighters of Stalingrad,' it boasted. 'We can offer our unbounded gratitude for this immense debt we owe to every single fighter at Stalingrad, and that is but a weak repayment. The name Stalingrad should, must, and will pull us upward if destiny and the war's changing circumstances bring dark and dangerous hours. And the name Stalingrad will from now on be connected to the phrase: Now more than Ever! Total War begins for us right now, encompassing the last man and the last woman in all their activities. More than ever now there is but one thing: victory, for which the heroes of Stalingrad fought, suffered, and died!'

'Heads must roll after the war!' said the foot soldier on the Eastern Front with bitter humour, adapting one of the Nazis' battle slogans: 'Wheels must roll!'

Fritzi was working back at the Ministry of Food by then, administrating distribution to the regions, as well as for General Unruh, finding useful jobs for *Wehrmacht* soldiers not currently fighting at the Front, both in the Reich and in Occupied France. And then there was the 'night job', making contact with reliable collaborators for Operation Valkyrie, as it came to be known, as he travelled the country ostensibly checking the local food depots. He was so stretched he hardly had time to sleep. In addition, his boss, Herbert Backe, the Secretary of State at the Ministry of Food, turned out to be another Erich Koch – corrupt, constantly promoting Nazi Party members to jobs for which they were not qualified. Fritzi decided to hand in his resignation. Perhaps he jumped before he was pushed. One way or the other, he was given a hearty farewell party on 31 March, and Fritzi being Fritzi, he partied in style, dancing and singing and drinking heavily. In the early hours, he was found lying unconscious across the rails of the Berlin S-Bahn. The driver of the train only just saw him in time. Some said it was a murder attempt. Others, suicide. Most likely it was pure exhaustion. But happily, his resignation left him with more time and energy to pursue his 'night job' which he did in typical Fritzi style, furiously and uncompromisingly, for the next 15 months, till July 1944.

He wrote to Charlotte on Sunday 4 April 1943, recuperating from his 'accident', sitting at a writing table, looking out over the Wannsee lake: 'The burden of work has exhausted me spiritually and physically. I realise more and more how necessary it is to be single-minded and live my life like that.' He was reading about Cromwell and he could see how single-minded that man had been. 'As for myself, I now sense in everything I do, clearly, that it's neither here nor there whether Fate picks me to undertake a certain task or demands that I give up my life for it. It only matters that I follow my conscience, as God speaks to me.' Darker and darker went the letter, obliquely referring to what lay ahead. 'That the Ship of Life can't rest as peacefully as the old barges in the lagoon which we saw on our honeymoon is obvious. Instead we have storms now, and so it happens that a ship, from time to time, will be shattered. It can't be any other way once one has dared to set off on the high seas. Otherwise one would have decided to become a bargeman instead.'

'Fritzi Schulenburg was arrested at three one morning because, on the arrest of a fellow officer for rebellious speech-making, someone had mentioned that Schulenburg had been searching Potsdam for "reliable" officers,' wrote von Hassell in his diary on 20 April 1943. 'Schulenburg was released after a few hours, having defended himself skilfully, but the matter still smoulders . . . I have been warned four times that my telephone is being tapped, and that I am probably being watched in other ways . . . Dohnanyi, his wife and brother-in-law Dietrich Bonhoeffer have been arrested . . . Oster has been dismissed and it is feared the whole project may break down.'

Fritzi got away with his overnight interrogation. But he knew he was being watched.

*

Time was running out, thought the conspirators. At Army Group Centre Henning von Tresckow was still trying to find support for an assassination attempt at the Eastern Front. It needed several generals to agree to swift action following the assassination, to order the troops on side. But where else could the deed be done, Henning asked Fabian and the other conspirators for the hundreth time. And by whom but an army officer?

'I'm not getting anywhere with Manstein,' Henning told Fabian in the privacy of his own quarters at Army Group Centre's HQ, now at Krasny Bor near Smolensk. Henning had been working hard on the Field Marshal, but to no avail. Like Kluge, Manstein wouldn't hinder the conspirators but he wouldn't help them either. Too scared.

'He understands it all,' said Henning, 'he even agrees. He trembled with his whole body when I told him we'd regret for ever our inaction when we stood before God's judgement. But you know Manstein . . .'

Henning turned his attention to Hitler's adjutant, the unsuspecting General Schmundt. The Führer, as Supreme Commander, should really visit Army Group Centre for once, he told Schmundt, in order to properly acquaint himself with the situation on the Eastern Front and to give his heroic troops some heart and hope after Stalingrad. Schmundt wasn't as clued up as Kluge and Manstein. It worked. Hitler was arriving in ten days' time, and what's more, he was coming with a big entourage. In two planes. From his Wolf's Lair HQ at Rastenberg all the way to Smolensk. On 13 March 1943.

Henning and Fabian quickly rethought their plans. Not a shooting but a bomb, smuggled onto Hitler's plane while he was handing out medals to his brave soldiers. This had the added advantage of looking like an accident, which wouldn't cause rebellion among the troops. Henning knew something about bombs, but he needed to get a reliable fuse. The English ones were known to be the best, and, luckily, a contact in Berlin was able to 'acquire' some for him. Day after day Henning and Fabian went off to a far field on the banks of the great Dnieper river to test them. The bomb was small enough to fit into a packet containing two bottles of Cointreau. The new plan was for Fabian to ask one of Hitler's lieutenants to do Tresckow a favour: 'Could he very kindly take a couple of bottles of Cointreau back to Rastenberg with him, for General Stieff. Tresckow had lost a bet to him. It was all a bit of a joke.' Stieff was on the Führer's staff at Rastenberg.

The day arrived. It was still freezing winter on the Eastern Front, the wind bitter, the landscape white in deepest snow.

'*Gott im Himmel!* In God's name! You're not planning anything today are you?' an alarmed Kluge asked Henning.

'No, no,' assured Henning with a little laugh. 'Much too early. We're not ready yet.'

The top *Wehrmacht* personnel were ordered to present themselves at Kluge's HQ at Krasny Bor. A motorcade went to meet the Führer at Smolensk airport, but the Führer refused to get into his allotted car. His own fleet of cars had arrived with its own SS security, and it was his own chauffeur Erich Kempka who drove him to Kluge's bunker. Trains from Smolensk to Krasny Bor were stopped for the duration and SS guards were posted all along the line, rifles and machine guns at the ready. Hitler brought his own food and his own doctor, Morell, who tested the food before Hitler ate it. The great Führer's eating habits were terrible: bringing mouth down to plate, not fork up to mouth – four sorts of vegetables, and only non-alcoholic drinks. And there was no smoking.

It was one of those short visits captured for the newsreels: beloved Führer visiting his brave soldiers on the Eastern Front and so on. Soon they were all getting back into their cars making a speedy way back to the airfield. Henning was in the Führer's motorcade. Fabian was in another car, at the back, carrying the packet with the two bottles, securely wrapped. At the airfield he set the timer on the fuse, then joined Henning von Tresckow who was standing next to the unsuspecting Lieutenant. He handed him the packet. They laughed at the good joke of the lost bet and the Lieutenant climbed into the plane with a cheery wave.

'Anna' was the code name for the plot. They reckoned the plane should explode somewhere over Minsk. Henning and Fabian and the other conspirators rushed back to their quarters and waited, feverishly, for news. It never came. Then came news that the Führer's plane had landed safely at the HQ in East Prussia. *Gott im Himmel!* What on earth had gone wrong? Henning quickly rang the Lieutenant and told him they'd made a stupid mistake. They'd given him the wrong packet. Fabian von Schlabrendorff, his Adjutant, was anyway arriving the next day by courier plane, so he'd come and retrieve the packet. And take the bottles to General Stieff himself.

Either the Lieutenant was very stupid or very busy. Either way, Fabian arrived the next day and managed to retrieve the packet. It was still lying, unopened, on the Lieutenant's desk. He left as quickly as was polite and went to find Stieff, a fellow-conspirator, to give him the Cointreau and the news such as he understood it. Then he was off to Rastenberg railway station where a wagon-lit was always at the ready to take army personnel to and from Berlin. He hid in an empty carriage and gingerly undid the packet of dynamite. There was the fuse – completely blackened and useless. What had happened? Was it the temperature, even more freezing up in the air than on the ground? He knew German artillery often didn't work in the extreme cold of the Russian winter. Was that it? There was no telling.

On the train journey to Berlin Fabian tried to think of ways to divest himself of the dynamite. First, he thought of Kleist von Schmenzin, the man he'd so admired when he was a young boy working on his country estate in Pommern, and again years later when they met, both committed anti-Nazis by then. But over the years Kleist had gone more and more into himself. He remained in touch with the Beck/Goerdeler group of resisters, but there was something '*ausgeloscht*', extinguished, about him these days. It was really only a matter of time before he was arrested, was how Kleist saw it.

Fabian settled instead on Professor Sigismund Lauter, the doctor who had attended him all those years ago when he was sick. Lauter still had his elegant apartment in the Kurfürstendamm, still entertaining various 'friends', including some who were on the run. He let Fabian in without a word, took him into the drawing room where stood a fine antique cupboard, put the packet inside and locked it. A quick handshake and Fabian left as discreetly as he'd come.

It was profoundly disheartening. But once embarked, the *Wehrmacht* conspirators weren't giving up. The next chance came sooner than expected. An exhibition about the military successes of Army Group Centre was to be the highlight of that year's Celebration Day of Heroes on 21 March. Major Gersdorff was the one deputed to demonstrate some captured Russian weapons to the Führer. He put himself forward as the next assassin. Tresckow told Fabian to stay in Berlin and hand over the remaining bomb to Gersdorff at the Hotel Eden. But at the last minute, Adjutant Schmundt changed the plans. Perhaps he'd heard rumours. The timing was changed, and Gersdorff was replaced by General Field Marshal Model to demonstrate the weapons. The war wounded and their guests plus a raft of generals, admirals and Nazi Party functionaries were seated by the time the Führer arrived, accompanied by Joseph Goebbels in a black Mercedes, densely protected by a phalanx of SS guards of Honour. Göring, Himmler, Admiral von Donitz, Bock and Field Marshal Keitel awaited. Inside the band played a quick few bars of Bruckner's 7th Symphony. Hitler only spoke for 15 minutes. Then he raced through the exhibition and was out and away within 10 minutes. Gersdorff still had the bomb in his briefcase. He raced to the toilets and pulled out the fuse.

Axel von dem Bussche, Fritz-Dietlof von der Schulenburg's friend from his months in France, was the next to volunteer as an assassin. He had his reasons. He'd been stationed in the Ukraine, at Dubno, since late 1942. It was a lovely town, thought Axel, surrounded by fields and woodland and the Ikva River. On summer evenings, the

local townspeople liked to walk along its banks. Water from the river
was brought to the centre of town by horse and cart. In the bitter winters ice blocks were stored deep in the ground and lasted all through
the summer. At night, the streets were lit with gas lamps. The town
had one of the largest Jewish communities, wealthy and poor alike:
doctors, tradesmen, actors at the local theatre, photographers, teachers, market dealers, knife sharpeners. There were four synagogues.
The Kantor had a beautiful voice.

One day a man from the civil administration of the District had
come to Axel's Commanding Officer: they were to surround and
secure the local airfield early the next morning, for an 'Action'. The
Commanding Officer refused. The next morning one of his officers
came in: 'Herr Oberleutenant, I think you should come out to the
airfield and see what things are happening there. You need to see it at
once.' He went, taking Axel with him. In woodland past the airfield,
they found a scene beyond mortal comprehension: deep pits dug in
the ground, surrounded by SS, and a queue of people, naked, old and
young, men, women and children, a kilometre long, and behind them
truckloads more, being harried by an SS *Einsatzgruppe* and local
police screaming orders to get out, '*Raus! Raus!* Undress! And throw
your clothes back into the trucks.' You could hear the shooting from
the pits. Axel and his officer were standing some distance away, in the
October sunshine. At first, they couldn't take it in. The Jews, for they
were the town Jews, were harried into the pits to lie face down, head to
toe, like herrings, then shot in the back of the head with machine guns.
'We have to stop them!' said Axel. 'Arrest them!' His officer was not
a bad man, but he refused. 'You see,' he said, 'all that would happen
is they'll send an SS battalion and shoot us all. We can't stop it.' He
was a small man, looking up at Axel. 'This will only stop once we're
all walking round in rags.' Axel said they should do it anyway, at all
costs. 'You know, Bussche,' he answered, 'he's even taken our honour
away from us now.'

The next day Axel sent a coded message to Fritzi Schulenburg,
offering himself as the assassin. It was more a suicide gesture than
a heroic one, he admitted later. It was one of six known attempts on
Hitler's life. Who knows how many unknown attempts?

'Schulenburg also showed up again,' wrote Helmuth von Moltke
on 10 September 1943. 'I have never had such a stimulating and
uncontroversial talk with him.' The reason it was 'uncontroversial'

is because Fritzi, the old card-player, was keeping mum, even to members of the Kreisau Circle – because he knew they would never approve an assassination. 'It takes a long time to get Fritzi completely in line with us, but he is well on the way to being so,' Moltke wrote from Berlin to his wife Frieda at Kreisau after another meeting when Fritzi had apparently offered positive critical comments to one of their latest papers. 'The slight distance which Fritzi always kept from us has visibly diminished and is well on the way to disappearing completely,' he added on 25 November. Moltke was an exraordinarily committed and courageous conspirator, working as a lawyer at the *Abwehr* now, a cover in order to be close to other conspirators, all preparing to take over government as soon as a coup was effected. But he was still for a coup – not an assassination. Fritzi knew there was only one way to rid Germany of Hitler: to assassinate him 'before he brings Germany into total destruction.'

By November 1943, the conspirators managed to arrange some home leave for Axel von dem Bussche and he arrived at the house of a priest in the Berlin district of Zehlendorf, awaiting instructions. Fritzi joined him and they spent two nights talking and preparing. Then they went to see General Olbricht, Chief of Staff of the Reserve Army, to discuss final details: someone somewhere had arranged a demonstration of new uniforms to Hitler at the *Wolfschanze*, Wolf's Lair HQ in East Prussia. Luckily, the Führer was very interested in the cut and style of uniforms for his *Wehrmacht* heroes, especially the leather greatcoats. Axel was the man chosen to demonstrate the uniforms. The necessary explosives would arrive with the uniforms. Lieutenant Stieff at the Wolf's Lair would see to it that Axel reached his room at the Guest House.

Axel waited two days in that guest room for the uniforms to arrive from their warehouse in Berlin. They were the worst two days of his life. '*Mensch!* Christ! Hold your nerve!' he kept telling himself. He was 24 years old. The uniforms never arrived. November 1943 was the start of Bomber Harris's carpet bombing of Berlin. The first raid was on the night of 18/19 November, the second on the night of 22/23. Harris used 440 Lancaster bombers. The weather was good, with no rain, causing several firestorms. Much of Berlin was left in ruins, including the warehouse.

Schicksal, fate, the Führer might have pronounced, had he known.

CHAPTER ELEVEN

BACK IN THE REICH

The Communists in the Reich were still fiercely fighting the Nazi regime in 1943 – those who were still alive and not incarcerated in a concentration camp or one of the Gestapo prisons. But you wouldn't know it from the accounts of resistance and opposition written in the first years after the war. It was all Prussian aristocrats and Social Democrats then. Even Ernst Thälmann, the leader of the German Communists, into his tenth year of solitary confinement by 1943, was all but forgotten. Or left out. Only in East Germany was he remembered in those early accounts of exceptional human bravery and endurance. Because in the West, after the war and well into the 1960s, the new enemy was Communism. And there were no Communist heroes.

But Thälmann was always a hero to his daughter Irma. One day, when she was ten, Irma's form teacher set the pupils an essay: write about what interests you most. Some wrote about sport, some about hiking, some about collecting stamps. Irma wrote about the Five-Year Plan. Her *Vater* was always talking about the Five-Year Plan. So now she set about finding good illustrations for her essay from the *Red Star* newspaper and the *Worker's Illustrator*. When she handed the essay in, the teacher objected. They didn't allow politics in class. That evening when she told *Vater* about it, he said the influence of school was bad – part of the capitalist system. For example, he said, they were being raised to hate the French, but French workers had the same problems as their own dock workers in Hamburg. And the children were just as hungry. It was the same in England. And in America. *Vater* had been to America in his youth and seen it for himself.

In 1943, Ernst Thälmann was still in Hanover prison – still allowed the odd visit by Rosa and Irma. They knew why: the Nazis were frightened of *Vater*. They didn't want trouble from their Communist workers in the factories and, if news got out that Thälmann was being badly treated or – *Gott im Himmel!* – executed, there would be plenty of trouble. And news always got out, one way or the other. In fact, Suffenplan, the administrator of the prison, was these days minded to treat his most important prisoner with a certain respect, whether from fear or a sneaking admiration neither Irma nor Rosa could work out. *Vater* was allowed reading material, and sometimes writing material too. Once Irma was even able to take a photograph of her *Vater* in his cell.

'On the left of his cell stood the bed,' wrote Rosa later, 'on the right a small table with the necessary cups and cutlery. In the corner, a pail for slops and toilet. No running water. And a small barred window.' When Thälmann requested another prisoner be allowed into his cell to play a game of chess, Suffenplan at first allowed it. But when Opitz, the local Gestapo chief, heard about it he refused it immediately. He also refused Thälmann's request for a lengthening of his daily hour's exercise in the prison courtyard. Opitz was a Nazi ideologue through and through. On Thälmann's 52nd birthday he made a point of visiting him in his cell, just to tell him that the world outside had completely forgotten about him. See – no flowers, no letters, no cards even, he jeered. Was he stupid, or what? Thälmann knew he was lying. So did everyone else. But Thälmann couldn't leave it there, even if it resulted in another beating. 'We'll win in the end,' he said as Opitz was leaving. 'The Soviet Union has already existed for twenty years. The Third Reich won't last that long!'

The war years were hard for Irma and her mother Rosa. They couldn't get work permits. They were under surveillance. Food and coal were scarcer and scarcer and without the help of the Party they might have starved. But as Allied bombing increased, causing destruction and chaos, it made civil administration more difficult for the Nazis, which was good news for Irma and Rosa. In the confusion, they were left alone more often now and were able to go about their business quietly helping the comrades in one way or another as long as they took reasonable precautions.

In 1942, Irma had met Heinrich Vester at a clandestine Communist Party gathering. They married soon after. Heinrich came from Singen, far from Hamburg, in the south of Germany. But Irma still managed to spend time in Hamburg with Rosa in spite of the increasingly sporadic railway service. And she still managed to visit *Vater* in prison, as and when Suffenplan allowed it. In July 1943 a permit for a prison visit came through. Irma made her way to the railway station with a small suitcase, meaning to spend a few days with *Mutti* and the comrades in Hamburg afterwards.

'It was an unforgettable experience, visiting *Vater* in his prison in Hanover in 1943. I went from Singen. As I came into his cell, he already knew I was arriving,' Irma wrote years later. It was the same as before: soldiers doing flak duty on the roof of the prison sema-phored the information to him. They were his link to life. As soon as the Nazi guards left Thälmann alone in his cell he went to his barred window and got the news – about the bombing raids, the Russian advances, about other Communist prisoners – and about Irma's arrival at the prison gates.

'Hitler will come and go, but the German Volk and state will remain,' he wrote on Irma's slate, shorthand: 'These soldiers are fight-ing the Hitler system. They are courageous.' *Vater* was always hopeful of the future, noted Irma, he always went on fighting. Staying silent in his cell was not his way. He knew that invading Russia was Hitler's greatest mistake and also his greatest crime against the German Volk. *Vater* would accuse the prison guards: 'All your talk! But when you went to school, as I imagine you did, you just learned how to repress the Volk. You have no love for your own German Volk, only your own skins!'

As soon as the guards left the cell, Irma and *Vater* took out their slates and chalk, chatting all the while about *Mutti* and the family and the hot July weather for the benefit of the listening device which had been installed before Thälmann's arrival. 'I'm giving you some important material to take with you,' wrote *Vater* before wiping it off. 'Distribute it among the comrades.' He passed her a thin exercise book which she stuffed in her knickers – a place even the Nazi guards would be embarrassed to search. *Vater* knew when the watch changed, so Irma was able to get out of the prison and back to the railway station without a problem. *Vater*'s writings she took with her turned out to have two purposes: to repeat to the comrades his firm belief that the Soviet Union was bound to defeat the Nazis in the end, and more basically, to prove to them that he was still alive. Still fighting.

It was the last week of July 1943 when Irma arrived in Hamburg from her visit to her *Vater* in Hanover, and the occasion of the worst Allied bombing raid on the city, aptly code-named Operation Gomorrah. The heatwave had left the ground tinder dry. After the Royal Air Force and United States Air Force had dropped their bombs, there were tornados of fire rising high into the skies, leaving the centre of Hamburg in ruins and 42,000 dead.

'I'd hardly arrived before the sirens went off. Bombers! That night was the biggest raid on Hamburg,' wrote Irma. 'It was indescribable. People jumped burning into the water. It was like daylight. The asphalt on the street was burning. People were burnt to death in their cellars. Hamburg burnt for weeks. Trains and railways were bombed. When the people ran to open ground they were shot down by American and English planes. Our relations wanted to get back to the village of Bargteheide. *Mutti* thought it better to stay in one of the big bunkers in Hamburg. But I took them. But then I wanted to get back. Our apartment was used by various comrades who were homeless.'

Thälmann heard about it from a Gestapo official from Hamburg who had business in Hanover. The man told Suffenplan that no one was still alive in Hamburg, and Suffenplan told *Vater*. 'He had no peace after that,' wrote Irma. 'We didn't know. And were worried ourselves about *Vater*, imprisoned in his cell like a bug. I wrote to him immediately, but he never got the letter. Finally I got a call from Berlin to go there and get a visitor's permit. *Vater* had created such a protest. He wanted to know if I was alive.'

A second visit was arranged for August, but when Irma arrived a Gestapo official was pleased to tell her that her *Vater* was no longer in Hanover but in Bautzen, east of Dresden. So Irma, her *Vater*'s daughter to the last, immediately re-routed. But first she went to visit an aunt in the Weisswasser district of Berlin, to hand over *Vater*'s exercise book because she feared her apartment in Singen and Rosa's apartment in Hamburg, which had survived the bombing, might be searched by the Gestapo. She stayed in Berlin for four days. The aunt baked a cake of sorts for *Vater* and Irma had presents from friends in Hamburg, as well as some fresh clothes and various other foodstuffs in her suitcase. It was very heavy but she dragged it onto a tram, then onto two trains, stopping and starting all the way.

Eventually she arrived at Bautzen. Her suitcase was too heavy to carry all the way to the prison, a picturesque medieval building up on a hill, so she looked around for a porter to help her – someone she could trust. Odd how easy it was to know whom to trust in those days, just by a look. She found an old man standing by with a wooden cart.

'Can you take me to the prison?' she asked.

'Are you visiting your brother?'

'My *Vater*,' she replied, with a certain look.

The old man smiled. 'You know, we have one here now – a workers' leader. Maybe it's him.'

'What do you think of him?'

'I like him.' He gave her a once over. 'I bet he's your *Vater*.'

'You're right. I'm the daughter of Ernst Thälmann.'

It made her happy to say it out loud like that.

'Everyone in Bautzen knows he's here,' said the porter as they walked along, once they were out of earshot. 'The Nazis were very secretive about it but news got out straight away. They arrived with a whole column of cars, as though Thälmann was a criminal. Everyone was tense. But the walls of prisons have ears. The news went round our small town like lightning.' That put Irma in a really good mood.

The prison under Administrator Plischke was much worse than Hanover. His first words to Irma: 'Where have you been? You were meant to be here four days ago.'

Apparently the Gestapo had been looking for her. So now they did a suitcase search – messed up all the clothes, took what they wanted for themselves. Finally, Irma was led to *Vater*'s cell.

At first they just stood close together, in silence – they were so happy and grateful that each was still alive. *Vater* had suffered a lot in Hanover, Irma could see. The prison had been bombed. It was sixty degrees in the cell.

'The women were calling out for their children. I was helpless. I'll never forget that night,' said *Vater*, bereft now of their usual slates and chalk. 'Innocent women and children are dying in this war, a war being run for the benefit of international capitalism,' he added for the benefit of the Bautzen guards. 'Irma, this war is a barbarity!'

The prisoners had been forced to remain in their cells during the bombing of Hanover, like wild animals, rattling the bars which were hot as fire. 'Tell me, how can you come to terms with your conscience? Why don't you let us out?' Thälmann had asked Suffenplan. His answer: 'I don't have permission.'

'Irma, these people have no sense of responsibility, they don't have to think even, they just have to obey orders – even for murder.'

The guard on duty at Bautzen wanted to stop *Vater*, but *Vater* was in such a mood that nothing could stop him from telling the world what he thought. 'This war will end with the total destruction of the Fascist system!'

Apparently *Vater* had been moved by order of the courts on 11

August 1943 – brought to Bautzen in a heavily guarded Gestapo car with Suffenplan, via the Harzgebirge mountains where they'd spent a night high up in a Gasthof hotel. There were some people from Hamburg staying there who'd been bombed out of their homes. As they sat outside at a table, they recognised Ernst Thälmann. What can they have thought? They said nothing, just smiled. There was another stopover near Leipzig in another eating place which was full of military. Again, he was instantly recognised. People kept coming in to have a look. Suffenplan started to get nervous. When they left at 6.30, everyone was standing outside, watching, smiling, saying a silent goodbye. It brought tears to his eyes, *Vater* told Irma.

'He told me to go back to Weisswasser, stay there for 14 days, then visit him again on my way back to Singen,' wrote Irma about her visit to Bautzen. 'He'd never done that before, asking us to visit. But he could see what was happening – the political and military situation – and he was of the opinion that the war would end soon, because the Soviet Army's advance couldn't be held back any more. However, the coming defeat would make the brutality and hate by the Fascists even greater – and *Vater* felt his life even more threatened.'

In a smuggled note to a fellow prisoner, Thälmann wrote: 'Will they let me out of my imprisonment and into the world again? No! Not if they can help it. It's even likely, as terrible and hard as it is to express it here, that the National Socialist regime, faced with the threat of invasion by the Soviet army and the general worsening of the situation within Germany, will do everything to erase the memory of Ernst Thälmann. The Hitler regime wouldn't hold back under those circumstances – they'd get rid of me and solve the problem once and for all.'

Irma came back after 14 days. She talked again to her old porter and told him her *Mutti* would visit Bautzen soon. She described *Mutti* to him and he said he'd look out for her. Then she went to the prison. It was a terribly hot day and *Vater* was thirsty. Couldn't she bring him some fruit? When she left the prison, she looked everywhere for fruit but couldn't find any. Someone told her quietly that there were some apples and pears in a certain shop, under the counter. She went but the woman wouldn't sell her any because she wasn't a regular customer. Irma explained she wanted it for her father in prison.

'Are you Ernst Thälmann's daughter?' asked the woman. Irma nodded. She gave her some apples. Irma asked if the woman could always supply *Vater* with fruit if one of the decent prison guards came to fetch it. Yes, agreed the woman. Irma sent her father a smuggled postcard from the railway station: 'Dear *Vater*! Send out for fruit to the Groshandlung R.' That's how things were in those days. It was Irma's last visit to her *Vater*. Rosa visited twice more, using her maiden name.

In October 1943 a soldier on home leave from the Western Front was visiting his old comrades at Bautzen prison where he'd been a guard before the war. He was called Walter Lesser and, curious about the famous prisoner, he asked to be allowed a short visit. He knew the prison administrator Herr Direktor Plischke well and got permission to go to Thälmann's cell.

'As I entered the cell Thälmann looked up from his book and stared at me, an unknown soldier, in amazement. But he said nothing. I'd never seen Thälmann before, but I recognised him from photographs and saw at once that it was really him. I still asked him if he was Thälmann, the leader of the German Communists. "Yes, I am that Thälmann," he replied with a little laugh.' Lesser told him he'd come home on leave from Brest in France and he'd heard Thälmann was in Bautzen prison. He was being sent to the Eastern Front next and he was keen to find out what Thälmann thought of the situation over there and of Germany's outlook in general. Thälmann looked at him in silence for a while, then spoke to him in a tone which, he said, allowed absolutely no contradiction: 'The war with Russia is Hitler's biggest mistake. Germany will never be able to defeat the Soviet Union, for the simple reason that, twenty years after the October Revolution, she is stronger than ever. But the German Volk is another matter. The German Volk wants friendship between the two States.' And that was the last anyone ever heard of Ernst Thälmann.

Throughout the years following the Nazi *Machtergreifung* and the years of war, there were thousands of resistance groups in the Reich – some like the Red Orchestra and the White Rose well-known, but most hardly even heard of. Among the workers especially there were undocumented clandestine groups in the factories and the shipyards and the light industries – former Trade Unionists and Churchmen, Communists and Social Democrats and anonymous people of all persuasions in local communities like the Engelmanns in Düsseldorf who took care to work in small and informal networks to keep them safe from the Gestapo spies and plants and local denouncers.

Who knows about August Kordahs, owner of the Germania bread factory in Duisburg, and his team of drivers led by Hermann Runge, delivering illegal literature along with the loaves of bread, quietly organising local resistance? They lasted till May 1935, when more than 200 employees and customers were arrested. Or the FAUD group? The Free Workers' Union of Germany, with over 4,000 members, allied neither to the Communists nor the SPD, who lasted till 1937. Who knows about Communist Walter Mickin and his group of former Communist workers' sports club members, arrested in 1935 along with 350 others? Who knows about Werner Blumberg and the 230 former SPD members, writing and distributing the *Sozialistische Blätter* newspaper in the Hanover area, all arrested in the summer of 1936? Or Hans Adlhoch, member of the Christian Lumber Workers' Federation and leader of the Catholic Workers' Movement? He was first arrested in June 1933, then repeatedly imprisoned and tortured, then incarcerated in Dachau concentration camp in 1944, finally dying in May 1945, just as the war ended. Who knows about the underground group of Hamburg shipyard workers who lasted till the end of 1942 when more than sixty were arrested and sentenced to death? Or the Herbert Baum Group which operated in and around one of the Siemens factories in Berlin and on 18 May 1942 set fire to an anti-Soviet exhibition organised by Joseph Goebbels? All were arrested within days. Before his execution Herbert Baum was tortured and dragged around his Siemens factory, ordered to identify any accomplices. He gave none away. Who knows about the resistance group around Karl Zimmet, Georg Jahres and Hans Huntzelmann of the ADV, the Anti-Nazi German People's Front in Munich, which lasted till late 1943 when the Gestapo discovered and arrested thirteen loosely connected groups with 300 members?

Better known perhaps was John Schehr who took over the leadership of the German Communist Party after Ernst Thälmann's arrest in March 1933. He was arrested nine months later, brutally tortured and murdered at Kilometerberg near Wannsee, along with three other leading Communists. Or Robert Uhrig, a toolmaker in the Ruhr area, who'd been arrested in 1933 soon after the Reichstag fire along with 11,000 other Communists. He returned to resistance work as soon as he was let out of the Gestapo prison at Luckau where he'd been sentenced to three years' hard labour, organising sabotage cells in

twenty factories around Berlin and maintaining links to other clandestine groups in Hamburg, Leipzig and Munich, as well as producing
the underground newspaper *Informationdienst*, with Beppo Romer
and dozens of others, the women often acting as couriers, the papers
hidden under a baby in a pram, or in a laundry basket. By late 1941,
that group had been infiltrated by a Gestapo plant and some 200
were arrested the following February, including Uhrig himself who
was sentenced to death by the *Volksgericht*. He served two years in
Sachsenhausen concentration camp before being guillotined in June
1944, in spiteful haste before the certain collapse of the Reich following the Allies' Normandy Landings at D-Day – his wife Charlotte
meanwhile arrested and despatched to Ravensbrück concentration
camp.

The list goes on and on.

'From the minute I sit down and write the first line, I am lost, a com-
pelling force is in command,' wrote Rudolf Ditzen, sitting at his desk
at Carwitz, chain-smoking and recovering from a hangover. 'Good
resolutions, the most sincere promises, go by the board – I must write.
A hundred times I have wondered what it is that drives me so.'

Back in summer 1942 he was writing *Our Home Life Now*, a second
volume of memoirs, following on from *Our Home in Days Gone By*.
Memoirs were the solution to all his problems, thought crafty Rudolf:
no interference from the Nazi censors, his publisher satisfied with
huge sales, his reading public happy as larks. He addressed them like
friends, letting them into a secret about the way he wrote his stories:
'Suddenly,' he confided, 'the material is exhausted.' A minute earlier
he might have been planning the next part of the tale, he explained,
but then quite suddenly, and even taking himself by surprise, 'the material is exhausted'. Fascinating, thought the reader, avid for any detail
about their favourite author Hans Fallada's home life and desperate for
any distraction from the war. Yes, yes, there was the Fallada family,
happy and content with their three charming children, their amusing
animals, their fresh vegetables and fruit from the garden, leading an
idyllic life in spite of everything!

'What I can't find words to describe to you (he used the informal
'*Du*' here, as though talking to a friend) dear reader, is the surroundings of our house, a little way out of the village, among fruit trees,
protected by tall firs, on a wide lake – only fifteen steps from the house

to the water's edge. The lake is deep, the water crystal clear, cool even during the hottest summer days. If it's one of those boiling August days, just before meal-time, we jump in, hot from the kitchen or the housework. Then we sit down together at table, a bit damp, but cooled and laughing . . .'

'I tell some terrible lies in it,' Rudolf admitted to a friend. 'More like a work of fiction really.'

'The beginning and end of this book and on every other page,' wrote Rudolf, quite lost in his own brilliant story-telling, 'is my wife Suse – even when she's not actually being talked about. She's the one who made me who I am today, taught me, the lost one, how to work again, gave me, the hopeless one, Hope. Through her belief in me, her loyalty, her patience, we have everything we own today, which gives us all so much joy.'

But in reality Rudolf's life had been on a steep downward slide for months. Suse went on being the dutiful housewife and mother but her patience had finally run out. Rudolf had moved into the guest room the year before. Suse spent days at a time away from Carwitz, mainly with the Burlages in Berlin. Willi Burlage had been Rudolf's doctor for many years, treating him in his clinic for his drinking and drugs and nerves, but now Rudolf had pretty much given up. Apart from sporadic attempts at abstinence, he just went on as before. Suse had to keep the keys to the medicine cabinet hidden because otherwise he helped himself to anything he could find. And he went on having affairs, sometimes right under Suse's nose, like the young woman from the village who came in to help out with the children. These days, when Rudolf had to go to Berlin on some business matter, he stayed in a hotel, not with the Burlages. He took to calling Willi Burlage 'Fatso'.

But he'd warned Suse, hadn't he? Before they married he'd already told her: 'I hope you realise that your prospect is one of financial insecurity, that I am in bad health, and that I can and must give you no children, and that I have been rejected by my social class.' In fact they'd gone on to have three children and he loved them all, so Suse could hardly complain could she? Apparently Suse didn't agree.

By June, Rudolf had moved into the gardener's room across the yard and he had to admit, even to himself, that his wife was finally giving up on him: 'Worst of all, the feeling gradually grew on me that even my wife was turning away from me,' he wrote later in *The Drinker*, the story of a man who gets into deep trouble with his business and his marriage and takes to drink, ending up a complete drunkard. Rudolf's writing had always been part-autobiographical, but not like this. *The Drinker* was even written in the first person – the only time he ever did it.

'At first the signs were almost unnoticeable, little things that anyone else would have overlooked,' Rudolf wrote, as though recalling real incidents in his own life, which they might easily have been. There was the birthday party when the Drinker's wife didn't offer him a slice of cake. He never ate cake, he admitted, but in the past his wife had always offered him a slice nevertheless. Then there was the case of the cobweb: three days it stayed there in his room untouched 'above the stove', but not a single cobweb in the rest of the house. And then there was the doormat: returning home worse for wear one evening, he found the doormat was missing. He called out to his wife Magda, but she didn't answer. He had to step into the hallway in his muddy shoes, sit on the bench, take his shoes off and walk around in stockinged feet! Just like the Drinker, Rudolf didn't realise how much he depended on his wife, on Magda/Suse – until it was too late.

These were the darkest days for Rudolf Ditzen, struggling with his addictions and his nerves, his battles with the Nazi cultural authorities, and the worsening war. There was another stay in a clinic. Then came news that Hubert Rader, their faithful gardener-cum-handyman, much loved by the children, had been killed at the Front. So had the brother of one of their maids. So had Suse's nephew, her sister Tilly's only son. Later it was their niece's fiancé. Meanwhile Rudolf's mother and sister and brother-in-law were having a terrible time in Celle, which was not far from bombed Hamburg. As was Suse's mother. Rudolf did everything not to have them to stay – he really couldn't bear that many people, let alone that many women, in the house. But come they did, sometimes one at a time, sometimes more. Meanwhile the Nazi terror regime marched on. Every day they heard of another horror – like their old friend Marga Kentner's boyfriend Alfred Schmidt, music teacher and secret Communist, who was arrested and despatched to Sachsenhausen concentration camp. When he was finally released, he was swiftly rearrested, brought before the *Volksgericht* and sentenced to death. It was that favourite trick of the Nazis: first give them hope, give them life, then snatch it away.

The regime thrived on denunciations. Sometimes it was for money, mostly it was out of sheer envy and spite. The Mayor of Carwitz had it in for him, said Rudolf, so all denunciations were taken at face value, no questions asked. When someone in the village reported the Ditzens, claiming their dog had been hustling their livestock, the dog had to be put down. Then someone else denounced them for stockpiling wood. Then came the denunciation that Rudolf was a drug addict, which played pure havoc with his nerves, especially considering the Nazis' euthanasia policy for the handicapped and the insane. On that occasion, Rudolf had to use all his powers to persuade the two officials who came to the house that he'd given up morphine years ago and that now he only took sleeping pills, administered and policed by his wife. On and on it went, his depression and nerves getting worse and worse. Not to mention the fact that the war was coming closer to Carwitz now that Allied bombing had intensified.

Yet still Rudolf wrote – because he simply couldn't live without it. Perhaps this accounts for the lowest ebb he ever reached, when he decided to write a book about the Kutisker case – a famous fraud case of the 1920s involving two Jewish financiers. Unsurprisingly, he was immediately given access to all the files in the Ministry of Justice, and even allowed to take some files home to Carwitz when bombing raids again threatened Berlin.

'I am planning a large-scale work, the story of a broker on the Stock Exchange, but obviously without any anti-Semitic content,' as he wrote disingenuously to his mother. But to his sister he admitted that he'd started to dictate the 'anti-Semitic' book in the hopes of getting permission for more paper from the authorities for his earlier novels. 'Even if I don't believe it will ever be published, I've still taken care to make it accurate. Even the most religious Jew wouldn't be able to fault it.'

He was still canny Rudolf: he just wanted to keep the authorities happy and get his paper allowance. And his advance. He had little intention of completing the book. Was he forgetting his taskmasters? Did he really think he could outwit Goebbels? 'I need a series of anti-Semitic books to be written, by good writers, mind you, like Fallada and Norbert Jacques,' Goebbels wrote in his diary on 29 May 1943 in the wake of Stalingrad. Rudolf managed to put the Ministry of Public Enlightenment and Propaganda off for a year, saying he was too busy. When his publishing house was bombed, he easily got a new publisher because the propaganda value of a Jewish novel by the famous Hans Fallada was so great. Meanwhile he got on with his two memoirs and a project titled *The Conquest of Berlin*, to be made into a film – an innocuous subject about a penniless young man who arrives in Berlin from the provinces during the 1920s and becomes a successful businessman. Ernst Rowohlt, back in Berlin after his dismissal from the military for being 'politically unreliable', knew the truth about the Kutisker book: it was 'a novel which will never be completed but which is good enough for an advance,' Rudolf told him. He was right about that. The advance was 40,000 marks. The average wage was 150 Reichmarks a month. The book was never published.

A fan sent Rudolf a crate of Burgundy for Christmas. A food parcel arrived out of the blue from a Swiss admirer. The Cultural Authorities asked him to go on a tour of German troops in the Sudetenland – just to meet them, perhaps read a few extracts to them, and write some short reports on their morale. Why not? thought Rudolf – a pleasant break from the everyday trials of wartime Carwitz, and some money too. He took Suse and the children with him. It was the summer holidays and they went horse riding and cycling. Then he was asked to go to France twice, on his own, to write so-called reports, where he had quite a fine time of it. But writing reports, however trivial, still implied a certain collaboration with the regime. That's life these days, he told himself. We have to live. We have to eat. I have to write. *C'est la vie.*

By mid-1943, the Russians had launched another counter-attack and the German army was in flat-out retreat. The Allies landed in Sicily. The bombing of German cities intensified and Carwitz was soon filled to overflowing with refugees from the Rhineland. Rations were reduced again – basic bread and fat as well as meat now. As to clothes and shoes, forget it. When the Ditzens passed through Berlin on their way to the Sudetenland they were shocked at the destruction and the beggars and the fighting in food queues. By November, Suse was insisting Rudolf go to Dr Zutt's clinic in Berlin. He was drinking heavily. She couldn't and wouldn't look after him anymore. He went. But on the night of 22 November the clinic was bombed and Rudolf had to return to Carwitz. That same night a bomb fell on Kurfürsten Strasse and killed Willi Burlage. Ernst Rowohlt, his lodger at the time, had gone out for the night.

'He was in the hallway of his house again. It was dark. He was in a bad way. He switched on the light and caught sight of himself in the long mirror: "So what's become of me!" cries a voice within me.' Rudolf wrote in *The Drinker* as though writing about himself. 'And my first impulse is to rush to Magda, to fall on my knees before her: "Save me! Save me from myself! Hold me to your heart!" But this impulse vanishes: I smile craftily at my image in the mirror. "That's just what she would like," I think. "And then – off with the old man and into a drunkards' home, while she gets hold of the business and the money!" Be cunning. Always be cunning.'

Did Rudolf know what happened to Mildred Harnack, the American who'd come to visit him in Carwitz, way back in 1934, with her friend Martha Dodd? Mildred had all along been an active member of *Die Rote Kapelle*, the Red Orchestra, one of the largest and most successful groups of resistance. It was based in Berlin but reached across the Reich and abroad, eventually involving some 400 people. Led by Mildred's husband Arvid, still employed at the Reich Ministry of Economics, and Harro Schulze-Boysen, still at the Reich Ministry of Aviation, it took care to remain a loose, informal network, including civil servants, journalists, students, teachers, artists, businessmen, diplomats and the military. Many of the members were women, often wives like Mildred or her friend, Libertas Schulze-Boysen. They documented Nazi crimes against humanity, helped Jews and others on the run to escape, assisted in acts of sabotage, distributed leaflets inciting the public and the military to resist, and passed on intelligence to the advancing Russians. Some of the members had Communist connections, others were ordinary people who felt impelled to resist the Nazi terror regime at whatever cost.

'The People are Troubled about Germany's Future,' went a lengthy typed leaflet written by Schulze-Boysen. 'Time and again, Minister Goebbels attempts in vain to scatter new sand in our eyes. The facts speak a hard and cautionary language. No one can deny any longer that our situation is deteriorating from month to month. No one can close their eyes any longer to the monstrosity of the events, to the catastrophe of National Socialist policy threatening us all. The major military successes of the early war years have not yielded decisive results. Most German armies are currently in retreat. Despite all the Armed Forces High Command fabrications the number of war victims is rising to millions. Almost every German house is in mourning. The workers are exposed to ever more severe coercion and over-exertion. The last reserves are being squeezed out of the population. There is barely anything left to buy. Money is losing its value. The army is swallowing up hundreds of thousands again and again. Industry and agriculture are suffering sorely from lack of labour. Tens of thousands of factories and farms are collapsing under the burden of war conditions . . .'

Another leaflet came in the guise of an open letter to 'a police captain' to be distributed at the Eastern Front: 'You have been promoted to captain in the East, as I heard. Did you excel in some way, in the end, within your police unit which is fighting the partisans? I can't believe it! You're not really one of those brutal and rough policemen for whom questions of politics and morals dissolve in bluster and beatings without the slightest consideration of humanity. You have always despised and hated those abhorrent creatures who accompany their cruelties with grinning cynicism and lack of character. Would I write to you otherwise if I did not assume you have not lost the ability and the courage to follow the dictates of conscience when it comes into conflict with a so obviously bestial "duty" as the ordered murder of the Soviet population?! In the state hospital in . . . I recently visited a number of police comrades who had been admitted from the East, for nervous breakdowns, all of them. You know the hospital atmosphere, that particular type of calm: the room had been livened up with flowers, patients were allowed to listen to music, and, to add to these ridiculously simple props of mental healing, much like in a novel, a few rays of sun shone into the room. Incidentally, there is a ward about which comrades told me with almost shy relief, where the even worse cases of nervous breakdown are kept: formerly vigorous police officers can only move around by hopping, like kangaroos, you know, and others crawl on all fours, shaking their heads placidly . . .'

A Gestapo plant had finally infiltrated the Red Orchestra in summer 1942. Harnack and Schulze-Boysen were arrested and tortured, accused of treason and espionage by the *Volksgericht* and sentenced to death in Plötzensee prison in December 1942, along with more than fifty others. For the leaders of such groups, the Nazis reserved their special fate: strung from meat hooks till they died.

As to Mildred – the American who'd first met her husband Arvid as a student in Wisconsin and come to Berlin with him when they married – Roland Freisler, the notorious judge of the *Volksgericht*, was minded to let her off with a lengthy prison sentence because, after all, she was a woman. But when Hitler heard of it he ranted and raved and personally ordered her to be put to death, by guillotine.

*

By mid-1943, Tisa von der Schulenburg had been back home in the Reich for four years. Tisa, the awkward one, had finally divorced her husband, Fritz Hess, not because he was a Jew, but because she just wasn't the marrying kind. She'd tried and tried to be a good wife, a normal wife, but it wasn't possible. In 1939 her mother had a stroke. Tisa left England and made her way back to her beloved Tressow, but it wasn't easy. War was imminent. She was filled with doubts and fears.

Returning to London afterwards – leaving her sick mother, leaving Tressow – was heart-breaking, but what else was she to do? In the event History decided it for her: arriving back at Croydon airport, the British officials became suspicious of her. What was she doing, going back and forth to Germany at this late date, with war on the horizon? How long had she been living in England? Who was her husband? Who was her father? What was her address? Did she have any links with Communists?

Before she knew it, Tisa was back on the plane to Cologne, met at the airport by her brother, Heini, still a convinced Nazi. She took the train to Lübeck and friends drove her to Tressow. As they neared the Schloss, Tisa's heart lifted: there were the blooming rape fields, deep yellow, with the heady perfume she'd yearned for all these years. And there was her beloved Tressow, with Weidemann, their faithful old retainer, standing at the entrance to welcome her. She cried and cried. A few days was all it took to travel back to a life she'd abandoned years earlier – back to her past, back home. Within weeks, England and Germany were at war.

That August her mother had a haemorrhage. Tisa sat for hours by her bedside in the hospital in Lübeck. There was a pear tree in bloom outside the window. First her brother Heini arrived from Cologne. 'It's over for me too. I've got cancer,' he said. He died a year later. The next brother to arrive was Wolfi, the good-looking one, the one Tisa had always argued with the most. He hadn't changed. He'd been working for years at the Reich Ministry of Sport, a valued member of the Nazi Party. Now that war was certain, he was able to choose his regiment. Sporty and tough as he was, he chose the *Fallschirmjäger*, the Parachute Regiment. The last brother to arrive was Fritzi.

He arrived too late for his mother's death. Once the hospital for-malities were over, Fritzi and Tisa, the old twosome, went to the *Dom*, cathedral, to sit and talk in peace. They'd always loved the medieval *Dom* with its solid towers and dark interior. They sat in a distant pew and talked in whispers. Since their brief meeting in the Gasthof on the eve of their father's death they'd hardly met. Now Fritzi repeated what he'd told her then: he was involved with General Beck and others in a plot to overthrow Hitler – ever since Sudetenland in 1938.

He'd taken the post of Police Chief of Berlin with the express purpose of assisting the new government once the coup had succeeded, in order to maintain law and order and prevent civil war breaking out. He only lasted a year in that post, most likely because the authorities already had their suspicions about him. He was transferred far away, to Breslau in Silesia, as District President, where he started to reform the administration, just as he had at Fischhausen. Charlotte and the children moved to Breslau after living on the Yorck country estate for some time. Peter Yorck was a distant relation of the Schulenburgs and already deeply involved in resistance work, specifically with Helmuth von Moltke at nearby Kreisau. Fritzi had joined them there on more than one occasion, and also in Berlin. In Schlesien, he was in contact with Oswald Wirisch, the Trade Union leader, because it was crucial – once the coup or assassination was effected and the new government in place – to have strong Trade Union leaders to keep the workers on side. All this Fritzi told Tisa in hushed tones in the Lübeck *Dom*, bringing her up to date.

Fritzi had changed since his marriage to Charlotte, Tisa noted – he was more relaxed, more confident. Very sure of himself and his actions. In a word, he was happy. He took life seriously, but never himself, humorous as ever – in fact he seemed quite careless of his own fate. Tisa looked at him as he talked in the gloom of the *Dom* interior: his high forehead, the scar on his cheek from student fraternity days, his strong nose, his sharp blue eyes. He was always a quick, quiet talker, inclined to be critical – but now Tisa could see there was a new self-discipline about him, an absolute determination to do what had to be done. He spoke to no one other than his fellow conspirators, he said, and he reminded Tisa to do the same. It was a question of life or death, and he meant to live – at least till the deed was done. And the deed was assassination. Not all the conspirators agreed, he admitted, but it was increasingly clear to Fritzi that this was the only way now. He'd always kept his cards close to his chest, thought Tisa, even as a child. He was a good bluffer, a good card player, and a clever fencer.

No one was to suspect what he really thought, and what he meant to do. At their father's state funeral Himmler had apparently asked him to join the SS. 'I've worn the outfit of the Prussian Civil Service for fourteen years and I don't mean to change it now,' he'd answered the *Reichsführer* SS with aristocratic politeness, and Himmler, the former chicken farmer, was persuaded. But perhaps Himmler had decided to keep an eye on Schulenburg from then on.

Tisa found Tressow changed. Not the Schloss itself, nor the land – the fields of wheat, the forests, the lakes – but the atmosphere. Her parents were dead. Johann Albrecht, her eldest brother running the estate now, was a Nazi. Heini was dying. Wolfi was away fighting somewhere, Fritzi in Breslau. It was just Tisa staying at Tressow now with Johann Albrecht who'd been badly wounded during the Great War. Weidemann, their faithful retainer, did most of the day-to-day work, helped by a few servants and farm workers who were too old to be called up. The visitors who arrived to pay their respects to her brother were not Tisa's sort, but bearing in mind Fritzi's warnings she greeted them with careful politeness. First came the local Nazi Party officials, people who'd been nobodies in the old days, now risen to positions of power and influence – dangerous people. Then came the neighbours, some good, some bad. She was guarded with them all. And with the estate workers. And the villagers. She never told anyone how she really felt.

Except for the two von Barner brothers, living at Trebbow, another lovely Schloss not far from Tressow. Trebbow and Tressow, the twin stars of Tisa's new life. The Barner brothers were old and trusted friends. On the day war broke out, Carl Ulrich von Barner was con-scripted into the army. That same evening, Tisa and Carl Ulrich got married – just a quick ceremony in the local registry office. Then she moved into Trebbow, to live there and oversee the running of the estate for the duration of the war, leaving Johann Albrecht and Weidemann at Tressow. Carl Ulrich left the next morning. His brother not long after. For a while, both brothers were stationed at Schwerin and free to return regularly to Trebbow to oversee the harvest. There were glori-ous days that autumn with tennis matches and swimming in the lake. Then both brothers were off to war and Tisa was left alone.

Trebbow was so like Tressow: a Schloss set in parkland, sweeping gravel drive and lawn at the front, courtyard and kitchen gardens at the back. A lake. Ancient oak trees. Entrusted by the Barner brothers to run the estate, Tisa did her best, budgeting carefully and getting on with everyone. Some old servants remained, just as at Tressow, including coachman Braun. But the estate was large and needed workers. As the war progressed more and more were foreign workers, sent to make up the shortfall – first Poles, then French POWs, later Russians. It meant getting on with local Nazi Party officials and, just as at Tressow, Tisa took care to play her role – much like an actor, she thought. The key thing was never to give Fritzi away with loose talk. So, when local Nazi Party officials came by, snooping, she greeted them politely, listened to their views about the war, even nodded mildly when they floated their nasty ideas on racial purity or the perfidy of the Jews – just biding her time till they left again.

Gauleiter Friedrich Hildebrand came, giving his Hitler salute. He was a typical Mecklenburger, wrote Tisa, stocky, middle-sized, not very intelligent, politically 'deep brown' as they called the committed Nazis. But not a bad man really. When she complained about the local *Gruppenleiter*, Hildebrand said she should always come directly to him for help. He'd been a friend of her father's. Tisa's only mistake was the '*Heil Hitler!*' salute. At first she tried to ban it from the estate – until someone quietly warned her about the dangers. She quickly changed her tune.

What had happened to the Germany she loved? She could hardly bear it. When she went on a rare visit to Berlin, she was appalled to find that all her old Jewish friends were gone – abroad, in concentration camps, or dead – their apartments taken over by loyal Nazi Party members. The worst time was when France fell, almost without murmur. Then the Nazis were jubilant and all sorts of people came out of the woodwork, cheering and jeering. The newspapers were full of lies: Hitler was doing as he promised, making Germany great again! She felt like a mad woman, she wrote in her private memoir of those times – a woman who could no longer understand the language of her own country. She and her few true friends kept their silence. They took care never to gather in large groups. When they met, they spoke in whispers.

Tisa's one consolation was the wireless. 'It stood next to my bed, and my bedroom had a double set of doors which were thickly padded,' she wrote. 'Every night I waited for my friend during those terrible years: the English transmission. And every night I waited for that voice: This is the BBC Home Service and it is so-and-so speaking. I waited for that

voice like waiting for the voice of a lover. You could get the best reception at one o'clock. Towards morning there was a lot of disturbance.
Later I could tune into the Forces Network, one for soldiers here, and
an English programme in the German language from the BBC World
Service, run by Germans, Jews and other opponents of the Nazis. But
it wasn't as clear as the Home Service. It was like a nightmare, hearing
about the fallen and the prisoners and the murdered. These times were
unforgettable. And all the while the beauty and stillness of the land in
the Prussian night.'

She was turned against her own country. And her own people. She
was frightened Hitler would win. Please God, don't let us win! Which
Germany are we talking about? The Germany of Goethe and Schiller?
Long gone. She was frightened of her own hate, she wrote.

She made Trebbow into a kind of asylum for fleeing friends and
refugees. And for her foreign workers. First came twenty Polish girls.
They'd been typists and shop girls in their past life – now they had to
learn haymaking and tending the livestock. They sang as they worked,
in their heavy boots with colourful scarves tied round their hair. Tisa
liked them and they liked her. Then the French POWs arrived and she
gave them work as foresters, bringing them extra food and clothing
in secret. Then, later, came the Russian POWs. She had to be careful
because Hanke, the Trebbow forester, was a *Blut und Boden*, blood
and soil member of the Nazi Party, believing everything the Party told
him. But he was loyal to the Barner brothers who'd always treated him
well. It became a power struggle between Hanke and Tisa because
Hanke knew Tisa couldn't fire him. Basically, he was a simple man,
a hunter and a man of nature and the forest, and in time they came
to grudgingly respect one another. As the local *Gruppenleiter*, Hanke
had to inform the villagers if one of their sons or fathers or brothers
had been killed. The villagers came to dread seeing him walking
down the single street, making for one of their small houses – but
which one?

During the bitter winters, with the newspapers full of false accounts
of the war on the Eastern Front, Tisa joined the women of the village
knitting socks and mittens and balaclavas for the soldiers, because
rumours were rife that they had no proper winter clothing. In the
long evenings, alone in the faded elegance of the Trebbow *salon*, Tisa
read her favourite books, especially Thomas Mann, now in exile in
Switzerland. He was her link to old Germany. She remembered his

children, the twins Erika and Klaus, from her days in Berlin, visiting Hugo Simon and his wife and their cultured friends. How beautiful they were, those twins!

She always kept a suitcase packed, just in case.

Fritzi had joined the *Wehrmacht*. Tisa wondered why. The war had changed everything, he said. He wanted to defend Germany, his *Heimat*, from the enemy. But he also had to fight the Nazis who had taken that *Heimat* away. In a sense, joining the *Wehrmacht* solved both at once: he could defend his country but he could also extend his contact to the only people who would be in a position to rid the Reich of Hitler – the army officers. That was General Beck's view and his own, too. After which, with any luck, they could negotiate a peace with the Allies and restore Germany to the *Heimat* she had been before the horror of the Nazi terror regime. Like so many resisters, Fritzi believed the *Wehrmacht* was now the safest place for him to be. But soon his secret friends at the Ministry of the Interior had him back in Berlin, at the Ministry of Food. They needed conspirators in the Reich, on the spot.

Charlotte and the children came to Trebbow from Breslau every summer for the whole school holidays. There were five children by now, four daughters and one son, named Fritz after his father. Once Fritzi was back in Berlin, he came to Trebbow quite often – wonderful times, Trebbow alive with children's voices and laughter, racing about the place on their bicycles, swimming in the lake, helping the foreign workers with the haymaking, bringing vegetables in from the kitchen garden, chopping wood in the forest with Hanke. Playing games with their *Vater*, who was a master of fun and invention. Finally, in 1943, with the Allied bombing raids getting worse and worse, the family moved to Trebbow full-time. They lived separately, on the top floor, but really it was just one big community, increasingly including friends fleeing Berlin. That was the year Charlotte gave birth to their sixth and last child, Adelheid. Fritzi chose Axel von dem Bussche, the friend he'd made in France, to be her godfather. Axel remained a close friend and loyal accomplice ever after.

'Christmas and New Year Fritzi was with us, at "the end of the world" as he so often called it,' wrote Charlotte in her private memoir. 'On New Year's Eve the children surprised us with a play, in which, to the delight of their father, they dressed up as the sun and the four seasons.' That January, 1944, Fritzi wrote his last will and testament and gave a copy to Tisa's husband, Carl Ulrich, and another to an old friend and colleague, Freiherr von Willisen. He told Charlotte he'd given Willisen the code word 'completion of testament' to use as a cover, should the assassination plot be discovered.

Over the next months Fritzi spent as much time as possible with the family at Trebbow. The place was filling up with refugees from bombed-out Berlin, including Mathias Wieman, the actor, and his wife, who devised evenings of poems and extracts of plays in the darkening drawing room. Fritzi also visited his eldest brother Johann Albrecht, still running the family estate at Tressow. And he and Charlotte visited old friends and colleagues together whenever possible, almost as though saying 'goodbye' – the Hardenbergs, Countess Döhnhoff, Count Heinrich Lehndorff, General Count Dohna, Ursula von Kardorff, Hermann Werne, and Axel von dem Bussche currently in a field hospital at Insterburg, seriously wounded – some known to History, many not. 'Next time you see me I'll either be a minister, or headless!' as he joked to their old friends the Kessels in Konigsberg.

When Bernt Engelmann came back to Düsseldorf on home leave from Caudebec-en-Caux in Normandy on the Western Front, he found the apartment empty. His father was abroad, his mother was away on one of her 'cures', that is, helping someone somewhere to evade the Nazi authorities. Tante Ney had left a message for Bernt to come to the bakery. He found her busy with customers as usual, chatting cheerfully to everyone, Nazi Party members included – but not too busy to fill Bernt in with the latest news, in the back room of the shop as usual. She needed urgent help with a woman called Irene Herz, she whispered. Apparently this Frau Herz was Jewish, living in Berlin, and on the run. Her husband and son had been picked up in the street by the Gestapo and taken to the goods-wagon railway station with hundreds of other Jews. Frau Herz was at work in the Siemens factory at the time and knew nothing about it. Her son, only eleven years old, just had time to hand over Maxi, their fox-terrier, to the woman who ran the newspaper kiosk on Oranien Strasse. When Frau Herz came back from work, she went to the kiosk to buy a newspaper and, to her surprise, heard Maxi barking in the back. Then she heard the terrible news, and she'd been on the run ever since.

'Here the most depressing things are happening at the moment,' wrote the journalist Ursula von Kardorff from Berlin to a friend. 'All

Jews up to the age of 80 are being deported to Poland. You see only tear-stained figures in the street. It is beyond measure and quite heart-breaking. Above all that one has to stand by and watch so helplessly and can do so frightfully little to help. They are only allowed to take with them one very small bundle the size of a briefcase.' The news-papers were trumpeting Joseph Goebbels' promise to make Berlin 'Jew-free' within months.

'You have to go and pick her up and bring her to Düsseldorf. She's got a new identity now, as a nurse. Luckily she's blonde – doesn't look Jewish at all,' said Tante Ney. 'We've got all the documents, but we have to get hold of a nurse's outfit . . . Anyway, go tomorrow, and wait for her outside the Hotel Central.'

Bernt's Onkel Karl, father of Gudrun, the cousin married to an SS *Obengruppenführer*, met him at the station in Berlin. He was touched that Bernt was paying them a visit. 'These damned English!' he opined, shaking Bernt vigorously by the hand. 'They're for the high-jump now! Another few weeks and they'll be begging the Führer for a peace-treaty.' It was the U-Boat successes in the Atlantic which gave him such hope. In February alone they'd sunk more than seventy merchant ships and tankers. 'They'll hardly have anything to eat soon!'

Onkel Karl was his mother's brother. How different they were.

'That'll be the end of their famous Empire! Without their colonies they'll be done for. That'll serve Churchill and all his terror attacks on Berlin right!' Onkel Karl's nights had been disturbed by Allied bomb-ing and his constitution wasn't up to it. Tante Elsbeth's nerves were at breaking point, he said. The night of 30 May had been the worst – over a thousand bombers had attacked Cologne apparently. He'd read it in the newspapers. And now it was Berlin again. *Unglaublich!* Unbelievable!

But as they left the station he whispered: 'How long do you think this war will go on?' Bernt must have looked surprised. 'You can tell me,' he said. 'We're alone now.'

He'd purposely left Tante Elsbeth at home so he and Bernt could talk. Tante Elsbeth was a heart and soul member of the Nazi Party, as were Gudrun and Horst-Eberhard, the SS *Obengruppenführer*. 'She still believes in total victory,' he said.

'And you don't anymore?'

Onkel Karl had his secret doubts ever since the lists of the Heroic Fallen on the Eastern Front had told their own story, it turned out.

Bernt told him that he and his parents had never believed Germany would win the war, not from the very first.

'But how long will it go on for?' Presumably Onkel Karl thought Bernt, based in Normandy with his communications unit, would be more reliably informed.

'Who knows? Not soon anyway,' said Bernt.

'How's your *Vater* by the way?'

'He's left England. In Australia now.' It had been one of those strokes of luck that Bernt's father, part Jewish, had managed to leave the Reich on a business trip before the Nazis got him. He was having a hard time of it, as they read in his letters delivered sporadically by the International Red Cross, but at least he was safe.

'Horst-Eberhard is beside himself about this Prague thing.'

'Is he dead?' Bernt meant Reinhard Heydrich, SS *Reichsführer* of the *Sicherheitsdienst*, who'd been assassinated. The newspapers hadn't yet fully informed the public. Yes, he was dead, confirmed his Onkel. Bernt couldn't have been happier.

'How's Gudrun?'

Onkel Karl sighed. 'She's pregnant, you know. Complications. Has to stay in Bad Tolz for the last few weeks.'

'Really . . . ?' Bernt had a quick think. 'Nurses in these private clinics . . . they have their special uniforms, don't they?'

'Yes . . . ?'

'I need one, Onkel Karl. Don't ask me why. But get one by tomorrow morning. Size 44.'

Perhaps Onkel Karl understood more than he was letting on. After a brief hesitation he said he was visiting Gudrun that same evening. They agreed to meet at ten the next morning outside the bank on Savigny Platz.

'By the way, Onkel Karl, I've got a present for her.' Onkel Karl was touched. But when he heard it was a little dog he wasn't quite so sure.

'He's called Maxi,' said Bernt, pleased with himself.

And sure enough, at ten o'clock the next morning, there was Onkel Karl outside the bank when Bernt arrived with Maxi on his lead. Bernt had met up with Frau Herz as planned, and now she was waiting in the ladies' toilets at the Hotel Central.

It was the one act of courage Onkel Karl ever committed. There, behind a bench, stood a small suitcase. 'You can keep the case,' he said before rushing off, Maxi trotting happily along behind him.

When Bernt and Frau Herz, now Nurse Maximiliane, arrived at Düsseldorf railway station, they were met by an SS officer in a smart uniform – Herr Desch, otherwise known as Fish-face. Tante Ney put Nurse Maximiliane up in her isolated cottage for a while, till they could get her out of the country.

Driver Krupa was waiting for Bernt at Rouen railway station when he came back from his home leave. That was a first. What was going on?

'They've arrested Erwin,' he said.

It was a terrible shock. Of course, Bernt knew they'd been taking risks all along, keeping themselves informed about the true development of the war by listening in to the BBC and, in the early years when they were still stationed on the Isle of Sylt, providing false numbers for the Allied bombers flying over. But it turned out Erwin had been doing a lot more than that. The military police had come to their barracks five days earlier and searched his room, then handcuffed him and taken him away.

Erwin and Bernt had been friends and collaborators since they first met at *Wehrmacht* training. They understood one another perfectly. Bernt knew that Erwin's father had done a long stint in a concentration camp in 1933, along with thousands of other Communists following the phoney Reichstag fire. When he was finally let out, he was unable to work or lead any kind of normal life. A strong, good man completely broken, Erwin said. And Erwin never forgave them.

'Where is he now?'

'Here in Rouen prison. Then it's Paris and a Court Martial.'

'What did he do?'

'Just rumours: passing Top Secret information to the Allies,' said Krupa. 'Major Zobel went white as a sheet, he was so scared he'd be blamed. The Double Doctor is in charge of our communications unit now.'

They drove on in silence for a while, thinking about what might happen to Erwin.

'I've just come back from Paris on a job myself,' said Krupa, meaning to cheer Bernt up. 'You wouldn't believe it. I saw Reichsmarschall Göring with my own eyes – as close up as I am to you now! He's even fatter in real life, wearing a huge cape. And rings on his fingers – honestly – with diamonds and rubies! And, you wouldn't believe it, make-up!' That did make Bernt laugh.

'We all knew why he was there. All the drivers knew. Filching stuff from the museums and private houses: whole crates of old paintings, tapestries, china and what-not . . . all shipped back to the Reich.'

Two days later, Bernt managed to persuade Major Zobel to get him a pass from the Occupying Authorities to visit Erwin in Rouen prison before he was transferred to Paris. Erwin was being kept in the central 'glass cage' of the prison which the Gestapo reserved for special cases. Bernt passed the guard a few cigarettes to make sure he had some time alone with him in his cell. He found him lying on a narrow iron bed, his head covered in bandages so you could only see one eye, his mouth, and his nostrils.

'These *Schweine*, pigs!' said Erwin out of the corner of his mouth. 'Just like they did to *Vater*.'

Bernt lit a cigarette and put it to his mouth.

'But they didn't get anything out of me . . . about Bruneval, you know?'

Bernt had no idea. Bruneval was part of the communications unit at British Command in Cap d'Antifer as far as he knew, but that was about it. Later he discovered what it was: Erwin knew the British had further developed their RADAR. From April 1943 on, they were able to detect German U-boats which had been decimating the merchant navy and troop ships in the Atlantic. Now the tables were turned: in May 1943 alone 40 U-boats were sunk, thanks to RADAR.

'Forget it,' said Erwin. 'But promise me,' he whispered: 'promise to do Plan 7.'

Plan 7. They'd discussed it so often – gone through the details again and again – their method of getting out of the *Wehrmacht*. Erwin knew all the military guideline loopholes and he'd designed Plan 7 specifically for Bernt. It was a dead cert, said Erwin. First Bernt had to feign illness – headache, stomach pains and so on, then they'd take his temperature. As soon as it went above 38 degrees you had to be despatched to the field hospital to be checked out, as stated in the *Wehrmacht* guidelines. To reach 38 degrees, all you had to do was rub the thermometer hard. Then the clever bit: Bernt's grandparents on one side were Jewish. Confess it, with a lot of hesitation, to Major Zobel – then he wouldn't press to have Bernt back in the Unit again, being a lily-livered sort. Especially after the whole incident with Erwin.

'*Mach's gut!* Good luck!' said Erwin. 'You'll be hearing from me. I won't be doing it the same way my *Vater* did . . .'

The next day the news went around like wildfire: Erwin had thrown himself under an oncoming train at Rouen station on his way to Paris. He'd been chained to a *Feld Kommissar* and he dragged him under too. Both were instantly killed.

Bernt was profoundly shocked and distressed. But it impelled him into Plan 7, and it worked like a dream, just as Erwin said it would. Off to the field hospital in Rouen he went, having first confided his terrible secret to Major Zobel. The hospital ward was run by a 70-year-old French nun in a starched white wimple. The young doctor was French too. They soon spotted that Bernt was one of the 'good Germans' who loved France and wanted nothing more than the end of the war, including victory for the Allies. Neither of them were minded to send him back to the Front, so they kept him busy helping out on the wards for as long as they could. Finally he was allowed sick leave to recuperate back home in Düsseldorf, the doctor having signed all the necessary medical reports.

In order to stay in Düsseldorf, Herr Desch found him a job with a firm called Wrobel & Co, doing essential war work. Bernt knew he was in good hands when he saw a copy of the London *Times* on Herr Wrobel's desk. By day, Wrobel & Co needed an English and French speaker to keep track of the Allies' iron and steel and munitions stocks. By night, they needed someone to carry on the good work of getting Jews and anyone else on the run from the Nazis out of the Reich. They'd found a new route via the Balkans which they hoped would see them through to the end of the war. The only problem was that the war seemed nowhere near ending.

The Gestapo arrived on their doorstep, in April 1943 – the month of the great round-ups and arrests. That was when Hans Oster at the *Abwehr* was arrested. Wilhelm Canaris, his Chief, was under suspicion from then on, and later also arrested. It made life very difficult for Wrobel & Co who relied heavily on *Abwehr* protection. In the event, the Gestapo found nothing incriminating in the office and left with nothing more than warnings. '*Verdammt mal!*' swore Herr Wrobel. 'These *Schweine!*' From then on they knew they were under surveillance and had to be extra careful.

So when Bernt heard a loud knocking downstairs at 6am on the morning of 2 March 1944 he feared the worst. It was bad timing. They'd had a small party the night before, at Herr Desch's, to celebrate Onkel Ney's birthday – just a dozen close friends, all part of the clandestine network, including Fräulein Bonse who was still busy with her decrypting and who brought the latest BBC news. Onkel Ney gave Bernt a package wrapped in brown paper and string to take home and hide somewhere safe. It contained documents and a pistol. His mother was away on one of her 'errands' again, so he was alone in the apartment.

Bernt went to the window and took a quick look. The black leather coat and the parked black car told him all he needed to know. He had no time to find a better hiding place for the packet. The knocking got louder. Was it that secretary at Wrobel's who'd denounced them? Bernt had never trusted her. He could hear heavy boots coming up the stairs. Keep calm, he told himself. 'What's going on! It's 6 o'clock! I was fast asleep!' Bernt said, opening the door. 'Identity card!' Bernt protested: 'I'm in the *Wehrmacht*.' The Gestapo man wasn't impressed. 'You're under arrest,' he said, taking out a pair of handcuffs. 'Why?' 'You know why.' The man just waited. Apparently, he wasn't going to search the apartment, just arrest Bernt.

As Bernt got dressed, he took a risk and left his dressing gown on the bathroom floor with the packet underneath – with any luck Frau Kurtz who lived on the third floor and had the keys to the apartment would notice and remove the packet before the Gestapo came back. The man in the black leather coat handcuffed him. The driver of the car got out and together the two black leather coats pushed Bernt into the back. As he ducked down Bernt cast a quick look upstairs – and there was Frau Kurtz behind her curtain.

'*Los! Raus!*' they shouted, kicking him down the stone steps to the cellar of the Gestapo interrogation building in Ulmen Strasse and into one of the cells. 'And all this for a filthy Jew,' added the man for good measure.

So now Bernt knew. It wasn't Wrobel & Co. It was one of their Jewish friends who'd been caught. Later he found out it was Dr Bernstein, arrested at Vienna station on his way to the Balkans and thence to freedom. Apparently, he'd been acting strangely out of sheer nerves, so they searched him and found, sewn into the lining of his coat, Bernt's father, Herr Engelmann's name and address in Australia. Dr Bernstein had promised not to write anything down, but what could you do? He was too scared. It was easy to trace Bernt after that.

Bernt was kept in isolation in his cell for several weeks. The puzzle of why the letters RK were chalked on the cell door was soon solved: a Roman Catholic priest arrived, prayer book and rosary beads and all. Bernt wasn't a Roman Catholic. 'I hear you want to confess, my son,' said the priest, giving him a blessing. Bernt knelt down. 'Your Tante Ney sends her best wishes,' prayed the priest. 'And Herr Wrobel too. He is in the best of health. Amen.' Bernt made the sign of the cross. 'Amen,' he enjoined.

After that it was a long downhill progression for Bernt. First to Ratingen Gestapo prison, then on to Anrath near Krefeld which was full of Dutch prisoners for some reason. There he remained, in isolation, for over two months. At the beginning of May 1944, he was hauled upstairs by a Gestapo *Kommissar* called Richter, demanding a full report of his activities 'protecting Jews'. Officially. Unofficially, seeing as the Reich was close to defeat, as anyone could see, Richter wanted Bernt to sign a statement saying that he'd always been treated well by *Kommissar* Richter, who now, in turn, was asking for clemency. 'He has helped me to the best of his capabilities, and thus saved my life,' Bernt duly wrote and signed.

'Do you actually know what this is all about?' asked a *Sicherheitsdienst* interrogator from Berlin during another session. 'It's *critical* that the Western powers know how important it is for us to work *together* against the Soviets and Communism.' Presumably they thought the English-speaker might be able to help them out some time in the future, thought Bernt. A week later, news of the Normandy Landings filtered through the cell walls: 7,000 ships, 16,000 planes, 620,000 men with 100,000 military vehicles of every sort were now on French soil, making for the Reich. The Luftwaffe only had 350 planes. Hitler hadn't expected landings in Normandy – he'd planned for Calais, fooled by Operation Fortitude, a clever deception devised by the Joint Planning Staff at the War Office in London. Now the Supreme Commander and Führer was having to transfer exhausted troops from the Eastern Front to the West. Most of them were thrilled to get away from the ferocious Russian advance.

Richter couldn't stop an order for Bernt's transfer to Flossenberg concentration camp which arrived on 1 September 1944, signed by SS *Reichsführer* Ernst Kaltenbrunner, the man who'd taken over the *Sicherheits Dienst* when Reinhard Heydrich was assassinated in Prague. There were eighty other prisoners on that particular transport – men and women of all nationalities. At one point Bernt was handcuffed to a Dutch professor, at another to a farmer who'd refused to swear the oath of allegiance to Hitler, at yet another to a German Jehovah's Witness.

Bernt remembered Ernst Kaltenbrunner well because he'd been the guest of honour at his cousin Gudrun's wedding.

CHAPTER TWELVE

THE END

On 15 May 1944, Julius Leber, the larger-than-life former SPD Reichstag member, was on his way to the lawyer Joseph Wirmer's apartment. He took the tram from his coal business in Berlin-Schöneberg, doubling back a couple of times as usual to make sure he wasn't being followed. There were meetings all the time these days, sometimes in private apartments, sometimes in hotels, sometimes in offices. Often they were held in the back room of Leber's coal business, because once he got out of Sachsenhausen concentration camp in May 1937 he went straight back to fighting the Nazi regime, unbent and unbowed, making contact with other resisters through his friends Ludwig Schwamb, Gustav Dahrendorff and Ernst von Harnack.

Leber was a lot thinner these days – no longer the ample ebullient man he'd once been. But looks can be deceptive – he was as combative as ever, taking the lead in all the discussions the groups were having. Some wives might have objected, especially as Leber and Annedore had two children, now in their teens and needing their father to be present after his four years' absence. But not Annedore. He called her 'Paulus' after her conversion on the way to Damascus to the cause of Social Democracy. Her conversion hadn't taken long – Leber could talk and persuade anyone, and he could make her laugh like no one else she'd ever met in her safe conservative life. She loved him and she admired him, even when he drank and womanised and recklessly courted danger. And she knew the dangers. 'Two hours after our victory Dr Leber will be hanging from a lamp-post in the market square,' as the local Nazis of Lübeck had threatened even before 1933. Leber's response was to beat them up whenever he could, physically as well as verbally. So it was inevitable that he'd be arrested soon after the Nazi *Machtergreifung*. He wasn't bothered. 'In general, it is not the present which occupies me the most,' as he'd written from prison in June 1933, 'it is the future. What we have today is a transition. I have not the slightest doubt about that. But what comes next is wrapped in profound darkness.'

The Battle of Stalingrad was a turning point for the secret fighters of the Nazi regime. By early 1943, and despite Dr Goebbels' best efforts of lies and dissembling, they knew the end was in sight and it gave them renewed determination. 'Klaus Bonhoeffer knew since summer 1943 that Stauffenberg wanted to actively attack the National Socialist regime,' went a later Gestapo report. 'He also knew that Generals Olbricht (Chief of the General Army Office at Army High Command), Mertz, Oertzen, Schwerin and Schlabrendorff on the military side were engaged in Putsch plans. On the civilian side, he knew of Goerdeler, Leuschner, Leber, Wirmer, FD Schulenburg, Hassell, Kaiser, Popitz, Habermann, Trott and Guttenberg . . .' During his interrogation, Bonhoeffer also mentioned Werner von Haeften, who was Stauffenberg's adjutant, in the safe knowledge that by October 1944 and after the hundreds of 20 July Plot arrests, all these names were already known to the Gestapo.

Julius Leber, too, found renewed strength for the fight in 1943. Through his three friends, Schwamb, Dahrendorf and Harnack, he now made contact with a much wider range of resisters. Remembering the failure of the Left during Weimar – the fatal lack of collaboration between the Social Democrats and the Communists – he was minded to meet anyone and everyone working to remove Hitler and the Nazi regime, whatever their previous political alignments. 'The aim: to create a unified Front between Right and Left and bring together the former Christian and Trade Union wings,' he commented. He'd already met Carlo Mierendorff, the political theorist, Wilhelm Leuschner, the Trade Unionist, and Klaus Bonhoeffer the lawyer and younger brother of theologian Dietrich Bonhoeffer at Ludwig Schwamb's apartment back in 1938. Now they introduced him to the Kreisau Circle of resisters around Helmuth von Moltke, and the Goerdeler/Beck group.

The Kreisau Circle were wary of Leber, the former SPD firebrand. Moltke preferred the other three former SPD members, Mierendorff, Theodor Haubach and Professor Adolf Reichwein. They came from educated backgrounds, whereas Leber was, in Moltke's view 'much less cultured than them'. The social gulf seems to have blinded Moltke to the fact that Leber was in fact extremely well educated, albeit not in the traditional way. Leber wasn't bothered – he wasn't much taken with them either, Prussian aristocrats as they mostly were, the sort he'd roundly attacked in the old days in his newspaper, the *Lübecker Volksboten*.

Moltke was an international lawyer drafted into the *Abwehr* by Canaris and Oster as soon as war broke out to join the anti-Nazis they were gathering around them, plotting to overthrow Hitler. His job in counter-intelligence allowed him plenty of scope to travel and secretly keep in touch with his friends in Britain. In fact, he was one of the many who'd gone to Britain before the war, begging for its intervention. All this Leber knew. And he could see that Moltke was a clever, witty, decent and courageous man. But the trouble with Moltke, as Leber saw it, was that he was given to theorising and planning more than to action. He was also deeply religious and thus against the taking of life or, to put it more accurately, assassination. A plot to remove Hitler from power, yes. Long discussions about the *Neue Ordnung*, the new political system once the Nazis had been removed, certainly. But assassination? No. Leber, on the other hand, was for killing. He'd fought the Nazis in Lübeck for too long not to know that they were brutal killers themselves. He'd done four years in concentration camps which told him the same. He was for removing Hitler by any means, fair or foul. Talking, thought Leber, got you nowhere.

Leber first makes an appearance in Moltke's letters from Berlin to his wife Freya in Kreisau on 6 August 1943 under the codename 'substitute Uncle', because he was being put forward as a replacement in the group for the Trade Union leader Wilhelm Leuschner. Two days later he appears again: 'As soon as this letter is finished, I'll bicycle out to Peter (Yorck) from him to Adam's (Trott) where Seltzer and Husen will join me, back from there to Peter and the beginning of a night session with Friedrich (Mierendorff), Theo (Haubach) and perhaps our Substitute Uncle.'

Moltke's apartment was like the General Post Office, plotters coming and going all the time. 'I didn't write yesterday,' he wrote, 'the day was too full, and I wasn't alone for a minute.' Seltzer had come at 2.30, Peter at 3, Adam and Haeften at 3.30, and on till bedtime at 2am. The next day at the office, it was the same: Stauffenberg at 11, then Adam, then Hans, then home for lunch with Peter and Husen, then a quick bicycle ride to Conrad's, with Friedrich (Mierendorff) already waiting back at the apartment, staying till midnight talking on and on, planning for the new government after the Fall of the Nazis.

Leber had to concede their political ideas were sound, inspiring even, and in fact not that far removed from his own ideas as expressed in his early political writings: a democratic system along English lines, embracing a wider section of society, all within the context of a unified Europe, to make sure such a war could never happen again. In 1943 this was a revolutionary idea, and one with a clear future. But there was never enough concession made to the workers, insisted Leber – those who'd been fighting in vain for their rights long before the Nazis came to power – hounded and brutally treated, first under Bismarck, then Weimar, and finally under the Nazis who ended by forcing them into a war they didn't want. No, said Leber, he wouldn't subscribe to any new political system which didn't give the worker his fair and equal due. In a word, Socialism. And that, most of the old Prussians found hard to swallow.

But there was one Prussian aristocrat who saw things as Leber did: Fritz-Dietlof von der Schulenburg. It hadn't taken Fritzi long to realise that the Socialism of National Socialism was a hollow promise – a mere ruse to get the workers' vote. 'Our *whole* life must be Socialist,' as he'd written to his boss, Koch, on 12 July 1933. 'It's still possible to achieve: for example by visiting the workers in their impoverished homes, and the fishermen suffering from Haft sickness, and the poor immigrants, and the farmers, and those living on the dangerous borders of our Region – all this achieves more good than any amount of propaganda, and gives us a real insight into the soul of the Volk, in a way nothing else can.' But he soon learned he was barking up the wrong tree, first with Koch and later with the whole Nazi regime. 'The time will come,' as he wrote to Charlotte on 24 August 1933 with premature optimism, 'when the loud mouths and false Leaders will be scattered to the winds.' That year he and Charlotte invited the unemployed of his administrative district for a Christmas feast.

In 1943 it was Fritzi who made the first move to meet Leber. Knowing about Leber's recent involvement with Kreisau, he sent a message by courier to his coal business. A date was agreed: he was to come to Leber's home in Eisvogel Weg on 22 November, taking all the usual precautions. Just as Fritzi arrived, there was an air-raid alarm – sirens wailing, people in panic running for cover. The Lebers quickly led the great Prussian into their modest cellar. There Julius Leber offered Count Schulenburg the safest place. To their amazement the young Count not only refused, he insisted on going back up into the house. For what? To collect some cushions and the coffee! No air-raid is going to put me off, he indicated to Leber, whose rumbustious reputation he already knew because as a teenager Fritzi had

attended the *Gymnasium* in Lübeck where Annedore's father was the
Principal. Later he'd kept in touch with Herr Doktor Rosenthal, even
after Rosenthal lost his job through *Gleichschaltung*. No, Fritzi knew
all about Julius Leber. That's why he contacted the man in the first
place. And the more he knew, the more he liked.

As Annedore wrote later, the two men were reserved with one
another at first, because you had to be careful with everyone these
days. But they soon realised that, unlikely as it was, they had a great
deal in common – were, in fact, rather alike. Fritzi had originally
believed in the 'Socialist' part of National Socialism because he knew
from his own experience that the *ancien régime* political and administrative system was in dire need of reform. A later Gestapo report
confirmed that Fritzi already had doubts about it as early as 1934, following Georg Strasser's murder, and that by 1938 he was fully engaged
in Opposition activity.

Now, at the end of 1943, he and Leber joined forces, each determined to be rid of the man leading Germany into catastrophe. Political
theories were all well and good, they agreed, but what was needed first
and foremost was action. 'You can't make politics with literary and
theoretical debate,' as Fritzi put it, no doubt thinking of the Kreisau
Circle. Leber didn't need telling. A fully functioning government and
administration had to be ready to step into the political vacuum once
the Nazi regime was gone. Thereafter the key was good leadership
– someone strong enough and charismatic enough to carry the Volk
through the chaos of the immediate post-Nazi and post-war period.
It didn't take Fritzi long to realise that they had such a man in Julius
Leber. By late 1943, the Beck/Goerdeler group and Kreisau were listing
Goerdeler or Ludwig Beck as the future Chancellor, the lawyer Wirmer
as future Minister of Justice and Fritzi Schulenburg as Minister of the
Interior. Fritzi let it be known that he thought Leber the better man for
the post, and that he would be happy to serve under him as Secretary
of State.

But first they had to kill Hitler.

After the success of that first meeting with Leber, Fritzi quickly
arranged a second, this time with Claus Count Schenk von Stauffenberg
present – another aristocrat, albeit not Prussian, and another man of
action. Like Fritzi, Stauffenberg had started by supporting the Nazi
regime, but unlike him, he never became a member of the Party. He
was a career army officer first and foremost and, like most of his

fellow officers, he smarted under the terms of the Treaty of Versailles and welcomed Hitler's early successes to reclaim some of the lost territory. He'd fought in Poland, France and Russia and in North Africa as part of Rommel's *Afrika Korps* where he was severely wounded, losing his right hand, two fingers of his left and the sight in one eye. He'd spent months in hospital. But by late 1943 he was back at work, based in Berlin as a staff officer with the Reserve Army under General Olbricht, an anti-Nazi from early on, working closely with Ludwig Beck. In fact, Stauffenberg was already in touch with several conspirators, including the Kreisau Circle at home and Henning von Tresckow at the Eastern Front. He knew about the failed attempt to assassinate Hitler by Tresckow and Schlabrendorff, and now, favourably placed in his new post, he was poised to take a leading role in the fight.

'Pfaff (Goerdeler) confirms that the preparations are really going ahead now,' wrote Hassell, listed to be Foreign Minister in the post-Nazi government, in his diary on 13 November 1943. 'The determination to act, both in Berlin and at the Front, is set. When I asked Pfaff if that included the "*Kernpunkt*" he became a bit vague.' That was because *Kernpunkt,* the key point, referred to the assassination plot, and Goerdeler was one of those who worried about the taking of life.

What Hassell didn't know was that Fritz-Dietlof von der Schulenburg was acting as a link between all the groups. At the lawyer Joseph Wirmer's apartment, he'd introduced Karl Goerdeler to Kleist-Schmenzin, Fabian von Schlabrendorff's old friend who'd gone to England in 1938 to see Churchill to beg for British intervention. Elsewhere he'd arranged the meeting between Stauffenberg and Axel von dem Bussche when Axel offered himself as the next assassin. And he was the link between Stauffenberg and Julius Leber's group of Social Democrats. Fritzi moved from one Opposition group to another, from General Beck, his father's old friend, to Canaris and Oster at the *Abwehr,* to Helmuth von Moltke and Carl Goerdeler and Kreisau, to Fabian von Schlabrendorff when he was on one of his clandestine errands to Berlin, and thence back to Tresckow and Army Group Centre still fighting it out at the Eastern Front.

From time to time, he also went to meetings at Moltke's apartment in Berlin but he kept his cards so close to his chest that Moltke got the false impression they were finally getting Fritzi on side for a coup, and away from an assassination. 'Peter (Yorck), Marion, Fritzi and I went to church with a sermon by Lilje, on the horrors and gravity of history, which was very good,' wrote Moltke from Berlin to his wife Freya in Kreisau on 5 December 1943. 'Fritzi came back for lunch, at which we ate your chickens, which were very delicious. Fritzi was nice and seems to be on his way back to us. He was here till 7 o'clock, debating with Reichwein, who had in the meantime joined us . . . I am waiting anxiously to see whether we can tie Fritzi more closely to us again.' What Fritzi had told his sister Tisa back in 1939, that from now on he'd be wearing a mask, even to friends if necessary, was evidently true. It's not that he didn't trust and admire Moltke, it's just that he knew with his usual certainty that Moltke was wrong and that he was right. 'I am of course stupid, Moltke is clever,' he joked with Charlotte. The point being, as he wryly noted: 'They are not inclined to be involved in an assassination.'

After Carlo Mierendorff was killed by a bomb while visiting an aunt in Leipzig in December 1943, it was Fritzi who persuaded the Kreisau Circle to accept Julius Leber in his stead. And it was Fritzi who introduced Leber to Stauffenberg – which turned out to be another of the great, unexpected collaborations. He also introduced Fabian von Schlabrendorff's friend, Kleist-Schmenzin, to Goerderler in another of those meetings in Wirmer's apartment, where Kleist-Schmenzin told Goerdeler about his pre-war trip to England to meet with Churchill. 'The role of Schulenburg was uppermost,' as a later Gestapo report noted.

In the meantime, whenever he could, Fritzi took the train from Berlin to Schwerin and on to Trebbow to see Charlotte and their six children, all safely housed with his sister Tisa, surrounded by the dark Mecklenburgh forests and the silent lakes and wide fields of wheat – far from the Allied bombing on the one hand and the hounding of the Nazis on the other.

Prussian aristocrats and former SPD members weren't the only resisters reinvigorated by Stalingrad. 'Around summer 1943 a group of leading Communist functionaries, including Anton Saefkow and Franz Jacob, later Bernhard Bastlein, began anew to build up a strong Communist organisation, targeting the factories and industries and the *Wehrmacht* army,' it was later noted by the Gestapo.

Saefkow and Jacob had been part of a Communist cell in Hamburg even before the 1933 *Machtergreifung*. Bernhard Bastlein was one of their leaders – all followers of the great Ernst Thälmann, and all in and out of Gestapo prisons and concentration camps. But by summer 1943 Saefkow and Jacob were free again and living in Berlin, renewing contact. Bastlein was still incarcerated at Berlin Plötzensee prison till January 1944 when the prison was hit in an Allied bombing raid and he was able to escape in the chaos. Saefkow had meanwhile made contact with Ernst Rumbow, another old Communist comrade who'd spent years in concentration camps and Gestapo prisons, surviving severe torture. Together they wrote long papers on future Communist policy, distributed by couriers in far-flung Saxony, Thüringen and Magdeburg, calling on the Volk in the *Heimat* to resist the Nazis, with their duplicitous lies and their terrible war crimes. They also made contact with the *Freies Deutschland*, Free Germany movement, orchestrated by exiled German Communists and German POWs in Russia. There was little contact with Soviet Communists, given the conditions of war – other than the secret and highly dangerous tuning in to Radio Moscow. The focus was regime change in Germany.

By spring 1944, all the plotters, whether Communist or Prussian aristocrat or Social Democrat, knew time was running out. There were too many Gestapo spies and plants, too many arrests, too many interrogations under torture, too many executions. Some wondered whether it was even worth proceeding with the assassination plot, given the extreme dangers and the fact that the war would surely be ending very soon. The Allies had already declared at the Casablanca Conference of January 1943 that they would only accept an Unconditional Surrender. Wouldn't it be better to save the lives of the best among them rather than have them all executed in the event of a failed assassination attempt? Stauffenberg rejected that idea vehemently. Henning von Tresckow agreed: 'The assassination attempt must take place at whatever cost. Even if it does not succeed, we must still act. For it is no longer a question of whether it has a practical purpose; what counts is the fact in the eyes of the world and of History, the German Resistance dared to act. Compared with that nothing else is important.'

Stauffenberg and Tresckow had been of the same mind since they first met in July 1941 at Army Group Centre HQ, then based in

Borissow, the scene of unspeakable Jewish massacres. They talked, from the start, of assassination. Could they shoot Hitler, surrounded as he always was by rings of SS security? Better a bomb, perhaps. Then they could blow up other top Nazis at the same time, which the Generals around Ludwig Beck insisted was essential if a coup was to succeed. But at that time they decided it was too soon, given that the Volk, fed by Goebbels' propaganda, hardly knew truth from lies, and the *Wehrmacht* soldier at the Front still believed in his oath of loyalty to the Führer.

It was a different story, however, when they met again in August 1943, at Olbricht's apartment along with General Ludwig Beck. Tresckow was shocked at Stauffenberg's appearance – the missing hand, the missing fingers, the eyepatch. But he found him in excellent heart and utterly determined on assassination now. 'I must do something to save our Reich,' Stauffenberg wrote to his wife Erika. 'As army officers, we share the responsibility for what's happening.' One thing they already knew: the assassin had to be an army officer – someone with access to Hitler's inner circle, because the security round the Führer was so tight that he rarely left the safety of his bunkers, whether in Berlin or the *Wolfschanze*, the Wolf's Lair at the Eastern Front. The great Führer's preference was to stay behind his triple ring of SS security up at Berchtesgaden in the Austrian alps. When he did go out in public it was rarely for more than an hour, the venue and route always changing at the last minute. Rumour had it, he wore not only a bullet-proof vest but a bullet-proof cap too. In other words, everyone around the Führer knew there were assassination plots afoot. They just didn't know by whom or when.

By January 1944, Helmuth von Moltke and Julius Leber were beginning to work constructively together, Moltke finally accepting that Leber was a key player and a great politician, though they still couldn't agree on the future role of the Trade Unions nor any of Leber's more radical Socialist ideas. But there was mutual respect – not least because, on Leber's part, he knew that Moltke had been an active opponent of the Nazi regime from the very start, appalled by the *Anschluss*, the invasion of Czechoslovakia and Poland, the declaration of war, the conquest of France – and all the rest of it. Leber and Moltke met twice that January 1944, once at Peter Yorck's, once at Leber's coal business. But then came the great shock: on 19 January Moltke was arrested by the Gestapo.

Now everyone knew the enemy was closing in. There had been a sweep of arrests of late – probably as a result of a Gestapo spy called Dr Reckzeh who'd infiltrated a social group around Elizabeth von Thadden who held social parties to disguise their Opposition work. Under extreme torture, Goerdeler's name had been mentioned. And Moltke's. The immediate result was that all Opposition work in Moltke's section of the *Abwehr* came to an abrupt halt. Canaris was removed and the *Abwehr* was placed under *Reichsführer* Heinrich Himmler's personal control. Goerdeler got away but was forced to go on the run, staying no more than a few nights here, a few there, helped by a raft of courageous anonymous people, until finally, on 12 August 1944, the Gestapo caught up with him and arrested him.

On the night of Moltke's arrest, Stauffenberg had immediately contacted Peter Yorck to confirm that he intended to be the next assassin. He also contacted Fritz-Dietlof von der Schulenburg and Adam von Trott to tell them the same. Over the next weeks he travelled everywhere making contact with several groups of conspirators and seeing so many people in his office at Bendler Strasse that General Fromm, Commander in Chief of the Reserve Army, asked who, *Gott im Himmel*, were they all?

By April, plans were in place. Stauffenberg travelled to Trebbow and spent the night talking everything through with Fritzi. Olbricht had managed to promote Stauffenberg as his Chief of Staff in the Reserve Army at Bendler Strasse which meant he could accompany him to occasional meetings with the Führer's entourage. It was the first step. But plans needed to speed up. The Allies were standing at the gate on both Fronts, East and West. And the Nazi regime was closing in to take last-minute revenge.

Julius Leber and Adolf Reichwein also speeded up their plans. They decided to contact the Communists Saefkow, Jacob and Bastlein, using a go-between named Ferdinand Thomas, a contact of their former SPD colleague Dr Schmid. Thomas had been sentenced to three years in a concentration camp for 'courier work' in 1936 and was trusted by the Communist group. Even so, Saefkow and Jacob sent Judith Auer, one of their long-time couriers, to check him out. Then they agreed to go ahead.

Which is why, on 15 May 1944, Leber was making his way to the lawyer Wirmer's apartment for a meeting with Schulenburg, Goerdeler and Leuschner, preparing to tell them of his and Reichwein's decision to meet the Communists. But first there were the usual things to discuss – disagreements about future Trade Union involvement and the role of the *Wehrmacht*, workers' rights and, critically, peace negotiations with the Allies. Here again, there was a split in opinion: with whom best to negotiate? The conservative group round Goerdeler were for the Western Allies, but the younger group, led by Leber, Schulenburg and Stauffenberg, favoured the Russians. Goerdeler was determined to exclude Russia entirely, still believing that the Western Allies would be prepared to cede some territory back to Germany. Leber quickly disabused him of this naivety – it was 'illusionist' he said – impossible either to leave Russia out of the equation or to expect any territorial concessions from the Allies. In fact, there was no avoiding a total occupation of Germany by the victors, whether before a coup or after, he said. With that, some wondered again whether plans for an assassi-nation should proceed at all, given an Allied victory was so close and the Russians were already poised outside Warsaw.

Leber decided to wait before telling the others of his and Reichwein's decision to meet the German Communists. Instead he reminded them: 'If you want the successful downfall of the Nazis, you have to have a clear and positive aim, in order to be able to re-orientate the misled masses.' As soon as Hitler was assassinated the telephone wires to the Führer HQ would be cut and all remaining top Nazis, wherever they were, arrested. They agreed that wireless broadcasts and the press would need to go into action immediately to reassure the Volk. They already had people in place for that, but as Leber pointed out: 'One by one, each corruption and crime of the fallen Nazi regime will have to be repeated to the Volk through broadcasts and the press,' again and again, just as Hitler and Goebbels had done, because the Volk had effectively been brainwashed. If the Nazis could do it, so could they.

It was critical Army officers remained free of suspicion. Field Marshal Witzleben, a long-time conspirator, would make the announcement in a wireless broadcast: 'The Führer Adolf Hitler is dead! An unscrupu-lous clique of non-military Party leaders have taken advantage of the situation and attempted to shoot the iron fighters in the back, in order to take power . . .' Later the Volk would be told what the New Order entailed: 'A reinstatement of human rights, law and order, and the socialising of key industries, and general tolerance of race, religions, and class, and the reinstatement of Jewish rights,' as Carl Mierendorff, with Leber and Reichwein, had formulated back in June 1943. But for now they just had to understand that their Führer was dead and the thousand-year Reich was at an end.

There was another meeting on 16 June, in the Hotel Esplanade. Then another on 21 June, in Peter Yorck's apartment on the Hortensien Strasse, including Adam von Trott, Julius Leber, Adolf Reichwein and Theodor Haubach. This is when Leber and Reichwein told the others they intended to meet up with the Communists Saefkow and Jacob and Bastlein. But wasn't it too risky, the others asked? How could you trust the devil? Reichwein reminded them he'd known and trusted some of the Communists in the Red Orchestra group, including Arvid and Mildred Harnack, those old friends of Rudolf Ditzen, both arrested and executed in 1942. For his part, Julius Leber reminded them he'd met and worked with many Communists, including Jacob, in Sachsenhausen concentration camp. The fact remained: they couldn't run a post-war government without them. Time was running out, and they were going ahead.

In fact, the meeting had already been arranged – at Dr Schmid's surgery in Köpernicker Strasse – for the following evening, 22 June. Present were Leber, Reichwein, Saefkow, Jacob, Ernst Rambow, the go-between Ferdinand Thomas and Dr Schmid himself. Leber and Jacob greeted each other warmly, old friends as they were from Sachsenhausen days. Leber's opening question to the Communists: who had the say-so in the present KPD organisation? Was it the Germans, or was it Russia? Jacob confirmed it was the Germans. Jacob in turn asked Leber about the SPD membership. Leber confirmed they were prepared to work with the Communists, not wanting to repeat the mistakes of the past. 'But let's concern ourselves with the future, not the past,' he added, meaning the future after 'Day X'. He wanted reassurance that things wouldn't run the way they had in Russia: dominated by the Party, attacking the churches and the Christian Trade Unions. And what about the big industries and businesses? Jacob and Saefkow assured him they could work together.

That evening Leber reported back to his old colleague and friend Gustav Dahrendorff: 'The main point was: the Communists agreed to a Democratic system, and gave an assurance that this would be future practice.' This was credible because, even before the Nazi *Machtergreifung*, at the KPD German Communist Conference in 1932, Ernst Thälmann himself had stated he was in favour of working with the Social Democrats and their Trade Unions in order to defeat the Nazis. Still, Leber didn't give the Communist group any specific details about 'Day X', the when and the how of the assassination. And he never mentioned the name of Stauffenberg. A next meeting was agreed, for 4 July at the *U-Bahn* on Adolf Hitler Platz – a little joke.

What Leber and Reichwein didn't know is that Bernhard Bastlein had been arrested. It had happened on 30 May immediately after a meeting between Bastlein, Ernst Rambow and a man called Hans Schmidt, which had taken place informally, on the corner of Schönhauser Allee. Schmidt had left early. Bastlein was picked up, but Rambow got away. Gestapo files show that Bastlein, the old Hamburg fighter, gave almost nothing away under interrogation and torture – he only knew the code names, he insisted, nothing else. As late as 1 July 1944, the Gestapo still didn't know who 'Hans', 'Alfred', 'Paul', 'Walter', 'Stefan' and 'Fritz' were. Bastlein only admitted to knowing Saefkow and Jacob because he knew the Gestapo already had their names.

Who was the traitor? It turned out to be Ernst Rambow, the old Comrade Saefkow had known even before 1933. They'd trusted Rambow completely because he'd been arrested by the Nazis in 1934 and incarcerated for six years, till 1940. They didn't know that somewhere along the line, after severe torture, he'd been 'turned'. Later he'd fetched up in Berlin and was apparently working as a shoe mender when he and Saefkow met up again. In fact, he was already working for the Gestapo, under the control of one Hermann Schulz. Rambow informed Schulz about the 30 May meeting, and the 22 June meeting. And the proposed 4 July meeting. His own fate was a terrible one, caught between the twin evils of Nazism and Communism: after the horror of informing on his former comrades, he was arrested by the Allies in July 1945 and handed over to the Russians. Seeing him as a traitor either way, they sentenced him to death on 25 September 1945.

Jacob and Saefkow, meanwhile, had several meetings to prepare for the next meeting with Leber and Reichwein on 4 July. In the event, Leber didn't turn up – he still couldn't fully trust the Communists and he decided to wait and see. Reichwein felt differently and went to Adolf Hitler Platz at 6pm. The group was planning to move on to the badly bombed apartment of Magdalena Pechel, wife of Rudolf, the former chief of the *Deutsche Rundschau* news agency, arrested in 1942. Bernhard Bastlein, code name 'Hermann', was meant to be there too but was securely incarcerated by then. The three made another date for the next day, at the Tiergarten station, to include Leber. It never happened because Reichwein, Jacob and Saefkow were all arrested that same evening. Rosemarie Reichwein, realising what had occurred, immediately informed Peter Yorck of her husband's disappearance. Yorck telephoned Leber to warn him. In vain. The Gestapo arrived at his coal business the following morning and arrested him.

News travelled fast. Stauffenberg was badly shaken by Leber's arrest. He and Leber had been working closely together during the previous weeks on the frankly Socialist programme for the new government after 'Day X'. Now he raced to finish his plans for Hitler's assassination, turning to General Fromm, Commander in Chief of the Reserve Army at Bendler Strasse, for help. Fromm took the decisive step and promoted Stauffenberg to his own staff, thereby giving him the critical access to Hitler's inner circle. Fromm had so far kept himself away from direct assassination plots and some said he didn't know what was afoot when he agreed to promote Stauffenberg, but that is stretching credibility too far. It was back to the mask problem.

In fact, Fromm had warned Hitler as early as January 1942 that a war on two Fronts could not be won once the Americans joined the fight, and that they should broker for peace as soon as possible. The result: for two years he'd been excluded from military strategy meetings. But by early 1944 he was back in precarious favour. That January he confided to his wife and daughter Helga that the assassination attempt could only succeed if all the top hierarchy of Nazis were blown up, not just Hitler. So he took the decisive step of promoting Stauffenberg to his own staff, surely knowing it would mean his own death if the plot failed. Albrecht Mertz von Quirnheim, another strong anti-Nazi, took Stauffenberg's position under Olbricht. Bendler Strasse was ready to act.

'The world lies under the cloud of the Invasion,' Ulrich von Hassell wrote in his diary on 12 June 1944, following the Western Allies' landings in Normandy. 'It's quite grotesque that, after the long tension of waiting, *both* sides greet it with a relieved "at last".'

By 10 July things were worse: 'Catastrophe looms larger and larger on the horizon,' von Hassell wrote. 'Up till now it looked as though things would go on for quite a long time yet. But now there are several indications that the end is coming sooner.' The Eastern Front was collapsing, with 'fleeing German soldiers', hopelessly futile attempts of the depleted Luftwaffe, and a shocking lack of weapons and armaments.

Nor was von Hassell an admirer of Hitler's 'miracle weapon' the V-bomb, which would only make 'this terrible war' even worse and ruin any hope of a half-way decent peace treaty. The Invasion was making swift inroads after a slow start, while Italy was constantly going in reverse. And you could just 'forget about the U-boat war.' On top of all this, his old friend and colleague Ludwig Beck was ill and pessimistic now – not so much about the likely success of the assassination plot as about the possibility of a future German government being able to come to terms with the Allies. It didn't stop von Hassell setting off through the bombed streets of Munich to give one of his lectures – this time on the great poet, Dante. And it didn't stop him repeating a joke doing the rounds: Count Bobby (idiot): 'I should like to serve at the Führer's HQ.' Staff surgeon: 'Are you crazy?' Count Bobby: 'Is that one of the requirements?'

Von Hassell's last diary entry was on 13 July 1944. He and his beloved wife Ilse had spent some very uncomfortable hours in their cellar during another bombing of Munich which was being heavily targeted now. Their daughter Almuth had only just made it home to Ebenhausen in time, riding through the burning streets on her bicycle. 'No post. No newspapers. No telephone.'

Claus von Stauffenberg and his fellow conspirators were readied to act, just waiting for the opportunity. Bendler Strasse remained the Headquarters of Operation Valkyrie, both for the assassination plot and the co-ordination of events after 'Day X'. The coup telegram was ready and prepared for Field Marshal von Witzleben to send out to all military HQs once Hitler was dead. The Reserve Army under Fromm and Olbricht had two million men at its disposal to maintain order once the deed was done. And they would be supported at home by the Berlin police under Arthur Nebe.

We have Oster's word for it that Arthur Nebe, Chief of Police and member of the SS, was on side, contrary to all appearances. He'd been a professional policeman before the *Machtergreifung* and quickly adapted to the new Nazi regime, whether out of conviction or opportunism no one knows. For a short time, he even led the *Einsatzgruppe* attached to Army Group Centre, the centre of the military conspirators. Again, no one knows why. Was he already in touch with Tresckow? Did Oster send him? He served a few months at the Front, taking part in horrific acts of extermination, though his defenders say he tried to save as many lives as he could. It was the eternal dilemma: after the war it was often almost impossible to tell who was genuinely wearing a mask in order to play their part in the conspiracy, or who later claimed to be wearing it to save their own skins. In Nebe's case the best way to look at it is backwards: the Nazis kept their most brutal punishment for those they considered their worst enemies and traitors: hanging by piano wire, the slowest and most painful death – like animals, as Hitler had it. This was Nebe's fate, on 21 March 1945, in last-minute revenge, just before the final collapse of the thousand-year Reich.

Fritz-Dietlof von der Schulenburg had meanwhile been travelling the length and breadth of the country for several months, contacting reliable police officers and politicians and administrators to take over at a local level as soon as they received the code-word 'Valkyrie'. His method, as the Gestapo later heard, was to tell no one anything more than what was essential to their own part in the operation. Information was organised in a series of circles: a small inner circle knew everything, the next circle knew about the assassination plan but none of the details, a third wider circle knew that a coup was planned, and a fourth outer circle were merely alerted in a general way, readied to act as and when they were told. Former Trade Unionists, teachers, clerics, civil servants, policemen, community leaders – the network stretched far and wide, encompassing thousands in its outer reaches. No names were used and Fritzi made certain his contacts were reliable by contacting only those recommended by known and trusted others. Any doubts, and they were left out.

In the course of his duties, he was able to visit Copenhagen and liaise with sympathisers there who in turn would alert people in Sweden and England after 'Day X'. He also managed, on a working visit to Paris, to meet up with conspirators there, including General von Stulpnagel, Military Commander of Occupied France, and Stulpnagel's right-hand man, Caesar von Hofacker, Stauffenberg's cousin, who was part of a long-established resistance cell acting as liaison with conspirators in the Reich. He even managed to contact his old Prussian Civil Service colleague, Dr Seifarth, now in France working as an administrator by day, on resistance work by night. And back in the Reich, ever since he'd written a paper on 'Bomb damage and reconstruction', he had easy access to the Ministry of the Interior, the 'day job' happily going hand in hand with the 'night job', discussing and planning critical administrative matters such as resettlement, housing and organisation of the new *Länder* after 'Day X'. Thanks to army officers like Fabian von Schlabrendorff who were regularly in Berlin, he never lost contact with the plotters around Henning von Tresckow at Army Group Centre. Back and forth Fritzi went, up and down the country and across borders, knowing that the Gestapo was suspicious of him since his brief arrest in April 1943. With his wide circle of devoted friends and 'disciples', and his own gift for understanding people, and his impenetrable mask, he was the ideal person for the job.

On 7 June 1944, Stauffenberg, as General Fromm's Chief of Staff, accompanied him for the first time to the Berghof and an emergency meeting with Hitler and his cronies. The Allies had just landed in Normandy and the Invasion had begun. General Fromm had evidently managed to hide behind his mask of loyalty since his reinstatement, and Stauffenberg was amazed how easy it was to gain access once he was a member of the inner circle. He played his part as the returning war hero with his Iron Cross, standing to attention, biding his time, knowing that sooner or later there'd be another meeting at another Führer HQ.

Meanwhile he and his fellow conspirators were busy with the technicalities of producing a bomb which would kill as many top Nazis as possible along with their Führer. Any action was fraught with danger and terrible ironies. 'The man who does it, must do so in the knowledge that he will go down in German history as a traitor. If he does not do it, however, he will be a traitor to his conscience,' Stauffenberg told a friend that July. He knew the assassination attempt might fail, so he instructed his wife Nina that, in the event, she was on no account to stay loyal to him but should refute his actions completely. Someone had to stay alive to look after their four children.

On 6 July, there was another meeting with the Führer at the Berghof. And another on 11 July. Each time Stauffenberg was barely searched, which was just as well since he now had the pack of dynamite and fuse and pliers in his briefcase. But on each occasion neither Göring nor Himmler were present, so he waited for the next opportunity – the Generals still insisting that killing the Führer but leaving the other top Nazis alive was as good as useless. The next opportunity came soon. On 15 July, General Fromm and Stauffenberg were summoned to a meeting at the Wolf's Lair at Rastenberg. Back at Bendler Strasse Olbricht put Operation Valkyrie on alert.

The flight to Rastenberg took little more than an hour, followed by a short drive from the military airfield to the Wolf's Lair. Again, Stauffenberg was astonished by how easy it was to pass through the three SS security rings surrounding the HQ. The Guest Bunker was situated in Inner Security Ring III which also housed the Führer Bunker and the *Lager* Bunker, where military strategy meetings took place, as well as the key *Nachrichten* Bunker, housing the wireless and telegraph links to the outside world. Here, unbeknown to the Nazi leadership, the Chief, General Erich Fellgiebel, was in place ready to give the order to cut all wires except those connected to the Bendler Strasse as soon as Hitler and his cronies had been killed. There was only one problem: the SS had their own line, over which he had no control.

There is a photograph of the moment the Führer walks across from the Führer Bunker to greet the new arrivals. General Fromm is bowing, stretching out his hand in greeting. Stauffenberg, to Fromm's left, is standing smartly to attention, looking straight at Hitler. Field Marshal Wilhelm Keitel, Chief of Staff, hovers. Others, all in uniform, go about their business in the background with the dark East Prussian forest rising beyond.

What can Stauffenberg have been feeling? His briefcase was in the Guest Bunker. The military strategy meeting in the *Lager* Bunker would start at 13.00. News from both Fronts, East and West, was worse and worse, but everyone around the Führer acted as though victory was still within grasp. The Führer himself appeared to have entered Never-Never-Land. If anyone dared to express any doubts, he flew into one of his rages. Dr Morell, his private physician, was in constant attendance because Hitler was effectively a drug addict by then.

Then Stauffenberg discovered that neither Himmler nor Göring would be present at the meeting. What to do? As soon as he had a minute to himself, he made his way to the *Nachrichten* Bunker. General Fellgiebel put him through by telephone line to Merz von Quirnheim, waiting with the other conspirators at Bendler Strasse. They were downcast, nonplussed. 'Do it anyway,' said von Quirnheim. But Stauffenberg decided, once again, to wait. They flew back to Berlin, taking the briefcase with them. Another meeting was planned for 20 July. Maybe this time he'd be lucky.

That evening, 15 July, Horst Werner Dittmann was making his way home to Marien Strasse when an open-topped military jeep came hurtling towards him down the road. Dittmann ran *Jaeckels*, Fritzi's favourite bookshop in Berlin, and over the years they had become happy like-minded acquaintances. 'It braked suddenly,' Dittmann recalled later, 'and Count von der Schulenburg jumped out and raced up to me. He must have recognised me and told the driver to stop. He quickly asked me if I had a cellar where he could leave a packet for a few days. It obviously contained explosives, though he avoided using the actual word, but made it pretty clear nevertheless. I said yes but pointed out that I had been watched by the Gestapo for the past few weeks. "That's no good then!" he shouted, already running back to the jeep. And off it sped . . .'

That same evening Fritzi went to see Ursula von Kardorff, the journalist and family friend who often stayed at Trebbow. 'On 15 July, Fritzi came to see me and brought me a copy of *Grimms' Fairy Tales*. He was different – outwardly calm, but you could feel the inner tension. His gaze, usually so clear and firm, darted about everywhere.' He'd come to ask her to visit Annedore Leber and tell her they'd found out where the Gestapo were holding her husband: in their Prinz Albrecht Strasse HQ. Annedore had been interrogated for several hours after Leber's arrest and their home had been searched. They found nothing.

The children, Katharina and Matthias, were staying with relations in the country. When the Gestapo finally let her out, she'd gone into hiding in a hospital run by nuns. That's where Ursula would find her.

News of the delayed attempt on Hitler's life soon reached Fabian von Schlabrendorff and Henning von Tresckow at Army Group Centre. They were based at Ostrow in Poland, north-east of Warsaw, the *Wehrmacht* in flat-out retreat now, beaten back again and again by the swiftly advancing Russians. Fabian was still going back and forth to Berlin, liaising with the civilian conspirators, so he was able to see his wife and children from time to time. Tresckow hadn't seen his family since his last home leave in April. His wife Erika recalled that when she saw him off at Berlin *Haupt Bahnhof* on his way back to the Front, he had an expression of 'goodbye' as he waved to her out of the carriage window.

Of late, Fritzi was becoming uncharacteristically reckless, no doubt because of the several missed assassination attempts. On 12 July he'd gone to see Dr Medicus at the Department for Military Personnel and informed him he couldn't leave for France for another ten days. It was a dangerous move because Heinrich Himmler had personally ordered his immediate transfer to Lyons. Evidently the *Reichsführer* still had his suspicions about the Count. But following the news that Stauffenberg had failed to detonate the bomb on the first assassination attempt at the Berghof, Fritzi decided that he had to delay his departure and run the risk of Himmler finding out about it. He made a fleeting visit to Trebbow. He no longer had a fixed address in Berlin.

On 16 July, there was a meeting in the Stauffenberg apartment in Tristan Strasse in Berlin. Present were the two Stauffenberg brothers, Claus and Berthold, Fritzi Schulenburg, Caesar von Hofacker and Adam von Trott. Between them they agreed that their next assassination attempt had to succeed, even if it were only Hitler who was killed. Time was running out fast, and the fact that recently Hitler, Himmler and Göring were rarely in the same place at any one time suggested they knew an assassination attempt was imminent. They agreed that future peace negotiations should proceed with the Russians as well as the Western Allies. For the Russians they would rely on Count von der Schulenburg, Fritzi's relation who'd been the German Ambassador to Moscow, and General Koestring who'd been his military attaché there before the war. For the Western Allies they'd have Adam von Trott, with his many British friends, and still working at the German Foreign

Office in Wilhelm Strasse. Field Marshal Witzleben wasn't mentioned, presumably because he was against dealing with the Russians. There was no avoiding an unconditional surrender, they agreed, but the swift ending of the war was all that mattered now: the saving of millions of lives, on all sides, the saving of German cities from further bombings, above all, the saving of the German name and Honour. The German Volk would not thank them at first, but in the future, they would come to understand.

The next morning Fritzi went to see Ursula von Kardorff again. 'He was less tense this time,' she wrote, 'and ate a hearty breakfast.' Ursula had been to see Annedore, and Fritzi was relieved to hear that she hadn't given any names away. He asked Ursula to take her a bunch of roses. 'You have to go and see her again and tell her I'm going to France in three days' time.' He was tense. 'And tell her we're doing our duty! Nothing more. Be careful. You don't know the danger you might be putting yourself into, and I don't want to be responsible for that.'

The next day he came for the third and last time. 'I've never seen him so nervous. But still full of vitality – happy even. He told me two men had been asking after him, where he was staying. He thought they might have been quite harmless but doubted it.' His eyes had that restless look again which worried her. 'He had something wild about him ... He meant to go to Mecklenburg that night to see his wife.'

Charlotte hadn't heard from Fritzi since his last clandestine visit. There had only been a visit from one of his friends, told by Fritzi to go to Trebbow and collect Reichwein's books which were on his writing desk, and to hide them somewhere safe. 'On 18 July late in the evening the Schwerin station master rang up to say my husband was on the road, on foot, from Schwerin to Trebbow, and I should go and meet him with the car,' Charlotte wrote in her memoirs. 'He could only stay one night. I was to wake the children up, so we could celebrate my birthday, which was on 20 July. That night he told me he was "going over the top" and that it had a fifty–fifty chance of success. But he was so assured about it, I never thought it might fail. Early the next morning, at 7 o'clock on 19 July, I drove my husband back to the local station at Lübstorf.' It was the last time Charlotte saw him.

The reason for Fritzi's precipitate visit to his family at Trebbow was that Fromm and Stauffenberg had been ordered to attend another military strategy meeting with Hitler the following day, 20 July. And this time, as Stauffenberg told General Ludwig Beck, he was going to plant the bomb 'come what may'. He sent Annedore Leber a message: 'We know what our duty is.'

Olbricht again ordered Operation Valkyrie on standby. The Panzer tank corps of the Reserve Army stood at the ready, as did the Berlin Police under Arthur Nebe. Stauffenberg held last-minute meetings with his fellow officers at Bendler Strasse, taking control of everything. The place was a hive of activity and tension. Everyone knew this was the moment. Stauffenberg sent his driver to collect his briefcase from the barracks in Potsdam and bring it to Tristan Strasse. It contained two packets of dynamite, a 30-minute fuse and some pliers. The fuse was English. Stauffenberg's Adjutant Werner von Haeften carried a second identical briefcase, the one containing a briefing lecture about the situation at the Eastern Front. A plane was organised to bring them back to Berlin after the bomb exploded. Stauffenberg tried to telephone his wife Nina and the children who were staying with his mother in Lautlingen, but he couldn't get a connection. He spent the night at his brother Berthold's apartment in Tristan Strasse. The next morning Berthold drove him to the military airport, bound for the Wolf's Lair.

They arrived at the Inner Circle Security Zone at 10.30 hours, just in time for breakfast. Fromm had excused himself, saying he had to go to his daughter's home in West Prussia. At 11.30, Wilhelm Keitel informed Stauffenberg the meeting had been brought forward by 30 minutes. Werner von Haeften and Stauffenberg held their nerve and raced to activate the bomb. One of the staff officers came to tell them to hurry up – the meeting was due to start. Hastily they made their way across the 400 metres to the briefing room, each holding a briefcase. At the entrance to the *Lager* Bunker Keitel's adjutant took Staffenberg's briefcase and carried it into the room. Stauffenberg told him to put it on the floor nearby so he could more easily reach his notes. The meeting had already been underway since 12.30, with Hitler and 23 officers standing round a heavy oak table spread with maps. The windows were open because it was a hot day. Neither Himmler nor Göring were present. Stauffenberg took his place at the long side of the table, one down from Hitler, with a General standing in between. The Führer raised his hand in silent greeting and carried on talking. The briefcase was too far from the Führer so Stauffenberg surreptitiously moved it, placing it against one of the table legs. No one noticed. Then he made an excuse to leave the room, murmuring an apology and leaving his cap on the table to indicate he was coming back. At 12.42 Hitler asked what had become of Stauffenberg and sent a General out to find him. Stauffenberg was with von Haeften and General Fellgiebel 200 metres away. That's when the bomb exploded.

Stauffenberg and von Haeften ran to the waiting car and drove off fast. Behind them, as they left, they could see the wounded staggering from the exploded Bunker. There was debris everywhere, papers and maps flying through the air, men screaming and shouting. No one could have survived, they thought. They reached the outer Security Ring before the alarm went off and the sentries let them through. It was 12.50. Once they landed at the Berlin airfield, at 15.45, Werner von Haeften telephoned Bendler Strasse to confirm the assassination had been a success and that Hitler was dead.

But General Fellgiebel had meanwhile telephoned General Fritz Thiele, the Chief of Wireless Operations at Bendler Strasse, to say that the Führer wasn't dead, merely wounded. Thiele didn't know whether it was true or not – in a world where everything was lies he thought Fellgiebel might have been arrested and be speaking at gunpoint. Highly distressed and confused, he decided to go for a walk round the streets of Berlin to decide what to do and whom to tell. At 15.15, he returned and went to tell Olbricht that the bomb had exploded killing and wounding many, perhaps also the Führer. But perhaps not. Olbricht, who'd put Operation Valkyrie on the next level of alert and had no intention of reversing the order, went looking for Fromm, who wasn't in fact with his daughter in West Prussia but in a meeting in his office. He barged in unannounced. Hitler was dead, he said. But Fromm had heard different rumours. He asked to be put through to General Keitel at the Wolf's Lair. No, the Führer wasn't dead, Keitel told him, merely wounded. Fromm immediately saw the dangers: as Commander in Chief of the Reserve Army, now on standby, he'd be the one blamed for the plot. The duty wireless operator was ordered to recall the announcement 'Der Führer Adolf Hitler ist tod!'– the Führer Adolf Hitler is dead. Then he put Olbricht under arrest and told him to reverse all Operation Valkyrie orders. Olbricht refused.

In contrast to the confusion at Bendler Strasse, the situation at the Wolf's Lair was clear. Fellgiebel had managed to cut all the

telephone wires – except the SS line. Within an hour *Reichsführer* SS
Himmler had been informed and soon arrived at the scene, taking
control of everything, including the Reserve Army. Where was
Stauffenberg, he wanted to know? His cap had been found, but not
the man.

Stauffenberg and von Haeften arrived back at Bendler Strasse at
16.40. The place was in chaos. Stauffenberg immediately took control of everything. First, he assured Olbricht and Fromm that Hitler
was certainly dead. Himmler lied about everything, so why believe
anything he said? No one could have survived that blast. But Fromm
didn't believe him. Olbricht told Fromm if he didn't activate Operation
Valkyrie immediately, the Reich would go under, and he with it. At
16.45, Field Marshal von Witzleben sent a telegraph message from
the Reich War Ministry to all military districts: 'The Führer Adolf
Hitler is dead . . . In order to maintain law and order in this situation
of acute danger the Reich Government has declared a state of martial
law and has transferred the executive power to me together with the
supreme command of the Wehrmacht.'

General Wilhelm Beck, as future Chancellor, had arrived at Bendler
Strasse by then, dressed in civilian clothes, and was waiting to make
the wireless announcement to the Volk that Hitler was dead. But in the
confusion of truth and lies, no one really knew what to do. At 17.42
Bendler Strasse listened with the rest of the Volk to an announcement
on the wireless about the assassination attempt: '*Der Führer lebt*' –
The Führer is alive.

The telephone kept ringing at Bendler Strasse, Stauffenberg answering the same query again and again: is it true or is it one of their
lies again? It's a lie, he repeated again and again. But it might have
been true for all Stauffenberg knew. He insisted Operation Valkyrie
go ahead – either way.

Joseph Goebbels meanwhile managed to contact Major Otto Ernst
Remmer at the Wolf's Lair, who confirmed that there had been a failed
military putsch and that the Führer was most definitely alive. Four
men had been killed outright, nine were seriously wounded. Hitler
came to the telephone. 'Do you recognise my voice?' he said.

Hitler had been saved by the solid oak table leg. He wasn't killed
but he was seriously wounded, though this was never admitted. He'd
staggered from the bunker with his hair on fire, trousers torn off at
the waist and tunic torn. His legs were badly burnt, both eardrums

were damaged and his right arm was partially paralysed. For the rest of his now short life he suffered from a bad tremor. People who met him were shocked to see a frail old man, very far from their image of the Great Führer.

By 21.00, troops were surrounding Bendler Strasse. 'It's over,' said von Quirnheim, looking out of a window and down into the courtyard. Claus von Stauffenberg went into his office and tried to ring their co-conspirators in Paris. All the telephone lines had been cut. Stauffenberg, Olbricht, Beck and Quirnheim retreated into Fromm's room. Fromm, in a last-ditch attempt to distance himself from the plotters, came in and ordered them to be arrested. Beck asked to be allowed to shoot himself. Fromm agreed – as one Prussian General to another – and Beck retreated into another office with his pistol. In the event, he only managed to wound himself and later had to be put out of his misery by an officer who shot him in the head. So ended General Wilhelm Beck's fight against the Nazi terror regime, begun with his resignation in 1938. 'Final decisions about the continuity of our Reich are at stake here,' he'd written to Brauchitsch in his secret memo on 16 July 1938. 'Exceptional times require exceptional actions. Other upright men in responsible positions of state will join the military men on their course.'

At 22.00 came a German wireless broadcast: 'For the second time in this war started by Jewry, a foul and murderous attempt has been made on our Führer's life . . . Providence protected the man who holds in his hands the destiny of the German people. The Führer remains unhurt . . . The feeling of gratitude for his salvation is the supreme, the overwhelming emotion of all Germans. It finds its expression in the demonstrations of loyalty and love of the Führer which have already poured in from all over Germany . . .'

At fifteen minutes past midnight the plotters were taken down to the courtyard where a firing squad was already lined up. Olbricht had asked to write a last letter to his wife. Stauffenberg had taken the responsibility for everything upon himself, saying the others were only following his orders. Headlights from military vehicles were used to light up the dark courtyard for the shooting: first Olbricht, then Stauffenberg, then Werner von Haeften, then Quirnheim.

At 1am came Hitler's broadcast to the Reich: 'German racial comrades! I do not know how many times an assassination attempt against me has been planned and carried out. If I speak to you today, I do so for two reasons: first, so that you may hear my voice and know that I myself am uninjured and well. Secondly, so that you may also learn the details about a crime that has not its likes in German history. A very small clique of ambitious, wicked and stupid criminal army officers forged a plot to eliminate me and virtually the entire staff of the German leadership of the armed forces. The bomb which was planted by Colonel Count von Stauffenberg burst two metres to my right. It very seriously injured a number of associates dear to me; one of them has died. I myself am completely uninjured except for some very small scrapes, bruises or burns. I regard it as a confirmation of my assignment from Providence to continue to pursue my life's goal as I have done hitherto . . . The group represented by these usurpers is ridiculously small. It has nothing to do with the German armed forces, and above all with the German *Wehrmacht*. It is a very small coterie of criminal elements which is now being mercilessly excised . . . We will settle accounts the way we National Socialists are accustomed to settle them.'

Fabian von Schlabrendorff and Henning von Tresckow heard the news of Stauffenberg's failed assassination attempt at Army Group Centre's HQ, now based at Bialystock just over the border with East Prussia, only a few kilometres from where they'd started with Operation Barbarossa three years previously. They were attending another of those tedious lectures on Party ideology when an officer came in and announced that there had been a failed attempt to assassinate the Führer. Shocked, Tresckow asked the officer to give him the exact wording of the message. He couldn't believe it because at four that same afternoon von Quirnheim had telephoned to say the assassination had been a success and that Schlabrendorff was to make his way immediately back to Berlin.

Then came the wireless announcement at 17.42 confirming that the Führer was alive. They still couldn't believe it – it was probably Nazi lies again. They decided to sit it out and carry on as normal. They had their evening meal in the officers' mess – with all the talk about the failed assassination attempt – and then they went to bed. But at 1am came Hitler's own voice on the wireless transmitter: 'A very small clique of ambitious, criminal, stupid officers . . .' They sat in silence, trying to take it in – and what it meant for them. Henning was pale. 'I will shoot myself,' he said. He couldn't see an alternative. If he was arrested and tortured he might break and divulge some names. He was thinking of his family, of Wartenburg, of his friends, as well as the wider circle of plotters. He knew the brutality of the Nazis too well. If he killed himself, making it look like an accident, at the Front, the revenge might be limited to the 'small clique'.

The next morning came the news that Stauffenberg, Olbricht, Haeften and Quirnheim had been executed by firing squad. 'Now the whole world will vilify us,' Tresckow told Fabian and the others. 'But I am firmly convinced we did the right thing. I consider Hitler to be the arch enemy not only of Germany, but the whole world. When I stand before my God in a few hours and give an account of my deeds, I think I can say with a clear conscience that I did it in the fight against Hitler . . . I hope God will not allow Germany to be destroyed. None of us can complain about our death. Whoever joined our group had to put on the Robe of Nessus. A person's moral integrity only begins at the point when he is prepared to die for his convictions.' He was calm and collected. Before he left he answered all his usual telephone calls from 8.15 to 9.40, and gave his last orders and advice. Then he called for his driver to take him up to the Front. There he blew himself up with a hand grenade – to make it look like an accident, not suicide.

On 28 July, Ilse von Hassell was woken at 3am by a violent ringing of the doorbell at Ebenhausen. It was the Gestapo. 'Where is your husband?' She knew it had never been her husband Ulrich's intention to hide once the news of the failed assassination became official. 'He's in Berlin,' she said in her usual direct way. She and their daughter Almuth were arrested and taken to the bombed-out Gestapo building in Munich. They were let out later, but the children of the Hassells' younger daughter Fey were taken away as part of the Nazis' 'Sippenhaft' revenge programme, removing the children from their parents and taking them to SS Lebensborn children's homes. It was the same for many of the plotter families.

The morning after Ilse and Almuth's arrest the Gestapo stormed into Ulrich 's office in Berlin. They found him sitting at his desk, waiting for them. First he was sent to Ravensbrück concentration camp near Mecklenburg where he managed to smuggle out a letter to his family reassuring them that he was fine: the weather was so good he was able to sit on the steps of his hut and eat his meal in the open air, he wrote. On 18 August he was brought back to Berlin in chains, first to Moabit prison, badly bomb damaged, then to the Gestapo HQ in Prinz Albrecht Strasse. He was sentenced to death by the *Volksgericht* on 8 September 1944 and sent to Ploetzensee prison to await his execution later that same day.

'My beloved Ilschen,' he wrote from Ploetzensee. 'Thirty years ago today I received the French bullet which I carry about with me still. On this day also the *Volksgericht* pronounced its sentence and, if it is carried out, as I imagine it will be, thus comes to an end the supreme happiness which I have known thanks to you. It was certainly too precious to last! At this moment I am filled with the deepest gratitude towards God and towards you. You are at my side and you give me peace and strength. This thought mitigates the fiery agony of having to leave you and the children. May God grant that your soul and mine may one day be reunited. You are alive, however, and that is one great consolation I have amidst all my anxieties for you all, including the material ones; and, as regards the future of our children, knowing that you are strong and courageous – a rock, but a dear, sweet rock for them. Remain as you are, good and kind, and do not grow embittered! God bless you and Germany! I hope that you will receive my memoirs as my legacy, as a memorial to our happiness and in token of my gratitude. My affectionate greetings to Grandmama, Aunt Mani, Wolf and to all my friends.

'In deepest love and gratitude, I embrace you, your Ulrich.'

Fritz-Dietlof von der Schulenburg had gone to Bendler Strasse on 20 July in order to help organise matters once Hitler had been assassinated. 'I met Fritzi Schulenburg in the corridor,' wrote Hans Karl Fritzsche, another of those unknown conspirators, in his memoirs after the war. 'He confirmed that the game was up, because it turned out Hitler really was still alive. But he added: "We have to carry on regardless – we have to drink this poisoned chalice down to the dregs. We have to give up our lives for it. Later people will understand." He pulled me into an empty office. We sat side by side on an army bed. He took some papers from a briefcase and tore them up into small pieces and threw them in the waste paper basket. He told me it was his wife's birthday that day. Then he shared a *Landwurst* sausage with me which he'd received from his wife in Mecklenburg that morning. Then he left to go and see Stauffenberg.'

Fritzi was arrested in the building along with dozens of others and taken to Prinz Albrecht Strasse. There he was interrogated on several occasions by SS *Obergruppenführer* Ernst Kaltenbrunner who had been promoted to Chief of the *Reichssicherheitsamt*, the Reich Security Office, once Reinhard Heydrich had been assassinated in 1943. On 20 July Heinrich Himmler had immediately summoned Kaltenbrunner to the Wolf's Lair and ordered him to prepare daily reports for Hitler and Martin Bormann on his interrogations. The first arrived on Bormann's desk on 21 July 1944. It was written from Prinz Albrecht Strasse and began, like all the following reports till the last on 15 December 1944: 'Most esteemed Party Comrade BORMANN! *Heil Hitler!* Your devoted KALTENBRUNNER, SS Obergruppenführer and Chief of Police.'

Much of the daily grind of interrogation was done by *Oberstrumbannführer* von Kielpinsky. By 24 July they were able to list the leaders of the plot: Beck, Olbricht, Stauffenberg and his brother, Berthold, Quirnheim, Schulenburg, Haeften, Witzleben and Major General Hoepner. To say the reports were exhaustive hardly covers it: in the end they ran to hundreds of closely typed pages, happily discovered later by the Americans and held in their National Archives in Washington, DC.

For those being interrogated, each had to make their own decision as to whether to speak or not. Fritzi decided to speak. Without naming names other than those already known to Kaltenbrunner, he was minded to have his motives and reasons on record. Who knew, perhaps his words would survive for posterity. He was interrogated over a period of three weeks, during which time he gave a typically exact and coherent account of the events leading up to 20 July, as well as the motives and the plans for the new post-Nazi government. He made it clear that there were four different circles of knowledge about the plot and future plans, with only the very small inner circle knowing all the details, and the outer circle knowing none at all.

'The interrogations of the Stauffenberg group (above all Schulenburg) leave open the possibility that a large number of those involved and connected to the plans had indeed been told nothing,' noted Kaltenbrunner on 18 August 1944.

Fritzi gave nine separate reasons why he decided to take action against the Nazi regime, confirming that 1938 and the Fritsch affair had been the starting point for many, but that as far as he was concerned the Nazi Party had already abandoned their early simplicity and straightforwardness long before. 'I was particularly struck by the way a whole upper echelon soon rejected all the basic beliefs which they'd preached in the early days.' Kaltenbrunner amplified on this by quoting from the wireless broadcast which the conspirators had prepared for use once Hitler and his cronies had been assassinated. 'While our soldiers fought and bled and fell, men like Göring and Goebbels, Ley and others led a life of luxury, filling their cellars and estates with stolen goods, while demanding that the Volk suffer . . .' The Party had become dominated by a Will to Power, said Schulenburg, a fight of Party against State, abandoning the rule of law in favour of a Police State, dangerously centralised, browbeating the Volk with force and propaganda, and attacking Christianity. As far as the Nazis' foreign policy was concerned, it turned the whole world against Germany. As far as the occupied territories were concerned, they did everything to alienate the local population.

Kaltenbrunner concluded that Count von der Schulenburg had been central to both the plot and the plans for a new government. On 10 August 1944, he was put on trial by the *Volksgericht*, presided over by the abusive, screaming judge Roland Freisler. There is no transcript of Schulenburg's trial, only a few snatches recorded for the

Deutsches Rundfunk, German wireless, and a verbal account given by an unnamed member of the SS who was among the invited Party members. He later spoke to Werner Friedler, the editor of *Deutsche Allgemeine Zeitung*, who in turn wrote a coded letter to Charlotte, delivered by the Wiemanns who were still living as house guests at Trebbow after their apartment in Berlin was bombed out. Friedler code named Fritzi 'van Gogh' and gave 'a felicitous picture of the single-mindedness and sureness with which he handled himself to his end. And of his courage and lightly laughing superiority with which he defended himself. In contrast to many others who became unsure and exhausted.' He stood by what he'd done without reservation, in order to save Germany from unspeakable misery, he stated, standing unbowed before Freisler. He expected to be hanged for it, but this would cause him no regret. 'Did you give no thought to your wife and children, Count Schulenburg!' Freisler asked him in phoney concern. '*Schurke Schulenburg!*' responded Schulenburg, sharply sarcastic: 'You villain Schulenburg!'

There are two photographs of Fritzi standing before the court in an ill-fitting jacket – someone else's, a humiliation deliberately used by Nazis – and no tie, but hair neatly combed and hands coolly folded, looking straight ahead. In the first we see the Nazi Party members who'd been invited to the spectacle seated behind him, with the unknown SS officer no doubt among them. In the second, taken from the opposite angle, we see the other accused seated in front along with some lawyers, and a unit of SS *Totenkopf* behind. His last words, relayed to  Charlotte by Werner Friedler: 'We took this task upon ourselves, to save Germany from unmentionable suffering. I know I shall be hanged for it, but I don't regret my actions.' He was sentenced to death and hanged in Plötzensee prison that same day. He was 42.

Julius Leber had been in captivity since June 1944, latterly in

Brandenburg prison where he was severely tortured. On 26 July he was finally able to get a letter out to Annedore. 'My dear Paulus!' he began in his usual way. 'Today, after three most oppressive weeks, I can finally send you a sign of life. For me this is an endlessly joyful feeling, because thoughts of you, my dearest young one, have been the whole world to me. Again and again the knowledge of your unshakeable love and fellowship brought everything back into perspective. So I can write this letter to you today filled with love and trust. I start with a small request: I'm writing without my spectacles. They were left behind in the office.'

She should try and keep the coal business going at all costs to have a future income for herself and the children. 'Send me a small photo of yourself! I have so much I want to say to you, my dear wife, so much I want to ask. I have one consolation: I know you'll be strong and courageous whenever there's danger . . . Send our children wishes from their loving father, and keep loving me! Your old Julius.'

Following the 20 July assassination attempt, Leber had been transferred to a Gestapo interrogation unit at Drogen. Here he had to make the same decision as all the others who'd been arrested: whether to speak or not to speak. Like Fritz-Dietlof von der Schulenburg, Julius Leber decided to speak, and very likely for the same reasons: he wanted his ideas and his motives recorded for posterity. For the next ten days he was interrogated off and on by either Kaltenbrunner or Kielpinsky. Since he wasn't involved in the immediate events leading up to the assassination attempt, already being in prison by then, he was of less interest than Schulenburg, but of interest nevertheless as one of the main architects of the future government. From other interrogations as well as Leber's, it became clear that there were two factions among the plotters – Goerdeler and the Conservative faction on the one hand, the Socialist faction with Leber and Reichwein and their Trade Union collegue Leuschner, including Schulenburg and Stauffenberg, on the other. The former were for 'Westpolitik', dealing solely with the Western powers, the latter were determined to deal with the Soviets as well.

Throughout, Leber stood by the workers and their rights. He insisted on a 'radical Socialist policy'. Kaltenbrunner discovered it was Leber who'd pointed out to the others that there was no avoiding the Allies' occupation of the whole of Germany after an unconditional surrender, with no conquered territory remaining. He also discovered that Leber was listed as future Minister of the Interior, a position originally considered for Count Schulenburg till Schulenburg stated he'd be happy to serve under Leber instead.

The main, indeed only advantage of Drogen was that for the duration of the interrogations Leber was able to lead a more or less decent life. 'My dear Paulus!' he wrote to Annedore on 31 July, regaining some of his old bounce. 'As you see, I'm still writing without my spectacles! Perhaps they went to Brandenburg. Unfortunately I only have one pair. One really ought to be more careful in life and have two of everything. I'm writing in haste!'

There followed a list of things he hoped she'd be able to send him: a razor, a comb, a small mirror, some socks, a nightshirt, writing paper, stamps, pencil, tobacco (wonderful!), a pack of cards for Patience, the spectacles. And a bit of cake and sugar, he added as a hopeful afterthought. He'd been waiting all day for a letter from her, it being the first possible day for one to arrive.

'I long as never before for a sign of life from you! To know how things are for you, my dear Paulus, and how our little ones are doing. Above all though, I am filled with joy about the possibility of seeing you. Your old Julius.'

It wasn't to be. No post from Annedore. Nor news. Nor spectacles. Briefly there was the hope of a visit, but it turned out to be a false hope – a little extra torture. Annedore was herself arrested and kept in custody for two months. On 5 August, Julius Leber was transferred to Ravensbrück concentration camp, along with his old Social Democrat colleagues Gustav Dahrendorff, Theodor Haubach and Hermann Maas. There news finally got through to him about Annedore's arrest, in the porous way news always eventually filtered through the walls and barbed wire of the concentration camps.

'Any contact is strictly forbidden,' wrote Gustav Dahrendorff about life in Ravensbrück. 'Two SS guards watch over us to keep the prisoners far apart so we can't communicate with one another . . . We see a bit of sky. We breathe in the air. Each one tries to catch the eye of a friend. We suspect our fate – a bet with death, as Haubach once called out to me. Julius Leber gives me a strong look as we pass one another, his body taut and his face friendly and defiant at the same time, saying: "Don't let yourself go! See to yourself!" He had the look of a man who'd gone into himself, in sheer determination, still strong, still unbroken.' Others saw Leber's exceptional self-discipline too, wrote Dahrendorff. In this place of nameless pain, he seemed 'a man of inner greatness.'

Isa Vermehren, a female colleague from Lübeck, crossed paths with Leber three times in Ravensbrück and they were able to exchange a few words. He was worried for his wife, he whispered. But 'for such a fine and great idea, the loss of one's own life was a fair price to pay'. He and Annedore had fought for a 'great cause' and he asked especially that Isa tell the Lübeck workers he'd done 'everything in his power to fight the Nazis, and that it wasn't in his hands that things had turned out as they had'. He sent them his best wishes and told them to 'fight on and remain true to the cause'. When Isa first saw him he was in civil clothing but the next time he was in the usual concentration camp stripes. His face was blue with bruises. But his expression remained defiant, serious, concerned. 'Even the concentration camp guards seemed impressed by his dignity and unbending self-confidence.'

On 28 September 1944, Leber was transferred from Ravensbrück to Moabit prison in Berlin – the same prison in which Ernst Thälmann spent his first years of solitary. On 14 October, he was transferred to the Gestapo HQ in Prinz Albrecht Strasse together with Gustav Dahrendorff, Adolf Reichwein, Hermann Maas and Dr Loeser, Mayor of Leipzig, to await their trial. On 20 October at 9.00 the *Volksgericht* trial began, with screaming Roland Freisler presiding once again. Dr Loeser's case was dismissed. The other four, Social Democrats all, were charged with both treason and high treason.

'We sat in two rows with ten policemen: Julius Leber and Adolf Reichwein in the first row, Hermann Maas and I in the second,' wrote Dahrendorff. 'The President, Freisler, dealt with the so-called evidence categorically as though it were fact, in an aggressive and provocative manner, and loudly. The accused were hardly given a chance to defend themselves. Each time any of us tried we were shouted down by Freisler. At no point was it a genuine court proceeding. The whole thing, taking place in the main *Saal* of the *Volksgericht*, had the look of a show trial. The greatest part of the seating was taken up with invited guests, including SS officers, Gestapo personnel, and war wounded. Also some press, who outwardly at least had to give the appearance of obedience.'

But one man among the press – Paul Sethe – was a secret sympathiser, another mask-wearer, who published his account of Leber's trial after the war: 'The accusations and abuse rained down on the accused like a volcano,' he wrote. 'It lasted about two hours, and you could feel your heart beating all the time, sinking lower and lower as the sentence came closer, wrapping Julius Leber in the shadow of death. But Leber's voice remained calm and measured throughout – no trembling, no uncertainty, no words spoken too fast or too slow, not one sign that Julius Leber was frightened of the man seated on the bench. The only sign of strain: again and again he rose up on his toes, up and down, up and down. "That's incorrect," he'd point out quietly and politely. Or: "You're mistaken in that once again, Herr President."' Freisler was visibly disturbed by it. After recess, when Freisler re-entered the Court to pronounce sentence, 'Leber sat there quietly, in full control – not one blink on that large and impassive face, casting his eyes over and beyond the men in their red robes with contempt and complete indifference.' There is a photograph of him standing there awaiting his fate, gaunt, a thin shadow of his former ebullient rotund self – but upright, looking straight ahead.

Dahrendorff was sentenced to a lengthy period in a concentration camp, from which he was freed eventually by the advancing Russians. The remaining three were all sentenced to death. Reichwein and Maas were hanged that same day in Plötzensee prison. But Leber's death sentence was held over till 5 January 1945 – no doubt for further interrogation and torture.

In prison Julius Leber was allowed two cigarettes a day and he was allowed to write Annedore an occasional letter and he could receive some too. 'The hardest thing to bear is the loneliness,' he wrote to Annedore. 'Day after day goes by, and my mood goes up and down. Today is such a gloomy, desolate, grey day, rain non-stop, so my mood is likewise. But then a shaft of sunlight shines through my little window, and my spirits rise again . . .' In another letter: 'The last months have struck deep into my soul. My gratitude to you is as great as is my trust in the strength of your will and your heart. My love for you knows no bounds. For weeks now, I have been living alone within myself. I kiss you, and am always with you.' And again: 'You are the home for my soul. One can't say anything greater than that to another human being. And that is what you are to me!'

His last letter was written on 1 January 1945. 'My dear wife!' he began, more formally than usual, as though he knew this was good-bye. 'All my thoughts and good wishes have been with you and the children, even more than usual during these last feast days. What good things can I wish for you and the children for this new year? What will it bring you? My thoughts constantly range far into and beyond the year 1945, trying, hesitatingly, to look into your future. What will Life hold for you and the children?' He'd been expecting to love and protect them for their whole lives. 'Oh Paulus! How often have I sought you out in my thoughts, palpitating with longing for you all, again and again, but first and last, for you, my dearest and truest and proudest wife.'

He had her letter of 28 December before him, written immediately after a visit she had been allowed. It gave him strength and comforted him in his loneliness. 'And when those dark hours overcome me, I think back to your visit – how you sat and talked, and how bravely and proudly you looked at your future – and then everything becomes easier for me again.' He was worried for her health. He thought that right now, in the middle of the fight, the heart could keep going. But what of the reaction afterwards? And when he thought of the children, especially Matthias, their sensitive one, his soul shuddered to its depths. 'As I write this, out of my deepest heart, a different feeling streams from my soul: a feeling of unending pride in you, your strength and your whole self! In this pride and beautiful feeling, accept a loving Goodnight kiss from, your old Julius.'

Leber was finally hanged at Plötzensee prison on 5 February, just as the Western Allies crossed the Rhine, the Russians crossed the border into Germany, and Winston Churchill, Franklin D. Roosevelt and Joseph Stalin began the Yalta Conference in the Crimea to decide the fate of post-war Germany.

Fabian von Schlabrendorff had managed to escape the Gestapo for a few days after 20 July but they soon caught up with him, along with nearly all the rest of the plotters, including Hans Oster at the *Abwehr* section of the Reich Ministry of War.

'After 20 July it wasn't long before General Oster was arrested in Dresden and brought to the Gestapo prison in Prinz Albrecht Strasse. That's where I saw him again,' wrote Fabian later. 'Our cells were near each other. For months we saw each other every morning, going early to the washrooms. Speaking was forbidden, and there were always prison guards. But that didn't stop Oster saying to me on 1 January 1945, to the surprise of the Gestapo, very loudly: "I wish you a good and happy New Year." There was no reaction at all from the guards, so amazed were they. Oster's manner in the washroom revealed a man absolutely free, unlike any other men I have known. He moved around completely naked, as though it was the most natural thing. Even the guards had to respect it. He took absolutely no notice of them. They were like air to him. Oster loved the showers and made a big performance out of it, like a feast, to the annoyance of the Gestapo and the joy of his fellow prisoners. Once I witnessed him being taken, handcuffed, to the cellars. His face showed complete indifference. It reminded me of a saying from school: "Free is man, even if he be in chains." That was the first time I realised what that saying really meant. He looked more like an old-style cavalier. His expression showed nothing but disdain for his interrogators.' Oster hated Hitler with all his might. He told his interrogators he'd put himself at General Beck's disposal immediately after the Fritsch affair in 1938.

One day Oster was standing by the door of his cell and he was able to whisper as Fabian passed: 'They got Nebe.' Nebe was the

mask-wearer *par excellence* – an early member of the SS, later Chief
of the *Reichskriminalhauptamtes*, Criminal Investigations Bureau in
Berlin. In those days, recalled Fabian, 'he had lunch with Kaltenbrunner
every day and found out everything the Gestapo was up to. Which he
duly passed on to Oster. Occasionally he told me too, when I was on
one of my trips to Berlin, sent by Henning von Tesckow to inform
Nebe about the worsening conditions on the Eastern Front. Sometimes
we corresponded too, always in code.'

Oster wasn't the only familiar face Fabian spotted in the Gestapo
prison. One day he saw Dietrich von Bonhoeffer being led from his cell.
Bonhoeffer had been a thorn in Hitler's flesh from early on because he
and the pastors of the *Bekennende Kirche*, church, including Martin
Niemöller the famous pastor of Dahlem, had spoken out against Hitler
and the Nazi terror regime quite openly, telling them, 'This is where
your power ends, and ours starts.' On another occasion, when several
prisoners were being pushed down into the cellars during an Allied
bomb attack on Berlin, he spotted Kleist von Schmenzin, who gave
absolutely no sign of recognising him. During his Gestapo interrogations Fabian was surprised he'd never been asked about his old friend
Schmenzin. But now he knew the reason why: Schmenzin had never
mentioned Fabian's name. The Gestapo, decided Fabian, were brutal,
but not that clever.

In all some 5,000 people were arrested in connection with the 20
July plot, including distant family members who knew nothing of
it. Thousands more Communist and Social Democrat officials were
rounded up, and many killed. Including Ernst Thälmann, who, after
eleven and a half years in solitary confinement, was finally executed
on 18 August at Buchenwald along with 24 others.

In early 1945, Fabian was transferred to Flossenburg concentration camp in a green police van, together with some other prisoners
unknown to him, seated on two facing wooden benches in the back.
Looking out of the small van window Fabian could see signs of the
thousand-year Reich falling apart, chaos and confusion everywhere –
people fleeing, official cars making a getaway. A road sign showed him
he wasn't far from his home town of Buch am Forst and he thought
briefly of trying to escape. But it was impossible. Instead he ended up
in solitary confinement, which suited him fine. Every other day he was
allowed out in the exercise yard with two SS guards – nice farm boys,
curious to know who he was. 'Oh, we've got quite of few of your lot

here,' they told him, 'an Admiral, a General, and a high-up military judge.' It wasn't hard for Fabian to work out who they were. At night he could hear the voices of other prisoners, mostly English POWs. Every evening they sang 'It's a long way to Tipperary.'

On 3 February 1945, Fabian von Schlabrendorff's path crossed with Kleist-Schmenzin again. It was the day of Fabian's trial before the *Volksgericht*, presided over, once again, by Roland Freisler. There were three accused that morning, all shackled, hands and feet. One was Major Staehle, the plotters' liaison on the General Staff. The other was Kleist-Schmenzin. After the depositions had been read out, it was Kleist-Schmenzin whose case came up first. He didn't care to defend himself. When Freisler challenged him, asking whether he had anything to say for himself, he answered: 'I have always considered Hitler and National Socialism as the arch enemy of the German Reich. I always fought against it, with all my strength.' Nothing more. Even Fabian was shocked. There stood an unbroken man, he thought.

Fabian's turn came next. Freisler had just called for his file when the sirens went off. It turned out to be one of the heaviest American daylight bombing raids on Berlin. The three accused were hustled out of the Court and down into the cellar air-raid shelter by the Court police, along with Freisler, the lawyers, and anyone else. Down in the cellar the three accused, still shackled, were seated apart, each separated from the other by one of the policemen. Minutes later there was an almighty crash. Freisler was visibly shaken and kept trying to use the telephone line to get more information. The line was dead. In his confusion, he was still carrying Fabian's files under his arm.

Minutes later, the Court suffered a direct hit and the gallery above, columns and all, came crashing through the cellar ceiling, pinning the Superintendent down at one end and felling Freisler at the other. They were plunged into darkness. Later they heard rescuers digging through the rubble. 'Freisler is dead,' said someone.

The Court police led the three accused, still shackled, out of the cellar through the rubble and into the back of a waiting Gestapo car. They could see the Court was on fire as the car drove zig-zag along Bellevue Strasse. Nothing was recognisable – no building left standing, no street signs, no people. Everything enveloped in black. You could hardly see your own hand in front of you, wrote Fabian in his memoir. On the way he tried to talk to Kleist-Schmenzin. He didn't react. He could see the dangers better than Fabian. Somehow they got back to the Gestapo prison in Prinz Albrecht Strasse, though getting into the courtyard was difficult because most of the building was gone. They were bundled out of the car and separated. Before he was taken away Kleist-Schmenzin gave Fabian one last, direct look, full of warmth and friendship. 'It was our goodbye.'

Fabian was taken down into the prison bunker. There among the crowd of he saw Oster and Franz Halder. 'Freisler is dead!' he shouted out.

A few days later he found himself in front of the Court again, together with Major Staehle. It had moved to a small courtroom in Kleist Park and now it was Vice President Krohne who presided over the proceedings. Fabian and Staehle were seated side by side on the bench. When no one was looking Staehle drew a cross on his trouser leg, murmuring 'Kleist'. Guillotined, it later transpired. While Staehle's case was heard Fabian was taken off to a room where three Court policemen were playing Skat cards. How strange this is, he thought – caught here between their life and my death. Then he was called back into the Court. Suddenly he galvanised himself and defended himself 'with all my might', using his old legal training. He insisted he'd given his evidence under Gestapo torture and it could therefore not be allowed. Krone was nervous, Fabian could tell, reminding everyone in the courtroom that they were under rules of silence and that nothing was to be put down in writing. After the midday recess, once the Court was recalled, Krone gave his verdict: Fabian von Schlabrendorff's defence of false evidence under torture was admitted. Out of the blue, Fabian was a free man. Krone stood up and shook his hand and wished him good luck. He even awarded Fabian compensation. Not that he ever received it. But remember, wrote Fabian von Schlabrendorff in his memoirs, it was the last few weeks of war. No wonder Krone was nervous. The Russians were already standing at the gates of Berlin.

CHAPTER THIRTEEN

AFTERMATH

'One day in January 1933 I was sitting with my esteemed publisher Rowohlt in an unpretentious Gasthof in Berlin, enjoying a convivial dinner, our lady wives and a few bottles of good Franconian wine keeping us company,' wrote Rudolf Ditzen, the author Hans Fallada, in September 1944, with happy hindsight. 'The effect wine had on me was entirely unpredictable: generally it made me belligerent, self-opinionated and boastful. But this evening it hadn't.' In 1933 things were still looking fairly good for Rudolf, apparently: Ernst Rowohlt still had his publishing house, Rudolf's marriage to Suse was still up and running, his writing was still flowing as nicely as the wine. And here was his friend and esteemed publisher sitting opposite him in happy companionship, 'a huge 200 pound baby, alcohol evaporating from every pore in his body'.

As the evening wore on, Rowohlt 'reached a state when he wished to make a contribution of his own to the general entertainment: crunching a champagne glass between his teeth and eating the lot'. It was Rowohlt's party piece. And it was probably time to leave. But neither of the men had any intention of doing so, when 'into this supremely relaxed and contented scene there now burst an agitated waiter, to remind us that beyond our perfectly ordered private world there was a much larger outside world, where things were currently in a state of extreme turmoil. "The Reichstag is burning! The Reichstag is burning! The Communists have set light to it!"'

Never mind that Rudolf, recalling this happy evening several years later, got the date wrong – the Reichstag fire being in February. He never had been too worried about accuracy anyway, as he was the first to admit. In high good humour, the two friends summoned the waiter to fetch a cab. They wanted to go straight to the Reichstag to see the fire for themselves and join in the fun. Their wives stopped them. Just as well, mused Rudolf those many years later. 'Or our lives could have come to an end that day.' On reflection they thought it wouldn't perhaps be that bad. Wrong. People started to be arrested 'left, right and centre' with a suspicious number 'shot while trying to escape'.

Rudolf and Rowohlt both knew they were 'compromised', known anti-Fascists and 'friends of the Jews'. Then came the Nazi burning of 'degenerate books' in May 1933. Rudolf described his agonised deliberations about whether to leave Germany, like so many other writers, including Thomas Mann. But he couldn't do it, he wrote. 'I love Germany.' So he stayed. But at what cost? Constant anxiety.

Perhaps he got the date of the Reichstag fire wrong because he was writing this account with no notes, from memory – in Neustrelitz-Strelitz prison. It was a prison for 'mentally ill criminals', and he'd been incarcerated there in September 1944 following a drunken and generally addled attempt to shoot Suse in their kitchen at Carwitz, Suse having finally given up on her husband and filed for divorce in July of that year. He wasn't surprised. 'Almost from the beginning of our marriage I had relationships on the side,' he wrote to a friend. 'Sometimes my wife knew about them, sometimes she suspected something, sometimes she had no idea.' And that was without all his drinking and addiction problems.

Rudolf was locked up in Ward III, 'surrounded by murderers, thieves and sex offenders', with prison guards coming in and out the whole time, checking on him. But he wasn't bothered. Because he was writing – like fury. For some inexplicable reason his request for paper had been granted by the prison *Kommandant*, probably to keep him out of trouble, but all the more inexplicable because for the past year the Nazi Ministry of Public Enlightenment and Propaganda had refused him paper on the basis that he was not a sufficiently 'reliable' author. He'd kept them at bay by promising a book on the Kutisker financial scandal, involving two 'nasty Jews', which was just what Joseph Goebbels needed in his recently declared 'Total War' effort. Rudolf had accepted the 40,000 Reich Mark advance, but privately he had no intention of finishing the book, as he confided to Rowohlt. With any luck the war would finish first. But now, here he was with pencil and plenty of lined paper and all the hours *der liebe Gott* gave, to write his heart out. First he wrote *The Drinker*, then a couple of children's stories. And then, finding no one stopped him, he turned to his reminiscences of the Nazi period.

He knew it was a dangerous undertaking, what with the prison guards constantly looking over his shoulder. But he wrote in tiny,

illegible writing, upside down and in the spaces between, using abbre-
viations for good measure. 'It's a children's story,' he told the guards,
who, stupidly, believed him. 'I prefer not to think about what will
happen to me if anyone reads these lines,' he wrote. 'But I have to write
them down *before* the war ends . . .'

Crafty Rudolf knew as well as anyone that the war would soon
end, and that, once out of danger from the Nazis, every Fritz would
be writing his white-washed reminiscences. So he wrote and wrote,
all day and often all night too, and by mid-October it was done. Then
he applied for home leave, just for one day. He needed to collect some
notes for his Kutisker book, he said. Incredibly, it was granted. Was
the *Kommandant* a secret admirer of the famous Hans Fallada? Not
only did he get his day leave, he managed to smuggle out the manuscript of *A Stranger in My Own Country*, as it was later titled, and
hide it somewhere safe.

Mostly it was a true account of the horrors of the Nazi terror regime
– a rare courageous act on his part, since if it had been discovered
and deciphered, he would certainly have ended up in a concentration
camp. And it is true that he and Suse had given a home and work
to several people, whether Jews or opponents of the Nazis, who had
lost their jobs and were more or less on the run. But there was also
a bit of exaggeration: Rudolf may never have been a formal member
of the Reich Literary Chamber as he claimed, but he did apply for it.
Because, without it, there would be no paper, no publisher, no next
book – and that Rudolf couldn't survive. Prison, yes. Not writing, no.
And he'd made many compromises many times, adjusting a character
here, a story-line there, to fit in with the requirements of the Nazi
authorities. But he always managed, in his writing at least, to stand
up for the 'little, decent man', speaking to his many readers who were
quietly keeping their heads down, waiting for the terrors of the Nazi
regime to end. As he wrote to his mother Elizabeth: 'I know I am a
weak man, but not a bad man.'

He was let out of the prison sooner than expected. By 13 December
he was living back home with Suse in Carwitz, hoping for a recon-
ciliation. He promised to stop drinking, having affairs, and to give
her more money. She probably knew it was pie-in-the-sky. But he also
made the house and their smallholding over to her, so giving Suse
and their three children a secure home and living. They celebrated
Christmas together as a family, like in the old days. After Christmas,

in the spirit of the promises he'd made, Rudolf said he was going to Feldberg to tell his current mistress, Ulla Losch, that their relationship was over. Off he set through the snow, determined to put things right. He didn't come home that evening. The next day he and Ulla got engaged. They were married on 1 February 1945 in Berlin. It was a quiet sort of wedding, reported Rowohlt, interrupted by an air-raid.

Ulla Losch was 22, pretty and vivacious. Wealthy too, and already a widow. How could Rudolf resist? Except that her vivaciousness was fed by a serious morphine habit, and her background wasn't quite what it seemed: she'd been working at the Losch Soap factory when the boss, the much older Herr Losch, became besotted with her, divorced his wife and married her. Then died suddenly four years later. By the time Rudolf came across Ulla she was the talk of Feldberg, having moved there with her mother and young daughter to get away from the bombing raids on Berlin. Ulla was elegant in a way quite unheard of in Feldberg, even before the war, with immaculate make-up and painted nails. The people seemed to like her for it rather than resenting it, because she was also friendly and helpful. Few other than the local chemist knew of her addiction, not at the beginning at least.

Once she became the new Frau Ditzen people weren't quite so sure. Their sympathy was with Suse. But they had bigger matters to worry about than Herr and Frau Ditzen. Who would reach Feldberg first, the Russians or the Americans? They lived in terror, rumours of horrific acts of reprisal spreading like wildfire. In the event it was the Russians, on 29 April 1945. It was a Sunday. 'Terrible days,' wrote Rudolf's mother in her diary, describing how five Russian soldiers suddenly appeared in their kitchen. 'Poor Suse had to suffer a lot.' More and more Russians arrived, most looking 'Asiatic', and Suse was raped more than once. It was happening everywhere.

In Berlin Wilhelm Pieck, who'd been Ernst Thälmann's right-hand man, returned from exile in Moscow along with several other former German Communists and Social Democrats, including Walter Ulbricht, who later followed Pieck as President of East Germany. It was Soviet official policy at that time to try and win over the defeated population, rooting out old Nazi Party officials and installing new local mayors, former anti-Nazis, wherever possible. The Russian *Kommandant* in Feldberg was called Major Sidelnikoff, and by early May Rudolf Ditzen had made it his business to get to know him and reassure him of his credentials. Luckily he had his manuscript of *A Stranger in My Own Country* to hand, written, as he pointed out, well before the end of the war. By the end of May he'd been made temporary Mayor of Feldberg. 'The Russians come as your friends,' announced the new Mayor, without much conviction.

There were perks with the job. In a sharp reversal of fortunes, prominent local Nazis were relieved of their large houses which were duly handed over to decent anti-Nazis instead. It wasn't the same as Jews being hounded out of their homes by the Nazis during the 1930s since it wasn't part of an ideology of racial extermination, but it was a revenge nevertheless. Ditzen, the new mayor, was allocated a spacious house in Feldberg, in Prenzlauer Strasse. It had belonged to a lawyer who'd committed suicide along with his wife, joining thousands of others who simply couldn't face the future after the collapse of the German Reich. He invited Suse, his three children and his mother, Elizabeth, who was still living with Suse at Carwitz, to come and live with them for the time being. They were happy to accept. In the topsy-turvy chaotic world of post-war Germany, Ulla and Rudolf made the family welcome, and, somehow, everyone got on.

As Mayor of Feldberg, Rudolf had endless and insurmountable problems to deal with, working long hours to the point of exhaustion. First there was the huge influx of refugees from East Prussia. Then there was the looting and the stealing – by local Germans as much as by the Russian troops. Then there were the die-hard local Nazis who were refusing to work and went about destroying property rather than repairing it. And there were the usual neighbour disputes, with bitter recriminations and denunciations on both sides. But Rudolf had his own problems to deal with. 'On 12 August 1945 the Mayor Ditzen – presumably as a result of his alcohol and morphine addictions – suffered a collapse,' reported one of his employees. 'He arrived early one morning at the Kommandatur in nothing but his nightshirt and broke all the windows, thereby wounding himself.' Apparently his new wife was in a similar state and tried to commit suicide by slitting her wrists. They both ended up in hospital. They weren't alone – the wards were full to bursting with despairing people who'd had breakdowns or tried to commit suicide, everyone at the end of their wits, seeing no hope in the future after six years of the Nazi terror regime followed by five years of war.

When Rudolf came out of hospital he and Ulla moved to Berlin.

They'd had enough of Feldberg. First, they went to Ulla's old apartment in the one-time desirable Schöneberg district. They found it badly bomb damaged, with other people living in it – in other words, they found it in the same state as the rest of Berlin. It was incredible that people could still be alive in places which looked like nothing but piles of masonry, they thought, whole districts flattened and gone. But there they were, these starving people, emerging from bombed-out cellars into the daylight, pushing old carts with their few remaining possessions along blasted roads, looking for somewhere to live and something to eat. And there were Rudolf and Ulla, living in three rooms of what had once been Ulla's elegant apartment, with the windows blown out and having to fetch water from a stand-pipe up the road, taking their place in the long queue. Worse still – far from helping Ulla kick her morphine habit, Rudolf joined her.

None of it stopped him from writing however, banging away at his old typewriter. It helped that in these immediate post-war weeks and months the returning Communists and Social Democrats were finally working together to establish a democratic anti-Fascist regime. One of the tools to achieve this, they agreed, was to restore an active cultural life: a free press, the *Berliner Rundfunk* wireless station, theatre and music and cinema, a *Kulturbund* to replace the Nazi Ministry of Culture, and, as far as Rudolf was concerned, the re-establishment of the book publishing business, free from political interference.

The *Kulturbund* was run by Johannes Becher, a man from a similar background to Rudolf but who'd taken a different path when faced with the rise of Fascism, joining the Communist Party and, once the Nazis took power, fleeing into exile, first to Paris, then Moscow. Becher had worked with the *Freies Deutschland* Committee in Moscow, contacting German prisoners of war who had previously been Communists or Social Democrats, and made regular wireless broadcasts to Germany. Now he was back in Berlin looking for the kind of artists and writers who could help with the cause of rebuilding post-Fascist Germany. Foremost among the writers, as far as Becher was concerned, was Hans Fallada, one of the finest pre-war writers, who could spin a tale of the highest literary quality without losing the popular touch. They met some time in October through the grapevine of returned or resurfaced artists and intellectuals who vouched for Rudolf's anti-Nazi credentials.

Becher arranged for Rudolf and Ulla to move to a large house with a garage and garden in the Pankow district of Berlin where most of the Russian administration and army officers now lived. Ulla's daughter Jutta went with them, soon to be joined by Uli and later Lore, during school terms, with Suse visiting from time to time, bringing vegetables and fruit from her thriving smallholding. Becher, a near neighbour, provided them with better ration cards and got Rudolf some work on the *Tagliche Rundschau*. Christmas 1945 was spent with Becher and guests, including Wilhelm Pieck. By January 1946 Rudolf had signed a contract with the new Aufbau publishing company, to write a novel, *Der Alpdruck*, The Nightmare, about grim life in post-war Germany.

The central character Dr Doll, a writer, is clearly based on Rudolf himself, a man struggling to come to terms with his 'feeling of utter helpless shame', which is part of the post-war 'malady of the age, a mixture of bottomless despair and apathy'. As Rudolf's new patron, Johannes Becher put it: 'The contradiction he (Doll/Rudolf) embodied was not just private and personal. He embodied and represented, in his mental and spiritual crisis, a general German condition.' Or, as Rudolf put it in the foreword to the novel, addressing his reader in his usual confiding way: 'It may perhaps be of some value as a *document humain*, a faithful and true account (to the best of the author's abilities) of what the ordinary German felt, suffered, and did between April 1945 and the summer of that year.'

'Always, during those nights around the time of the great collapse, Dr Doll, when he did eventually manage to get to sleep, was plagued by the same bad dream,' Rudolf began, describing the wait for the Russians – the fear, the humiliation, the guilt – thereby instantly drawing his reader in. 'Well into the night, after a day filled with torment, they stayed sitting by the windows, peering out onto the little meadow, towards the bushes and the narrow cement path, to see if any of the enemy were coming – until their eyes ached, and everything became a blur and they could see nothing.' In the event Dr Doll, like Rudolf, is chosen as local mayor by the Russians. Like Rudolf, Doll has to deal with hopeless and recalcitrant locals. Like Rudolf, Doll also has to deal with a wife who is an addict and is himself addicted, mostly to drink. And like Rudolf, Doll ends up having a breakdown.

No wonder Rudolf told his readers he hadn't enjoyed writing the book but had written it because it seemed 'important'. He tried his best to bring some hope to the ending: 'Life goes on, and they would outlive these times, those who had been spared by the grace of God, the survivors,' he wrote. 'Life goes on, always, even beneath the ruins. The ruins are of no account; what counts is life – the life of a blade of grass in the middle of the city, in among the thousand lumps of shattered masonry. Life goes on, always.' Perhaps people might learn something, he hoped, 'learn from their suffering, their tears, their blood.'

Next Becher handed Rudolf a Gestapo file found among those left behind by the fleeing SS. It concerned an ordinary middle-aged, working-class Berlin couple, Otto and Elise Hampel, who, after Elise's brother was killed in France in 1940, decided to take their own, secret action against the Nazi regime. They told no one and joined no resistance group but started writing postcards denouncing the terror regime and left them in the hallways of apartment blocks and offices, for people to find and read. The story was heaven-sent for Rudolf, champion of the decent little man – and the hundreds of thousands of anonymous people who'd resisted the Nazi regime in small ways and large. He changed their names from Hampel to Quangel and made their loss more dramatic by making it the death of their only son, Otto – but otherwise he remained faithful to the original, only adding a cast of typical Fallada characters to the tale, sweeping the reader along from the opening line to the very last. The first draft of 600 pages only took him 24 days to write.

'The postwoman Eva Kluge slowly climbs the steps of 55 Jablonski Strasse. She's tired from her round, but she also has one of those letters in her bag that she hates to deliver, and is about to have to deliver, to the Quangels, on the second floor,' starts Rudolf. How many millions of his German readers had had the same desperate experience? The loss of a son, a father, a husband at the Western or Eastern Front? Hans Fallada, writing in the present tense, had them taut with anticipation before the end of the first paragraph. 'Before that, she has a Party circular for the Persickers on the floor below. Persicker is some political functionary or other – Eva Kluge always gets the titles mixed up. At any rate, she has to remember to call out "*Heil Hitler!*" at the Persickers' and watch her lip.' So there we have it: Eva Kluge, 'just an ordinary woman, but as a woman she's of the view you don't bring children into the world to have them shot.'

Up and down the stairwell of 55 Jablonski Strasse Eva Kluge goes, introducing the reader to the various tenants who will make up the story of this book, each representing an aspect of the lives of ordinary people in Nazi Germany in 1940, at war. Apart from the Quangels on the second floor and the Persickers on the first, there's Judge Fromm on the third – an elderly cultivated man who quietly helps people fleeing the Nazis, including his Jewish neighbour Frau Rosenthal who later finds refuge in Judge Fromm's apartment. A petty thief and Gestapo informer, Emil Borkhausen, lives in the back courtyard. And there is Trudel Hergesell, Otto Quangel's fiancée who works at a local armaments factory and joins a resistance cell there, and Kuno Kienschaper, Eva's adopted son, a good German, as well as her useless husband, Enno. Lastly, the man deputed by the Gestapo to hunt down the writers of the postcards, *Kommissar* Escherich.

It's *Kommissar* Escherich who makes the book into a headlong thriller. Because Escherich is a perfectionist, marking the location of each found postcard – they were nearly all found – with a little flag on a large map of Berlin, till, at last, he catches his prey. But is he proud and pleased? No, he's left with a sneaking admiration for the courage of the Quangels – perhaps the only person to be converted by them, as Rudolf tells his reader with a wry smile at the end of the book.

Like the fictional Quangels, the Hampels were finally caught in late 1942 and executed in April 1943. It was the same month as Rudolf's friends, Mildred and Arvid Harnack, and several others of the Red Orchestra Group were executed, as well as Dietrich Bonhoeffer, the pastor and theologian, his sister, Christine, and brother-in-law Hans von Dohnanyi.

By the time Rudolf delivered *Jeder Stirbt für Sich Allein*, Alone in Berlin, to the publisher, his own  life was on a steep downward spiral. The relationship with Ulla was grinding to a halt, largely due to her continuing morphine addiction. 'I have thought so much about our life at Carwitz lately,' Rudolf wrote to Suse on 9 June 1946. 'A small comment from Uli pointed me to the fact that, there too, much must have changed. He said the swing had been taken down. In theory I know, of course, that your lives there are completely changed, and all sorts of other things will have changed too, but the memory still holds hard onto those old pictures.'

Rudolf's health, after years of addiction to drink and drugs and fighting the Nazi regime, was exhausted. He died a few months later, on 5 February 1947, aged 58.

The thing that kept Irma Thälmann and her mother Rosa going during the last year of the war, before their arrest, was their shared memories of *Vater*, his letters which they read and reread, and the constant support, financial and otherwise, of their Communist comrades – those not yet arrested. The last visit to *Vater* in Bautzen prison, whence he'd been transferred after the heavy bombing of Hanover, was back in August 1943. Since then they'd heard nothing but rumours.

Irma was 23 now, living in Singen in South Germany, having married a fellow Communist comrade, Heinrich Vester, two years earlier. Heinrich had meanwhile been arrested for refusing to sign a statement saying that Frau and Irma Thälmann had contact with Communists abroad and Soviet prisoners of war in Germany, listened secretly to the BBC and Radio Moscow, and went about telling everyone that the Soviet Army would be victorious in the end. Irma hadn't seen him since. She worked in her brother-in-law's workshop in Singen as a lathe operator, and went to visit *Mutti* in Hamburg as often as possible, taking trains as and when they operated, which was entirely unpredictable now that Allied bombing raids had intensified in all-out war.

One of their favourite memories was of the November 1932 elections, the last free elections before the Nazis' *Machtergreifung*, when the Communists gained six million votes – how Irma had been allowed to attend the big Communist rally with *Mutti*, and how *Vater* had suddenly appeared in the midst of the crowd to wild cheers of 'Teddy! Teddy' and given another of his note-free mesmerising speeches, bringing it to a rousing end, right arm raised, fist clenched. Irma and Rosa could quote favourite parts of his speeches by heart: 'We know a land where no Fascism reigns, where it would be unthinkable that Fascist murderers could go about streets, free to practise their bloody acts against the working man and woman, as in Germany today. That land is the Soviet Union. And that land, where there is no unemployment, gives the proletariat of every country the example of a revolutionary solution – the build-up of Socialism. So we feel tightly bound to the international proletariat everywhere in their anti-Fascist fight.'

Best of all were *Vater*'s letters – those which remained. When Irma married Heinrich and moved to Singen she took them with her, along with any other incriminating papers – because they knew that sooner or later the Hamburg Gestapo would come and search the Thälmann home again in their usual brutal way.

'Even if our name is despised in Germany today, I know it's also spoken with joy by many,' *Vater* had written to Irma in 1936 for her seventeenth birthday. 'You are the only child of a man who has dedicated his entire life to the Workers' Movement. You have to lead your life to show that you, as my daughter, are worthy of this. Soon the responsibilities which such a life demands will get greater for you, and in fighting them you will find out the strengths and the weaknesses in your character. The highest task in this battle is and remains always the way you handle yourself, and your basic attitude to the task. Without that there is no improvement, no going forward to something better. That's an ancient law. Keep a deep respect for your mother's wisdom.' He told her to read Goethe and Schiller and let herself be transported by them. That was important. Otherwise, where else could she find her inspiration to do battle? 'I can't be beside you, to guide you,' he ended, 'but I am always with you in spirit, watching over you as you go your way. Your *Vater*.'

Some of Irma's most powerful memories were of the prison visits, especially in Hanover where the administrator Suffenplan allowed a certain amount of freedom, albeit always within the confines of the prison cell. Was he a secret admirer of *Vater*'s? It was hard to tell. But Irma certainly managed to get away with all sorts when she visited – not least 'smuggling' in a Zeiss camera hidden in her underwear and taking some photos of him. How on earth did she manage to get away with that? But there sits Ernst Thälmann reading at a small table in his cell, head bent, wearing a shirt and waistcoat, looking composed and collected and concentrated, older but unbowed. The great question: why didn't the Gestapo execute him like so many others? Irma and Rosa thought it was because they knew that news of his death would get out quickly, passed from person to person like wildfire, and then there would be trouble. Trouble beyond their control.

On 16 April 1944, the month of the sweeping arrests, Irma was woken in the early hours with loud banging and shouting at her door. She leapt from her bed, heart beating with the shock of it. 'Open up! Gestapo!' They turned the place upside down – every cupboard, every book, every piece of clothing, stomping around in their black boots. Everything she'd smuggled out from *Vater* was there: his trial indictment, his letters, some photos of him in his Hanover cell. They searched everywhere but they found nothing. Irma was an old hand at this kind of thing and cleverer than them.

'You're under arrest!' they shouted at her. 'We'll soon wipe that smile off your face!' After three days, she was transferred to Hamburg, her name changed to Martha Suhren – Thälmann wasn't a name to use in Hamburg. In July she was transferred again, this time to Berlin-Charlottenburg. On 28 September 1944, in the early hours of the morning she was put in a large black police van with some others. They stopped at a prison somewhere, probably Plötzensee she later decided, where the van let out the other prisoners, and she was left alone. Her seat backed on to the partition behind the driver's seat.

'Have you read the news about the bombing of Buchenwald?' she heard the policeman in the front seat say to the driver. 'Amazing that Thälmann and Breitscheid were killed, isn't it?' Irma knew that Breitscheid, a leading Social Democrat and active anti-Nazi, had been arrested in 1940.

Irma couldn't take it in at first. *Vater* was in Bautzen surely? She banged on the wall. 'Please. What have you just said? Who died in Buchenwald?'

'What's it to you?'

Irma was in high alarm. 'Please tell me! Ernst Thälmann is my *Vater*. I must know! Please, tell me the truth.' Then they answered: 'If we'd known who you were we wouldn't have talked. It's in the papers. Apparently Ernst Thälmann was killed when Buchenwald was bombed.' Later it transpired that was a lie – yet another to add to the long list. The announcement in the newspapers was to hide the fact that both men had been murdered in those final months of the war, just before they could be liberated by the advancing Russians, exactly as Thälmann himself had predicted.

Rosa Thälmann had gone to Bautzen and tried again and again to get news of her husband, to no avail. Then she went to Gestapo HQ in Berlin with the same result. The truth only came out a year later, once the war was over. After Berlin she'd travelled to Singen to see Irma. That's when she found out Irma had been arrested. She herself was arrested a few days later. When Irma was in the local prison, a woman in the next cell called out. 'Who are you really?' When Irma told her she was Thälmann's daughter the woman told her: 'Your mother sends her love. Stay brave, she says. She was transported to Ravensbrück three days ago. We shared a cell for two nights. Everyone knows the war and Fascism are coming to an end. The Red Army isn't far from Berlin. They will set us free, also your *Vater*. Your mother doesn't believe the stories about his death.'

The next morning the transport continued on to Ravensbrück. As Irma stood in a long row of prisoners, a woman with a red armband came along: 'Where is Irma Vester? Fall out! Come this way!' Irma had her own name back apparently. She stepped out of the line. 'Keep very quiet Irma,' said the woman who turned out to be one of the camp inmates, on a *Lagerpolizei*, camp police, work detail. 'Don't attract attention. Your mother is fine. You will see her today. Do as I say.'

Ravensbrück, 50 miles north of Berlin, had been built in 1939 as a concentration camp exclusively for women – nearly all of them political prisoners: German Communists and Socialists, Polish and Russian partisans, French resisters, some Dutch, a few Italians, many Jewish women, some nuns, some gypsies, and, by the time Irma arrived, some children too. Four women from the British SOE, Violette Szabo, Cecily Lefort, Lilian Rolfe and Denise Bloch were all killed at Ravensbrück. In total more than 120,000 women were incarcerated there from 1939–45. Of these some 50,000 didn't survive, either dying of starvation, disease or exhaustion, both physical and mental. Over 2,000 were killed in the camp's gas chambers. Some were used in medical experiments, all were used as slave labour in and around the camp or its satellite camps, many working in local factories like Siemens.

As Irma was marched through the camp she saw row upon row of *Blocks* stretching far into the distance, housing over 15,000 women. Hers was already overcrowded. 'People were lying head to tail and over one another like herrings. Many had nowhere to lie at all and stood about, falling asleep leaning on others. It was terrible. Screaming, beatings, swearing – like being in hell. Late that night, long after the *Block* warden had ordered silence, I was led to the camp office and given my striped work clothes by some women of the *Lagerpolizei*. One of them took me aside: "We're going to *Block* 32, the Death Block. It's where all the partisans from the Soviet Union and Poland are. Your mother's there. It's the best place to be. No betrayal there. You can spend the night with her. Don't be afraid. Nothing will happen to you or your mother. We'd rather die." It was wonderful,' Irma wrote. '*Mutti* and I talked the whole night. She was ill then, but surviving. The Camp *Kommandant* had told her *Vater* was killed when Buchenwald was bombed. We didn't believe it. We comforted one another, but we were both anxious. *Mutti* gave me good advice on how to handle myself: don't show your hate of the Fascists so openly. She was already *Lager* experienced. The next morning at five o'clock, the comrade fetched me back to the other *Block*. Ten minutes later we were marched off on our work detail.'

The camp guards were female SS, large, brutal women with plenty of sadists among them. The administration was exclusively SS male. Later they appeared, one by one, at the Hamburg Ravensbrück trials, the war crime tribunals held in 1947, but for now they held the power – the *Blockführerinnen*, the barracks' overseers, going about with dogs and whips. Elfriede Müller was one of the worst, known as 'the beast'. Irma took no notice – she was her *Vater*'s daughter after all.

'When mother and I were in Ravensbrück we met women of all sorts: partisans, university students, simple workers – wonderful women,' Irma wrote years later when all the horror was over. 'We'll never forget Galina and Schura and the Soviet doctors. They were very concerned with mother – always at her side, looking after the health of the wife of Ernst Thälmann. They found extra food, did extra washing, talked German and made her hard life as good as possible. How impressive they were. How clean. Their block was the cleanest and best organised in the camp. You could have eaten off their floor. And they were bright and happy and always ready to help. Especially the women in the Death Block for Polish and Russian partisans. In there they maintained discipline and comradeship. Everything was decided by committee, and every Sunday they had an hour of political information. Sometimes they got hold of a Nazi newspaper, but they also got information from the German prisoners. They collected it up for their hour of discussion. As far as mother could tell there weren't many members of the KPD Party among them, but they led the discussions, and there was never any fighting. Only plenty of debate.'

Irma was sent to do kitchen duty in one of the satellite camps called *Waldbaustraflager*. She had a bad time with one of the sadist SS warders who addressed her exclusively as 'Communist pig!' The Polish women warned Irma to be careful: that warder was looking for an excuse to get her. So Irma heeded *Mutti*'s advice and showed no sign of her burning hate. Until one day the warder attacked her, taunting her: 'That Communist dog Thälmann is dead. Good thing!'

Then Irma went wild and attacked the woman with a kitchen knife. It was in November 1944.

There was chaos after that. The SS camp guards charged in, beating Irma to the ground with their batons and whips, dogs barking and straining at their leashes, then dragged her out into the deep snow, through the camp, stumbling in her wooden clogs, falling over again and again, to the *Kommandant*'s office. 'I'd like to string you up from the nearest tree as they did to your Communist criminal father,' he said. But he knew if he did that to Ernst Thälmann's daughter he'd have a riot on his hands. Instead she did six weeks in the underground bunker, starving, walls iced up, water frozen in the bucket. Finally, on 31 December, she was let out into the blinding light of day and white snow and returned to the main camp at Ravensbrück.

On 26 April 1945, the SS left the camp with the prisoners on a death march. Only the sick, including Irma and Rosa, were left behind with a few Polish, Russian and Czech women who'd been the helpers. For three days, they were left to their own devices, finding what food they could and comforting one another, with the bedraggled remnants of the once victorious German army marching past the camp, watched by the haggard half-dead women prisoners in their striped camp uniforms. It was a desperate sight. 'Everyone was very anxious, waiting every minute for the Red Army. Then we heard the tanks in the distance. At midday on 29 April we saw the first tanks rumbling towards us, the red flag flying high on the turrets. At last! Anyone who could still walk ran into the road. It was the best moment of our lives – freed by the Soviet Army! We climbed up onto the tanks to embrace the soldiers, crying with joy. The Russian women told the soldiers I was the German among them, and who I was. Then they doubled their greetings for the daughter of the great leader of the German Communist Party, Ernst Thälmann.'

Irma and Rosa couldn't accept that *Vater* was dead – and such a short time before the Soviet Army came to liberate him. 'What's the point of living, now he's dead?' they told each other. But then they felt ashamed. *Vater* had taught them how to act by his own example, and that only by suffering the hardships could greatness be achieved. They told themselves: 'The great task *Vater* worked for and lived for has been achieved. The Capitalists have had their power taken from them in our section of Germany. The fateful split in the Left, between the KPD and SPD, is healed, and they have united to create the Socialist State.' On

7 October 1949 the DDR, German Democratic Government, of East Germany was formed. Wilhelm Pieck, Ernst Thälmann's old comrade, at its head as the first President.

At Trebbow, in Mecklenburg, there was constant anxiety during those last months of the war. They knew the Soviet Army wasn't far away and they'd heard the rumours: women raped, even old ladies, houses burnt, pillaged and looted – brutal Communists taking revenge on their old enemy, the Fascist Nazis. As far as the Russians were concerned all Germans were Nazis. Except German Communists, that is, many of whom were fighting with the Russians – which was hard to believe, but true.

'How often I've studied the local map,' wrote Countess Charlotte von der Schulenburg years after the war, 'usually through a magnifying glass, of Brandenburg and Mecklenburg, seeking out the beloved towns and villages, the streams and lakes, and the country roads. Then I feel like someone looking down from a great astronomical distance, trying to find the Lost Land, filling it with pictures from memory: *that's* where the path led over the field to the edge of Wiesenthal, *this* is where the little bridge was, *here's* where the crossing was with the high trees, and *here's* where the stream led into the lake.' It was heartbreaking, but she couldn't stop.

'Ah, Trebbow. You arrive at the little station at Lübstorf from Schwerin, catching sight of Schwerin lake on the right-hand side of the railway track, off and on all the way. The horse-drawn carriage was always waiting for us at the back of the railway station – Bruss the coachman, with his impressively weathered, friendly face, sitting proudly on the front seat, greeting us with a wave of his whip. Two beautiful carriage horses, already restive. Sometimes it was the dark green *Wagonette* with benches either side in the back, sometimes it was the *Shooting-brake*. Off we went at a trot along the country road. After a while there was a slight incline, then a wood, and that's where the Trebbow boundary began. When we came out of the woods the flat fields spread out wide either side of the tree-lined road which led straight to Trebbow.' Charlotte might put down her magnifying glass for a while, but she always went back.

'In 1940 Fritzi became a soldier. Carl Barner and Tisa, Fritzi's only sister, invited me and the children to Trebbow for the summer. What should we do all alone in Breslau after all? We went to Trebbow every summer after that, from late spring to early autumn. Sometimes we visited nearby Tressow too. It was always a great adventure travelling from Breslau with our mountains of luggage. It was war after all, and everything was laborious and difficult – just getting a taxi or finding a seat in a railway carriage for a mother with so many children. That first year Puppi was a few months old, in my arms. Lala was looking after the older children and endless bags of toys and baby bottles and nappies. A change of trains in Berlin, a night with friends, and then across to Lehrter railway station the next morning to get the train taking us north, to Mecklenburg.

'Finally in summer 1943, I gave up our apartment in Breslau and we moved lock, stock and barrel, to Trebbow. Tisa gave us a lovely set of rooms on the first floor which I could furnish as I liked. Fritzi was able to bring his beloved books, and there we all sat, round our same large dining table, on our same old dining chairs with the French *petit point* embroidery.' Tisa had the rooms on the ground floor. Carl Ulrich was away at war.

So much had happened since those happy days. Too much. Too much tragedy. Too much unhappiness. Charlotte's consolation was the map and the magnifying glass.

'I searched out that other life, when Fritzi was still with us. *There*, at the small railway station in Lübstorf, is the last time I saw him. That's why the landscape of Trebbow has such a deep meaning for me. It is the background to my life of happiness. Then came the events of the summer of 1944, then the sadness of the following winter, right up to our flight from Mecklenburg in April 1945.'

Charlotte dreamed about Fritzi. She wrote him letters. She read the poems he loved. She went for long walks over the wide fields and into the dark Trebbow forests, just to be alone, away from all the noise and chaos. 'Fritzi is often with me,' she wrote to herself on 21 April 1945, 'his strong, loving spirit showing me powerfully what's indestructible. I can almost feel the pressure of his hand with his linked fingers, see his eyes, his strong nose, his high forehead. Again and again, it seems impossible to me that he's dead, in spite of all the evidence and logic.' She told herself that she had to learn to be alone. Only the children stopped her from giving up altogether.

Tisa and Charlotte had been to Berlin twice in the months after Fritzi's execution, desperate to find out what happened, in vain. No news, no trace. There was no last letter from Fritzi. There was nothing. So back to Trebbow they went, hopeless, picking their way through the rubble and craters to Lehrter station. Charlotte clung to the possibility that Fritzi had escaped to France.

On 5 August 1944 the journalist Werner Fiedler came to visit. He was the friend of the Wiemanns who said he'd try and find out something for Charlotte. On the same day *Gauleiter* Friedrich Hildebrand turned up at Trebbow with some of his SS men. Privately, in the high-ceilinged drawing room, he told Charlotte he'd try and protect her and the children, but he could only do that if she promised not to leave Trebbow – no travel, no telephone calls, no visitors. He was doing it for the sake of her father-in-law Count von der Schulenburg, he said, who'd always treated him well.

Tisa, hovering in the background, knew what he meant. Hildebrand had been nothing more than a humble, uneducated farmhand before he joined the Nazi Party, then rose and rose through the ranks to reach his present elevated status which allowed him to behave with such magnanimity. What could they do? Charlotte accepted his offer graciously. She knew the Nazis were taking many of the children of the plotters into *Sippenhaft*. Tisa, the awkward one, seethed with anger. But they needed his protection. Some of the villagers were accusing the Schulenburgs of being traitors. Many servants had left. When Charlotte finally tracked down Hercher, Fritzi's so-called defence lawyer at his trial, he told her: 'Yes, your husband made a very intelligent impression. How could he do that!' He'd only spent half an hour with Fritzi, on the eve of the trial, so he didn't have much to add – only that the Count was smoking a pipe, reading. Even the only remaining Schulenburg brother, Johann Albrecht, still living at nearby Tressow, accused Fritzi of being a traitor. It was unbelievable really: he sent a letter to Himmler disowning his own brother. Perhaps he'd gone mad, thought Tisa. Johann Albrecht, wounded in the 1914–18 war, was dying of cancer.

That summer Carl Ulrich came home on leave. Charlotte's mother came to stay and help with the children and the household. There were so few servants left. Then Hildebrand asked Carl Ulrich to come and see him in his offices in Schwerin. They all went. Charlotte and her mother and Tisa waited in the *Dom*, cathedral, for his return. Tisa, sitting in one of the ancient wooden pews in the gloom, thought of the time she and Fritzi had sat in the Königsberg *Dom* back in 1938, at the time of their father's death, when Fritzi had sworn her to secrecy about the plot to kill Hitler. 'Go back to England, there will be a war and this war will be terrible over here,' he'd told her then. 'After the war you may return, because this war will be the end of Hitler, *we* will see to it.' And now here they were back where they started, waiting for news. Carl Ulrich came back. 'Fritzi's dead,' he said. No one spoke a word.

Later that same month, Werner Fiedler sent some news. He'd made contact with an old acquaintance who was a member of the SS and had been present at Fritzi's trial. Over a glass of wine one evening, Fiedler managed to get the full story from him – or as full as it would ever be. He gave Erika Wiemann a coded letter to pass to Charlotte, using Van Gogh as a cover. 'The research which I'm using for my book,' he wrote, 'gives a most felicitous picture of the unswerving and clear way he handled himself to the very end, his courage, and even his gently mocking manner at the Art Exhibition, when he was defending himself against his glib critics.' Apparently Fritzi made a last, brief statement to the court, standing very upright, looking straight at screaming Freisler: 'We took this task upon us, to protect Germany from an unspeakable suffering. It is clear to me that I will be hanged for it, but I do not regret my actions and hope they will be fulfilled in another, happier time.' Fiedler couldn't write it down, so he learned it off by heart.

Back at Trebbow, Tisa took in wave upon wave of soldiers and refugees from the Eastern provinces. The refugees helped on the estate in return for meagre food rations, mostly potato soup cooked in two great tubs in one of the out-houses. Then they moved on, joining an endless trek of humanity walking West, escaping the Russians, the roads crammed with the old, the young and the infirm, mostly women and children – their men killed or missing or in a Soviet POW camp. Throughout the autumn they trekked, then through the heavy snows of winter and into the pale green of spring, pushing prams and carts and bicycles laden with their few possessions, thousands dying on the way. So this was the thousand-year Reich. This is what it had come to.

By April 1945, the Russians had reached Schwerin. Charlotte and Tisa discussed late into the night and finally knew they had to leave Trebbow, their home, the place they loved. There were some distant family relations of Carl Ulrich in Holstein, in the West. They'd have to flee in the dead of night, telling no one. But how could this be done? Only Klara, the childrens' nurse, was trustworthy.

A few nights later they put the children to bed as usual, then woke them at midnight, pressing fingers to their lips. Ssshh! don't say a word, don't make a sound. It was like Christmas, Puppi said, jumping up and down, excited. The other five were quiet as mice, sensing something serious was happening. They dressed in layers and layers of clothes and loaded their most precious possessions, including the trunk of Fritzi's papers. Bruss brought the carriage and horses from the stables. They threw a large carpet over the top to act as a shelter, like a tent. Charlotte climbed up onto the front seat and took the reins with Fritz, now aged seven, beside her. Klara sat in the back with the other children, Neiti now aged two lying on the floor, squeezed between the boxes and cases and clothes. Tisa went ahead in the two-hander, leading the way – down the gravelled drive, slowly, so as not to make a noise, the horses of the Brake pulling hard with all the weight. Once on the country road they went faster, leaving Trebbow – the beloved fields, the beloved woods, the beloved lakes – far behind.

They managed to get as far as Travemunde, where they needed to get across the Trave river – into freedom. But the bridge had been bombed and there was just one ferry, with the flotsam of the world waiting in a long queue to cross. Charlotte jumped down from the Brake and went up to an officer. She had her six children in the back, she protested – couldn't he let them through? She was very persuasive when she had to be, was Charlotte, and soon enough a soldier came down the line and waved them forward. Tisa in her two-hander too. Somehow they made it to Holstein, to Carl Ulrich's relations and their large country house – already filled to bursting with refugees and soldiers and freed POWs, just like at Trebbow. But they welcomed the Schulenburgs in, found them something to eat and settled them, first in the downstairs hall, later in a single attic room – Charlotte, Klara and the six children all crammed in. Once safely delivered, Tisa returned to Trebbow. There was still so much to do.

So there was Tisa, in her two-hander, making her way back East while the whole world trudged West. Who was this mad woman in her carriage? they asked themselves. Where was she going? By the time she got back to Trebbow – who knows how – the SS and most of the soldiers had fled, just one step ahead of the Russians. But the refugees were still there, more and more of them, displaced, lost, in despair. What on earth was she to do?

In the event it was the Americans who arrived at Trebbow – up the long tree-lined drive through the parkland they came, six American jeeps, white star emblazoned on their sides. Apparently they'd been negotiating terms with the Russians in Schwerin. Now here they were, parked up in a line outside the front entrance of Trebbow, coming up the steps, casually saluting Tisa who stood there, ready to greet them. Carl Ulrich was away again – who knew where?

How surprised the Americans were to find that the mistress of the grand country house spoke fluent English. How could they know that she'd spent years in England, and that her ex-husband Fritz Hess still sent her food parcels from London – whenever possible. This place was ideal for billeting, the Americans could see at a glance. But there were 120 refugees living there now, women and children, crammed into the top floors. Tisa expected the American officer to turf them all out, but he didn't. She was allowed to stay in her own room. The officers moved into the ground floor. The rank and file moved into the farm outbuildings. 'Where's the booze?' asked one. 'None left,' said Tisa.

There was no electricity, so the mill couldn't function, the baker couldn't bake, the slaughterer couldn't slaughter. The dairy was quiet. Tisa told the Americans she needed to go to Schwerin to sort something out. They took her in one of their jeeps, and cheerfully 'liberated' a couple of generators which they hauled back to Trebbow. The Russians were billeted the other side of Schwerin lake and came looking for supplies. The Polish and Russian POWs, freed from their camp, did the same. The villagers, those who'd been Nazis, locked themselves in their houses, terrified. Nothing happened at Trebbow itself because there was a large 'V' sign painted on the entrance, signifying they'd been anti-Nazi. Most of their neighbours on the surrounding landed estates had fled. Hanke, their forester, was arrested by the Americans. He'd shot dead some US airmen who'd ejected from their burning plane and come down in one of the Trebbow fields. They'd been 'trying to escape' he said, and he was only obeying orders. Whose orders? the Americans interrogated, reversing the natural order of things as they'd stood for the past twelve years in the Greater German Reich. *Gauleiter* Hildebrand's, came the answer.

By the summer another unit of Americans had moved in and Tisa had to move out. She settled herself in the stables, in one of the horse stalls. She painted it blue, brought down a bed and a chair from the house, and hung a rug over the partition for privacy. She retrieved her mother's silk dressing table chair, the one Tisa used to sit on as a child, watching *Mutti* brushing her hair. There was water, swallows flew in and out, and the weather was glorious. She placed a table and chair under the lime tree in the cobbled courtyard and ran the estate from there. Later the Americans found her a caravan and tent from one of the disused German army camps. By day she worked in the tent, set up by the lake, and swam early every morning. Nights she spent in the caravan, nicely done up, with roses from the garden on the table. She and the Americans worked happily together, her English useful to them as they tried to bring some order to the chaos of dividing Germany up into four zones – American, British, Russian and French. Carl Ulrich had been taken prisoner somewhere, but more than that Tisa did not know. Later, once it became clear that Trebbow would be in the Russian zone, she moved to the British zone and, again making use of her English, found work helping the British occupying authorities.

Through the grapevine Charlotte and the children had meanwhile moved to Schloss Hehlen. It was another of those country houses with a large estate, belonging to one of the Schulenburg relations. The place was full of the usual post-war flotsam, and Jonny von der Schulenburg, a cousin, long since divested of a wife and something of a drinker, welcomed them with cheerful generosity, open-armed. Once again, the family lived in grand rooms, once again with no money. The children loved Jonny and loved the freedom. Charlotte began to take up the threads of her future life. She bartered her remaining jewels for food on the black market. They stayed for seven years. But she needed to earn a living. Eventually she found a job as a housemother and teacher in a boarding school, taking her children with her.

Gradually she made contact with other widows of the executed plotters – the only people who could understand how she felt. To add to their despair, their husbands were rarely seen as heroes. In the twisted psychology which prevailed after years of a terror regime with all its propaganda and lies and brutality, followed by a war which had killed millions, many still accused the plotters of treachery. It was as though they couldn't bear to blame Hitler, their Führer, the man who had promised to make their *Vaterland* great again. It was incredible. And terrible.

Most of the widows of the July 20 plot had one consolation denied Charlotte: they had a last letter, telling them how much their husbands loved and treasured them. Freya von Moltke, Mika Stauffenberg, Ilse von Hassell, Annedore Leber. But Charlotte had nothing. Then, one day in 1954 a letter arrived in the post. It came from Annedore Leber. She and Freya von Moltke had been researching the stories of the plotters and resisters for a book. Among some documents they'd found Fritzi's last letter to Charlotte, written in Plötzensee prison on the day of his execution. The Gestapo had ordered it destroyed, but one brave secretary in the Reich Justice Ministry had found it, copied it and hidden it away. In the post-war chaos the letter had got lost, but now, here it was, miraculously, in Charlotte's hands.

'I remember, the sun was shining brightly through the window as I held the piece of paper in my hand,' Charlotte wrote. 'It was unfathomable – suddenly here were his words in front of me, almost ten years after he'd written them:

My above everything beloved darling,
    You must know it all by now: Today I was sentenced to death by hanging by the *Volksgerichtshof*, to be carried out here at Plötzensee prison.
    My thoughts were with you on the black day, the 20th July, seeking you out. In the following weeks too, when I was sitting with the Gestapo police – I was talking to you every day, through the distance, and stroking each of my children. All my passionate thoughts and feelings surrounded you and the children.
    My professional life is nothing more than a memory now, full of hope and adventure though it was.
    I found my complete happiness with you, my darling you, and I thank you for it from the bottom of my heart. Our love is immortal and will last for ever. Don't mourn me, but live as though I were looking over your shoulder, living and laughing with you all!
    You must remain at Trebbow, come what may, and attach yourself to it. That's the right thing to do. Kiss each and every one of my children, with them I had nothing but joy, my lively genii. And you, my darling genius of love, hold me as close and dear as I do you, as tight and as trusting as it was from the very first. What we were together was finally unreachable, but the story will right itself in the end and set us free. You know it was

the love of our *Vaterland* which drove me to do what I did.

Forgive me all the worry, anxieties and difficulties which I have brought on you!

Send greetings to all our friends

All, all my love,

always your Fritzi

ACKNOWLEDGEMENTS

I would like to thank, first and foremost, the families of the six characters in *The Good Germans*. Without them, the book could never have been written. They have supplied memoirs, letters, photographs and personal memories. Between us, and through the six stories, I hope we have been able to remind our readers what it must have been like to be one of the two thirds of Germans who never voted for the Nazis, but had, nevertheless, to suffer the Nazi terror regime, the war which inevitably followed, and the terrible aftermath with all its guilt and recriminations. Not everyone amongst that two thirds showed the kind of bravery which distinguishes our six, but they all had to live through those terrifying times. Many others, quite unknown, were as brave. Only look at the statistics: contrary to popular myth, the Germans never managed to match the Allies in their war production – not in artillery, nor tanks, nor planes, nor ships. Sabotage by millions of anonymous workers is the answer. *The Second World Wars* by V.D. Hanson, Basic Books 2020, gives chapter and verse.

In order of appearance in the book: I'd like to thank Kirsten Engelmann, the widow of Bernt Engelmann. After the war Engelmann became a highly respected journalist, with a special mission: to out as many former Nazis as possible. Then comes Annette von Schlabrendorff, Fabian's granddaughter, who kindly liaised for me with his four sons, filling in the details. After the war Fabian took up his law profession, and in that capacity tried to get compensation for his resistance friends, those who survived, including Ernst Niekisch, the former editor of the journal *Widerstand*. Achim Ditzen is the last of Rudolf and Suse's three children. I thank him for several interesting and helpful telephone calls. The plan was to meet in Berlin, but Covid-19 intervened. The same, too, with Vera Dehle-Thälmann, Irma's daughter. She confirmed many details of Irma and Rosa's story, including the life they led after the war in Communist East Germany, keeping the memory of Ernst Thälmann alive. For Irma the fall of the Berlin Wall in 1989 was like a betrayal. Adelheid Gowrie, the sixth and last of Fritzi and Charlotte's children was my main source for the von der Schulenburg story. Beyond giving me her mother and aunt Tisa's memoirs and letters, she was something of an inspiration for this book. Special thanks go to her. Lastly I thank Katharina Leber's children David Heinemann and his sister Julia, the grandchildren of Julius and Annedore, who has carried on his mother's and grandmother Annedore's mission to keep the memory of Julius, the great Social Democrat, and his circle of resisters alive.

Gerd Stratmann was an indispensable help to me in tracing the families of these six characters. The only one I knew personally at the start was Adelheid Gowrie, known as Neiti. I might ring Professor Stratmann up in Berlin and tell him that one of my characters was Bernt Engelmann, but where was his family? Within days he'd call back with a name, an email address or a telephone number. It never failed. Some took longer, because the link went through the female line and the names had changed, but sooner or later there he was, back on the line. At other times he found key texts and documents, passing them on with a few comments of his own by way of context. Luckily I speak German. Best of all was his cheerful can-do attitude, never giving up on a lead. I thank him with *herzlichen Dank*.

The Gedenkstätte Deutscher Widerstand, German Resistance Memorial Centre, in Berlin was a key source for this book. I thank the Director, Dr Johannes Tuchel, very much for his generous help with documents, books, articles and photographs. His own work 'Kontakte zwischen Sozialdemokraten und Kommunisten im Sommer 1944 – Zur historischen Bedeutung des 22 Juni 1944' published in *Dachauer Hefte 11* in 1995, charting the contact and collaboration between Julius Leber and his Social Democrat colleagues with the German Communists round Anton Saefkow and Franz Jacob in June 1944 in the lead-up to the 20 July Plot, was indispensable to this book. I would recommend anyone on a visit to Berlin to spend some hours in the Memorial Centre. It is a deeply affecting and impressive record of the extraordinary bravery shown by so many, known and unknown, during the Nazi period. The fact that it took Germany until 1980 to found such a memorial seems to tell its own story.

I would also like to thank Erika Becker and Stephan Knuppel at the Hans Fallada Archives. They provided documents and photographs from the archive, and a most delightful tour of the house in Carwitz, which has been left very much as it was in Rudolf and Suse Ditzen's day, surrounded by Suse's garden and situated by one of those beautiful silent lakes so typical of the Mecklenburg area. A wonderful place to visit.

The book is dedicated to Anthony Sheil, agent and friend. His last act of friendship to me before he died was to pass me on to his colleague at Aitken Alexander Associates, Clare Alexander. What a bit of luck! It only took Clare two weeks to place *The Good Germans* with Weidenfeld, so persuasive is she. I thank her for it. And also for some very useful pieces of advice offered along the way. She couldn't have found a better home for the book than Weidenfeld. Between them, the editors Alan Samson and Aruna Vasudevan knocked it into shape, clipping and smoothing it here and there, Alan with a broad stroke, Aruna with a very fine one, focusing brilliantly on the detail. I thank them both. As I do the rest of the production team at Weidenfeld, deftly led by Clarissa Sutherland.

Lastly I'd like to thank the London Library. When I was setting out to write this book I expected to spend a lot of time in German libraries reading the speeches and letters and texts of my six characters. I'll just pop into the London Library before I go, I thought. You never know. And, sure enough, there in the back stacks, hidden away in the gloom and dust of seventy years, I found them: books written by one or other of my characters, published way back in the 1950s and 1960s. I have to assume an unknown German, a former resister perhaps, had decided to emigrate to London after the war, bringing their books with them, and bequeathing them to the London Library for safe keeping before they died. Incredibly, Irma Thälmann's memoir of her father, published in 1954, had never been taken out by anyone from that day to this. Likewise the slim, faded volume of Thälmann's speeches and texts, published in East Berlin in 1951. It's hard to describe the joy of being the very first to open a musty volume after over seventy years. Schlabrendorff's memoir, Annedore Leber's memoir, one of Bernt Engelmann's, all there in the back stacks. And Hans Fallada's books too, of course, which were, by his own admission, largely autobiographical. Not to mention numerous unknown memoirs by unknown Germans fleeing the country which had caused them so much suffering. I salute them, one and all.

ILLUSTRATIONS

Sources and permissions (by reference to photo number)

The families of our six characters have very kindly allowed us to reproduce the personal photographs in this book.

9, 20, 21, 24, 28, 35, 37: Dr Johannes Tuchel, Director of the Gedenkstätte Deutscher Widerstand, German Resistance Memorial Centre, Berlin, has kindly given permission for us to use these images

3, 14, 15, 25, 39: The Hans Fallada Archiv at Carwitz, Literaturzentrum Neubrandenburg, kindly allowed us to use the Fallada images

2: Look and Learn

7: With thanks to Landesarchiv, Berlin

8: Thormann Archive, with thanks to Peter Badel

18, 27: Alamy Ltd

33: Akg Images

36: Hans Hoffmann Collection, Bavarian State Library Munich/ Image Archive

NOTES

CHAPTER ONE: The Swastika

7   'Get that thing down': B. Engelmann, *Im Gleischritt Marsch*, memoir, vol. 1, p. 11.

8   Reichstag elections, November 1932: M. Housden, pp. 14, 15 and 23.

9   'Like a blazing fire . . .': Engelmann, *Im Gleichchritt Marsch*, memoir, vol. 1, p. 51.

10   Election results: Housden, pp. 14, 15 and 23.

10   'Three-quarters of the population lived in a single room . . .': Williams, p. 10.

11   'As soon as I have the power . . .': Housden, p. 12.

11   'There is no greater or more shameful . . .': Bredel, p. 17.

12   Schlabrendorff background: Begegnungen, memoir, pp. 11, 25, 30.

13   Ernst Niekisch: Schlabrendorff, p. 75.

17   'headaches, dizzy spells . . .': Walther, p. 54.

17   The suicide pact duel, Walther, 59.

17   ' . . . a decadent person . . .': Williams, p. 20.

18   ' . . . because I was just a lowly employee . . .': Walther, p. 79.

19   'Everything in my life . . .': Williams, Introduction.

19   Railway ticket costs: Williams, p. 61.

20   'But that's life . . .': Williams, p. 66.

20   'A thoroughly degenerate psychopath': Walther, p. 70.

20   'Prisoners who have served long sentences . . .': Williams, p. 80.

20   Election results: Housden, pp. 14, 15 and 23.

21   'I have never been so happy . . .': Williams, p. 85.

21   'poor Germany': Walther, p. 180.

22   Schleswig Holstein vote: Williams, p. 93.

23   'My parents often told me . . .': Irma Vester-Thalmann Erinnerungen, memoir, p. 11.

25   Hamburg uprising: Irma memoir, p. 13.

26   'Hamburg was a great city': Bredel, p. 25.

28   Liebknecht: Bredel, p. 46.

29   Thälmann speech, 10 July 1932: Bredel, p. 17.

CHAPTER TWO: The Nazis Take Power

30   Fritzi's wedding: Krebs, p. 94.

31 Rosenkranz rose-wreath and childhood: Tisa memoir, p. 9.

32 'You're like a boy': Tisa memoir, p. 22.

35 'By autumn 1932, Fritzi had been transfered to Heiligenbeil ...' and fishermen in crisis: Heinemann, pp. 10–18.

35 'I've become a National Socialist ...': Heinemann, p. 25.

36 Hitler and Goebbel's speeches: Heinemann, pp. 203, 318.

38 Thälmann's speech and arrest: Merson, p. 29; Irma memoir, p. 36.

39 25 January 1933: Irma memoir, p. 40.

40 Herbert von Bismarck: Schlabrendorff, Begebnungen memoir, p. 168.

40 Reichstag fire arrests: Merson, p. 32. Also see Merson for further arrests of Communists: 'Unbekannte Dokumente' in BzG and for 'Berichte des Thalmann-Kuriers', 1964 and 1965. It left a small group: Dahlem, Florin, Pieck, Scher, Schubert, Schulte, Ulbricht and perhaps Merker. None were betrayed and only Schehr was arrested in November 1933. By the end of May, they had decided the situation was too dangerous and divided into two sections, Home and External, with their base in Paris.

40 SA raids: Peukart, p. 90.

41 Torture: Housden, p. 28.

41 Thälmann's arrest: Irma memoir, pp. 23, 42.

42 Wels' speech: Housden, p. 30; Anger, p. 19.

43 'Masterly ...': Williams, p. 107.

44 Berliner Illustrierte: Philip Brady's introduction to Little Man, What Now?

45 Ditzen quotes: Williams, pp. 93, 102, 119.

45 'It is a story about a marriage ...': Walther, p. 186.

45 'The despair and the love ...': Brady, p. xi.

45 'What we need ...': Williams, p. 117.

48 'People have said to me ...': Brady, p. xxv.

49 'SA troop in their brown shirts ...': Sebastian Haffner, Defying Hitler, p. 124.

49 Theodor Eicke: Engelmann, Im Gleichschritt Memoir, vol. 1, p. 114.

50 Ernst Niekisch: Schlabrendorff memoir, pp. 77, 81.

51 Sigismund Lauter: Schlabrendorff memoir, p. 60.

52 'The day will come ...': Beck, p. 122.

53 'Socialism isn't party political ...': Leber, Ein Mann, p. 102.

53 'He who provokes the demonstrationing worker ...': Beck, pp. 122, 128.

53 'Today the worker stands': Leber, Ein Mann, pp. 82, 88.

54 31 January: Beck, p. 129.

54 'Now it's clear for all to see ...': Leber, Ein Mann, p. 90.

55 Leber's arrest: Leber, p. 275; Beck, p. 130.

56 'Carefully, I went through the train ...': Annedore's memoir; Beck, p. 133.

CHAPTER THREE: 1933 and All That

57   'A beautiful green Thursday . . .': Leber, *Ein Mann*, p. 251.

57   'He who wants to earn the name of politician . . .': Beck, p. 69.

57   '. . . she found a rooftop near the prison . . .': Annedore memoir.

58   'I've just discovered that one of the prisoners . . .': Beck, p. 137.

58   'No newspapers yesterday . . .': Beck, p. 216.

59   'In the last two days, the elm . . .': Leber, *Ein Mann*, p. 251.

59   'His old enemy Wittern . . .': Beck, p. 102.

61   'He was sentenced to . . .': Leber, *Ein Mann*, pp. 251–3; see his trial transcripts 27/5/33, as reported in *Lübecker Generalanzeiger*, Beck, p. 129.

62   'So now we're outlawed once and for all . . .': Beck, p. 116.

63   'His warm heart for everyone in need . . .': Krebs, p. 89.

64   'I would regret it . . .': Heinemann, p. 36.

65   'I imagined much different after the *Machtergreifung* . . .': Heinemann, p. 41.

65   'The Focke-Wulf factory in Bremen . . .': Housden, p. 43.

66   Army statistics: Grunberger, p. 182.

66   'The boss gave a talk at one of the last workforce meetings . . .': Housden, p. 40.

66   *Kraft durch Freude* movement: Housden, p. 41.

67   *Volkswagen* and *Volksempfange*, the people's wireless/radio: Adam Tooze, *The Wages of Destruction* (Penguin 2007), p. 147.

67   The Volk: Housden, p. 23.

68   'bottling peas and beans . . .': Tisa memoir, pp. 51, 75.

69   The Simons and Fritz Hess: Tisa memoir, pp. 84, 92.

70   Tisa's marriage and leaving Germany: Tisa memoir, p. 94.

71   Brothers and father Nazis: Tisa memoir, p. 99.

72   Frau Ney and the group: Engelmann, *Im Gleichschritt Memoir*, vol. 1, p. 160.

74   Herr Desch: Engelmann, *Im Gleichschritt Memoir*, vol. 1, p. 167.

75   Bernt's friends: Engelmann, *Im Gleichschritt Memoir*, vol. 1.

77   'Rosa . . . these hours . . .': Irma memoir, p. 21.

77   'After the Reichstag fire by the murder worker . . .': Irma memoir, p. 41.

78   Hitler salute: Housden, p. 72.

78   'Total dominance over the Reich . . .': McDonough, p. 13.

79   'We train our youth to use their bodily strength . . .': Kater, p. 18.

79   'A mentally ill person costs the community . . .': Housden, p. 73.

79   'Our *Gymnasium* was quite an old-fashioned place . . .': Housden, p. 76.

80   'The meaning of 1 May . . .': Irma memoir, p. 44.

82   Prison visit: Irma memoir, p. 51.

83   Funeral of Thalmann's father and Thalmann's letter: Irma memoir, p. 56.

CHAPTER FOUR: Early Years of Nazi Rule

85   *Volksgerichtshof*, The People's Court: Koch, Introduction.
85   Hitler and Goebbels quotes: Koch, pp. 24, 4.
88   The Sponats: Walther, p. 213.
89   The twins, Lore and Edith: Walther, p. 216.
89   'Quite honestly . . .': Williams, p. 146.
90   'a genuine old farmhouse': Walther, p. 218.
90   Suse, 'the most wonderful woman in the world': Williams, p. 144.
92   '. . . to write a foreword to bring the book more in line with Nazi regulations . . .': Williams, p. 153.
92   'The only possible thing would be to emigrate . . .': Kuhnke, p. 103.
93   Martha Dodd, 'It was a lovely spring day when we started': Dodd, *Through Embassy Eyes*, 1939.
95   'Please, my son, don't write anything political . . .': Kuhnke, p. 42.
96   Description of Ernst Rowohlt: Dodd, p. 75.
96   'Anyone who is committed to politics . . .': Schlabrendorff, memoir, p. 77.
98   Carl von Ossietzky: Mommsen, p. 9.
98   'All the churches are the same . . .': Housden, p. 46.
98   Martin Niemöller: Housden, p. 47; Schmidt, Pastor Niemöller, 1959.
99   Niemöller, '*When the Nazis came for the communists . . .*': McDonough, p. 66.
100 Kleist-Schmenzin's escape: Schlabrendorff, memoir, p. 112.
100 New Years Eve: Engelmann, *Im Gleichschritt Memoir*, vol. 1, p. 124.
102 Pastor Klotzel: Engelmann, vol. 1, p. 132.
103 'I must admit, I've really been shaken by the Strasser thing . . .': Heinemann, p. 185.
103 Fritzi and Charlotte retreat to the country: Krebs, p. 115.
104 Fischhausen, east of the Elbe: Heinemann, p. 44.
105 Letter to Erich Koch: Heinemann, pp. 188, 313.

CHAPTER FIVE: Hard Times: 1935

107 'We were still in bed when the doorbell rang . . .': Irma memoir, p. 57.
109 *Mutti*'s prison visit, Irma memoir, p. 60.
111 Thälmann's letter, 'My dearest Rosa! . . .': Irma memoir, p. 64.
111 '*Vater*'s thoughts were often with the great . . .': Irma memoir, p. 66.
113 Statistics for Communist functionaries, cells and presses since January 1933: Merson, pp. 182, 225; Housden, p. 28.
113 Communist presses: Allen, p. 858; Pikarski and Ubel, p. 22; Merson, p. 116; Housden, p. 33.
113 Bavarian Autobahn leaflet: Pikarski and Ubel, p. 54; Housden, p. 33.
114 SPD activities: Marslock and Ott, p. 218; *Bremen im Dritten Reich*; Housden, p. 32.

114 Catholic resistance: Housden, pp. 50, 51.
115 'Hitler announced to the world that compulsory military service . . .': Engelmann, *Im Gleichschritt Memoir*, vol. 1, p. 214.
116 'It was Friday 6 March . . .': Engelmann, vol. 1, p. 216.
121 General Jodl and Hitler's translator, Paul Schmidt: Engelmann, vol. 1, p. 229.
122 Letters to Annedore: Beck, pp. 143, 153, 155; *Annedore Fur und Wieder*, p. 183.
123 'Only now is it becoming clear to me . . .': Leber, *Ein Mann*, p. 262.
124 'You found my last letter too short . . .': Leber, p. 259.
125 SOPADE Report: Beck, p. 156.
125 'Christmas lies before us . . .': Leber, *Ein Mann*, p. 262.
125 'Co-operate in large international projects': Hilton, p. 1.
126 Swiss Olympic Committee comments: Hilton, p. 31.
127 Broadcasting statistics: Hilmes, p. 2.
127 'German sport has only one task . . .': Hilton, p. 13.
128 German Youth and sport: Housden, p. 74.
129 Hitler on Youth, '. . . I am beginning with the young . . .': Housden, p. 68; H. Rauschning, 'Hitler Speaks': p. 246.
129 Goebbels' party: Dodd, p. 202.

CHAPTER SIX: The Nazis Tighten the Screw

131 'The title says it all': Walther, p. 217.
132 Rudolf's letter to his sister: Williams, p. 160.
132 'Once we had a Hans Fallada . . .': Walther, p. 249.
132 'I just stood up and said they had better choose . . .': Williams, p. 165.
133 Ernst Rowohlt: Dodd, p. 74.
134 'I can no longer write what I want to write . . .': Williams, p. 168.
134 Rudolf's transfer to La Charite Hospital: Walther, p. 259.
134 *Berliner Illustrierte* serialisation, 10,000 Reichmarks: Walther, p. 262.
135 Objections to the character of 'Herr Doktor Kimmknirsch': Williams, p. 179.
135 Rowohlt, 'a broken and tragic figure': Dodd, p. 74.
136 'end up in a drawer': *Wolf among Wolves*, p. 799.
139 'I used to think courage meant . . .': *Wolf among Wolves*, p. 799.
140 'It is now so wonderful here that it makes my heart glad . . .': Williams, p. 184.
140 Goebbels, 'A terrific book!': Williams, p. 186.
141 *Heimwerk Samland* and *Wein Stube*: Krebs, p. 120.
141 'When Schulenburg appeared in the village . . .': Krebs, p. 125.
143 'Summer parties in the garden of the Schulenburgs' official residence . . .': Krebs, p. 126.
143 Wilhelm's death: Tisa memoir, p. 104.

145 Back in England, Tisa memoir, p. 106.
146 'Koch has lately been complaining . . .': Heinemann, p. 45.
146 Fritzi 'leaving Fischhausen was hard . . .': Krebs, p. 138.
146 Klaus von der Groeben: Krebs, p. 140.
147 'At first he didn't want me, but his other suggestions for the post were rejected . . .': Heinemann, p. 47.
147 February 1938 memo about language: Heinemann, p. 48.
147 Paper, March 1938: Heinemann, p. 194.
148 Funeral of a Communist, Adam Schaefer: Mason, p. 315.
148 Letters from Sachsenhausen, Leber, *Ein Mann*, p. 262.
149 Informers: Dodd, p. 233.
149 'You either have to rule . . .': Leber, *Ein Mann*, p. 177.
149 'Thoughts on the Banning of German Social Democracy', *Gedanken zum Verbot*: Leber, *Ein Mann*, p. 187.
151 Gustav Dahrendorf: Beck, pp. 162, 144.
152 Annedore Leber quotes: Leber, *Die Toten*, pp. 4, 6.
153 Hitler and Goebbels quotes: Taylor, pp. 384–6.
153 SOPADE report: Housden, p. 73.
153 Hitler Youth: Housden, p. 78.

CHAPTER SEVEN: Turning Point: 1938

155 Prison visit: Irma memoir, p. 36.
155 Hamburg shipyard resistance: Meehan, p. 64.
156 *Vater* and Irma letters, Irma memoir, p. 71.
157 Trying to find a job: Irma memoir, p. 66.
157 Karl Liebknecht: Bredel, p. 47.
157 Thälmann letters: Thälmann Briefe, p. 163.
159 Thälmann's transfer: Bredel, p. 164.
160 Lenin and hate: Bredel, p. 96.
160 Thälmann speech: Bredel, p. 104.
160 *News Chronicle* on Thalmann: Bredel, p. 146.
161 Wilhelm Pieck's leaflets, 'Free Ernst Thälmann!': Irma memoir, p. 69.
162 'There is a real danger': Bredel, p. 22.
163 'I believe that it was God's will': Clay, *Trautmann's Journey*, p. 56.
164 'When he walked into a room, he always stood out . . .': Schlabrendorff, Begegnungen, memoir, p. 121.
164 Werner von Fritsch, Commander-in-Chief of the Army: Schlabrendorff, p. 120.
165 Himmler quote, 'It is absolutely essential for you . . .': Meehan, p. 42.
165 Kleist-Schmenzin: Schlabrendorff, p. 121.
165 'You do not believe this is the end . . .': Ian Colvin, p. 210.
166 Quote, Hambros' bank employee: Meehan, p. 52.
166 'In Berlin the best opinion is that Hitler . . .': Shirer, p. 124.

166 the many informers to London: Meehan, pp. 3, 48.

168 New democratic government ready in wings: Meehan, p. 3.

168 'A Herr von Kleist': Docs of British Foreign Policy, p. 683 onwards, in Appendix under 'Unofficial German Approaches, Aug–Sep 1938'.

169 Nevile Henderson letters: Docs of British Foreign Policy, pp. 58, 63, 78.

169 Lazy Halifax: 'The Foreign Secretary said he was very lazy and disliked work ...': Meehan, p. 13. Note: Tim Bouverie's *Appeasing Hitler* gives excellent chapter and verse on this whole subject.

170 'Sir Nevile Henderson was an emotional man ...': Colvin, pp. 210, 214.

170 Sir Robert Vansittart and Cadogan: Meehan, p. 19.

170 Beck memo: H. A. Jacobsen, *Germans against Hitler* (Press and Information Office of the Federal Government of Germany, 1969), pp. 23–4.

171 Colvin's report: Colvin, p. 218.

171 Ewald von Kleist-Schmenzin in England: Four Documents of British Foreign Policy, p. 683 onwards.

174 Hans Oster: Schlabrendorff memoir, p. 173.

175 Churchill's reaction: Meehan, pp. 1 and 2.

175 'International atmosphere stormy': Hassell diary, p. 49, unabridged German version.

176 Kristallnacht: Engelmann, *Im Gleichshritt Memoir*, vol. I, p. 284.

177 Public reaction to Kristallnacht: Meehan, p. 54.

178 Kulle, 'Are you mad?': Engelmann, vol. I, p. 304.

179 Werner's father, 'the Communist, had been arrested ...': Engelmann, vol. I, p. 321.

180 Herr Desch and Fräulein Bonse: Engelmann, vol. I, p. 325.

CHAPTER EIGHT: The Road to War: 1939

182 Descriptions of Fritz-Dietlof: Krebs, p. 140.

183 Fritzi in Berlin: Heinemann, p. 46.

183 March 1938 lecture: Krebs, p. 165.

184 Hitler and 'dry nit-picking pen-pushers' and Fritzi's response: Heinemann, pp. 51, 53.

184 'We are obliged to depopulate ...': Housden, p. 13, source: H. Rauschning, *Hitler Speaks*, 1939. Note: Rauschning was present at many of Hitler's early Table Talks, but soon broke away, giving up his Nazi Party membership, and by 1936 he had emigrated, ending up in America. Historians are divided about the exact accuracy of his quotes, but not their general import. One of his earliest critics was the Swiss Wolfgang Hanel, a Holocaust denier. Later, David Irving.

184 Fritzi's visit to Witzleben: Heinemann, p. 50.

185 The radio reports: Shirer, pp. 159–62.

185 Graf von der Schulenburg, Fritzi's father's death and burial: Krebs, p. 148.

186 Tisa goes back to Germany: Tisa memoir, p. 112.

188 *Vater*'s death and aftermath: Tisa memoir, p. 116.

189 'Flew over my area of Silesia . . .': Heinemann, p. 54.

190 Cadogan quote: Meehan, p. 20.

190 Colvin and Kleist-Schmenzin meeting in the Casino Gesellschaft Club:
     Schlabrendorff memoir, p. 136.

191 Fabian in England: Schlabrendorff memoir, p. 139.

192 Gerd von Tresckow: Schlabrendorff memoir, p. 186.

193 Tresckow, 'Hitler wants war . . . And that will be the death of Germany':
     Schlabrendorff memoir, p. 190.

194 'Among the upper classes, the Gestapo . . .': Dodd, p. 235.

195 10,000 in exile, 'fled and emigrated': Merson, p. 182.

195 Dresden police report: Housden, p. 37; Mason, *Arbeiterklasse und
     Volksgemeindschaft*, p. 722.

196 Alma Stobbe: Engelmann memoir, p. 78.

196 Gestapo report: 'In March of last year, several new personalities in the
     Communist Party formed an alliance . . .': Engelmann memoir, p. 80.

196 Communist sabotage: Merson, pp.187–8. Note: statistics of war produc-
     tion in Hanson show that German output, contrary to the usual statistics
     quoted, was far behind the British and American output. This could have
     been down to the highly effective sabotage cells in the German arma-
     ments factories.

198 Harnack and 'Erdmann': Housden, p. 34; Merson, p. 196.

198 The Red Orchestra statistics: Benz and Pehle, p. 281.

199 Leber, 'My greatest happiness . . .': Beck, p. 160.

199 Niekisch on Esterwegen Concentration Camp, 'It was barbaric . . .':
     Niekisch, *Das Reich der niederen Daemonen*, p. 121.

200 'The Will To Power is no more than a slogan . . .': Leber, p. 177.

200 Schwamb: Annedore Leber memoir, *Die Toten*.

201 'Two small rooms in the little house . . .': Beck, p. 169.

372 Births, marriages and deaths: *The Times*, with thanks to the Times
     Room, London Library.

203 'The ideal German should be: as blond as Hitler, as tall as Goebbels, and
     as slim as Göring,' joke: Housden, p. 168.

203 Euthanasia, Hadamar: Housden, p. 57.

203 Statistics of euthanasia: Christopher Browning, NYB, October 2018.

204 Kurt Gerstein: Housden, p. 170.

205 Intended assassination: Georg Elser, McDonough, and Pridham, vol. 4,
     p. 592.

206 'All Germany is talking about the attempt on Hitler's life at Bürgerbräu
     . . .': Hassell diary, p. 141, unabridged German version.

207 KPD announcement: Merson, p. 213.

CHAPTER NINE: Into the Darkness

209 *Iron Gustav* film contract: Walther, p. 282.
209 'The *Vater*, he held the power . . .': Manthey, p. 134.
209 Else Bakonyi: Williams, p. 280.
210 'This month is marked in black in my diary . . .': Foreward to *Iron Gustav*, Williams.
210 'It's one thing to sit at your writing desk . . .': Manthey, p. 130.
211 'Rudolf seriously thought of emigrating . . .': Williams, p. 197.
213 Rudolf's earnings per month: Walther, p. 287.
214 Fall of France, June 1940: Clay, p. 74.
215 Heydrich, 'In all previous actions . . .': Housden, p. 149; Federal Archive R19/395.
215 'Wolff told me . . .': Hassell diary, p. 157, unabridged German version.
216 Hitler, 'I wish to have a population which is racially impeccable . . .': Rees, p. 146.
216 Franck, 'We can only talk of these things . . .': Rees, p. 150.
216 *Der Ewige Jude*, 'Wherever rats appear . . .': Clay, p. 78.
217 Christmas 1940: Williams, p. 212.
218 Rationing: Engelmann, memoir, vol. 2, *Bis alles in Scherben fallt*, p. 15.
218 Rosa's memories: Irma memoir, p. 78.
220 'After the Fascist army . . .': Irma memoir, p. 80.
220 'Terrible that it's come to this!': Irma memoir, p. 62.
221 Semaphore and slates and camera: Irma memoir, p. 83.
222 Prison visit: Irma memoir, p. 80.
222 'The Instructors are still getting through . . .' and other KPD activity: Merson, p. 188.
222 Thälmann in contact with KPD: Thalmann Briefe, p. 10.
223 International Mineworkers Federation: Merson, p. 203.
223 War Economy Decree, September 1939: Mason, p. 309.
224 Marie Jalowicz Simon: Simon, *Gone to Ground*, p. 24.
224 20 Marks a week: Engelmann memoir, vol. 2, p. 140.
224 Catholic Poles: Housden, p. 59.
225 Isle of Sylt: Engelmann, memoir, vol. 2, p. 31.
230 Swing Youth: Housden, p. 86.
231 Into France: Engelmann, memoir, vol. 2, *Bis alles in Scherben fallt*, p. 98.

CHAPTER TEN: A War on Two Fronts

233 'Hitler launched Operation Barbarossa . . .': statistics: Martin Collier and Philip Pedley, *Hitler and the Nazi State* (Heinemann, 2005), p. 86.
234 Clandestine Resistance group White Rose's pamphlets: I. Scholl, *The White Rose, 1942–43* (Weslyan University Press, 1983), pp. 73, 78.

235 'So Fabian had good reason to disappear into the army . . .': Schlabrendorff Begegnungen memoir, p. 192.

235 Helmuth von Moltke, 'Dear Yorck . . .': Balfour, p. 127.

236 Henning, 'War is madness . . .': Scheurig, p. 67.

236 Description of Schlabrendorff and the group round Henning: Scheurig, p. 98.

236 Description of Henning, 'Though he was a military man through and through . . .': Scheurig, p. 33.

236 Hitler's plans to invade Russia: Schlabrendorff, p. 197.

237 'The Soviet Kommissars': J. Keegan, p. 186.

237 Hitler, 'Dear Herr Stalin . . .': R. Murphy, *A Diplomat Among Warriors*, p. 257.

238 Führer Befehl: Schlabrendorff, p. 198; Scheurig, p. 102.

239 Hitler's visit to Borissow: Schlabrendorff, p. 200.

240 General Halder, 'He's playing warlord again': the Halder diaries, in Keegan, p. 193.

240 'Then came Führer Order 33': Clay, p. 117.

241 Ulrich von Hassell's country house at Ebenhausen: Foreword, Hassell diaries, unabridged German version.

241 'A few days ago Sch(labendorff) reserve lieutenant and lawyer, turned up, . . .': Hassell diary, unabridged German version, p. 278.

242 Goebbels and propaganda quotes: Kellner, p. 142.

243 Catholic Bishop Galen quotes: Ibid.

243 Goebbels, reported in the *Frankfurter Zeitung*, 14 December 1941: Kellner, p. 156.

244 Meeting with Field Marshal von Bock: Schlabrendorff, p. 211.

245 Fritzi, 'I want my children to be brought up with a deep and personal sense of religion . . .': Heinemann, p. 200 onwards, private letters.

246 Dr Seifarth's testimony about Schulenburg and Hitler's assassination: Heinemann, p. 55.

246 Fritzi's turning point 1938: Archiv Peter, Kaltenbrunner Berichte an Bormann und Hitler uber das Attentat von 20 Juli 1944, Geheime Documente aus dem ehemaligen Reichsicherheitshauptamt, Karl Heinrich Peter, Spiegelbild einer Verschworung, pp. 212, 501, and, earlier, p. 259, pub. Stuttgart 1961.

246 The *Grafenkreis*, 'the circle of Counts': Heinemann, p. 92.

247 Fritzi's meetings with Kreisau and Tresckow (Smolensk): Heinemann, p. 99.

247 Fritzi to Charlotte, June 1940, 'I feel truly freed!': Heinemann, p. 64.

247 Fritzi and Axel von dem Bussche: memoir by his friends, p. 136.

248 Fritzi's letters to Charlotte, 'Last night we went on maneouvres . . .': Heinemann, p. 208.

249 Fritzi's diary, 20 June to November 1941: Krebs, p. 209.

249 '"parasitic" Capitalism': Krebs, p. 219.

250 Fritzi meets Hassell in Berlin: Hassell diary, unabridged German version,

p. 288.

252 Fritzi, 'Ali, pray for Charlotte and the children . . .': Krebs, p. 234.

253 'Kluge was like the moon . . .': Schlabrendorff, p. 223.

253 Hassell, 'a bad month lies behind us . . .': Hassell diaries, unabridged German version, p. 338.

254 Fabian's visit to Beck, 'Beck himself opened the door . . .': Schlabrendorff, p. 269.

255 Battle in Stalingrad, 'Then came Stalingrad . . .': Kellner, p. 232.

255 Hitler Youth magazine on Stalingrad, 'The homeland will never know the likes . . .': Ibid.

256 Fritzi to Charlotte, letter, 4 April 1943, 'The burden of work has exhausted me . . .': Heinemann, p. 208.

256 'Fritzi Schulenburg was arrested . . .': Hassell diary, unabridged German version, p. 362.

257 'I'm not getting anywhere with Manstein . . .': Schlabrendorff, p. 224.

257 Army Group Centre assassination attempt: Schlabrendorff memoir, p. 227.

257 The bottle bomb, 'The bomb was small enough to fit into a packet containing two bottles of Cointreau . . .': Scheurig, pp. 127–45.

260 Lauter hid the dynamite, 'Fabian settled instead on Professor Sigismund Lauter . . .': Schlabrendorff memoir, p. 61.

260 The Gersdorff bomb attempt, '[Gersdorff] put himself forward as the next assassin . . .': Schlabrendorff memoir, p. 143.

260 Dubno, Ukraine and Axel von dem Bussche as assassin: by his friends, pp. 225, 149.

261 'It was one of six known attempts on Hitler's life': Der Spiegel, 20 July issue, p. 104.

261 'Schulenburg also showed up again . . .': Balfour, p. 201; Krebs, p. 265.

262 Axel and the uniforms, von dem Bussche's assassination attempt: by his friends, p. 139; and his interview in The Restless Conscience documentary, director Hava Kohav Beller.

CHAPTER ELEVEN: Back in the Reich

263 No Communist heroes: Merson, p. 2. For example, Alan Bullock in The Third Reich, claimed the German Communist Party collapsed in 1933 with little resistance. Likewise Wheeler-Bennett, in The Nemesis of Power, William Shirer, in The Rise and Fall of the Third Reich, Richard Grunberger, in A Social History of the Third Reich, and Terence Prittie, in Germans Against Hitler, with a Foreword by Hugh Trevor-Roper, criticised by Professor Geoffrey Barraclough as 'a lone voice'. Things only began to change mid-1960s, e.g. with T. W. Mason's Labour in the Third Reich and Horst Duhnke's Die KPD von 1933 bis 1945.

263 Irma's essay, 'write about what interests you most': Irma memoir, p. 27.

264 Thälmann, 'On the left of his bed . . .': Bredel, p. 164.

265 Irma visits *Vater*, 'It was an unforgettable experience . . .': Irma memoir, p. 83.

266 Irma, 'I'd hardly arrived before the sirens went off . . .': Irma memoir, p. 85.

266 Irma's Bautzen visit, 'Her suitcase was too heavy . . .': Irma memoir, p. 87.

269 Walter Lesser, visit to Thälmann in Bautzen: Bredel, p. 173.

269 Communist worker resistance, Housden, p. 135; Merson, p. 309. By 1945, some 30,000 KPD members had been murdered, executed or found dead in a concentration camp, and see also: 'Resistance from Worker's Movement', Gedenkstätte Deutscher Widerstand, Berlin, German Resistance Memorial Centre.

271 Rudolf Ditzen/Fallada, 'From the minute I sit down and write the first line . . .': John Willett, Introduction, *The Drinker*.

271 'What I can't find words to describe . . .': Fallada, *Heute bei uns zu Haus*, pp. 57, 9.

272 Ditzen, 'I tell some terrible lies in it . . .': Williams, p. 220.

272 Ditzen to Suse, 'I hope you realise that your prospect is one . . .': Willett, Introduction, *The Drinker*.

274 Kutisker case novel, 'a famous fraud case of the 1920s . . .': Walther, pp. 340, 343; Williams, pp. 216, 233.

274 Letter to sister about 'anti-Semitic' book: with thanks to the Hans Fallada Archive.

274 Goebbels diary entry, 29 May 1943: Walther, p. 337.

276 'He was in the hallway . . .': Willett, *The Drinker*, p. 79.

276 Red Orchestra leaflets: with thanks to Dr Johannes Tuchel at the Gedenkstätte Deutscher Widerstand, German Resistance Memorial Centre, Berlin.

278 Tisa's brother Heini, 'It's over for me too': Tisa memoir, p. 122.

279 Helmuth von Moltke and Oswald Wirisch: Krebs, p. 190; Peter, p. 466. Note: For Fritzi contacts re: 20 July plot see: Archiv Peter, pp. 212, 501, 259.

279 Fritzi's happy marriage to Charlotte, 'In a word he was happy . . .': Tisa memoir, p. 123.

279 Fritzi in Breslau: Krebs, p. 186.

280 Tisa's marriage to Carl Ulrich von Barner and move to Trebbow: Tisa memoir, p. 126.

281 Tisa's wireless, 'It stood next to my bed . . .': Tisa memoir, p. 129.

283 'Christmas and New Year, Fritzi was with us . . .': Charlotte private memoir, with thanks to Adelheid Gowrie.

283 Fritzi's visit home, and his will, January 1944: Krebs, pp. 284–6.

284 Fritzi and Charlotte visits to old friends: Krebs, p. 292.

284 Bernt's summer 1942 leave: Engelmann, memoir, vol. 2, p. 233.

284 Journalist Ursula von Kardoff, Berlin, 'Here the most depressing things are happening . . .': Fulbrook, p. 222.

287 Driver Krupa to Bernt, 'They've arrested Erwin': Engelmann, vol. 2, p. 321.

287 Göring in Paris: Engelmann, vol. 2, p. 228.

287 Bruneval, part of the communications unit at British Command in Cap d'Antifer: Engelmann, vol. 2, p. 222.

290 Bernt's arrest, 2 March 1944: Engelmann, vol. 2, p. 375.

CHAPTER TWELVE: The End

293 Leber, 'In general it is not the present . . .': with thanks to the Gedenkstätte Deutscher Widerstand, German Resistance Memorial Centre, Berlin.

294 Klaus Bonhoeffer: Peter, Kaltenbrunner Berichte, for contacts between conspirators.

294 Leber, 'The aim: to create a unified Front . . .': Krebs, p. 172.

294 'Leber was, in Moltke's view "much less cultured than them"': Beck, p. 176.

295 Leber codename 'substitute Uncle': Moltke, *Letters to Freya*, p. 329.

296 Fritzi letter to Koch, 12 July 1933: Krebs, p. 111.

296 Meeting between Leber and Fritzi, 22 November: Annedore Leber memoir; Beck, p. 182.

297 'A later Gestapo report' on Fritzi: Archiv Peter: Kaltenbrunner Berichte, p. 273.

297 Fritzi, 'You can't make politics with literary and theoretical debate . . .': Archiv Peter: Kaltenbrunner Berichte, p. 300.

297 Fritzi favours Leber, 'the better man for the post': Mommsen, p. 202.

298 'Pfaff (Goerdeler) confirms that the preparations are really going ahead now . . .': Hassell diary unabridged German version, p. 400.

298 'Schulenburg was acting as a link between all groups . . .': Archiv Peter: Kaltenbrunner Berichte, pp. 206, 357, 300; Beck, p. 182.

299 Fritzi to Charlotte, 'I am of course stupid . . .': Balfour, p. 202.

299 Gestapo Report, 'The role of Schulenburg was uppermost': Archiv Peter: Kaltenbrunner Berichte, p. 206. For other Fritzi entries see Kaltenbrunner Berichte an Bormann und Hitler uber das Attentat von 20 Juli 1944, Geheime Documente aus dem ehemaligen Reichsicherheitshauptamt, Spiegelbild einer Verschworung, 212, 501, 259, 285 around summer 1943, Prosecution statement at Leber's trial. With thanks to Dr Johannes Tuchel at the Gedenkstätte Deutscher Widerstand, German Resistance Memorial Centre, Berlin.

299 Anton Saefkow, Franz Jacob and others: Tuchel Kontakte, p. 82 onwards.

300 Tresckow quote, 'The assassination attempt . . .': Mommsen, Introduction, p. 7.

301   Moltke and Leber's Socialist ideas: Beck, p. 181.

301   Moltke's arrest, 19 January 1944: Balfour, p. 297.

302   'Stauffenberg travelled to Trebbow ...': Archiv Peter: Kaltenbrunner Berichte, p. 305.

302   15 May 1944 discussions Leber–Schulenburg: Tuchel Kontakte, p. 82 onwards.

303   Leber on need for propaganda – crimes 'repeated to the Volk through broadcasts and the press': Beck, pp. 186, 192.

303   Field Marshal Witzleben anouncement in a wireless broadcast: *Der Spiegel*, 20 July issue, p. 105.

303   The New Order, Leber and Reichwein: Tuchel Kontakte, pp. 88, 90.

304   The New Order: Beck, p. 188; Roon, p. 589.

304   June 1944 meetings: Tuchel Kontakte, p. 90; Beck, p. 195; Merson, p. 286.

305   Bastlein's arrest, 30 May, and traitor Ernst Rambow: Tuchel Kontakte, p. 85.

305   There were about 400 in the Saefkow group, some 90 of whom were executed. With thanks to Johannes Tuchel of the Gedenkstätte Deutscher Widerstand, Berlin.

306   Leber's arrest by Gestapo: Merson, p. 286, Annedore Leber memoir.

306   Stauffenberg moves fast, 'he raced to finish his plans for Hitler's assassination ...': Momsen, p. 203.

306   Fromm confides in wife and daughter: *Der Spiegel*, 20 July issue, pp. 104, 106.

306   'The world lies under the cloud of an Invasion', 12 June 1944: Hassell diary, unabridged German version, pp. 430, 433, 437.

307   Arthur Nebe, Chief of Police: see Keyserlingk-Rehbein diagram of several links of resisters to Nebe in *Suddeutsche Zeitung*, 19 July 2019; with thanks to Professor Gerd Stratmann.

308   Schulenburg's method: Archiv Peter: Kaltenbrunner Berichte.

308   The wider circle: Krebs, p. 270.

308   Caesar von Hofacker: Krebs, p. 252.

308   Seifarth in France: Krebs, p. 255.

309   Contact with Tresckow: Krebs, p. 245.

309   Stauffenberg's appointment was not official till 1 July 1944.

309   Fromm hiding behind his 'mask of loyalty': *Der Spiegel*, 20 July issue, p. 107.

309   Stauffenberg, 'The man who does it ...': Housden, p. 106.

309   Stauffenberg delays attempt, then first attempt: *Der Spiegel*, 20 July issue.

311   Dittmann: Krebs, p. 295.

311   Fritzi's visit to Ursula von Kardorff: Krebs, p. 296.

312   Fabian von Schlabrendorff and Henning von Tresckow at Army Group Centre: Scheurig, p. 183.

312   Fritzi visits Dr Medicus, Department of Military Personnel, to delay his

trip to France: Krebs, p. 294.

312 Future peace negotiations involve Russia: Krebs, p. 296.

313 Fritzi asks Ursula von Kardoff to take roses to Annedore: Heinemann, p. 165.

313 'On 18 July, late in the evening . . .': Charlotte private memoir; with thanks to Adelheid Gowrie.

314 July 20 assassination attempt, military strategic meeting with Hitler: *Der Spiegel*, 20 July issue, pp. 109–14.

316 Witzleben's telegram stating Hitler was dead: Noakes, vol. 4, p. 621.

317 Beck quote from the memo: Housden, p. 103.

317 German wireless broadcast, 'For the second time in this war started by Jewry . . .': Noakes, vol. 4, p. 621.

317 Hitler's broadcast, 'German racial comrades!': Housden, p. 93.

318 Back at Army Group Centre: Scheurig, p. 190; Mommsen, Introduction.

319 Hassell arrest: Hassell diaries, p. 242; Wolf Ulrich's account.

321 Schulenburg at Bendler Strasse: Heinemann, p. 169; Annedore Leber and Freya von Moltke, *Fur und Wieder*, p. 114.

321 Schulenburg interrogation: Archiv Peter: Kaltenbrunner Berichte, pp. 256, 273, 416, 326, 455.

322 Schulenburg central to plot: Archiv Peter: Kaltenbrunner Berichte, p. 206; *Suddeutsche Zeitung* article, 19 July 2019, plus diagram showing all lines of contact leading to Schulenburg, 19 July 2019; with thanks to Professor Gerd Stratmann.

323 Friedler's account: Heinemann, p. 171.

323 Schulenburg's statement to the Court: Koch, p. 216; Krebs, p. 304.

323 Fritzi's last statement to Court: 'We took this task upon us, to protect Germany . . .': Heinemann, p. 172.

323 Leber's letter: Beck, p. 198 and 324.

324 Leber's interrogation: Archiv Peter: Kaltenbrunner, pp. 534, 179, 188, 497, 499, 546, 211, 212.

325 'my dear Paulus . . . I am filled with joy about the possibility of seeing you': Beck, p. 326.

325 Leber, 'a man of inner greatness'; Leber and Isa Vermehren in Ravensbrück: Beck, p. 200.

326 The trial and sentence: with thanks to Dr Johannes Tuchel at the Gedenkstätte Deutscher Widerstand, German Resistance Memorial Centre, and Beck, p. 202 and Mommsen Intro.

328 Leber's last letters: with thanks to Dr Johannes Tuchel at the Gedenkstätte Deutscher Widerstand, German Resistance Memorial Centre, Berlin; Beck, p. 332; and Annedore memoir.

329 Oster, Nebe, Bonhoeffer and von Schmenzin: Schlabrendorff, pp. 179–183, 279, 142.

330 In all 5,000 were arrested: McDonough, p. 56; Koch, p. 6, quoting Broszat. See German edition of Koch, 'In the Name of the Volk', for full accounts of trials.

330 Thälmann execution: Merson, p. 286.
330 Fabian at Flossenburg: Schlabrendorff, pp. 179–83.
331 Kleist-Schmenzin, 'I have always considered Hitler and National Social-
     ism as the arch enemy of the German Reich . . .': Schlabrendorff, p. 143.
332 'Freisler is dead': Schlabrendorff, p. 144.

CHAPTER THIRTEEN: Aftermath

335 Rudolf's extra-marital affairs, 'Sometimes my wife knew . . .': Williams,
     p. 231.
335 He had no intention of finishing the book, he told Rowohlt: Walther, p.
     340.
336 Rudolf applied to Reich Literary Chamber: Walther, p. 341; Williams, p.
     283.
336 'I know I am a weak man, but not a bad man': with thanks to the Hans
     Fallada Archive at Feldberg; Williams, p. 266.
337 Ulla Losch: Walther, p. 346.
337 Rudolf's mother's diary, 'Terrible days . . .': Walther, p. 368.
338 The Russians as friends: Walther, p. 369.
338 Lawyer committed suicide: Walther, p. 370.
338 Rudolf found in nightshirt at Kommandatur: Walther, p. 374.
339 Ulla's old apartment, Schoneburg district, Berlin: Walther, p. 377.
339 Johannes Becher and the *Kulturbund*: Williams, p. 249; Walther, p. 379.
339 Rudolf moves into a nice villa: Walther, p. 392.
340 Christmas 1945, with Becher and Wilhelm Pieck, Walther, p. 388.
341 'The first draft of 600 pages only took him 24 days to write': Walther,
     p. 413.
342 Rudolf to Suse, 'I have thought so much about our life . . .': Federlese,
     p. 58.
343 Irma, 23, living in Singen: Irma memoir, p. 91.
343 Thälmann speeches, 'We know a land where no Fascism . . .': Bredel,
     pp. 130, 134.
344 Thälmann to Irma, letter, 1936, 'Even if our name . . .': Irma memoir,
     p. 71.
344 Smuggling in the camera: Irma memoir, p. 81.
345 Irma's arrest: Irma memoir, p. 91.
346 Irma at Ravensbrück: Irma memoir, pp. 95, 82.
348 Irma and Rosa rescued – by Russian Army: Irma memoir, p. 100.
349 'How often I've studied the local map': Charlotte private memoir, p. 7;
     with thanks to Adelheid Gowrie.
350 'Fritzi is often with me', 21 April 1945: Charlotte private memoir,
     p. 56.
351 Friedrich Hildebrand and SS arrive at Trebbow: Charlotte private
     memoir, p. 29.

351 'Yes, your husband has made a very intelligent impression . . .': Charlotte private memoir, p. 47.

352 Fritzi to Tisa, 'Go back to England . . .', and Fritzi's resistance from 1938: Tisa's letter to Fritz Hess; with thanks to Adelheid Gowrie (Schulenburg) the sixth and last child, known as Neiti.

352 Carl Ulrich, 'Fritzi's dead': Charlotte private memoir, p. 35.

352 Werner Fiedler and account of Fritzi's trial: Charlotte private memoir, pp. 36–8.

352 April 1945, Charlotte and Tisa, fleeing Trebbow: Charlotte private memoir, p. 57.

353 Tisa's story: Charlotte private memoir.

356 Fritzi's letter, via Annedore Leber: Charlotte private memoir, p. 104.

BIBLIOGRAPHY

Balfour, M. (1988). *Withstanding Hitler.* New York: Routledge.

Beck, Dorothea, Julius Leber (1983). *Sozialdemokrat zwischen Reform und Widerstand.* Munich: Siedler Verlag.

Benz, Wolf and Walter H. Pehle (eds) (1994). *Lexikon des Deutschen Widerstands.* Frankfurt am Main: S. Fischer.

Bouverie, Tim (2019). *Appeasing Hitler.* London: Bodley Head.

Bredel, Willi and Thalmann, Ernst (1951). *Betrag zu einem politischen Lebensbild.* Berlin: Dietz Verlag Berlin.

Broszat, M. (1986). 'The Third Reich and the German People', in H. Bull (ed.), *The Challenge of the Third Reich.* Oxford: Clarendon Press.

Broszat, M. (1991). 'A Social and Historical Typography of the German Opposition to Hitler', in David Clay Large (ed.), *Contending with Hitler. Varieties of Resistance in the Third Reich.* New York: Cambridge University Press.

Brysac, Shoreen Blair (2002). *Resisting Hitler: Mildred Harnack and the Red Orchestra.* Oxford: Oxford University Press.

Burleigh, M. and Wippermann, W. (1991). *The Racial State: Germany 1933–1945.* Cambridge: Cambridge University Press.

Bussche, Axel von dem, by his friends, Hase & Koehler Verlag, 1994.

Clay, Catrine (2010). *Trautmann's Journey.* London: Yellow Jersey Press.

Collier, Martin, and Pedley, Philip (2005). *Hitler and the Nazi State.* Heinemann.

Colvin, Ian (1965). *Vansittart in Office, Permanent Under Secretary of State for the Foreign Office, 1930–1938.* London: Victor Gollancz Ltd.

Coppi, H., Danyel, J. and Tuchel, J. (1994). *Die Rote Kapelle im Widerstand gegen den Nationalsozialismus.* Berlin: Edition Hentrich.

Dahrendorf, Ralf and Dahrendorf, Gustav (1945). *Der Mensch das Mass aller Dinge.* Hamburg.

Dodd, Martha (1939). *Through Embassy Eyes.* New York.

Engelmann, Bernt (1982). *Im Gleichschritt Marsch, 1933–1939.* Cologne: Kiepenheuer & Witsch.

Engelmann, Bernt (1983). *Bis alles in Scherben fallt, 1939–1945.* Cologne: Kiepenheuer & Witsch.

Fest, Joachim (1986). *Plotting Hitler's Death: The Story of German Resistance.* New York: Henry Holt.

Fulbrook, Mary (2018). *Reckonings, Legacies of Nazi Persecution and the Quest for Justice.* Oxford: Oxford University Press.

Geyer, Michael and Boyer, John (eds) (1994). *Resistance against the Third Reich 1933–1990.* Chicago: University of Chicago Press.

Gruchmann, L. (1970). *Autobiographie eines Attentaters.* Stuttgart: Deutsche Verlags Anstalt.

Grunberger, Richard (2005). *A Social History of the Third Reich.* London: Phoenix.

Haffner, Sebastian (2002). *Defying Hitler, a Memoir.* London: Weidenfeld & Nicolson.

Halder, F. (1960). *The Halder Diaries.* Stuttgart: Deutsche Verlags Anstalt.

Hamerow, Theodore S. (1997). *On the Road to the Wolf's Lair: German Resistance to Hitler.* Cambridge, MA: Harvard University Press.

Hassell von, Ulrich (1988). *Die Hassell Tagebucher, 1938–1944.* Munich: Siedler Verlag.

Hanson, V. D. (2020). *The Second World Wars.* New York: Basic.

Heinemann, Ulrich (1990). *Ein Konservativer Rebel, Fritz-Dietlof Graf von der Schulenburg und der 20 Juli Deutscher Wederstand 1933–1945.* Munich: Siedler Verlag.

Herbert, U. (1994). 'Labour as Spoils of Conquest, 1933–45'. U. Herbert.

Hilton, Christopher (2006). *Hitler's Olympics: The 1936 Berlin Olympic Games.* Gloucestershire: Sutton Publishing.

Hilmes, Oliver (2018). *Berlin 1936: Sixteen Days in August.* London: Bodley Head.

Hoffmann, Peter (1996). *The History of the German Resistance 1933–1945.* Montreal: McGill-Queen's University Press.

Hoffmann, Peter (1995). *Stauffenberg: A Family History, 1905–1944.* Cambridge: Cambridge University Press.

Holmes, Blair R. and Keele, Alan F. (eds) (1995). *When Truth Was Treason, German Youth Against Hitler: The Story of the Helmuth*

Hubener Group. Urbana, IL: University of Illinois Press.

Housden, Martyn (1997). *Resistance and Conformity in the Third Reich*. London: Routledge Sources in History.

Jacobsen, H. (1969). *Germans against Hitler*. Bonn: Press and Information Office of the Federal Government of Germany.

Jacobsen, Hans Adolf (ed.) (1988). *Opposition gegen Hitler under der Staatsstreich von 20 July 1944 in der SD-Berichterstattung*. 2 vols. Stuttgart: Mundus Verlag.

Junger, Ernst A. (2018). *A German Officer in Occupied Paris, The War Journals 1941–1945*, translated by Thomas S. Hansen and Abby J. Hansen. New York: Columbia University Press.

Kater, Michael H. (2004). *Hitler Youth*. Cambridge, MA: Harvard University Press.

Kellner (2018). *My Opposition, the Diary*. Cambridge: Cambridge University Press.

Keegan, J. (1989). *The Second World War*. London: Hutchinson.

Kershaw I. (1983). *Popular Opinion and Political Dissent in the Third Reich*. New York: Clarendon Press.

Kiaulehm, W. (1967). *Mein Freund der Verleger – Ernst Rowohlt und seine Zeit*. Reinbeck.

Klemperer, von, Klemens (1992). *German Resistance to Hitler: The Search for Allies Abroad, 1938–1945*. Oxford: Clarendon Press.

Klemperer, Victor (1999). *I Will Bear Witness, 1933–1941: A Diary of the Nazi Years*. London: Modern Library Paperback Edition.

Klonne, A. (1960). *Hitlerjugend: die Jugend und ihre Organisation im Dritten Reich*. Hanover: Papyrossa Verlag.

Koch, H. W. (1997). *In the Name of the Volk, Political Justice in Hitler's Germany*. London: I. B. Taurus.

Krebs, Albert (1964). *Fritz-Dietlof Graf von der Schulenburg*. Leibniz-Verlag.

Kuhnke, M. (1996). *Besuch bei Fallada, Federlese*. Neubrandenburg: Literaturzentrum Neubrandenburg.

Leber, Annedore (1957). *Das Gewissen Entscheidet, Berichte des deutschen Widerstandes von 1933–1945*. Berlin: Mosaik Verlag.

Leber, Annedore, with Willy Brandt and Karl Dietrich Bracher (1954). *Das Gewissen steht auf. 64 Lebensbilder aus dem deutschen Widerstand 1933–1945*. Berlin: Mosaik Verlag.

Leber, Annedore, 1954. *Die Toten*. Berlin: Mosaik Verlag.

Leber, Annedore (1957). *Conscience in Revolt*. London: Vallentine

Mitchell & Co. Ltd.

Leber, Annedore and von Moltke, Freya Grafin (1961). *Fur und Wider: Entscheidungen in Deutschland 1918–1945*. Berlin: Mosaik Verlag.

Leber, Julius (1952). *Ein Mann geht seinen Weg, Herausgegeben von seinen Freunden*. Berlin: Mosaik Verlag.

Leber, Julius (1965). *Briefe aus dem Gefangnis an seine Angehorigen*. Berlin: Dietz Verlag.

Manthey, J. (1963). *Hans Fallada*. Reinbek: Rowohlt Verlag.

Mason, T. W. (1993). *Social Policy in the Third Reich*. Oxford: Berg.

Mason, T. W. (1975). *Arbeiterklasse und Volksgemeindschaft*. Opladen: Westdeutscher.

Mayer, P. (1968). *Ernst Rowohlt*. Reinbek: Rowohlt Verlag.

McDonough, F. (2001). *Opposition and Resistance in Nazi Germany*. Cambridge: Cambridge University Press.

McDonough, F. (1999). *Hitler and Nazi Germany*. Cambridge: Cambridge University Press.

Meehan, Patricia (1992). *The Unnecessary War, Whitehall and the German Resistance to Hitler*. London: Sinclair-Stevenson.

Merson, Allan (1985). *Communist Resistance in Nazi Germany*. London: Lawrence & Wishart.

Moltke, Helmuth (1991). *Letters to Freya 1939–1945*. London: Collins Harvill.

Mommsen, Hans (2003). *Alternatives to Hitler*. London: I. B. Taurus.

Moorhouse, R. (2006). *Killing Hitler, The Third Reich and the Plots against the Führer*. London: Jonathan Cape.

Niekisch, E. (1953). *Das Reich der niederen Dämonen*. Hamburg: Rowohlt Verlag.

Nicosia, Francis R. and Stokes, Lawrence D. (1990). *Germans Against Nazism: Nonconformity, Opposition and Resistance in the Third Reich. Essays in Honour of Peter Hoffmann*. New York: Berg.

Noakes, J. and Pridham, G. (eds) (1974). *Documents on Nazism, 1919–1945*. Exeter: University of Exeter Press.

Noakes, J. and Pridham, G. (eds) (1988). *Nazism: A Documentary Reader*. Exeter: University of Exeter Press.

Pehle, Walter (2001). *Lexikon des Deutschen Widerstandes*. Frankfurt: Fischer Taschenbuch Verlag.

Peter, Karl Heinrich (ed.) (1961). *Spiegelbild einer Verschworung. Die Kaltenbrunner Berichte an Bormann und Hitler uber das Attentat vom 20 Juli 1944. Dokumente aus dem ehemahligen*

Reichsicherheitshauptamt. Stuttgart: Seewald Verlag.

Peukert, Detlev (1980). *Die KPD im Widerstand, Verfolgung und Untergrundarbeit am Rhein und Ruhr, 1933 bis 1945*. Wupperthal: Peter Hammer.

Peukert, Detlev (1987). 'Youth in the Third Reich', in Richard Bessel (ed.), *Life in the Third Reich*. Oxford: Oxford University Press.

Peukert, Detlev (1988). *Die Edelweiss Piraten. Protestbewegung jugentlicher Arbeiter im Dritten Reich*. Bonn: Bund.

Peukert, Detlev (1991). 'Working Class Resistance. Problems and opinions' in David Clay Large (ed.), *Contending with Hitler, Varieties of Resistance in the Third Reich*. New York: Cambridge University press.

Peukert, Detlev (1993). *Inside Nazi Germany. Conformity, Opposition and Racism in Everday Life*. London: Penguin.

Pikarski, M. and Uebel, G. (1978). *Der Antifascistische Widerstandskampf der KPD im Spiegel des Flugblattes, 1933–45*. Berlin: Dietz Verlag.

Rees, Laurence (1997). *The Nazis, A Warning from History*. London: BBC Books.

Roberts, Andrew (2018). *Churchill, Walking with Destiny*. London: Allen Lane.

Roon, G. van (1971). *German Resistance to Hitler. Count Moltke and the Kreisau Circle*, translated by Peter Ludlow. London: Van Nostrand Reinhold Company.

Sandross, Hans-Rainer (2007). *Die Andere Reichshauptstadt: Widerstand der Arbeitsbewegung in Berlin von 1933–1945*. Berlin: Lukas Verlag.

Scheurig, Bodo (1973). *Henning von Tresckow, Eine Biographie*. Berlin: Stalling.

Schlabrendorff von, Fabian (1979). *Begegnungen in funf Jahrzehnten*. Tubingen: Rainer Wunderlich Verlag.

Schmadecke, J. and Steinbach, P. (eds) (1985). *Der Widerstand gegen den Nazionalsozialismus: Die Deutsche Gesellschaft und der Widerstand gegen Hitler*. Munich: R. Piper Verlag.

Schollgen, G. (1991). *A Conservative against Hitler: Ulrich von Hassell: Diplomat in Imperial Germany, the Weimar Republic and the Third Reich, 1881–1944*. Basingstoke: Macmillan.

Shirer, William (1941). *Berlin Diary*. New York: Alfred A. Knopf.

Siefken, Heinrich (ed.) (1991). '*Die Weisse Rose*: Student Resistance to National Socialism, 1942/1943: Forschunergebnisse und Erfahrungsberichte – A Nottingham Symposium'. Nottingham: Nottingham University.

Simon, Marie Jalowicz (2014). *Gone to Ground*, translated by Anthea Bell. London: Profile Books.

Schwerin, Detlef Graf von (1991). *Dann sind's die besten Kopfe die man heutet*. Zurich: Piper Munchen.

Snyder, Timothy (2017). *On Tyranny, Twenty Lessons from the Twentieth Century*. London: Tim Duggan Books.

Steinbach, Peter and Johannes Tuchel (eds) (1994). *Widerstand in Deutschland 1933–1945: Ein historisches Lesebuch*. Munich: Verlag CH Beck.

Steinbach, Peter and Johannes Tuchel (1998). *Illegale KPD und Bewegung 'Freies Deutschland' in Berlin und Brandenburg 1942– 1945*. Berlin: Gedenkstätte Deutscher Widerstand.

Steinbach, Peter and Johannes Tuchel (2006). *Georg Elser*. Berlin: Bebra Verlag.

Thälmann, Ernst (1965). *Briefe aus dem Gefangnis*. Berlin: Dietz Verlag.

Tuchel, Johannes. 'Kontakte zwischen Sozialdemokraten und Komministen Sommer 1944', in Wolfgang Benz, et al. (eds), *Dachauer Hefte, 11. Orte der Erinnerungen 1945–1995*. Dachauer booklets.

Tuchel, Johannes (2014). *Und Ihrer all wartet den Strick: Das Zellengefangnis Lehrterstrasse 3 nach dem 20 July 1944*. Berlin: Lukas Verlag.

Vester-Thälmann, Irma (1954). *Erinnerungen an meinem Vater, Das neue Wort*. Stuttgart: Das Neue Wort.

Walther, Peter (2018). *Hans Fallada, Die Biographie*. Berlin: Aufbau Taschenbuch.

Williams, Jenny (1998). *More Lives Than One, A Biography of Hans Fallada*. London: Libris.

INDEX